38.00

Programme for **I**nternational **S**tudent **A**ssessment

Where immigrant students succeed – A comparative review of performance and engagement in PISA 2003

D1466278

OECD
ORGANISATION FOR ECONOMIC CO-OPERATION AND DEVELOPMENT

ORGANISATION FOR ECONOMIC CO-OPERATION AND DEVELOPMENT

The OECD is a unique forum where the governments of 30 democracies work together to address the economic, social and environmental challenges of globalisation. The OECD is also at the forefront of efforts to understand and to help governments respond to new developments and concerns, such as corporate governance, the information economy and the challenges of an ageing population. The Organisation provides a setting where governments can compare policy experiences, seek answers to common problems, identify good practice and work to co-ordinate domestic and international policies.

The OECD member countries are: Australia, Austria, Belgium, Canada, the Czech Republic, Denmark, Finland, France, Germany, Greece, Hungary, Iceland, Ireland, Italy, Japan, Korea, Luxembourg, Mexico, the Netherlands, New Zealand, Norway, Poland, Portugal, the Slovak Republic, Spain, Sweden, Switzerland, Turkey, the United Kingdom and the United States. The Commission of the European Communities takes part in the work of the OECD.

OECD Publishing disseminates widely the results of the Organisation's statistics gathering and research on economic, social and environmental issues, as well as the conventions, guidelines and standards agreed by its members.

> *This work is published on the responsibility of the Secretary-General of the OECD. The opinions expressed and arguments employed herein do not necessarily reflect the official views of the Organisation or of the governments of its member countries.*

Reprinted 2006

PISA™, OECD/PISA™ and the PISA logo are trademarks of the Organisation for Economic Co-operation and Development (OECD). All use of OECD trademarks is prohibited without written permission from the OECD.

© OECD 2006

No reproduction, copy, transmission or translation of this publication may be made without written permission. Applications should be sent to OECD Publishing: *rights@oecd.org* or by fax (33 1) 45 24 13 91. Permission to photocopy a portion of this work should be addressed to the Centre français d'exploitation du droit de copie, 20, rue des Grands-Augustins, 75006 Paris, France (*contact@cfcopies.com*).

Foreword

Successful integration of immigrant populations is essential for ensuring social cohesion in immigrant receiving nations. Immigrants bring a wealth of human capital which, if nurtured carefully, can positively contribute to the economic well-being and cultural diversity of the host country. Yet, tapping into this potential remains a major challenge for policy makers. What barriers exist for young immigrants today? Can school contribute to reducing those barriers and in turn help young immigrants succeed in their adopted country?

Drawing on data from the OECD's Programme for International Students Assessment (PISA), this report entitled *Where immigrant students succeed – A comparative review of performance and engagement in PISA 2003* shows that immigrant students are motivated learners and have positive attitudes towards school. Despite these strong learning dispositions immigrant students often perform at significantly lower levels than their native peers in key school subjects, such as mathematics, reading and science, as well as in general problem-solving skills. The differences are most pronounced in Austria, Belgium, Denmark, France, Germany, the Netherlands and Switzerland. In contrast, there is little difference between the performance of immigrant and native students in three of the traditional settlement countries, Australia, Canada, New Zealand, as well as in Macao-China. Of particular concern is the fact that in the majority of countries at least one in four immigrant students do not demonstrate basic mathematics skills as defined in the PISA 2003 assessment. As such these individuals could face considerable challenges in their future professional and personal lives.

It is striking that immigrant students in all 17 countries covered in this report express similar, if not higher, levels of motivation than their native counterparts, particularly given the large performance differences across countries. This is an important finding for policy makers, as schools could build upon these strong learning dispositions to help immigrant students succeed in the education system.

The report contextualises these results with specific information on immigrant students' social background and the language they speak at home. Results show however that performance differences between immigrant and native students cannot solely be attributed to these student characteristics. The report also provides information on countries' approaches to immigration and the integration of immigrants. It shows that some countries, where there are either relatively small performance differences between immigrant and native students or the performance gaps for second-generation students are significantly reduced compared to those observed for first-generation students, tend to have well-established language support programmes with relatively clearly defined goals and standards.

This report complements both *Learning for Tomorrow's World – First Results from PISA 2003*, which focuses on knowledge and skills in mathematics, science and reading, and *Problem Solving for Tomorrow's World – First Measures of Cross-curricular Competencies from PISA 2003*, which profiles students' problem-solving skills.

This report was written by Petra Stanat and Gayle Christensen at the Max Planck Institute for Human Development, Berlin[1]. They conceptualised the report, designed the survey, performed all analyses and wrote the chapters. The publication was completed with the support of the countries participating in PISA, the experts and institutions working within the framework of the PISA Consortium and the OECD. The report was prepared at the OECD Directorate for Education under the direction of Claire Shewbridge and Andreas Schleicher, with advice from the PISA Editorial Group. The authors would like to thank Jürgen Baumert, Director of the Center for Educational Research at the Max Planck Institute for Human Development in Berlin, for supporting the project, as well as Georges Lemaître from the OECD's Directorate for Employment, Labour and Social Affairs for his valuable comments on Chapter 1 of the report. Special thanks also go to Michael Segeritz, Alexandra Shajek and Nina Bremm for their assistance with the research and data analyses. Technical advice was provided by Keith Rust and Wolfram Schulz.

The development of the report was steered by the PISA Governing Board, chaired by Ryo Watanabe (Japan). Annex C of the report lists the members of the various PISA bodies as well as the individual experts and consultants who have contributed to this report and to PISA in general.

The report is published on the responsibility of the Secretary-General of the OECD.

Notes

1   Petra Stanat is now at the Friedrich-Alexander University Erlangen-Nürnberg, Germany and Gayle Christensen is now at Urban Institute, Washington DC, USA.

© OECD 2006   Where immigrant students succeed - A comparative review of performance and engagement in PISA 2003

Table of Contents

Executive Summary

———•———

Based on the assumption that the successful integration of immigrant students into the education system presents a central concern to many countries worldwide, this report analyses evidence from PISA 2003 on outcomes of schooling including how well immigrant students perform in key school subjects at the age of 15, as well as how they assess themselves as learners and what their general attitudes are towards school. Two groups of immigrant students are analysed: *first-generation students* who were born outside the country of assessment and whose parents were also born in a different country; and *second-generation students* who themselves were born in the country of assessment but whose parents were born in a different country, *i.e.* students who have followed all their schooling in the country of assessment. The report compares immigrant students to *native* students who were born in the country of assessment and who had at least one parent born in that country. The analyses include seventeen countries with significant immigrant student populations: the OECD countries Australia, Austria, Belgium, Canada, Denmark, France, Germany, Luxembourg, the Netherlands, New Zealand, Norway, Sweden, Switzerland and the United States as well as the partner countries Hong Kong-China, Macao-China and the Russian Federation. For the majority of these countries, as well as for England, Finland and Spain, information is presented on policies and programmes to help immigrant students attain proficiency in the language of instruction.

The report examines how immigrant students performed mainly in mathematics and reading, but also in science and problem-solving skills in the PISA 2003 assessment, both in comparison to native students in their adopted country and relative to other students across all countries covered in the report (the 'case countries'). In addition, the report explores to what extent immigrant students reported that they have other learning prerequisites, such as motivation to learn mathematics, positive attitudes towards school and strong belief in their own abilities in mathematics (self-concept). Throughout, the report attempts to identify factors that might contribute to between-country differences in immigrant student outcomes and as such could provide policy makers with information on potential intervention points to improve the situation of these students. To this end, the report contextualises the findings by examining countries' immigration histories and populations, general immigration policies and specific policies to help students learn the language of instruction. Although it is not possible to estimate the effects of these factors on immigrant students' school success using the PISA data, the analyses presented in the report provide a description of countries with varying differences in performance and learning characteristics between immigrant and native student populations.

> *PISA results suggest that high levels of immigration do not necessarily impair integration.*

There is not a significant association between the size of the immigrant student populations in the case countries and the size of the performance differences between immigrant and native students. This finding contradicts the assumption that high levels of immigration will generally impair integration.

Immigrant students are motivated learners and have positive attitudes towards school. Such strong learning dispositions can be developed by schools to help these students succeed in the education system.

The findings indicate that immigrant students report similar or even higher levels of positive learning dispositions compared to their native peers. First-generation and second-generation students often report higher levels of interest and motivation in mathematics and more positive attitudes towards schooling. In none of the countries do immigrant students report lower levels of these learning prerequisites. The consistency of this finding is striking given that there are substantial differences between countries in terms of immigration histories, immigrant populations, immigration and integration policies and immigrant student performance in PISA 2003. It suggests that immigrant students generally have strong learning dispositions, which schools can build upon to help them succeed in school.

Despite these strong learning dispositions immigrant students often perform at levels significantly lower than their native peers. However, performance levels vary across countries.

While immigrant students generally exhibit strong learning prerequisites, the size of the performance differences between native students and immigrant students varies widely in international comparison. The differences are most pronounced in Austria, Belgium, Denmark, France, Germany, the Netherlands and Switzerland. In contrast, immigrant and native students perform at similar levels in three of the traditional settlement countries, Australia, Canada, New Zealand, as well as in Macao-China.

In Canada, Luxembourg, Sweden, Switzerland and Hong Kong-China, second-generation students perform significantly better than first-generation students. The gap between immigrant and native students in these countries appears to decrease across immigrant generations. This pattern may, in part, reflect effects of integration policies and practice that help to mitigate achievement differences over time and generations, although it may also be due to differences in the composition of the first- and second-generation student populations. Definitive conclusions cannot be drawn from PISA as data were collected at a single point in time. In order to study changes in educational outcomes across generations longitudinal studies would be required.

In the majority of countries at least 25% of immigrant students could face considerable challenges in their future professional and personal lives as they do not demonstrate basic mathematics skills in the PISA 2003 assessment.

PISA 2003 classifies students into six proficiency levels according to the level of mathematical skills they demonstrate. Level 2 is considered to represent a baseline level of mathematics proficiency on the PISA scale at which students begin to demonstrate the kind of skills that enable them to actively use mathematics; for example they are able to use basic algorithms, formulae and procedures, to make literal interpretations and to apply direct reasoning. Students who are classified below Level 2 are expected to face considerable challenges in terms of their labour market and earnings prospects, as well as their capacity to participate fully in society.

The findings indicate that only small percentages of native students fail to reach Level 2, whereas the situation is very different for immigrant students. More than 40% of first-generation students in Belgium, France, Norway and Sweden and more than 25% of first-generation students in Austria, Denmark, Germany, Luxembourg, the Netherlands, Switzerland, the United States and the Russian Federation perform below Level 2.

© OECD 2006 Where immigrant students succeed - A comparative review of performance and engagement in PISA 2003

Second-generation students in most countries show higher levels of proficiency compared to first-generation students, and smaller percentages of second-generation students fail to reach Level 2. Nevertheless, in over half of the OECD case countries, more than 25% of second-generation students have not acquired the skills to be considered able to actively use mathematics according to the PISA definition. In Germany, more than 40% of second-generation students perform below Level 2. In Austria, Belgium, Denmark, Norway, the United States and the Russian Federation at least 30% of second-generation students score below Level 2.

Background characteristics of immigrant student populations and school characteristics only partially explain differences in mathematics performance.

In most European countries immigrant students come from lower level socio-economic backgrounds and their parents often are less educated than native students' parents. This is also the case in the United States and Hong-Kong China. In contrast, the background characteristics of immigrant and native students are similar in Australia, Canada and New Zealand, the Russian Federation and Macao-China.

At the country level, there is a relationship between the relative mathematics performance of immigrant students and their relative educational and socio-economic background. However, performance differences remain between immigrant and native students in many countries after accounting for these background characteristics. For example, there are still significant performance differences between native and second-generation students in Austria, Belgium, Denmark, France, Germany, Luxembourg, the Netherlands, New Zealand, Norway and Switzerland. This suggests that the relative performance levels of immigrant students cannot solely be attributed to the composition of immigrant populations in terms of their educational and socio-economic background.

In several countries, many immigrant students attend schools with relatively high proportions of immigrant students. However, there is not a significant association between the degree of clustering within a country and the size of the performance gap between immigrant and native students. Therefore, the distribution of immigrant students across schools does not seem to account for international variation in performance gaps between immigrant and native students. Within countries, however, high proportions of immigrant students in schools may be related to performance levels, although the literature suggests that the evidence on this is mixed.

In most of the case countries immigrant students often attend schools with relatively disadvantaged student populations in terms of economic, social and cultural background. There is a more varied picture with respect to school resources and school climate. In three of the settlement countries, Australia, Canada and New Zealand, immigrant students and native students attend schools with similar resources and climates. In Belgium, immigrant students are likely to attend schools with less favourable characteristics. In other countries, the largest and most consistent differences occur for student factors related to the school climate and disciplinary climate. Immigrant students attend schools with less favourable conditions for at least one of these factors in Austria, Belgium, Germany, Luxembourg, the Netherlands, Sweden and Macao-China.

Similarly, performance differences in mathematics are not fully explained by the fact that some immigrant students do not speak the language of instruction at home. However, in several countries this relationship is quite strong and may warrant stronger language support in schools.

Countries also differ with respect to the proportion of immigrant students whose native language differs from the language of instruction. Accounting for the language spoken at home tends to decrease the performance differences between immigrant students and native students. In several countries, however, achievement differences remain significant. This includes both first- and second-generation students in Austria, Belgium, Denmark, France, the Netherlands and Switzerland; first-generation students in Luxembourg, Norway, Sweden, Hong Kong-China and the Russian Federation; and second-generation students in Germany and New Zealand. This indicates that the language spoken at home does not fully account for the variations in immigrant students' relative performance levels.

Nevertheless, immigrant students who do not speak the language of instruction at home tend to be lower performing in mathematics in several countries. Even after accounting for parents' educational and occupational status, the performance gap associated with the language spoken at home remains significant in Belgium, Canada, Germany, the United States, Hong Kong-China, Macao-China and the Russian Federation. Countries with a strong relationship between the language students speak at home and their performance in mathematics may want to consider strengthening language support measures in schools.

Policies to help immigrant students attain proficiency in the language of instruction have common characteristics but vary in terms of explicit curricula and focus.

An examination of language proficiency policies in Australia, Austria, Belgium, Canada, Denmark, Germany, Luxembourg, the Netherlands, Norway, Sweden, Switzerland, Hong Kong-China and Macao-China, as well as in England, Finland and Spain, shows that countries have some key characteristics in common. Very few countries provide systematic language support based on an explicit curriculum in pre-primary education (ISCED 0). The countries that have an explicit curriculum in place include the Canadian province of British Columbia and the Netherlands.

In primary (ISCED 1) and lower secondary (ISCED 2) education, the most common approach is *immersion with systematic language support*, that is, immigrant students attend regular classes to learn all standard academic programmes, but also receive targeted instruction to develop their skills in the language of instruction. In addition, several countries offer *immersion programmes with a preparatory phase in the language of instruction* for newly immigrated students, that is, immigrant students attend programmes to develop their language skills before they make the transition to regular classes. This approach occurs more frequently in lower secondary education (ISCED 2) than in primary education (ISCED 1).

Bilingual language support programmes given in both students' native language and the language of instruction are relatively uncommon. In England, Finland and Norway immersion with systematic language support may include some bilingual components. *Transitional bilingual programmes* with initial instruction in students' native language and a gradual shift toward instruction in their second language, however, do not play a substantial role in any of the countries presented in this report.

Similarly, very few countries generally offer supplementary classes in their schools to improve students' native languages. In Sweden, students have a legal right to native language tuition, and schools typically provide such classes if at least five students with the same native language live in the municipality. Schools in the Swiss Canton of Geneva also offer native language classes for the most common minority languages. In eleven countries or sub-national entities, the provision of native language tuition depends on the municipality or the individual school while in nine others native language instruction is left to families or community groups to arrange.

Despite these similarities in general approaches to supporting immigrant students in learning the language of instruction, the specific measures countries or sub-national entities implement vary considerably across a range of characteristics, such as the existence of explicit curricula and standards, the focus of the support (*e.g.* general curriculum vs. language development) and the organisation of the support (*e.g.* within mainstream instruction vs. in separate classes or language support as a specific school subject).

Several countries or sub-national entities have explicit curricula or curriculum framework documents in place for second language support. These include Australia – New South Wales and Victoria and Denmark for both immersion with systematic language support and immersion with a preparatory phase; Canada – Ontario, some German *Länder*, Norway, Sweden and Macao-China for immersion with systematic language support; and Canada – British Columbia and Luxembourg for immersion with a preparatory phase. The curricula vary considerably, however, in terms of content, level of specificity and scope.

> *Countries where there are either relatively small performance differences between immigrant and native students or the performance gaps for second-generation students are significantly reduced compared to those observed for first-generation students tend to have well-established language support programmes with relatively clearly defined goals and standards.*

It would, of course, be of considerable interest to determine the extent to which the different language support programmes contribute to relative achievement levels of immigrant students. This, however, is not possible on the basis of the available information. Nevertheless, it appears that in some countries with relatively small achievement gaps between immigrant and native students, or smaller gaps for second-generation students compared to first-generation students, long-standing language support programmes exist with relatively clearly defined goals and standards. These countries include Australia, Canada and Sweden. In a few countries where immigrant students perform at significantly lower levels, language support tends to be less systematic. Yet, several of these countries have recently introduced programmes that aim to support the learning of immigrant students. These developments may help to reduce the achievement gap between immigrant students and their native peers.

READER'S GUIDE

Data underlying the figures

The data referred to in Chapters 1, 2, 3, and 4 of this report are presented in Annex B. In these tables, as well as in data tables included in Chapter 5, the following symbols are used to denote missing data:

a The category does not apply in the country concerned. Data are therefore missing.

c There are too few observations to provide reliable estimates (*i.e.* there are fewer than 3% of students for this cell or too few schools for valid inferences). However, these statistics were included in the calculation of cross-country averages.

m Data are not available. These data were collected but subsequently removed from the publication for technical reasons.

n Data are negligible *i.e.* they do not occur in any significant numbers.

w Data have been withdrawn at the request of the country concerned.

Calculation of the OECD average

An OECD average was calculated for most indicators presented in this report. The OECD average takes the OECD countries as a single entity, to which each country contributes with equal weight. The OECD average corresponds to the arithmetic mean of the respective country statistics and for this report only applies to the selection of OECD *case countries* (see definition below).

Rounding of figures

Because of rounding, some figures in tables may not exactly add up to the totals. Totals, differences and averages are always calculated on the basis of exact numbers and are rounded only after calculation. When standard errors in this publication have been rounded to one or two decimal places and the value 0.0 or 0.00 is shown, this does not imply that the standard error is zero, but that it is smaller than 0.05 or 0.005 respectively.

Reporting of student data

The report uses "15-year-olds" as shorthand for the PISA target population. In practice, this refers to students who were aged between 15 years and 3 (complete) months and 16 years and 2 (complete) months at the beginning of the assessment period and who were enrolled in an educational institution, regardless of the grade level or type of institution, and of whether they were attending full-time or part-time.

Abbreviations used in this report

The following abbreviations are used in this report:

ESCS Index of economic, social and cultural status (see Annex A1 for definition)

HISEI Highest international socio-economic index of occupational status (corresponds to the highest occupational status of either the mother or father)

ISCED International Standard Classification of Education (the ISCED levels are explained in Annex A1)

SE Standard error

SD Standard deviation

SOPEMI *Système d'Observation Permanente des Migrations* (Continuous Reporting System on Migration). This was established in 1973 by the OECD to provide its European member states a mechanism for sharing of information on international migration.

Terminology used in this report

Native students or non-immigrant students: Students with at least one parent born in the country of assessment. Students born in the country who have one foreign-born parent (children of "combined" families) are included in the native category, as previous research indicates that these students perform similarly to native students.

Immigrant students: This group includes both *first-generation students* and *second-generation students* (see definitions below).

First-generation students: Students born outside of the country of assessment whose parents are also foreign-born.

Second-generation students: Students born in the country of assessment with foreign-born parents.

Case countries: This includes the 17 countries covered in this report. Fourteen OECD countries: Australia, Austria, Belgium, Canada, Denmark, France, Germany, Luxembourg, the Netherlands, New Zealand, Norway, Sweden, Switzerland and the United States; as well as three partner countries: Hong Kong-China, Macao-China and the Russian Federation.

Further documentation

For further information on the PISA assessment instruments and the methods used in PISA, see the *PISA 2003 Technical Report* (OECD, 2005) and the PISA Web site (*www.pisa.oecd.org*).

1

Countries' immigration histories and populations

INTRODUCTION

Migration movements form a central part of human history. In the social sciences, migration is most generally defined as "crossing the boundary of a political or administrative unit for a certain minimum period" where, in the case of international migration, the boundary involves the border of a state (Castles, 2000, p. 270; Skeldon, 1997). In the past two or three decades, interest in issues associated with international migration has increased among policy makers, educators, researchers and the general public. This development is partly due to the growth of immigrant inflows that most OECD countries experienced during the 1980s and the early 1990s resulting from the dissolution of the Eastern Bloc, political instability in many countries, the growing globalisation of economic activities and family reunion in the aftermath of labour migration movements during the 1960s and 1970s (OECD, 2001a). Worldwide, in the year 2000, approximately 175 million people lived outside their country of birth representing an increase since 1990 of 46% (Meyers, 2004, p. 1). Although many countries have implemented various measures to contain immigration levels, international migration movements remain a topic of global significance.

In addition to the question of how migration flows should be channelled and controlled, the issue of integration is a major concern. The process of integrating immigrants into society presents a major challenge for both the immigrants themselves and the host majorities in the receiving countries. It is a crucial issue in particular for the children of immigrants. Schools and other educational institutions play a central role in this process. As socialising agents, schools help transmit the norms and values that provide a basis for social cohesion. In diverse, multi-ethnic societies, this task is not only important, but also complex. Given the key relevance of education for success in working life, schools set the stage for the integration of immigrant groups into the economic system. To the extent that language barriers exist between immigrant groups and the host majority, a major task of schools is also to help students master the respective country's official language.

The Organisation for Economic Co-operation and Development's (OECD) *Programme for International Student Assessment* (PISA) provides a unique opportunity to examine the extent to which immigrant students succeed in the school systems of their host countries. *Learning for Tomorrow's World: First Results from PISA 2003* (OECD, 2004a) indicates that in most countries participating in PISA, immigrant students do not reach the same levels of achievement as their native peers. At the same time, the size of the performance gap varies considerably across countries. Using data from PISA 2003, this report analyses the situation of immigrant students in the participating countries in more detail (see also Baumert and Schümer, 2001; Baumert, Stanat and Watermann, 2006; Coradi Vellacotts *et al.*, 2003; Skolverket, 2005 for analyses based on PISA 2000). In order to contextualise the findings, the first chapter provides background information on immigrant populations and policies. It begins with an introduction to the concepts of immigration and integration used in this report. Next, it describes countries' approaches to immigration and integration and then provides a general characterisation of immigrant populations in the case countries. The chapter concludes with a description of the PISA database and the immigrant student samples for each of the case countries.

Not all of the 41 countries participating in PISA 2003 have significant immigrant populations, and for some countries the sample sizes of immigrant students in PISA are too small to conduct meaningful analyses (a more detailed explanation of the minimum criteria for inclusion of countries in the analytic chapters can be found in the description of the PISA database later in the chapter). As a result, this report focuses on 14 OECD countries: Australia, Austria, Belgium, Canada,

© OECD 2006 **Where immigrant students succeed - A comparative review of performance and engagement in PISA 2003**

Denmark, France, Germany, Luxembourg, the Netherlands, New Zealand, Norway, Sweden, Switzerland and the United States as well as 3 partner countries: Hong Kong-China, Macao-China and the Russian Federation. The OECD averages reported in the tables and graphs of the following chapters refer to the 14 OECD case countries only. Three additional countries, England, Finland and Spain participated in a supplementary survey on policies and programmes for language minority populations that is presented in Chapter 5.

IMMIGRATION AND INTEGRATION

International migration movements occur for a variety of reasons. The current literature on migration describes several types of migrants. Castles (2000, p. 269 f.), for example, lists the following eight migrant categories[1]:

1. *Temporary labour migrants*: men and women who migrate for a limited period (from a few months to several years) in order to take up employment.

2. *Highly skilled and business migrants*: people with qualifications as managers, executives, professionals, technicians or similar, who move within the internal labour markets of transnational corporations and international organisations, or who seek employment through international labour markets for rare specialised skills.

3. *Irregular migrants* (also known as undocumented or illegal migrants): people who reside in a country without the necessary documents or permits. They may initially arrive legally (*e.g.* as tourists, to visit family or with temporary work permits) but then stay beyond the expiration date of their visas. Labour migration flows include many undocumented migrants.

4. *Refugees*: according to the 1951 United Nations *Geneva Convention* relating to the status of refugees, a refugee is a person residing outside his or her country of nationality who is unable or unwilling to return because of a "well-founded fear of persecution on account of race, religion, nationality, membership in a particular social group, or political opinion." Signatories to the convention undertake to protect refugees by allowing them to enter and granting temporary or permanent residence status.

5. *Asylum-seekers*: people who move across borders in search of protection and make a claim for refugee status (according to the *Geneva Convention*), which may or may not be recognised. The definition of asylum seeker varies across countries. In most countries, however, the terms asylum seeker and refugee differ only with regard to the place where an individual asks for protection. The asylum seeker makes the claim for refugee status upon arrival in a country and the claim is considered on the territory of the receiving state. In many contemporary conflict situations in less developed countries, it is difficult to determine the cause of departure: whether it is due to personal persecution or the destruction of the economic and social infrastructure needed for survival. Only a fraction of asylum-seekers is recognised as refugees, another small proportion receives temporary protection. All others are refused.

6. *Forced migration*: forced migrants in a broader sense include not only refugees and asylum-seekers but also people who were forced to move due to environmental catastrophes or development projects such as new factories, roads or dams.

7. *Family members* (also known as family reunion migrants): people joining relatives who have already entered an immigration country under one of the above categories. This also includes

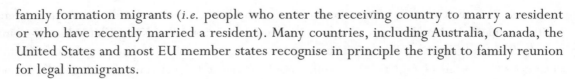

family formation migrants (*i.e.* people who enter the receiving country to marry a resident or who have recently married a resident). Many countries, including Australia, Canada, the United States and most EU member states recognise in principle the right to family reunion for legal immigrants.

8. *Return migrants*: people who return to their country of origin after having lived abroad.

An additional category of immigrants that does not appear in the list by Castles (2000) is long-term low-skilled labour migration. Although many countries would like this form of migration to be temporary, this is often not the case. In fact, a high proportion of immigrants in several European countries arrived as temporary low-skilled workers (*e.g.* "guest workers") but ended up staying for extended periods of time or permanently. Much of the migration into Southern Europe in recent years has involved unauthorised migrants taking on low-skilled jobs, who have been subsequently regularised by the receiving countries.

IMMIGRATION HISTORIES AND GENERAL APPROACHES TO IMMIGRATION AND INTEGRATION

A number of theories have been developed to account for international migration (for a comprehensive review see Massey, *et al.*, 1993). These models typically focus on labour migration, specifying factors that determine the initiation and development of international movement at the individual, household, national, and international levels. At the national level, receiving countries attempt to manage migration with immigration and integration policies.[2] State *immigration policies* establish the number and categories of immigrants accepted into the country and the types of residence and work permits granted. *Integration policies* concern the measures taken to promote the incorporation of immigrants in society. Both types of policy can be expected to influence the outcomes of immigrants and their offspring in the receiving country.

Immigration policies set the stage for integration (*e.g.* Bourhis, *et al.*, 1997). These policies, shaped by historical developments at international and national levels, differ across countries. In a comparative analysis of immigrant students' situation in schools, it is important to provide information on core characteristics of immigration processes including the relative size of immigrant populations, the primary forms of immigration, immigrants' level of skill within the receiving countries and naturalisation regulations. Such background information is necessary to contextualise findings on the situation of immigrant students within different school systems. This section will therefore provide a broad characterisation of approaches to immigration and integration within the countries included in the report. More specifically, it will discuss the most common model of categorising countries in terms of their immigration histories and general policies. Although this model cannot be regarded as definitive, it is useful for structuring the analyses presented in this report.

The literature typically distinguishes four groups of countries based on their immigration histories: 1) Traditional settlement countries, 2) European states with post-war labour recruitment, 3) European states with migration related to their colonial histories and post-war labour recruitment and 4) new immigration countries (*e.g.* Bauer, Loftstrom and Zimmermann, 2000; Freeman, 1995).

The *traditional settlement countries* include Australia, Canada, New Zealand and the United States. They were founded on the basis of immigration and continue to admit significant numbers of newcomers for permanent residence. These countries have extensive experience with immigration:

© OECD 2006   *Where immigrant students succeed - A comparative review of performance and engagement in PISA 2003*

"Although immigration flows and policies have fluctuated over the course of their national histories, their interaction with immigration and its social consequences is intimate, of long standing, and well-institutionalized" (Freeman, 1995, p. 887).

European states with post-war labour recruitment have also experienced significant immigration inflows at various times over the course of their histories, yet their development as nation states was not based on migration. The countries in this report that are included in this group are Austria, Denmark, Germany,[3] Luxembourg, Norway, Sweden and Switzerland. Mass migration to these countries occurred after World War II, when they actively recruited large numbers of workers to compensate for a shortage in labour during the 1960s and 1970s. Often, governments expected these workers to be temporary residents (hence the term "guest workers" used in some nations), yet many of the temporary workers permanently settled in the host country. Today, these European countries have sizeable immigrant populations. Within this group, the Nordic countries are sometimes distinguished on the basis of their stronger emphasis since the 1970s on humanitarian immigration.

The general pattern within the *Northern European states with colonial histories* including Belgium, France, the Netherlands and the United Kingdom, is quite similar to that in European states with post-war labour recruitment. As a result of their colonial pasts, however, immigrants in these countries are often from the former colonies and are more likely to speak the receiving country's official language.

Finally, the so-called *new immigration countries* have more recently transformed from immigrant-sending countries to immigrant-receiving countries. In addition to return migration (*i.e.* former emigrants, usually guest workers, returning to their home countries) during the 1970s and 1980s, immigration of foreign nationals increased considerably in these countries towards the end of the 20th century. Among the new immigration countries are Ireland, Italy, Greece, Portugal and Spain. In addition, the three partner countries included in this report (Hong Kong-China, Macao-China and the Russian Federation) have more recently begun to experience increased levels of immigration. In the Russian Federation, most immigrants are from states of the former Soviet Union. In Hong Kong-China and Macao-China, the largest immigrant group is from mainland China, although Hong Kong-China also has significant numbers of foreign domestic helpers who come mainly from the Philippines (OECD, 2004b).

Although the immigration experiences of countries within the four categories described above are obviously far from homogeneous, there is wide acceptance of this general categorisation based on common characteristics of immigration histories. More controversial, however, are attempts that have been made to group countries in terms of their general approaches to immigration and integration. For example, Freeman (2004) points out that countries do not typically have coherent national models of integration or incorporation in the sense of "incorporation regimes," which can be clearly distinguished and classified. Instead, he argues that countries "possess a patchwork of multidimensional frameworks" across different institutional sectors (p. 946). These include the *state sector*, the *market and welfare sectors*, and the *cultural sector*.

With regard to the *state sector*, there appears to be a relationship between immigration histories and regulations concerning the admission and naturalisation of immigrants. Although the relationship is far from perfect, it is possible to identify general policy approaches that distinguish the groups of countries described above (*e.g.* Castles and Miller, 2003; Freeman, 2004). The most obvious distinction is between the traditional settlement countries and the European states with post-war labour recruitment or colonial histories. The traditional settlement countries – Australia, Canada, New Zealand and the United States – tend to encourage immigration of whole families, set target levels for different types of immigration and provide relatively easy access to citizenship. In most cases, children of immigrants born in the receiving country automatically attain citizenship. Australia, Canada and New Zealand have policies in place that provide for the selection of immigrants on the basis of characteristics that are considered to be important for integration (*e.g.* language skills and educational background).

In the European states with post-war labour recruitment, employers selected labour migrants who could bring their families only if they met a number of conditions (*e.g.* adequate housing or sufficient income). These countries are more reluctant to issue permanent residence status and to grant citizenship. Children born in the country to immigrant parents do not automatically receive citizenship. In general, the situation in European countries with colonial histories is similar to that of European states with post-war labour recruitment. In some cases, however, the countries granted citizenship more readily to immigrants from the former colonies and it was easier for them to bring in close relatives.

Despite this general pattern, the immigration policies and practices of countries within one group vary considerably, and there is also a great deal of overlap in the policies and practices among countries of different groups. For example, in Australia, Canada and New Zealand the proportion of new immigrants who come for work or other settlement reasons is higher than it is in the United States where family migration represents a much higher percentage of new immigrants (OECD, 2005a). Also, the system of categorisation does not take state policies and practices related to illegal immigration into account, which can vary considerably across countries within one group.

The extent to which between-country differences in the *market and welfare sectors* relate to the integration of immigrants is unclear. There is some evidence that informal immigrant economies are more likely to develop in liberal market economies than in social market economies (Freeman and Ögelman, 2000). At the same time, however, the integration of immigrants in the market sector appears to interact closely with geographic factors and various government characteristics. In terms of welfare policies, most countries seem to give immigrants access to welfare state benefits largely independent of their citizenship status (Freeman, 2004).

Finally, the *cultural sector* involves state policies related to the recognition and expression of culture. These policies "produce incentive structures for the retention or loss of immigrant cultural characteristics and can seek to protect or transform the cultures of the receiving societies" (Freeman, 2004, p. 958). They address issues such as the practice of religion and the display of religious symbols, the stance toward immigrants' native languages, the role of women and child-rearing practices. These issues are subject to considerable controversy and heated debate. In the literature, countries are often located on a scale ranging from tendencies towards the marginalisation of immigrants to expectations for assimilation to state-endorsed multiculturalism (Freeman, 2004, p. 958). For example, Castles and Miller (2003) argue that Austria, Germany and Switzerland tend towards differential exclusion of immigrants; France, the Netherlands, and the United Kingdom towards assimilation and Australia, Canada, Sweden and the United States towards multiculturalism. As

© OECD 2006 **Where immigrant students succeed** - A comparative review of performance and engagement in PISA 2003

Freeman (2004) points out, however, these patterns are highly unstable and change constantly (see also Joppke and Morawska, 2003).

Overall, no clear-cut categorisation of different countries in terms of their approaches to immigration and integration policies exists. Yet, a few core differences emerge, especially among the traditional settlement countries, the European states with predominantly post-colonial and post-war labour migration, and the new countries of immigration. Whether it makes sense to divide these groups further into subgroups depends on the domain.

Because the categorisations suggested in the literature do not typically take educational policies and practices into account, their relevance for the education sector is unclear. This report therefore addresses the question of whether the results indicate that particular groups of countries show similar patterns of findings on the situation of immigrant students. It is important to note, however, that even if such patterns can be identified, it will be impossible to draw conclusions about their causes. Countries differ with respect to a multitude of characteristics and the design of PISA does not permit the isolation of causal factors. Therefore, the findings presented in this report are purely descriptive.

IMMIGRANT POPULATIONS

International comparative data on immigrant populations are often difficult to interpret. Sources assembling this information, such as the OECD's annual report on *Trends in International Migration*, have to rely on national panels, censuses, national registers or residence permit data that often use inconsistent categories. A key difference is the general definition of the immigrant population, which is based on individuals' nationality in some countries ("foreigners," "foreign nationality") and on their country of birth in others ("foreign-born"). Although there is currently a general shift towards using the birthplace-based definition, many of the available statistics suffer from this comparability problem. Also, certain subcategories of immigrants, such as "foreign workers," are often based on different concepts of employment and unemployment (*e.g.* OECD, 2004b, p. 369). Furthermore, undocumented immigrants are rarely captured in statistics. In some of the case countries, however, illegal immigrants make up a substantial portion of the foreign-born population. For example, recent estimates indicate that undocumented immigrants represent 26% of the total foreign-born population in the United States (Passel, Capps, and Fix, 2004).

While these limitations should be kept in mind, the OECD does provide background information on the immigrant populations in the OECD countries included in the report. Most of the information presented in the rest of this chapter comes from the publication series *Trends in International Migration* (*e.g.* OECD, 2005a). In 2005, the OECD developed a new database on international migrants using national censuses or large-sample surveys (OECD, 2005a). The goal of this effort was to develop more accurate and comparable statistics on immigrant populations. This new database is used where possible to compare differences for foreign-born and foreign-nationality immigrants (see Figure 1.1; Table 1.7). Because the data used in *Trends in International Migration* is limited to the OECD member countries, the partner countries represented in the empirical chapters of this report will not appear in the corresponding tables and figures.

Figure 1.1 shows the number of foreign-nationality (non-citizen) and foreign-born individuals as a percentage of the total populations in the case countries for the year 2002. The proportion

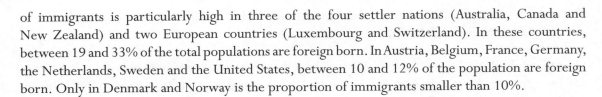

of immigrants is particularly high in three of the four settler nations (Australia, Canada and New Zealand) and two European countries (Luxembourg and Switzerland). In these countries, between 19 and 33% of the total populations are foreign born. In Austria, Belgium, France, Germany, the Netherlands, Sweden and the United States, between 10 and 12% of the population are foreign born. Only in Denmark and Norway is the proportion of immigrants smaller than 10%.

It is interesting to compare the foreign-born and foreign-nationality populations within the case countries (see also the last two columns of Table 1.7). In most countries, the differences in the relative sizes of these populations are fairly small, typically not exceeding five percentage points. As a rough proxy, this indicates that most individuals who have immigrated into these countries have not acquired their citizenship (although for accurate numbers on naturalisation it is best to examine the proportion of the foreign-born population that has the nationality of the host country). Notable exceptions are Australia and Canada where the foreign-born populations are about 15 percentage points larger than the foreign-nationality populations.[4] This should reflect the relatively liberal naturalisation practices in these countries. The opposite pattern emerges for Luxembourg where the foreign-nationality population is larger than the foreign-born population. This indicates that a large number of foreign-nationals living in Luxembourg were born there.

Figure 1.2 provides information on the proportion of different categories of immigrants who entered selected countries in 2002. Only those OECD countries for which largely comparable data are

Figure 1.1 ■ **Stock of foreign-born and foreign-nationality populations**

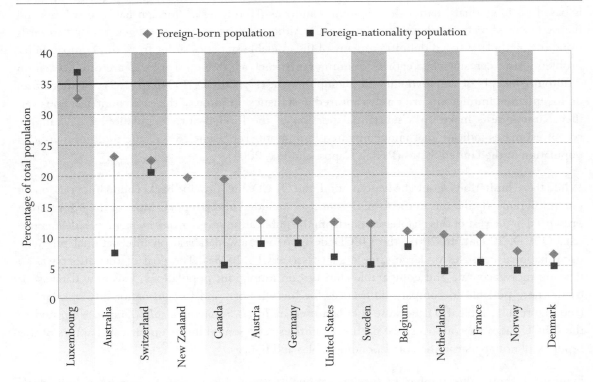

Note: Countries are ranked by decreasing order of percentage of foreign-born population.
Source: OECD PISA 2003 database, Table 1.1.

© OECD 2006 *Where immigrant students succeed - A comparative review of performance and engagement in PISA 2003*

Figure 1.2 ■ **Permanent or long-term immigration flows into selected OECD countries in 2002, by main immigration categories**[1]

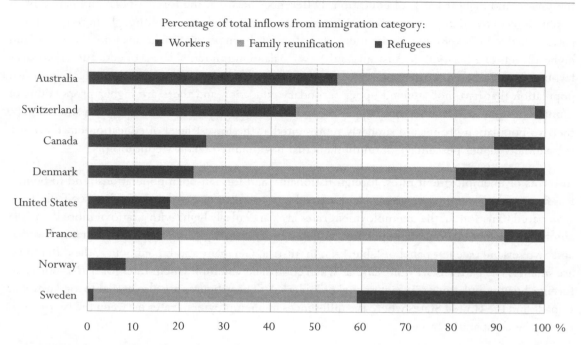

Percentage of total inflows from immigration category:

■ Workers   ■ Family reunification   ■ Refugees

Note: Countries are ranked by decreasing order of the percentage of workers in total inflows. Categories give the legal reason for entering the country. A worker who has benefited from the family reunification procedure is regrouped into this latter category even if he has a job in the host country while entering. Family members who join a refugee are counted among other refugees.

1. For Australia, Canada, Norway, Sweden and the United States, data concern acceptances for settlement. For Denmark, France and Switzerland, entries correspond to residence permits usually delivered for longer than one year. For Australia, category "Workers" includes accompanying dependents who are included in the category "Family reunification" for all other countries.

Source: National Statistical Offices, OECD calculations (see Table 1.2 for notes on data for Australia, France, Norway, Sweden and the United States).

available are included in the graph (see footnotes in Figure 1.2 for comparability limitations). The figure shows that the proportion of work-related immigrants is particularly high in Australia[5] (54%) and Switzerland (45%) and particularly low in Norway (8%) and Sweden (1%). In contrast, Sweden stands out with regard to refugees entering the country with a share of more than 40% among new immigrants in 2002. Compared to the other countries, the proportion of refugees is also quite high in Denmark (19%) and Norway (23%). Finally, family reunification plays a substantial role in all the countries, with particularly large shares in Canada (63%), France (75%), Norway (68%) and the United States (69%).[6]

Tables 1.3 and 1.4 present some data on the educational background and employment situation of immigrants in the OECD countries included in this report. Table 1.3 shows the proportion of the native-born and foreign-born populations aged 15 years and older by highest level of education attained. The disparities between the two population groups vary considerably across countries. In a few countries – notably Austria, Germany, the Netherlands, Switzerland and the United States – immigrants show substantially lower levels of education, with much higher proportions not having attained upper secondary level education. Belgium, Denmark and France show similar patterns, although the differences between the two population groups, substantial as they are, tend to be less pronounced. In Luxembourg there are substantially higher proportions of immigrants at both the lowest and highest levels of education. Differences between the foreign-born and native-born populations in Sweden are not substantial across the levels of education, although there is a similar pattern to that in Luxembourg, with more of the foreign-born population having both the lowest and highest levels of education. In Australia and New Zealand immigrants' levels of education compares favourably to the native-born population: there are comparatively lower proportions of foreign-born population that have not attained upper secondary education and there are higher proportions of immigrants that have attained both upper secondary and tertiary education. In Canada and Norway, the two population groups are similarly represented at the lowest level of education but there is a substantially higher percentage of immigrants that has attainted tertiary education.

In terms of unemployment rates, foreign-nationality and foreign-born populations tend to be in a less favourable position than national and native-born populations in most countries (see Table 1.4). Compared to nationals, the unemployment rates are particularly high (with a ratio of more than 2.5) among the foreign-nationality population in Belgium, Denmark, the Netherlands, Norway, Sweden and Switzerland (see left panel of Table 1.4). In Austria, Germany and Luxembourg, the differences are smaller. The patterns are quite similar when comparing unemployment rates for native-born and foreign-born populations (see right panel of Table 1.4). These figures are also available for Australia, Canada and the United States where the differences in unemployment rates between the two groups tend to be comparatively small.

Overall, the patterns of immigrant population characteristics reveal some differences and similarities among the traditional settlement countries and the European countries with post-war labour recruitment and colonial histories. Within the group of traditional immigration countries, the United States tends to differ. In terms of the proportion of immigrants residing in the different countries, three of the traditional settlement nations (Australia, Canada and New Zealand) occupy the highest ranks together with two particularly prosperous European countries – Luxembourg and Switzerland. The United States is similar to a group of European countries with somewhat lower (although not low in absolute terms) proportions of immigrants. Moreover, in most European countries and in the United States, immigrants tend to have lower levels of education than non-immigrants. This is not the case in Australia and Canada where immigrants' level of education is comparable or even higher than that of non-immigrants. Similarly, differences in unemployment rates between the two groups tend to be small in Australia, Canada and the United States.

RESEARCH QUESTIONS ADDRESSED IN THE REPORT

As previously noted, the OECD publication *Trends in International Migration* provides information on international migration movements on a regular basis. In recent years, the series has also begun to address questions related to the integration of immigrants. These analyses focus mainly on labour market integration while much less has been written about the integration of immigrant students in schools. With PISA, a database has become available that allows researchers to explore and compare the school success of immigrant students at an international level. Drawing on the immigration literature and the background information on countries' immigration histories and immigrant populations presented in this chapter, this report addresses the following set of questions related to immigrant students in the case countries:

- How do immigrant students perform in the PISA assessment domains compared to their native peers and how do relative achievement levels vary across the case countries?

- How do economic, social and cultural background characteristics of immigrant students relate to their achievement levels?

- Are the patterns for other learning prerequisites and outcomes, such as motivation to learn mathematics and self-concept in mathematics, similar to those for achievement?

- How do language support policies and programmes differ across the case countries?

- Do groups of countries emerge with similar patterns of immigrant student outcomes and do these groups correspond to categories distinguished in the literature?

- Which factors might contribute to between-country differences in immigrant student outcomes and what could be potential target points of interventions to improve the situation of immigrant students?

As noted throughout the report, the PISA data supply only descriptive information. Nevertheless, the analyses can provide new information and insights into these questions on the situation of immigrant students in many of the world's largest immigrant receiving countries.

IMMIGRANT STUDENTS IN THE PISA SAMPLE

The strength of PISA for examining immigrant students cross-nationally is that it provides an internationally comparable basis to explore students' learning across and within countries. In 2003, 41 countries participated (including all 30 OECD countries) and the survey includes information on students' background characteristics, approaches to learning and performance. In 2003 the focus of the assessment was mathematical literacy, with reading literacy, scientific literacy and problem solving as minor domains[7]. Literacy in each of the domains focuses on students' ability to apply their knowledge and experience to real-life situations.

In some countries participating in PISA, immigrants make up a very small proportion of the population. For these countries, the number of immigrant students included in the PISA database is not sufficient to yield reliable estimates of their achievement levels or relationships between performance indicators and other factors. To be included in the report, countries had to have a minimum of 3% of immigrant students (first-generation and second-generation students – see below) in the sample. In addition, at least 3% of students had to speak a different language at home to the language of assessment or other national language.[8] Countries' samples also had to have data for at least 100 immigrant students. Among the participating countries, 17 met these criteria: Australia, Austria, Belgium, Canada, Denmark, France, Germany, Luxembourg, the Netherlands, New Zealand, Norway, Sweden, Switzerland, the United States and the partner countries Hong Kong-China, Macao-China and the Russian Federation.

The student background questionnaire includes questions related to students' and parents' place of birth, allowing for comparisons between three subgroups throughout this report – first-generation students (foreign-born students with foreign-born parents), second-generation students (students born in the country of assessment with foreign-born parents), and native students (students with at least one parent born in the country of assessment). Students born in the country who have one foreign-born parent (children of "combined" families) were included in the native category, as previous research indicates that these students perform similarly to native students (Gonzalez, 2002).[9] Table 1.5 displays the proportion of each of the immigrant subgroups in the case countries.

First-generation students were asked to indicate the age at which they immigrated. One may expect that the performance of first-generation students is less a reflection of the receiving country's school system than the performance of second-generation students, as the majority of first-generation students have not spent their entire schooling experience in the receiving country. However, the average age at which immigrant students arrived in the OECD case countries is just over six years (see Table 1.6). Therefore, while the first-generation students missed the early years that may be critical for the integration process, many of them attended schools in the receiving country for the majority of their education, which may reduce the differences between the two immigrant groups. Nevertheless, differences between first-generation and second-generation students will be examined throughout the report.

The student questionnaire also allows for the exploration of the role of the language spoken at home, distinguishing between students mainly speaking a language that is different from the language of assessment, other official languages or other national dialects, and students mainly speaking a language that is the same as the language of assessment, other official languages or other national dialects. A limited number of countries participating in PISA also collected information on the specific country where the students or their parents were born and the specific language spoken at home. Where possible, this information is also presented throughout the report. However, because only a small number of countries collected this information, the majority of the analyses focus on the situation of immigrant student populations as a whole in the case countries. Furthermore, in some analyses, the groups of first-generation and second-generation students are combined to form a broader category labelled immigrant students.

To judge how well the PISA data on immigrant students represent the immigrant populations in each country, Table 1.7 compares the percentage of 15-year-old immigrant students (first-generation and second-generation combined) in the PISA 2003 sample to the percentage of immigrants in the population as a whole (see also Figure 1.1). The table indicates that the proportions of immigrants within the group of 15-year-olds and within the countries' populations as a whole are quite similar, rarely deviating more than two to three percentage points. While these comparisons do not ensure that immigrant students are accurately represented in the PISA samples, they do indicate that the proportions in the PISA sample are not substantially different from other estimates of immigrant populations.

Table 1.8 compares the three most common countries of origin for immigrant students in the PISA sample (where available) with the three most common countries of origin for the total foreign-born population in each of the case countries. The comparison is based on data from *Trends in International Migration* (SOPEMI) for 2002 (OECD, 2005). Again, this report uses migration statistics collected in each of the OECD countries with some countries providing information on foreign-born immigrants and others on foreign-nationality immigrants. Although the most common countries of origin do not align perfectly, there is a significant overlap in most of the case countries. This is particularly remarkable as there are numerous reasons why the results could diverge. The categories used in PISA are different from those used in the SOPEMI, and larger deviations are found in countries whose official migration statistics are based on nationality rather than on country of birth. For example, in Germany many immigrants from the former Soviet republics are immediately granted citizenship and are not counted in the German SOPEMI data (which uses nationality to categorize immigrants). In addition, differences should also result from cohort effects, as PISA focuses on 15-year-old students and their parents, while the SOPEMI includes the whole population of immigrants.[10] In the majority of the case countries where data are available, however, the broad trends for the most common countries of origin are similar in the two data sets.

The proportion of students in the PISA sample who speak a language at home other than the language of assessment also varies across countries (see Table 1.9). Luxembourg has the highest percentage of students who speak a different language at home (24%) followed by Canada (10%). In the rest of the case countries, the proportion is less than 10%. Table 1.10 shows the proportion of students by immigrant subgroup who speak a different language from the language of assessment. Not surprisingly, only a very small percentage of native students speak a different language at home: less than two percent in all of the OECD case countries. In the partner countries, the proportions tend to be a little higher. Among first-generation and second-generation students, much larger proportions of students speak a different language at home from the language of assessment. Again, the partner countries are exceptions to this trend, with immigrants in Hong Kong-China and Macao-China mostly coming from countries with the same official language as the receiving country and many immigrants in the Russian Federation coming from the former Soviet Republics. Among second-generation students in OECD countries, the proportion of students who speak a different language at home from the language of assessment ranges from about 28% in Australia and New Zealand to 64% in Luxembourg. The percentages are even higher among first-generation students ranging from 32% in Belgium to 83-84% in Luxembourg and Norway. Table 1.11 presents the most common languages spoken at home in each case country where this information was collected. As expected, these numbers are closely aligned with immigrant students' countries of origin.

The remainder of this report consists of five chapters. The next chapter compares immigrant and non-immigrant student performance in the case countries. In addition, it explores the relationship between students' home language and their levels of performance. Chapter 3 examines central background characteristics of first-generation and second-generation students in the case countries as they relate to achievement. In addition, it explores differences in the characteristics of schools that immigrant students and native students attend. Chapter 4 focuses on students' motivation, beliefs about themselves and perceptions of school, and how these essential prerequisites of learning vary among the three subgroups (first-generation, second-generation and native students). Chapter 5 presents the results from the supplementary survey of national policies and practices related to assisting immigrant students attain proficiency in the language of instruction.

Notes

_____

1   The descriptions represent modified versions of Castles' (2000) definitions.

2   Within a country regional levels of decision-making may also play a role.

3   Over the last two decades, the main form of migration to Germany has included individuals with German ancestry from the former Soviet Union and Eastern Europe. They receive German citizenship upon arrival, and official statistics typically do not count them as immigrants.

4   Data on the foreign population are not available for New Zealand. Therefore, the difference cannot be calculated for this country.

5   The figure for Australia given here includes accompanying family and is therefore inflated. The real proportion is around half that shown.

6   Note that some of the family reunification involves accompanying family of worker migrants. Also some of what appears under family reunification, especially the United States, involves the migration of relatives such as adult siblings or adult children, who constitute separate households.

7   Problem solving was an exceptional assessment of cross-curricular competencies carried out in the PISA 2003 survey. Future PISA surveys will include mathematics, reading and science as domains.

8   The percentages refer to weighted data.

9   Consistent with *Learning for Tomorrow's World: First Results from PISA 2003* (OECD, 2004a), students born abroad but whose parents are both native-born were also included in the native category. The number of cases with this constellation, however, is very small.

10   Indeed, certain migration waves are older (Italians in Australia or Belgium) and are unlikely to have many 15-year-olds still in school.

2

Performance of immigrant students in PISA 2003

INTRODUCTION

Although the past few decades have seen high levels of immigration to industrialised countries, it is only in recent years that international databases have become available with which to conduct quantitative studies on the situation of immigrant students. Such studies based on internationally comparable data show that there are significant differences in performance between immigrant and non-immigrant students in most immigrant receiving countries (Buchmann and Parrado, forthcoming; Skolverket, 2005; Christensen, 2004; Entorf and Minoiu, 2004; Baumert and Schümer, 2001; OECD, 2001b). The first results from PISA 2003 confirm these findings: native students are at an advantage (OECD, 2004a). In addition, the IEA's (International Association for the Evaluation of Educational Achievement) *Progress in International Reading Study* (PIRLS) indicates that performance gaps between immigrant and non-immigrant students are already apparent at the primary level of formal education (ISCED 1) (Schnepf, 2005; Schwippert, Bos and Lankes, 2003).

This chapter builds on the results of the first PISA 2003 report to provide a more in-depth analysis of achievement outcomes and differences between immigrant and native students and to examine the role of factors that may be of particular importance for immigrant student outcomes. The chapter has four sections. The first section describes the range of immigrant students' performance both in absolute terms and compared to native students in the receiving countries. As noted in Chapter 1, immigrant students are divided into two distinct groups: students who were born outside the test country and immigrated with their parents (first-generation students) and students whose parents immigrated but who themselves were born in the test country (second-generation students). The second section explores the role of the language spoken at home by students in explaining achievement differences. Many immigrants must learn a new language when they come to the receiving country and immigrant families often speak a different language at home to the language of instruction. This could be one of the biggest barriers to immigrant students' success in acquiring essential mathematics and reading skills. Therefore, an attempt is made to explore the association between the language spoken at home and students' mathematics and reading performance. Specifically, the section examines performance differences between immigrants whose spoken language at home is not the language of instruction and immigrant students who speak the language of instruction at home. The third section of the chapter investigates gender differences in mathematics and reading among both groups of immigrant students to examine whether these gaps are similar to native students in the receiving countries or whether alternative patterns emerge. The final section places the results presented in the chapter in the context of the general immigration policies and trends described in Chapter 1 to provide a comparative understanding of immigrant student performance internationally.

IMMIGRANT STUDENT PERFORMANCE IN THE OECD AND PARTNER COUNTRIES

First-generation students are likely to have most difficulty in terms of school performance, as they have directly experienced the challenges of immigration, such as learning a new language, adjusting to a new culture and social situation, or acclimatising to an unfamiliar school system. Figure 2.1a confirms that the greatest difference in mathematics performance occurs between first-generation and native students. The most pronounced difference of 109 score points is in Belgium. In the majority of the 14 OECD countries included in this study, the gap between first-generation and native students is more than 62 points: equivalent to a performance difference of a full proficiency level (see Box 2.1 for an overview of PISA mathematics proficiency levels). However, there is no significant performance difference in mathematics between first-generation and native students in Australia, Canada, New Zealand and Macao-China.

Box 2.1 ■ **Summary descriptions for the six levels of proficiency in mathematical literacy**

Level	What students can typically do
Level 6	At Level 6 students can conceptualise, generalise, and utilise information based on their investigations and modelling of complex problem situations. They can link different information sources and representations and flexibly translate among them. Students at this level are capable of advanced mathematical thinking and reasoning. These students can apply this insight and understanding along with a mastery of symbolic and formal mathematical operations and relationships to develop new approaches and strategies for tackling new situations. Students at this level can formulate and communicate their actions and reflections precisely regarding their findings, interpretations, arguments, and the appropriateness of these to the original situations.
Level 5	At Level 5 students can develop and work with models for complex situations, identifying constraints and specifying assumptions. They can select, compare, and evaluate appropriate problem solving strategies for dealing with complex problems related to these models. Students at this level can work strategically using broad, well-developed thinking and reasoning skills, appropriate linked representations, symbolic and formal characterisations, and insight pertaining to these situations. They can reflect on their actions and formulate and communicate their interpretations and reasoning.
Level 4	At Level 4 students can work effectively with explicit models for complex concrete situations that may involve constraints or call for making assumptions. They can select and integrate different representations, including symbolic ones, linking them directly to aspects of real-life situations. Students at this level can use well-developed skills and reason flexibly, with some insight, in these contexts. They can construct and communicate explanations and arguments based on their interpretations, arguments, and actions.
Level 3	At Level 3 students can execute clearly described procedures, including those that require sequential decisions. They can select and apply simple problem solving strategies. Students at this level can interpret and use representations based on different information sources and reason directly from them. They can develop short communications reporting their interpretations, results and reasoning.
Level 2	At Level 2 students can interpret and recognise situations in contexts that require no more than direct inference. They can extract relevant information from a single source and make use of a single representational mode. Students at this level can employ basic algorithms, formulae, procedures, or conventions. They are capable of direct reasoning and making literal interpretations of the results.
Level 1	At Level 1 students can answer questions involving familiar contexts where all relevant information is present and the questions are clearly defined. They are able to identify information and to carry out routine procedures according to direct instructions in explicit situations. They can perform actions that are obvious and follow immediately from the given stimuli.

668
606
544
482
420
358

Note: A difference of 62 score points represents one proficiency level on the PISA mathematics scales. This can be considered a comparatively large difference in student performance in substantive terms: for example, with regard to the thinking and reasoning skills, Level 3 requires students to make sequential decisions and to interpret and reason from different information sources, while direct reasoning and literal interpretations are sufficent to succeed at Level 2. Similarly, students at Level 3 need to be able to work with symbolic representations, while for students at Level 2 the handling of basic algorithms, formulae, procedures and conventions is sufficient. With regard to modelling skills, Level 3 requires students to make use of different representational models, while for Level 2 it is sufficient to recognise, apply and interpret basic given models. Students at Level 3 need to use simple problem-solving strategies, while for Level 2 the use of direct inferences is sufficient.

For second-generation students, one might expect very different results. These students are the children of immigrants. They were born in the receiving country and experienced all of their schooling in the same system as the native students. Nevertheless, in many countries, there are considerable performance differences between second-generation and native students. There are significant gaps in mathematics performance between the two groups in all countries, except in Australia, Canada and Macao-China (see Figure 2.1a). In three of the OECD countries – Belgium, Denmark and Germany – the disparity is greater than one proficiency level, while in Austria, the Netherlands and Switzerland the disparity is just below one proficiency level (more than 50 points difference). Germany is the country with the largest disparity. Second-generation students lag behind their native peers by 93 score points, which is equivalent to one and a half proficiency levels. This is particularly disconcerting, as these students have spent their entire school career in Germany.

Comparing the performance differences of first-generation and second-generation students may give some insight into the effectiveness of countries' school systems in developing immigrant students' mathematical literacy skills. First-generation students have typically only spent part of their schooling in the receiving country and may have had very different schooling experiences before they arrived there. The level of achievement they have reached at age 15 can therefore only partly be attributed to the school system of the receiving country. Their relative performance may serve as a rough baseline for the potential immigrant students bring with them when they enter the different receiving countries. In contrast, the achievement of second-generation students is largely determined by the receiving country's school system (although it will also be affected by the student's background). The gap in performance between first-generation and second-generation students may indicate the extent to which the different school systems succeed in supporting immigrant students' learning.

Table 2.1a shows that in most of the countries where there are significant gaps in mathematics performance between immigrant and native students, the difference tends to be smaller between second-generation and native students than between first-generation and native students. In five of the case countries – Canada, Luxembourg, Sweden, Switzerland and Hong Kong-China – second-generation students perform significantly better than first-generation students. The gap in these countries therefore seems to decrease across immigrant generations. This may indicate that spending more years in the school system in these countries reduces differences between immigrant and native students. In the other case countries, however, second-generation and first-generation students do not perform differently. In the case of Germany and New Zealand, second-generation students have significantly lower scores than first-generation students. Given the nature of the PISA data, this may also be a result of cohort effects (*i.e.* variation in the composition of the two subgroups).[1]

The results for mathematics performance in PISA are generally consistent with the findings in previous studies where achievement differences between native and immigrant students are largest in continental Europe and smaller in the settlement countries (*e.g.* Buchmann and Parrado, forthcoming). In addition, these findings seem to lend further support to the idea that it is more difficult to mitigate disadvantages in tracked systems, as the countries with the largest gaps between immigrant and non-immigrant students also have tracked systems (OECD, 2004a; Baumert and Schümer, 2001). The larger performance differences are also likely to be related in part to the profile of these countries' immigrant populations (OECD, 2004a). Where possible, this chapter will include additional analyses of individual immigrant groups.[2]

Figure 2.1a ■ **Differences in mathematics performance by immigrant status**

■ ■ Difference in mathematics performance between native students and second-generation students
■ ■ Difference in mathematics performance between native students and first-generation students

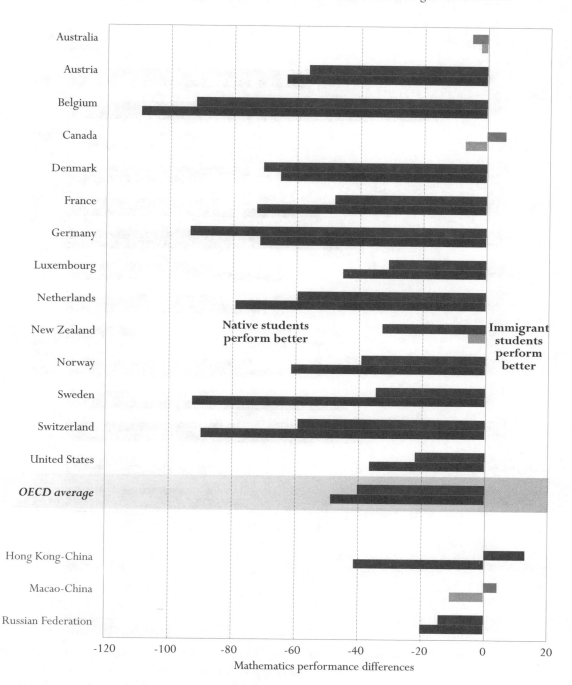

Note: Statistically significant differences are marked in darker tones.
Source: OECD PISA 2003 database, Table 2.1a.

Figure 2.1b ■ **Differences in reading performance by immigrant status**

■ ■ Difference in reading performance between native students and second-generation students
■ ■ Difference in reading performance between native students and first-generation students

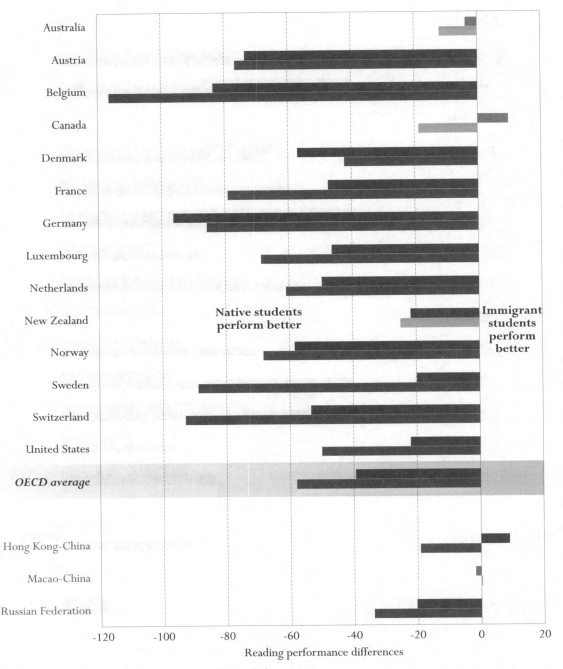

Reading performance differences

Note: Statistically significant differences are marked in darker tones.
Source: OECD PISA 2003 database, Table 2.1b.

© OECD 2006 Where immigrant students succeed - A comparative review of performance and engagement in PISA 2003

Figure 2.1c ■ **Differences in science performance by immigrant status**

■ ■ Difference in science performance between native students and second-generation students
■ ■ Difference in science performance between native students and first-generation students

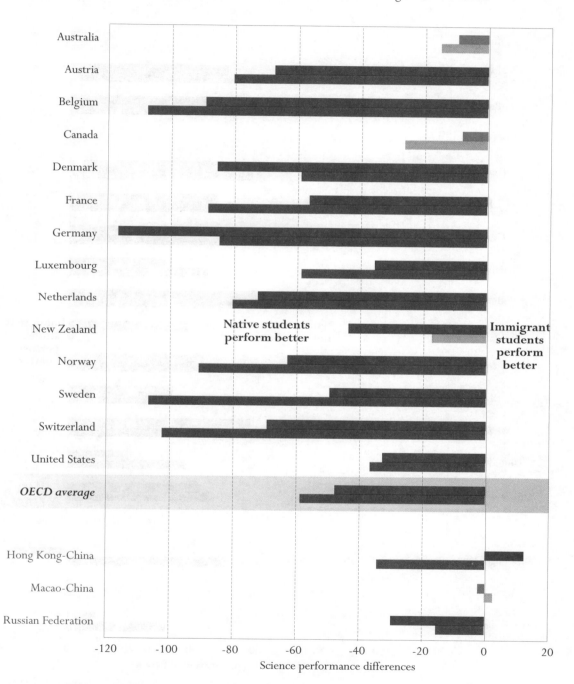

Science performance differences

Note: Statistically significant differences are marked in darker tones.
Source: OECD PISA 2003 database, Table 2.1c.

Figure 2.1d ■ **Differences in problem-solving performance by immigrant status**

■ ■ Difference in problem-solving performance between native students and second-generation students
■ ■ Difference in problem-solving performance between native students and first-generation students

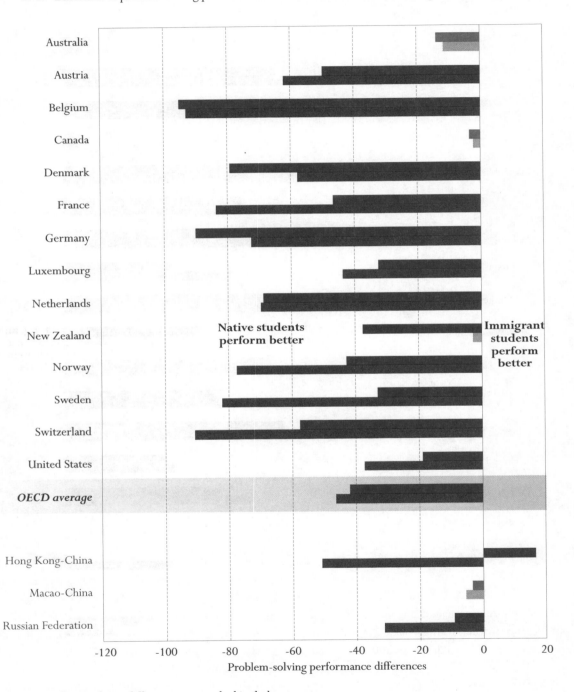

Problem-solving performance differences

Note: Statistically significant differences are marked in darker tones.
Source: OECD PISA 2003 database, Table 2.1d.

 © OECD 2006   Where immigrant students succeed - A comparative review of performance and engagement in PISA 2003

In the three other PISA assessment domains (reading, science and problem solving), there are also significant differences in performance between native students and immigrant students (see Figures 2.1b, c and d). The trends between second-generation and native students are similar across domains. There are larger differences in performance between first-generation and native students in reading and science than in mathematics and problem solving. The more pronounced disadvantages of immigrant students in reading and science may result from the greater need to master language in these subject domains. Previous research indicates that immigrant students whose native or home languages differ from the language of instruction may therefore be at a particular disadvantage in these domains (Abedi, 2003).

The remainder of this report will concentrate on performance differences in mathematics and reading. Table 2.2 indicates that there are high correlations for the performance of native, first-generation and second-generation students among the four assessment areas. In turn, it is not necessary to present results for all four assessment areas. This report focuses on mathematics as this was the major domain in PISA 2003 and a series of questions related to mathematics were included in the PISA student and school background questionnaires. In addition, the report will present results for reading, given the general importance that proficiency in the language of instruction has for immigrant students' learning in school.

The chapter will now turn to the absolute performance levels of the student groups as opposed to the differences in performance. Interestingly, even though large differences between second-generation and native students exist in a given country, the second-generation students may still perform above the OECD average or perform well compared to second-generation students in other OECD or partner countries. Figures 2.2a and 2.2b show the mean performance levels in mathematics and reading for native, second-generation and first-generation students in each country. The results should not be interpreted as an absolute ranking, as the statistics in the report represent estimates of national performance based on samples of students rather than the values that could be calculated if every student in each country had participated in the assessment. The degree of uncertainty related to the estimate is reflected by the standard errors (see Tables 2.1a and 2.1b). The figure therefore allows the reader to gain a rough indicator of the relative standing of different countries, but not an exact rank order of country performance.

Figure 2.2a shows that the mean performance in mathematics of second-generation students is significantly above the OECD average of 500 score points in Australia, Canada, Hong Kong-China and Macao-China. With the exception of Macao-China, second-generation students in these countries also perform significantly above the OECD average in reading literacy (see Figure 2.2b). Second-generation students in Austria, Belgium, Denmark, Germany, Norway and the Russian Federation have the lowest mean performance in reading and mathematical literacy. With the exception of the Russian Federation, there is a wide gap in performance in these countries between native students and immigrants (Table 2.1a). In contrast, the gap in performance between native and second-generation immigrant students is smaller where second-generation students perform above the OECD average.

Generally, the performance trends for first-generation students are similar to those described for second-generation students; the groups of countries with the lowest and highest mean performance tend to be the same. There are, however, two exceptions at the low end of the mathematics

Figure 2.2a ■ Performance on the mathematics scale by immigrant status

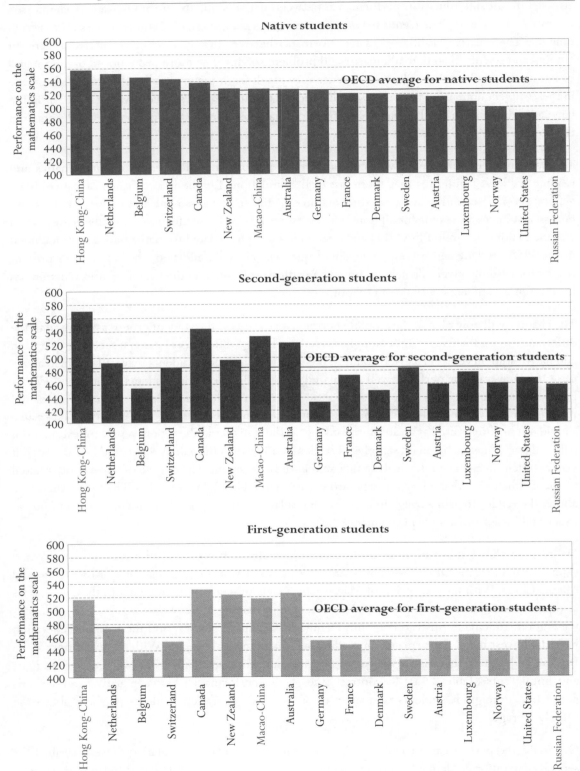

Countries are ranked in descending order of performance of native students on the mathematics scale.
Source: OECD PISA 2003 database, Table 2.3a.

© OECD 2006   Where immigrant students succeed - A comparative review of performance and engagement in PISA 2003

Figure 2.2b ■ **Performance on the reading scale by immigrant status**

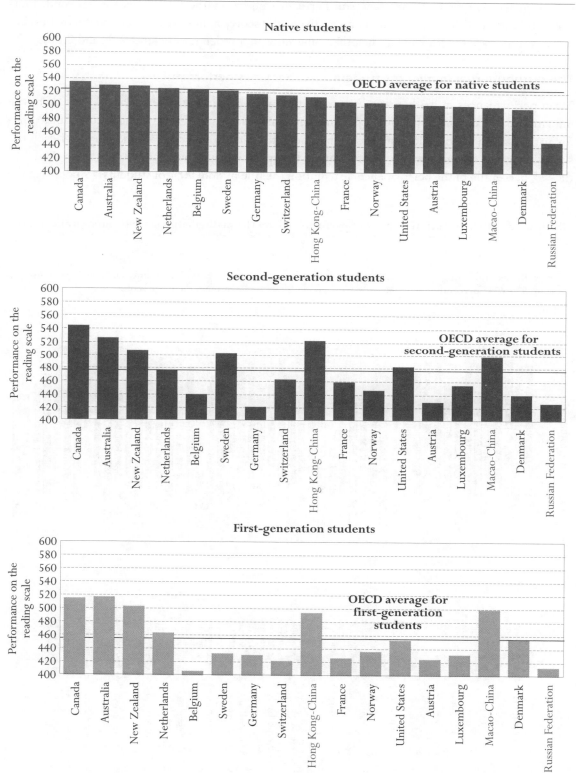

Countries are ranked in descending order of performance of native students on the reading scale.
Source: OECD PISA 2003 database, Table 2.3a.

performance spectrum. First, in Germany, first-generation students perform relatively better than second-generation students, yet they still perform well below the OECD average. Second, first-generation students in Sweden have comparatively low scores in both reading and mathematics, but this is not the case for students in the other subgroups in Sweden (see Figures 2.2a and 2.2b).

The distribution of immigrant students' mathematics performance

Mean performances in mathematics can mask the range of performance variation. It is therefore informative to examine how student performance varies across the entire distribution of outcomes for native, second-generation and first-generation students. In Figure 2.3a, the length of each bar shows the range of performance of students in the specified subgroup and extends from the 5th to the 95th percentile of the performance distribution (*i.e.* the middle 90% of students). Students at the

Figure 2.3a ■ **Distribution of student performance on the mathematics scale by immigrant status**

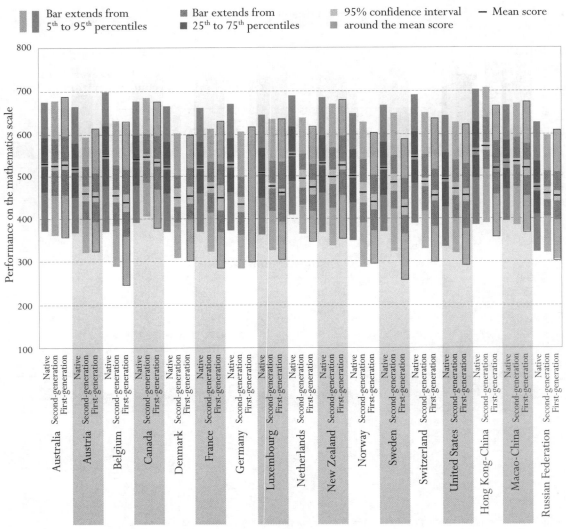

Source: OECD PISA 2003 database, Table 2.3a.

© OECD 2006   Where immigrant students succeed - A comparative review of performance and engagement in PISA 2003

top of each bar are among the higher performers (only 5% of students score higher) and students at the bottom of each bar are among the lower performers (only 5% of students score lower). The mean for each subgroup is depicted by a black line and the light grey or light red section around the mean represents the standard error of the mean. The mid-grey or mid-red section of each bar shows the range of scores for the middle 50% of students. In general, the bars for first-generation and second-generation students are longer, which indicates a wider range of performance within these groups compared to their native counterparts. Given both subgroups of immigrant students tend to have lower mean performances compared to their native counterparts, this means that the immigrant students at the lower end of the performance distribution (in the bottom segment of each bar) tend to perform at substantially lower levels than their low-performing native peers. In only a few countries – Australia, Canada, New Zealand and Macao-China – is the range of performance for native, second-generation and first-generation students similar (the bars are of similar length).

Figure 2.3b ■ **Distribution of student performance on the reading scale by immigrant status**

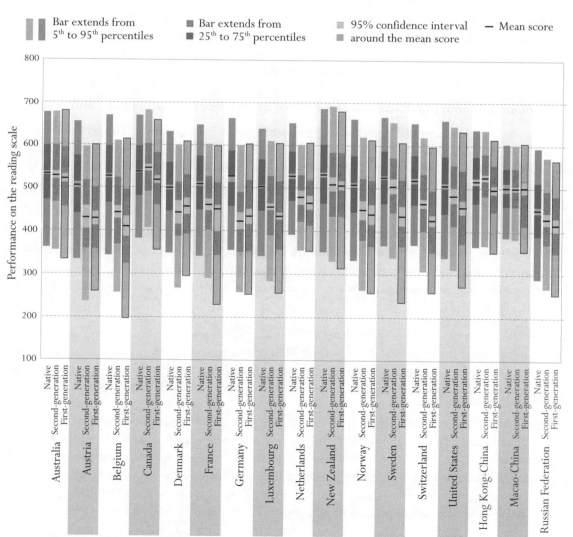

Source: OECD PISA 2003 database, Table 2.3b.

There are disconcerting differences along the low end of the spectrum of mathematics performance as well. The differences are particularly pronounced in Belgium where the lowest performing native students (only 5% of native students score lower) score 123 points higher than the lowest performing first-generation students. This gap represents the equivalent of two proficiency levels. In Sweden and Switzerland, the difference between these groups is equivalent to almost two years of schooling. In Germany, the 5th percentile of native students outperforms the 25th percentile of second-generation students.

Even when considering the mean performance of immigrant students, Figure 2.3a reveals large performance differences in several OECD countries. In half of the OECD countries – Belgium, Denmark, France, Germany, the Netherlands, Sweden and Switzerland – the middle 50% of native students all perform above the mean performance of first-generation students. This disparity remains for the mean performance of second-generation students in Belgium, Denmark and Germany. Similar patterns are observed for the distribution of student performance in reading (see Figure 2.3b).

Once again, these results show that in many European countries, as opposed to the three settlement countries, Australia, Canada and New Zealand, there are substantial performance differences between immigrant and native students. This pattern is most pronounced at the lower end of the performance distribution. Low-performing immigrant students often do substantially worse than low-performing native students, indicating that these students are particularly vulnerable to exclusion.

Performance of immigrant students by level of proficiency in mathematics and reading

The PISA 2003 assessment distinguishes six proficiency levels in mathematics. Box 2.1 presents the six proficiency levels and what students can typically do at each level. Of particular concern are students below Level 2, as these students may be considered at risk for not being able to actively use mathematics in daily life. According to the initial PISA 2003 report, Level 2:

> represents a baseline level of mathematics proficiency on the PISA scale at which students begin to demonstrate the kind of literacy skills that enable them to actively use mathematics as stipulated by the PISA definition: at Level 2, students demonstrate the use of direct inference to recognise the mathematical elements of a situation, are able to use a single representation to help explore and understand a situation, can use basic algorithms, formulae and procedures, and make literal interpretations and apply direct reasoning (OECD, 2004a, p. 56).

Based on this assumption, this implies that 15-year-old students who have not reached this level only have the most basic mathematical skills and are often unable to apply their mathematical knowledge in contexts where it might be needed to tackle everyday situations. This may have serious implications for these students' future educational and professional opportunities (OECD, 2004a).

As immigrant students tend to lag behind their native peers, they are at greater risk of not gaining essential mathematics and reading skills, which are vital for integration and success in the receiving country. Figure 2.4a shows the distribution of proficiency levels for first-generation, second-generation and native students. In the graph, proficiency Levels 5 and 6 were combined, as the number of immigrants reaching these levels is very small in some countries. The findings indicate that among native students, only a small percentage fail to reach Level 2, whereas the situation is very different for immigrant students. More than 40% of first-generation students in Belgium, France, Norway and Sweden and more than 30% of first-generation students in Austria, Denmark,

Figure 2.4a ■ **Percentage of students at each level of proficiency on the mathematics scale by immigrant status**

Percentage of students at PISA mathematics proficiency levels:

■ Levels 5 and 6
■ Level 4
■ Level 3
■ Level 2
■ Level 1
■ Below Level 1

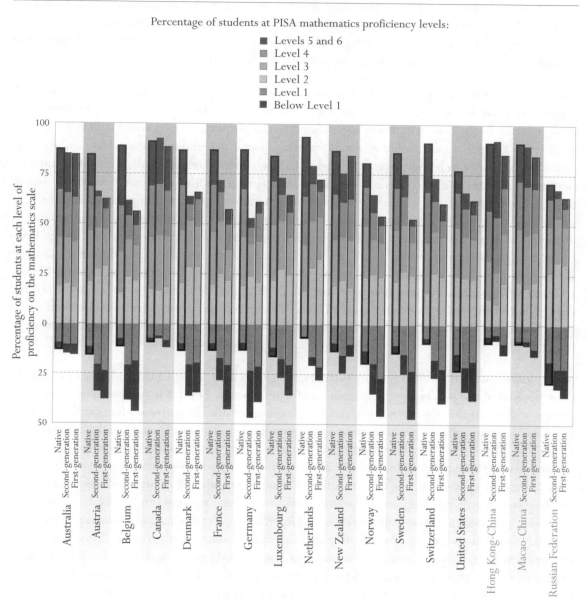

Source: OECD PISA 2003 database, Tables 2.4a, 2.4b and 2.4c.

Germany, Luxembourg, Switzerland, the United States and the Russian Federation perform below Level 2. In the Netherlands, more than 25% of first-generation students do not reach this level. These results indicate that in 12 of the 17 case countries, a substantial proportion of first-generation students perform at very low levels of mathematical literacy.

Second-generation students in most countries show higher levels of proficiency compared to first-generation students, and a smaller percentage of second-generation students fail to reach Level 2. Nevertheless, in over half of the OECD case countries, more than 25% of second-generation students have not acquired the skills to be considered able to actively use mathematics according to the PISA definition. In Germany, more than 40% of second-generation students perform below Level 2. In fact, more second-generation students than first-generation students fail to reach this level in Germany. In Austria, Belgium, Denmark, Norway, the United States and the Russian Federation at least 30% of second-generation students score below Level 2. The same is true for 25 to 30% of second-generation students in France, Luxembourg and Switzerland.

Again, based on research on assimilation tendencies for immigrants across generations, second-generation students are expected to be less disadvantaged in terms of achievement than first-generation students. This should also be reflected in the proportions of 15-year-olds not reaching proficiency Level 2, which should be smaller among second-generation students than among first-generation students. In France, Norway, Sweden and Switzerland the results do show this trend with at least 10% fewer second-generation students than first-generation students performing below Level 2. Nevertheless, the percentage of second-generation students failing to reach Level 2 is still substantially higher than the percentage of native students. Furthermore, in some countries, including Austria, Belgium, Germany and Denmark, the proportion of second-generation and first-generation students performing below Level 2 is similar (approximately 5% difference or less, although in Germany 6% more second-generation students than first-generation students do not attain Level 2) with large percentages of students in both groups failing to demonstrate the basic skills required at Level 2. For these countries, the pattern of findings suggests a need for additional support for immigrant children to ensure that they will reach a functional level of mathematical literacy.

A very different picture emerges for Australia, Canada, Hong Kong-China and Macao-China. In these countries, the percentage of students performing below Level 2 is comparatively low in all groups with less than 16% of first-generation, second-generation or native students failing to reach Level 2. The comparatively positive situation of immigrant students in Australia and Canada may be a result of selective immigration policies resulting in immigrant populations with greater wealth and education. Hong Kong-China and Macao-China are special administrative regions of China with most of the immigration coming from mainland China. As a result, differences in ethnic background and language between immigrant and native students in these two regions are likely to be small. However, it is clear that these countries succeed in providing a mathematical education where only relatively small proportions of students remain at low levels of mathematical literacy. In other countries, such as Belgium and the Netherlands, native students are among the top performers compared to the other countries, yet a large proportion of second-generation students fail to reach Level 2, even though they have received their education in the same school system as their native counterparts.

Figure 2.4b illustrates the percentages of students at each level of proficiency on the reading scale by immigrant group (for a full description of reading proficiency levels, please see Annex A2). As with mathematics, PISA emphasises reading literacy skills as a basis for lifelong learning (OECD, 2001b; 2004a). Students with skills at Level 1 are capable of completing only the simplest reading tasks (*e.g.* locating a single piece of information in a relatively simple text). This suggests that these students are at risk of experiencing severe problems in the initial transition from school to work and that they may not be able to take advantage of necessary further education and other lifelong learning opportunities (OECD, 2004a).

© OECD 2006 Where immigrant students succeed - A comparative review of performance and engagement in PISA 2003

Figure 2.4b ■ **Percentage of students at each level of proficiency on the reading scale by immigrant status**

Percentage of students at PISA reading proficiency levels:

■ Level 5
■ Level 4
■ Level 3
□ Level 2
■ Level 1
■ Below Level 1

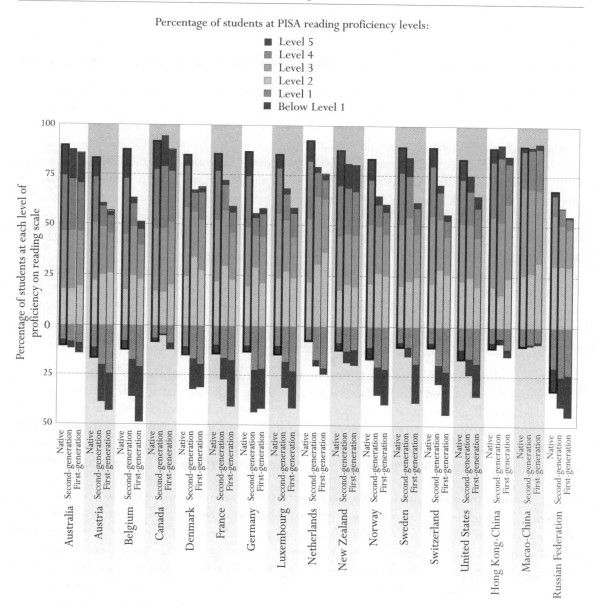

Source: OECD PISA 2003 database, Tables 2.4d, 2.4e and 2.4f.

Again, the trends in reading are similar to those in mathematics. With the exception of the Russian Federation, the percentage of native students who fail to reach Level 2 in reading is less than 20% across all of the countries included in this study. Among immigrant students, however, it is considerably higher. In 11 countries – Austria, Belgium, Denmark, France, Germany, Luxembourg, Norway, Sweden, Switzerland, the United States and the Russian Federation – more than 25% of first-generation students fail to reach Level 2. Similarly, in nine countries – Austria, Belgium, Denmark, France, Germany, Luxembourg, Norway, Switzerland and the Russian Federation – at least 25% of second-generation students perform at Level 1 or below. Germany has an especially high percentage of second-generation students in the very lowest category, with more than 20% of these students failing to reach Level 1 and more than 40% failing to reach Level 2. As in mathematics, countries with high percentages of immigrant students below Level 2 in reading may consider introducing support measures particularly geared to the needs of these student groups.

PERFORMANCE OF IMMIGRANT STUDENTS AND THE LANGUAGE SPOKEN AT HOME

Immigrant students are often exposed to more than one language. Many immigrant students must learn a new language when arriving in the adopted country. Other students may have been born in the country and gained some proficiency in the language of instruction but speak a different language at home. Education research indicates that speaking a language at home other than the language of instruction may further disadvantage students (Schmid, 2001). Evidence from both PISA 2000 and PISA 2003 shows that students speaking a language at home other than the test language tend to reach lower levels of performance than students who speak the test language at home (OECD, 2001b; 2004a). This is not to say that a multilingual environment is a hindrance to achievement. In fact, students with a high level of proficiency in both the language of instruction and the language spoken at home might benefit from a bilingual environment (e.g. Bialystok, 2001). In many immigrant families, however, using another language at home may indicate a situation of inadequate integration where parents do not have the skills necessary to assist with homework or students have not mastered the language of instruction because of limited exposure to it in their personal lives. These two factors may have a negative effect on students' ability to learn in the language of instruction.

Since many immigrant students may live in families where there is only limited understanding of the language of instruction at home (see Tables 1.10 and 1.11 for percentages of students speaking a language other than the test language in this study), it is essential to explore the role that language plays in order to better understand immigrant student performance in an international context. Such analyses may help to reveal potential target points for intervention. Providing additional support to second language learners may be one approach to improving performance of immigrant students.

Figure 2.5 shows the differences in mathematics performance between native students and four groups of immigrant students: second-generation students who speak the language of instruction at home, second-generation students who do not speak the language of instruction at home, first-generation students who speak the language of instruction at home and first-generation students who do not speak the language of instruction at home. Generally, the trends in performance for immigrant students introduced at the beginning of the chapter remain similar: in most countries, there are significant gaps in student performance in mathematics. Most notably, the gaps are even larger for second-generation and first-generation students who do not speak the language of instruction at home. The OECD average indicates that across OECD countries included in this study, second-generation and first-generation students who speak a language at home other than the language of instruction are at a similar disadvantage compared to native students, with performance gaps of 51 and 54 points respectively. For second-generation and first-generation students who speak the language of instruction at home, the performance disadvantage relative to native students is also similar: 25 and 29 points respectively.[3] These results underline the importance of this aspect of integration. More than 25 points separate first-generation students who do and do not speak the language of instruction at home. A similar difference is also seen for second-generation students.

© OECD 2006   Where immigrant students succeed - A comparative review of performance and engagement in PISA 2003

Figure 2.5 ■ **Differences in mathematics performance from that of native students by immigrant status and home language**

■ ■ Second-generation students who speak the language of assessment at home
■ ■ Second-generation students who speak a language at home most of the time that is different from the language of assessment
■ ■ First-generation students who speak the language of assessment at home
■ ■ First-generation students who speak a language at home most of the time that is different from the language of assessment

Statistically significant differences from native students are marked in darker tones.

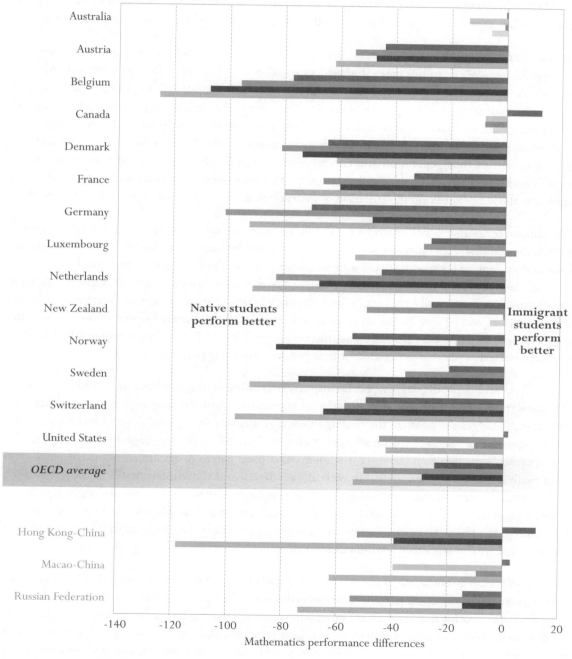

Source: OECD PISA 2003 database, Table 2.5a.

Based on the OECD average, it is not unexpected to find that in the majority of countries where there are significant differences in performance between immigrant and native students (Figure 2.1a), the performance disadvantage is larger for immigrant students (both second-generation and first-generation) who do not speak the language of instruction at home than for immigrant students who speak the language of instruction at home. This is the case in Austria, Belgium, France, Germany, Luxembourg, the Netherlands, Sweden, Switzerland, the United States, Hong Kong-China and the Russian Federation. In fact, in the United States there are no significant gaps between immigrant students who speak the language of instruction at home and native students. Yet, there are significant gaps for those who do not speak the language of instruction at home.

Australia and Canada are the only countries where no significant differences are found between the performance of immigrant students (second-generation and first-generation) who do not speak the language of instruction at home and native students. In other countries with relatively small performance gaps between immigrant and native students, such as New Zealand, Hong Kong-China, Macao-China and the Russian Federation, there tend to be larger gaps for immigrant students who do not speak the language of instruction at home than those who do (with the exception of first-generation students in New Zealand). These findings indicate that even in some countries with relatively small differences in performance between immigrant and native students, those not speaking the language of instruction at home perform significantly less well.

The pattern for performance in reading is similar to mathematics (see Table 2.5b). However, second-generation and first-generation students who do not speak the language of instruction at home are at a greater disadvantage for reading than for mathematics. The OECD average indicates that these students have substantially lower reading scores than native students with gaps of 56 and 70 points respectively. For second-generation and first-generation students who speak the language of instruction at home, the differences are 20 and 28 points respectively. Similar to the patterns observed in mathematics performance, students who do not speak the language of instruction at home independent of their immigration status (second-generation or first-generation) perform less well.

Tables 2.6a and 2.6b display the performance differences in mathematics and reading between the immigrant student groups overall after taking into account the language spoken at home. As expected, these results confirm the findings shown graphically in Figure 2.5 and further emphasise the importance of language for immigrant students. Controlling for language spoken at home, the performance gaps between immigrant students and their native peers are substantially smaller in both mathematics and reading. In Luxembourg, Norway and the United States, the performance differences between second-generation and native students in mathematics are no longer significant once language is taken into account. In New Zealand, Sweden and the United States the same is true for reading. In almost all of the countries included in the study, language spoken at home plays a considerable role in students' learning outcomes.

These results clearly indicate the importance of proficiency in the language of instruction for immigrant students across the OECD and partner countries in this study. The results show the need for more attention to be paid to improving literacy skills in both mathematics and reading for students with diverse language backgrounds. Policies focused on improving immigrant students' skills in the language of instruction could play a role in improving their educational outcomes and future success. Issues related to how OECD and partner countries provide language support for second language learners are explored in Chapter 5.

PERFORMANCE OF IMMIGRANT STUDENTS AND GENDER

In many OECD countries, there continue to be gender differences in tertiary qualifications with substantially fewer women entering the fields of mathematics and computer science than men. Initial findings from PISA 2003 show that females generally have lower levels of achievement in mathematics than males, although the gaps in performance tend to be small (OECD, 2004a). This section examines whether there are different trends in mathematics and reading performance for immigrant males and females compared to their native counterparts.

Figure 2.6a shows differences in mathematics performance by gender and immigrant status. In this case, native females are compared with native males, second-generation females with second-generation males and first-generation females with first-generation males. There is a fairly consistent trend across the case countries with males generally performing better than females. Among native students, the differences between males and females are significant in almost half of the case countries. The gender differences within the second-generation and first-generation student groups are not significant in most countries; however, they tend to follow the same pattern as native students. The fact that these performance differences in these subgroups are not significant should be interpreted with caution due to the small sample sizes that result when dividing the second-generation and first-generation student groups by gender.

Despite the small sample sizes, there are clearer trends in performance differences between males and females in reading, with native, second-generation and first-generation females generally outperforming corresponding males (see Figure 2.6b). These findings are in line with the findings of PISA 2000 where reading was the focus of the assessment (OECD, 2001b). In Austria, Belgium, France, Germany, Luxembourg and New Zealand, second-generation females outperform second-generation males on the reading assessment by more than 40 points. In these countries, the gender differences are larger for second-generation students than for native students. For first-generation students, there are performance gaps between females and males of more than 40 points in Austria, Belgium, France and Norway. In addition, they are larger than the differences for native students in these four countries. Overall, in most countries close attention needs to be paid to the reading performance of males, as males tend to lag behind their female peers regardless of their immigration status.

PERFORMANCE OF IMMIGRANT STUDENTS IN THE CONTEXT OF MIGRATION TRENDS IN THE RECEIVING COUNTRY

Thus far, the chapter has focused on broad differences in achievement between immigrant and native students. This provides general information on performance among the three subgroups, yet it does not allow for the investigation of how immigrants from specific countries perform. As noted in Chapter 1, immigrants living in the different OECD and partner countries come from a highly heterogeneous set of sending countries, and there tends to be substantial variation among immigrant groups in terms of their academic and economic success (*e.g.* Kao and Tienda, 1995; Borjas, 1999; Müller and Stanat, 2006). To the extent possible, the first part of this section explores some of these differences between subgroups of immigrants.

The diversity of first-generation and second-generation students in the case countries is difficult to capture in PISA 2003. Only a limited number of countries asked students to respond to questions related to where the student and their parents were born. In some cases, the number of students

Figure 2.6a ■ **Differences in mathematics performance by gender and immigrant status**

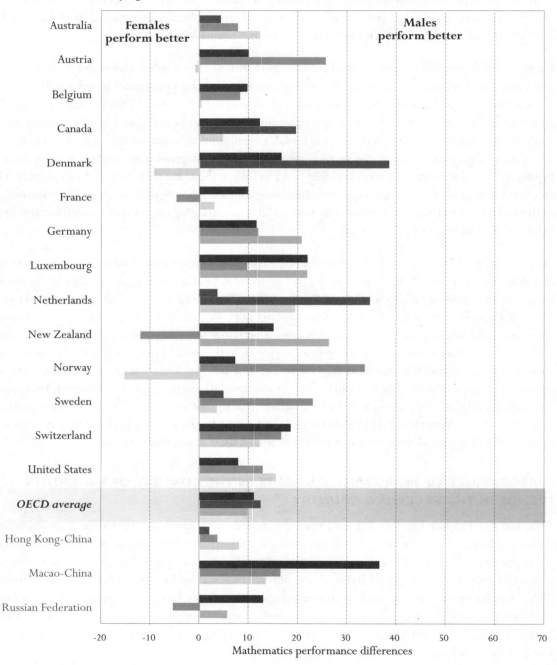

■■ Native students   ■■ Second-generation students   ■ ■ First-generation students
Statistically significant differences from native students are marked in darker tones.

Source: OECD PISA 2003 database, Table 2.7.

© OECD 2006 Where immigrant students succeed - A comparative review of performance and engagement in PISA 2003

Figure 2.6b ■ **Differences in reading performance by gender and immigrant status**

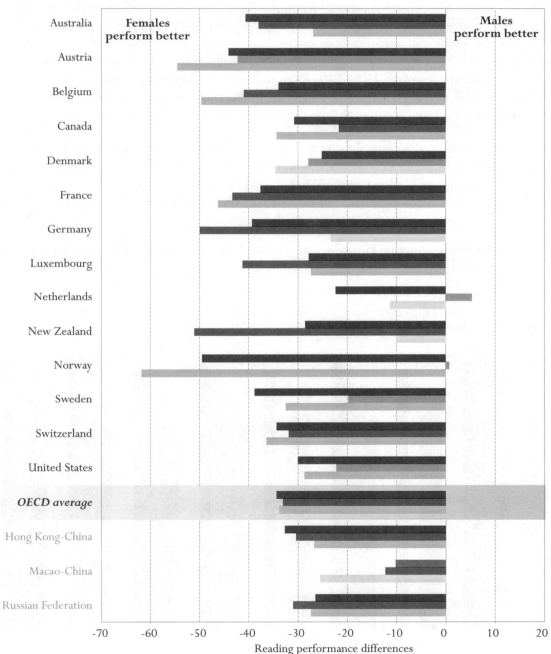

Native students   Second-generation students   First-generation students
Statistically significant differences from native students are marked in darker tones.

Source: OECD PISA 2003 database, Table 2.7.

from specific countries is very small and could not be included in the analysis.[4] Figure 2.7 shows the performance on the mathematics scales for native students and immigrant students from the three most common countries of origin for each case country where the information is available. The mother's country of origin was used for the analysis.[5] For this analysis, first-generation and second-generation students were combined. Shading in darker tones indicates that the difference between native students and the particular group is significant. The findings show that, within each of the countries, the results for different immigrant groups vary considerably. For example, in New Zealand, immigrant students from Samoa demonstrate significantly lower scores than their native peers (by 81 score points), while there are no significant performance disadvantages for immigrant students from the United Kingdom or China. In Australia, immigrant students from England and New Zealand do not exhibit significant differences compared to native students, while students from China even outscore their native counterparts on average by 49 points.

In the other countries, all immigrant student groups included in the analyses have significantly lower achievement scores than native students, but the difference varies by country of origin. For example, in Belgium, immigrant students with a Dutch background score 24 points less than the native students whereas immigrant students with a French or Turkish background have substantially lower

Figure 2.7 ■ **Performance on the mathematics scale of the three most common immigrant groups**

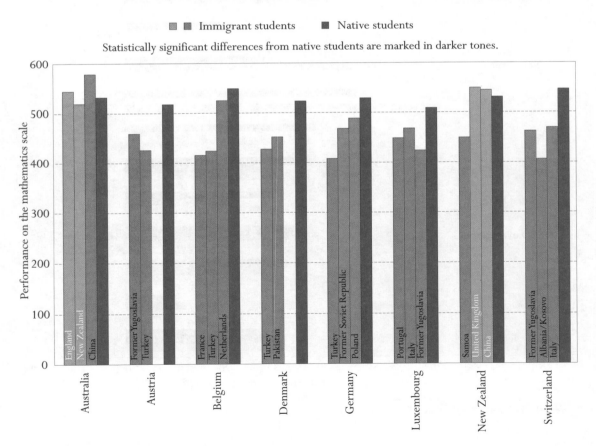

Source: OECD PISA 2003 database, Table 2.8.

© OECD 2006 Where immigrant students succeed - A comparative review of performance and engagement in PISA 2003

scores: 135 and 125 points, respectively. Performance differences of over 40 points can also be seen among the most common immigrant groups in Denmark, Germany, Luxembourg and Switzerland. In the United States, information collected on immigrant students from households where Spanish is predominantly spoken indicates that these students have significantly lower scores than native students (66 points). These results indicate that there may be a need for additional programmes or policies aimed at different immigrant groups with particularly low performance levels.

Two immigrant student groups are sufficiently represented in several countries to allow for comparative analyses. These include students whose families came from Turkey and from the former Yugoslavia. Figure 2.8 compares mathematics performance of these two groups with that of native students. Both groups have significantly lower scores than their native counterparts. In addition, both groups perform consistently below the OECD average of 500, and their mean scores are fairly similar across countries. Immigrant students from the former Yugoslavia have average scores ranging from 421 in Luxembourg to 460 in Switzerland. Students with a Turkish background have lower scores ranging from 405 in Germany to 436 in Switzerland. The gap in performance between Turkish students and native students is exceptionally large ranging from 92 points in Austria to 125 points in Belgium. The large performance disadvantages for both of these groups indicate that additional attention should be paid to the educational needs of these students.

Figure 2.8 ■ **Comparison of performance levels for immigrant students whose families came from Turkey and the former Yugoslavia**

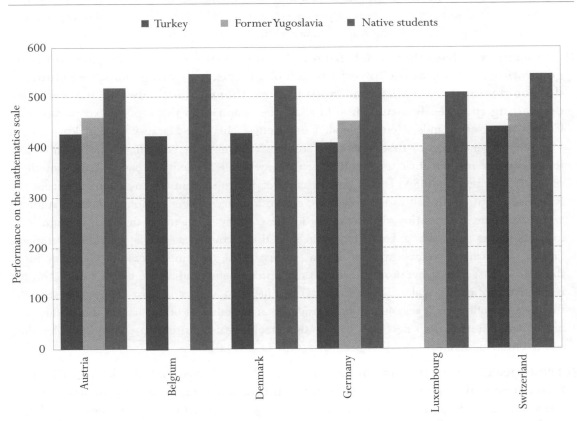

Note: Students from Turkey and the former Yugoslavia perform statistically significantly differently to native students in all countries.
Source: OECD PISA 2003 database, Table 2.9.

CONCLUSIONS

This chapter examined the performance of first-generation and second-generation students in mathematics and reading and compared it to the performance of native students. The chapter also explored the distribution of scores and proficiency levels for first-generation, second-generation and native students. Further analyses were conducted to examine the role of language spoken at home and gender for immigrant students. In addition, the chapter investigated the relative performance levels of several subgroups of immigrant students from different sending countries. A number of key findings emerge from these analyses:

(a) **While there are a few countries where first-generation, second-generation and native students show similar levels of performance, in the majority of countries there are significant differences between immigrant students and their native counterparts**. Immigrant students in Australia, Canada, New Zealand and Macao-China perform at similar levels to their native peers (with only second-generation students in New Zealand scoring lower in mathematics than their native peers). In a second group of countries – Austria, Belgium, Denmark, France, Germany, the Netherlands and Switzerland – both first-generation and second-generation students score almost one proficiency level below (and in some cases more) their native peers. Almost all of these countries with large disparities tend to have greater differentiation in their school systems with 15-year-olds attending four or more school types or distinct educational programmes (OECD, 2004a). This may contribute to the size of the performance gap, as may the composition of immigrant populations in these countries. A third set of countries falls somewhere in between these two groups. This includes Luxembourg, Norway, Sweden, the United States, Hong Kong-China and the Russian Federation.

(b) **In many countries there are substantial numbers of second-generation and first-generation students at the lowest proficiency levels, indicating that these students do not demonstrate skills that would allow them to actively use mathematics or reading in real-life situations**. In all of the countries in this report, except Australia, Canada, the Netherlands, New Zealand, Hong Kong-China and Macao-China, at least one in four second-generation or first-generation students (and in some cases many more) fall below the minimum mathematics and reading proficiency level needed for basic literacy in these subjects as defined by PISA. This is not the case for native students in any country, except the Russian Federation. In half of the countries, one in four second-generation students – students who have spent their entire school careers in the country – fail to reach this minimum level in mathematics and reading. Furthermore in the OECD countries Austria, Belgium, Denmark, France, Germany, Luxembourg and Norway, at least 10% (and in the case of Germany more than 20%) of second-generation students in mathematics and reading are below Level 1 on the respective proficiency scales. These students are unable to answer at least 50% of questions at the lowest proficiency level and can be considered at serious risk of not having the reading and mathematics literacy skills necessary to help them tackle real-life situations, to continue learning and to enter successfully into the work force (OECD, 2004a).

(c) **Not speaking the language of instruction at home is associated with significantly lower levels of performance for many immigrant students**. Immigrant students who speak a different language at home from the language of instruction tend to perform at lower levels than immigrant students who speak the language of instruction at home. Across the OECD countries, the difference between these two groups is 25 points in mathematics and more than 30 points in reading.

(d) Gender differences in mathematics performance tend to be similar across first-generation, second-generation and native students. Overall, gender patterns in mathematics performance are similar across groups with a tendency for males to outperform females. However, due to the smaller sample sizes, these are often not significant within the immigrant student groups. In reading, females tend to outperform males across all three sub-groups.

These findings are useful for education policy. First, they indicate that in a small group of countries, including Australia, Canada, and Macao-China (as well as New Zealand in most cases), immigrant and native students perform at high levels with only small (less than 20 score points) or non-significant achievement gaps. In the majority of countries in this report, however, there are significant differences in student performance with many immigrants failing to reach baseline performance levels defined by PISA. This is a problem not only for first-generation students, who are new to the receiving country and its school system, but also for second-generation students, who have completed all of their schooling in the receiving country. These findings point to a need for programmes and policies that focus on immigrant performance in those countries where immigrants lag significantly behind their native peers and where poor performance places students at risk for not having the mathematics and reading skills necessary to succeed in the receiving country. Furthermore, the findings related to language indicate that it is vital to ensure that immigrant students have the opportunity to gain adequate skills in the language used at school, as these appear to influence students' success in both reading and mathematics. The next chapter builds on these findings to consider the relationships among student background characteristics, immigrant status and performance.

Notes
_____

1 For example, in Germany the first-generation sample has a larger proportion of higher performing immigrant students from the former Soviet Republics while the second-generation sample has a higher proportion of relatively lower performing Turkish students.

2 Countries were given the option of collecting information on which country the student and his or her parents were born in. Australia, Austria, Belgium, Denmark, Germany, Luxembourg, New Zealand and Switzerland asked students this question. In all cases, the countries specified a list of countries that were most pertinent to their national immigrant populations.

3 As the analyses with the four different groups result in relatively small sample sizes in some of the case countries, second-generation and first-generation students who do not speak the language of instruction at home are combined into a single group for all further analyses. As noted above, these two groups generally tend to show similar trends in terms of achievement differences with their native counterparts.

4 If there are less than 30 immigrant students from a particular country, they were not included in the analysis.

5 The analysis conducted with the father's country of origin yielded very similar results.

Background characteristics, mathematics performance and learning environments of immigrant students

INTRODUCTION

Chapter 2 provided a detailed description of immigrant student performance within the case countries. The results indicate that in most countries first-generation students and second-generation students tend to lag behind their native peers. The literature suggests a variety of factors that may explain immigrant students' lower performance. Some of these explanations focus on characteristics associated with the immigration histories of the students and their families. The assimilation perspective tends to stress the importance of factors such as the age at which students arrive in the receiving country or the length of time the family has lived in the country (*e.g.* Alba and Nee, 1997). Other authors emphasise the role of language skills, arguing that a lack of proficiency in the receiving country's official language is the main hurdle for integration in the school system and labour market (*e.g.* Chiswick and Miller, 2003). Still other explanations focus on cultural factors. These include differences in basic assumptions that may cause immigrants to experience acculturative stress (stress associated with assimilating to a different culture) (*e.g.* Berry, 1992) or immigrants' general attitudes towards education and motivational orientations that may support or hinder the integration process (*e.g.* Fuligni, 1997). Cultural factors have also been used to account for differences in school success between immigrant subgroups focusing particularly on the relatively high achievement levels of students from some Asian countries (*e.g.* Stevenson *et al.*, 1993; Stevenson and Stigler, 1992).

While these ideas mainly refer to factors specifically related to students' immigration and cultural experiences, others stress the role of immigrant families' educational and social status (*e.g.* Fase, 1994; Jungbluth, 1999). According to these views, the disadvantages of immigrant students can largely be accounted for by their parents' socio-economic situation or level of education, which tend to be lower than those of parents in native families. If this were the case, models of social disadvantage could fully explain immigrant students' relative levels of school success, and it would not be necessary to consider aspects specific to immigration.

In addition to effects of individual background characteristics on school performance, other approaches emphasise the role of institutional factors. These include institutional discrimination with regard to grade retention, tracking decisions, referral to special education programmes or the extent to which textbooks reflect the diversity of students' cultural and language backgrounds (*e.g.* Gomolla and Radtke, 2002; Losen and Orfield, 2002). Also, several authors argue that community effects may influence the likelihood that immigrant students will succeed in school (*e.g.* Esser, 2001; Westerbeek, 1999). According to this view, segregation or self-segregation tendencies may cause immigrant populations to become isolated and therefore hinder integration. The evidence on this hypothesis is mixed, however (*e.g.* Coradi Vellacott *et al.*, 2003; Rüesch, 1998; Portes and Hao, 2004; Stanat, 2006; Westerbeek, 1999).

These different factors influencing immigrant students' school success most likely vary across countries and immigrant populations, and it is beyond the scope of PISA to test the different explanations. PISA is a cross-sectional study, *i.e.* data are collected at one point in time. Therefore, it is only possible to observe associations between various student or school characteristics and students' performance in the assessment and not to identify specific causes underlying the performance outcomes. Despite these limitations, however, it is useful to explore the relationship between immigrant students' background and academic performance within the case countries. Examining the associations among relative performance of immigrant students, educational and socio-economic characteristics of their families and immigrant status may have important implications for policy and educational practice. For example, if disadvantages linked to immigration status remain after accounting for parents' level of education and socio-economic status, schools may need to introduce support measures specifically geared toward immigrant students.

It is also important for analyses of differences in the outcomes of immigrant students across countries to consider the role of socio-economic and educational background factors for school success. Chapter 1 explained that countries' immigration histories and policies and therefore their immigrant populations vary considerably. In countries with selective approaches to immigration inflows, immigrants tend to be highly skilled and therefore have more education and work opportunities than in countries with less selective admission regulations. When examining performance differences between immigrant and non-immigrant student groups in an international context, it is essential to consider differences in the background characteristics of immigrant populations across countries.

PISA offers limited possibilities for taking into account immigrant population characteristics across the case countries. The data do not include information on the background of immigrant students' families at the time they entered the country. When the PISA data were collected, the immigrant students in the sample had already lived in the receiving country for some time. Therefore, their families' educational attainment, socio-economic status and other background characteristics reflect not only their situation at the time of immigration but also the extent to which they were able to adapt to their new environment. The policies and practices related to the integration of immigrants within a country should influence this adaptation process. Therefore, in countries with effective approaches to educational, social and labour-market integration, the situation of immigrant families may not only develop more favourably in terms of their children's school performance but also in terms of their economic, social and cultural status.

The effects of integration policies and practices on immigrant families' educational and socio-economic status should be most apparent in second-generation students. Their parents have already spent at least 15 years in the receiving countries, so the policies and practices in place in these countries should have had some effect and may therefore be reflected in the family characteristics. The families of first-generation students, on the other hand, have immigrated more recently, so their current socio-cultural status is more likely to reflect their situation at the time they entered the country. Accounting for families' educational and social status in analysing performance levels of first-generation students should therefore provide a rough estimate of the extent to which between-country differences can be attributed to variations in background characteristics of immigrant populations. It is important to note, however, that such an estimate is likely to be conservative as it may also absorb some of the variation associated with the effectiveness of immigration policies and practices that countries have in place.

Keeping this in mind, the first part of the chapter explores the role of immigrant students' background characteristics and their association with mathematics performance within the case countries. First, the chapter describes the level of parental education and economic, social and cultural status of immigrant and non-immigrant student populations for each of the countries included in the report. Next, the performance of these student groups in the PISA mathematics assessment is compared after accounting for parents' educational and occupational status. In addition, the analyses examine characteristics specifically associated with an immigration background (language spoken at home and age of the student at the time of immigration).

The second part of the chapter explores performance at the school level with the aim of locating differences between immigrant and non-immigrant students within the different school systems. This section describes how performance varies between and within schools. In addition, the schools that immigrant and non-immigrant students attend are characterised. As noted earlier, PISA can observe how certain characteristics are associated with performance variations but cannot identify causes for these differences. This is also the case at the school level. School systems differ considerably in terms of structural and contextual factors, such as tracking, streaming or residential segregation, and the meaning of results at the school level therefore varies across countries. Nevertheless, it is worth considering the extent to which immigrant and non-immigrant student populations within a country are likely to attend similar or different schools, as this may have important implications for targeting interventions.

IMMIGRANT FAMILIES' EDUCATIONAL AND SOCIO-ECONOMIC BACKGROUND

Often, people move to another country in the hope of improving their standard of living. This does not necessarily mean, however, that immigrants are among the most disadvantaged in the population of their native country. In fact, Chiswick (1999, 2000), Chiquiar and Hanson (2005) and others (for an overview see Chiswick, 2000) suggest that individuals who decide to settle in a new country tend to be a self-selected high-skilled group[1]. This was also shown in a recent international study of 22 countries (Liebig and Sousa-Poza, 2004).

Compared to the native populations in receiving countries, however, immigrants tend to be at a disadvantage in terms of their levels of skill and position within the social and economic hierarchy. Again, this depends partly on countries' immigration histories and the selectiveness of their immigration policies and practices. Countries requiring a certain level of education and training before issuing entry admissions should have more highly skilled immigrant populations than countries without such policies. Another consideration is the extent to which a country experiences an influx of illegal work migration, which is often associated with lower education and skill levels (*e.g.* Burgers, 1998; Rivera-Batiz, 1999). Indeed, countries differ considerably with regard to the level of irregular immigration and whether or not children of illegal immigrants participate in the public education system. For these reasons, large variations across countries in terms of immigrants' relative educational and social positions can be expected.

As discussed, the educational background of immigrant families should at least partially reflect their potential on entering the receiving country. This is particularly likely if the families immigrated relatively recently, as is the case for many first-generation students in PISA. Figure 3.1 displays the highest level of parental education in years of schooling by immigrant status. The bars indicate that the parents of first-generation students and of second-generation students have generally completed fewer years of formal schooling than the parents of native students. At the same time, the differences vary considerably across countries. The largest differences occur in Germany, with both the parents of first-generation and second-generation students having completed approximately five fewer years of schooling than parents of native students. In Austria, Belgium, Denmark, France, Luxembourg and the Netherlands, the educational disparities are also particularly pronounced for at least one group of immigrant students. Interestingly, the gap tends to be smaller for first-generation students than for second-generation students. This could reflect interruptions in school careers as a result

Figure 3.1 ■ **Highest level of parental education (in years of schooling) by immigrant status**

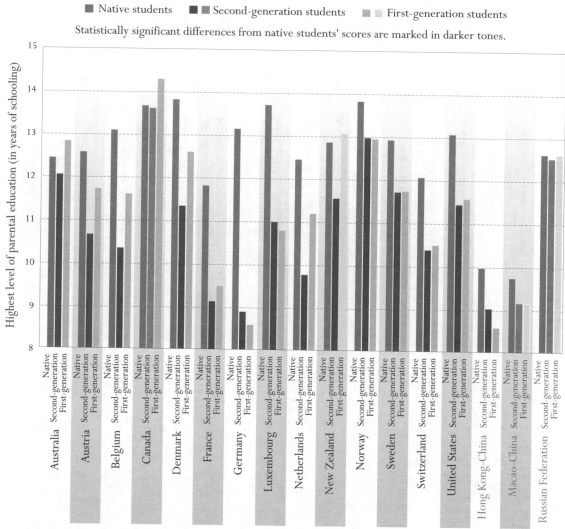

■ Native students   ■ Second-generation students   ■ First-generation students

Statistically significant differences from native students' scores are marked in darker tones.

Source: OECD PISA 2003 database, Table 3.1.

of immigration. Parents of first-generation students had their child before immigrating and are likely to have completed their schooling in the country of origin. Meanwhile, parents of second-generation students immigrated before the child was born and may have left their home country when they themselves were still of school age. Although the PISA data do not contain information on the course of parents' school careers, it seems plausible that differences in the likelihood of school-career disruptions due to immigration may contribute to this surprising tendency in the patterns of parental education for first-generation and second-generation students. Additionally, as discussed in Chapter 2 these disparities could also reflect changes in the composition of the immigrant groups.

In a minority of countries, the differences in parents' level of education between the immigrant and non-immigrant groups are relatively small. In Canada, New Zealand, Macao-China and the Russian Federation, the difference in the number of years parents have attended a school is not significant for at least one subgroup of immigrant students. Moreover, the difference in parental

Background characteristics, mathematics performance and learning environments of immigrant students

Figure 3.2 ■ **Distribution of the index of economic, social and cultural status (ESCS) by immigrant status (scores standardised within each country sample)**

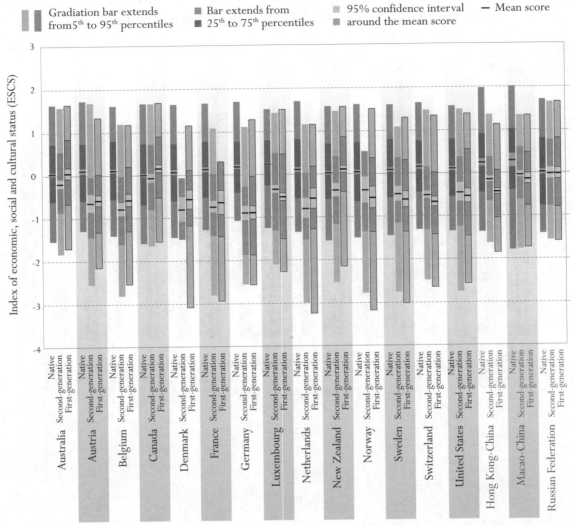

1. Due to small sample sizes, the 5th and/or the 95th percentiles could not be computed for these groups.
Note: Scores standardised within each country sample.
Source: OECD PISA 2003 database, Table 3.2.

education is one year or less for both second-generation and first-generation students in Australia, Canada, Norway, Macao-China and the Russian Federation as well as for first-generation students in Austria and New Zealand. In fact, parents of first-generation students in Australia and Canada have significantly higher levels of education than parents of native students.

Another important aspect of immigrant students' background is the extent to which their families are integrated in terms of socio-economic status. This can be examined by looking at the mean of the PISA index of economic, social and cultural status (ESCS) for both immigrant and native students (see Figure 3.2). Again, the differences between the groups vary considerably across countries. In most countries, immigrant families have, on average, lower economic, social and cultural status than native families. Generally in line with the results for parental level of education, notable exceptions to this trend are Australia, Canada, New Zealand and the Russian Federation. In Canada and the Russian Federation, neither first-generation nor second-generation students differ significantly from native students; in Australia and New Zealand only the families of second-generation students have a significantly lower socio-economic status than the families of native students.

With the exceptions cited above, immigrant students in most countries have more disadvantaged family backgrounds than native students. These differences can be based on varying distributions, however. For example, it might be that fewer immigrant students than native students come from the most advantaged socio-economic backgrounds or that more immigrant students than native students come from the least advantaged socio-economic backgrounds. To explore these patterns, Figure 3.2 presents the distribution of students (in terms of percentiles) on the index of economic, social and cultural status (ESCS). Focusing on the higher (most advantaged) and lower (least advantaged) ends of the ESCS distribution, it can be seen that immigrant populations in the case countries differ considerably in this regard. Three basic patterns emerge:

1. *Homogeneity among immigrant and non-immigrant student groups across the ESCS distribution*. In a small number of countries, the social situation of immigrant students is comparable to that of native students across the ESCS distribution. These countries include Canada and the Russian Federation. In addition, Australia shows a similar tendency. Although there are significant differences between second-generation and native students at some levels of the ESCS distribution within Australia, these are relatively small.

2. *Less favourable situation of immigrant students at the lower end of the ESCS distribution*. A more common pattern is that immigrant students at the lower end of the ESCS distribution are particularly disadvantaged compared to even the least advantaged native students while, at the same time, immigrant students at the top end of the distribution have similar levels of ESCS as their native counterparts. This pattern occurs most distinctly in Luxembourg, New Zealand, Switzerland and the United States.

3. *Less favourable situation of immigrant students at both ends of the ESCS distribution*. Most frequently, immigrant students have lower levels of economic, social and cultural status than native students at both ends of the ESCS distribution. This pattern is most pronounced in Belgium, Germany, the Netherlands and Sweden. It is also apparent in Austria, Denmark, France and Norway, although the group differences in these countries are not significant for all levels of the ESCS distribution.

In short, the differences in parental level of education and socio-economic status between immigrant and non-immigrant students vary widely across the case countries. In a few countries, all three subgroups have similar background characteristics. These include three of the settlement countries that were founded on the basis of immigration, namely Australia, Canada and (less consistently) New Zealand. In addition, a similar pattern emerges for the immigrant populations in the Russian Federation where immigrants come mainly from the former Soviet Republics. In the majority of countries, however, immigrant students are at a significant disadvantage compared to their native peers. The differences between immigrant and non-immigrant families tend to be particularly pronounced for students at the lower end of the ESCS distribution. In most cases, the pattern is similar for the families of both first-generation and second-generation students or even slightly less favourable for the latter group. Although this could indicate a lack of upward mobility, conclusions about developments across generations should be drawn with caution. Differences between families of first-generation and second-generation students may not only reflect upward or downward social mobility but also changes in the composition of immigrant groups that can be caused by fluctuations in immigrant inflow and admission patterns over time.

The findings show that immigrant and non-immigrant students differ in terms of their parents' level of education and socio-economic situation in most countries. Previous research indicates that these background factors are strongly associated with school success (*e.g.* Shavit and Blossfeld, 1993). Therefore, one might expect an association between immigrant and non-immigrant student group differences in terms of performance levels and educational and socio-economic background. The next section of the chapter will explore these relationships.

RELATIONSHIPS BETWEEN PERFORMANCE DIFFERENCES AND DIFFERENCES IN EDUCATIONAL AND SOCIO-ECONOMIC BACKGROUND AMONG IMMIGRANT AND NON-IMMIGRANT STUDENT GROUPS

Figures 3.3a and 3.3b show the association between differences in mathematics performance and parental education among immigrant and non-immigrant students for each country. The horizontal axis in the graphs represents mean differences between students from native families and students from either first-generation or second-generation immigrant families for parental education in years of schooling. The vertical axis represents mean differences between the two student groups in mathematics performance. On both axes, positive scores reflect an advantage for native students and negative scores represent an advantage for immigrant students. The gaps between the student groups for parental education and mathematics performance are clearly related: In countries where immigrant students perform at lower levels than their native peers the level of parental education in immigrant families also tends to be lower. With correlations of $r = .57$ ($p < .001$) for first-generation students and $r = .83$ ($p < .001$) for second-generation students the associations are moderate to strong. A similar pattern also emerges when considering differences in mathematics performance and families' economic, social and cultural status (see Figures 3.4a and 3.4b). Again, the correlations between the disadvantages of immigrant students in terms of performance and in terms of social background are quite strong (first-generation students: $r = .75$, $p < .001$; second-generation students: $r = .86$, $p < .001$). In Australia, Canada, New Zealand, the Russian Federation and Macao-China the gaps between native and first-generation students in terms of both performance and socio-economic status are particularly small. The distinct pattern for this group of countries anchors the regression line in Figure 3.4a.

The relationships depicted in Figures 3.3a to 3.4b suggest that international variations in performance differences between immigrant and non-immigrant students are related to similar variations in economic, social and cultural differences. This association should to some extent represent between-country differences in immigrant populations. At the same time, it may also reflect the effectiveness of integration policies and practices which can affect both the relative performance levels and the relative socio-economic status of immigrants. Again, among the countries with distinct patterns of disparities in terms of background and performance are Australia, Canada and, less consistently, New Zealand. In these settlement countries the differences between immigrant

© OECD 2006 **Where immigrant students succeed - A comparative review of performance and engagement in PISA 2003**

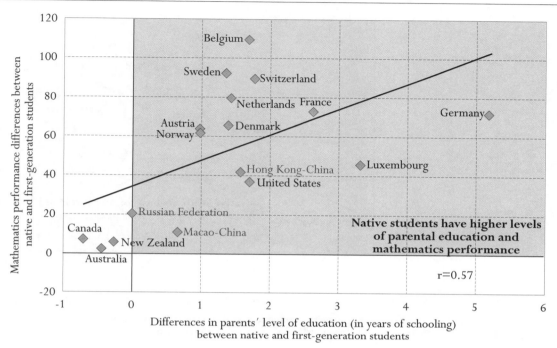

Figure 3.3a ■ **Differences between native and first-generation students in mathematics performance and parental education**

Source: OECD PISA 2003 database, Table 3.3.

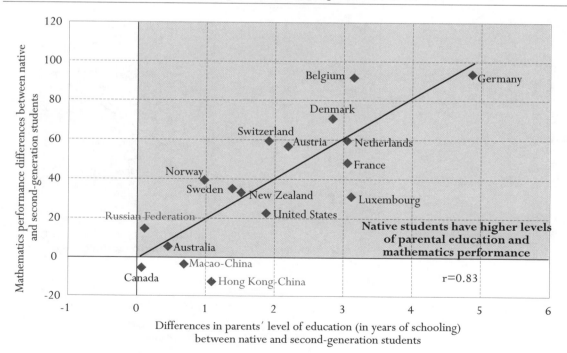

Figure 3.3b ■ **Differences between native and second-generation students in mathematics performance and parental education**

Source: OECD PISA 2003 database, Table 3.3.

Figure 3.4a ■ **Differences between native and first-generation students in mathematics performance and parents' economic, social and cultural status (ESCS)**

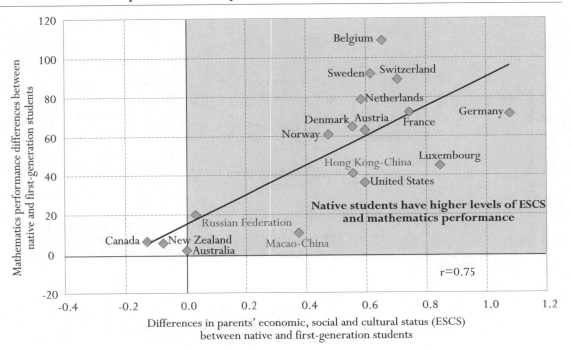

Source: OECD PISA 2003 database, Table 3.4.

Figure 3.4b ■ **Differences between native and second-generation students in mathematics performance and parents' economic, social and cultural status (ESCS)**

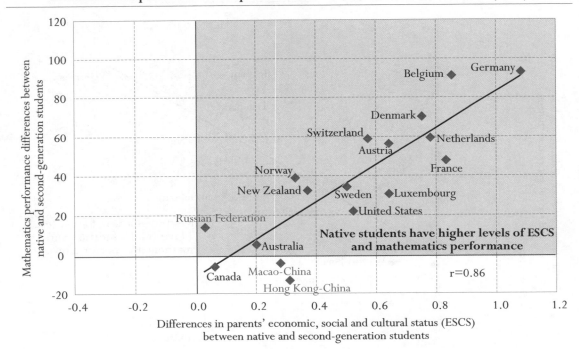

Source: OECD PISA 2003 database, Table 3.4.

and non-immigrant students for both performance and economic, social and cultural status are small. Another traditional immigration country, the United States, deviates from this pattern. Here, the disparities in performance and economic, social and cultural status are larger, although not quite as large as in some of the European countries included in the analyses. In the Russian Federation and Macao-China, finally, differences between immigrant and non-immigrant students are also small, which is most likely due to the unique composition of the immigrant populations in these countries (see description of immigrant populations in Chapter 1).

The relationships at the country level shown in Figures 3.3a to 3.4b, however, do not necessarily imply that the performance gaps between immigrant and non-immigrant students within countries can or should be attributed to these background factors alone.[2] That is, even after accounting for parental education and socio-economic status, immigrants may still be at a disadvantage with regard to performance. To explore this possibility, a series of regression analyses examines the extent to which parents' educational and socio-economic background account for performance differences between immigrant students and native students (see Table 3.5[3]). Instead of the composite index of economic, social and cultural status (ESCS), however, the indicator for parents' occupational status was used in the analyses. This was done to estimate the relative contribution of educational and occupational status separately (as they represent two distinct aspects of human capital) and to reduce collinearity. Not all students provided the necessary background information and they are therefore deleted from this part of the analysis (listwise deletion).[4] The proportion of missing background information varies across countries which reduces the comparability of the results of the regression analyses. In particular, results should be interpreted cautiously for those countries with high proportions of missing values (see Table 3.5 for details).

Model 1 in the series of regression analyses estimates the association of students' immigrant status and their performance in mathematics without taking into account any other background characteristics (see Table 3.5). Therefore, the coefficients indicate the extent to which the performance of immigrant students differs from the performance of their native peers. As shown in Chapter 2, the performance differences are significant for first-generation and second-generation students in most countries. However, neither group of immigrant students in Australia, Canada and Macao-China exhibits significant performance differences compared to their native peers. Similarly, first-generation students in New Zealand and second-generation students in the Russian Federation do not differ significantly from native students in mathematics performance.

The second model accounts for the parents' level of education, after having already accounted for the students' immigrant status. This decreases the size of the performance gap for immigrant students considerably in the majority of countries. It declines by 20 score points or more for second-generation and first-generation students in Germany, as well as for second-generation students in Belgium, Denmark and France. In several other comparisons, the reduction in the performance differences ranges between approximately 15 and 20 score points (first-generation and second-generation students in Luxembourg; first-generation students in Belgium, France and Switzerland; and second-generation students in Austria and the Netherlands).

Taking account of the parents' occupational status in addition to parents' educational level does not lead to large changes in the performance gap for immigrant students (see Model 3). This is likely due to the strong correlation between parents' educational levels and their occupations. Nevertheless,

Figure 3.5 ■ **Differences in mathematics performance between native and immigrant students before and after accounting for parental education and parents' occupational status (HISEI)**

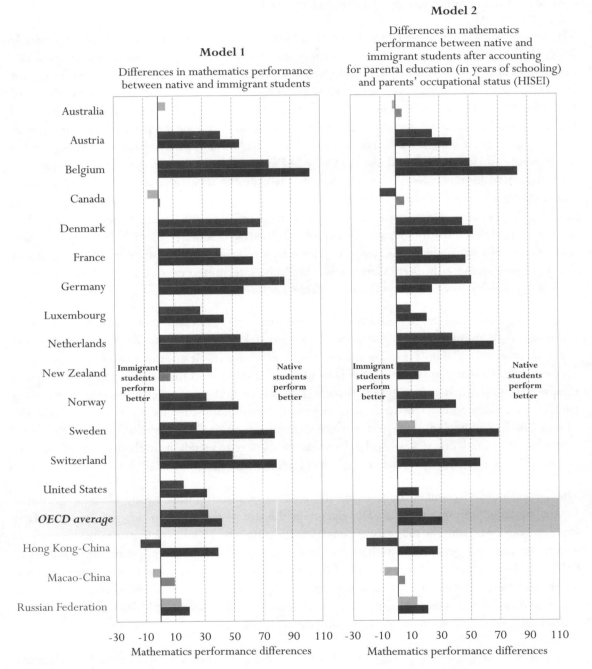

■ ■ First-generation students
■ ■ Second-generation students

Statistically significant differences from native students' scores are marked in darker tones.

Model 1

Differences in mathematics performance
between native and immigrant students

Model 2

Differences in mathematics
performance between native and
immigrant students after accounting
for parental education (in years of schooling)
and parents' occupational status (HISEI)

Source: OECD PISA 2003 database, Table 3.5.

© OECD 2006 Where immigrant students succeed - A comparative review of performance and engagement in PISA 2003

an additional decrease of 5 to 10 score points in the coefficient for the immigrant students results in several countries: for first-generation students in Austria, Belgium, Luxembourg, Norway, the United States and Hong Kong-China; for second-generation students in Germany; and for both first-generation and second-generation students in Sweden and Switzerland.

Despite the decreases in coefficients for immigrant students that occur after accounting for parents' educational and occupational background, the between-country differences in the performance gap remain substantial. Figure 3.5 shows the regression coefficients for immigrant students from Models 1 and 3 of the regression analysis. For the purpose of consistency with previous analyses, the sign of the coefficients was reversed. Therefore, the coefficients in Figure 3.5 indicate the extent to which native students outperform second-generation and first-generation students within each of the countries. Keeping in mind that the comparability of the estimates in absolute terms is limited, the rank order of countries with regard to the estimated differences in Model 3 is almost identical to that of Model 1. This pattern for the first-generation group in particular suggests that the cross-national differences in the mathematics performance gaps between native students and immigrant students cannot be explained solely on the basis of the educational or occupational status of their immigrant populations.

The findings from the regression analyses therefore indicate that the large performance differences in some of the European case countries are not just due to the lower human capital potential of their immigrants. In fact, the differences specifically associated with students' immigrant status rather than with their families' educational or occupational background are considerable in many countries.[5] This indicates a need for these countries to increase their efforts specifically aimed at the integration of immigrant students.

Again, a small group of countries does not show substantial differences in mathematics performance between immigrant and native students even before accounting for any background characteristics. This includes two of the settlement countries, Australia and Canada, as well as Macao-China and (for first-generation students) the Russian Federation. For these countries, it is unclear whether the small performance differences are due to the composition of their immigrant populations or to the effectiveness of their approaches to integration. Chapter 5 indicates that relatively structured and comprehensive second-language support programmes may contribute to this pattern in some countries.

As noted in Chapter 2, in a few countries second-generation students perform significantly better than first-generation students. This is the case in Canada, Luxembourg, Sweden, Switzerland and Hong Kong-China. Although the differences between the two immigrant groups may be partly due to cohort effects (*i.e.* more recent immigrants to the countries concerned having lower skill levels than earlier immigrants), this pattern may also suggest that these countries have particularly effective integration policies and practices. Chapter 5 explores policies and practices related to second-language support in some detail.

DISPARITIES SPECIFICALLY RELATED TO STUDENTS' IMMIGRANT STATUS

The section above indicates that performance differences between immigrant and non-immigrant students persist in many countries even after accounting for parents' level of education and occupational status. This suggests that these performance differences are, in part, specifically associated with students' immigrant background. As mentioned above, it is beyond the scope of PISA to explore the various explanations researchers have suggested to account for these disadvantages. Nonetheless, the international database allows for the analyses of two potentially important factors: language spoken at home and the age at which first-generation students arrived in the respective country.

Chapter 2 suggests that the language spoken at home plays a substantial role in mathematics performance. The following analysis considers the relationship between language use and mathematics performance while accounting for parents' educational and occupational background. Model 4 in Table 3.5 shows the results of introducing the language spoken at home as an additional factor in the regression analysis described before. This results in a heterogeneous pattern. In a number of countries, performance is strongly related to the language spoken at home even after accounting for parents' educational and occupational status. In the United States, students who do not speak the language of instruction at home score about 20 points lower than students who speak the language of instruction at home. In Belgium, Germany, Hong Kong-China, Macao-China and the Russian Federation, the performance disadvantage associated with not speaking the language of instruction at home is larger than 30 score points. The only other country for which the language spoken at home shows a significant negative association with mathematics performance is Canada (12 score points).

Adding the language spoken at home to the model tends to decrease the negative coefficients for immigrant students. In several countries, however, they remain significant. This includes the coefficients for both first-generation and second-generation students in Austria, Belgium, Denmark, France, the Netherlands and Switzerland; for first-generation students in Luxembourg, Norway, Sweden, Hong Kong-China and the Russian Federation and for second-generation students in Germany and New Zealand.[6] The decrease in the coefficients from Model 3 to Model 4 is largest for first-generation and second-generation students in Germany as well as first-generation students in the United States (15 score points). Changes of between 10 and 15 score points occur in Belgium (first-generation and second-generation students) as well as in the Netherlands and in Sweden (first-generation students).

The language spoken at home is therefore associated with substantial performance disadvantages in several countries. Whether or not immigrant families speak the host countries' official language at home may, to some extent, reflect their general level of integration. At the same time, however, the pattern does not necessarily imply that immigrant families should be encouraged to abandon their native languages. In fact, the literature on bilingualism clearly shows that it is possible for children to reach high levels of proficiency in more than one language (*e.g.* Bialystok, 2001). In line with this finding, immigrant students in some countries perform at similar levels as native students when they do not speak the language of instruction at home. Large disadvantages associated with the language spoken at home may suggest that students do not have sufficient opportunities to learn the language of instruction. Therefore, countries with substantial negative coefficients for students who speak a language at home that is different from the language of instruction in Model 4 may want to consider strengthening the language support measures available within their school systems.

Model 5 in Table 3.5, finally, includes all background characteristics from the previous analyses and adds the age at which students arrived in the receiving country. This factor is only relevant for the first-generation group.[7] The findings indicate that students who arrived in the receiving country at an older age tend to lag further behind their native peers in mathematics performance. In some countries, the relationship of students' age at immigration with performance is quite strong, and including this factor reduces the negative coefficient for first-generation students making it non-significant. This is the case for Denmark, France, Luxembourg, Norway, Hong Kong-China and the Russian Federation. In these countries, the negative coefficient for first-generation students decreases by 7 to 37 score points. In addition, the performance disadvantages for first-generation students are reduced by at least 15 score points in Belgium (48 score points), Germany (23 score points), the Netherlands (18 score points) and Switzerland (17 score points). This pattern reveals the important role of students' age at the time of immigration. Not surprisingly, there seems to be a strong tendency for immigrant students to reach higher levels of performance the longer they have spent in the receiving country's school system.

The results for age of immigration, however, do not imply that children from immigrant families who have completed all of their schooling in the host country will reach comparable performance levels to their native peers. As the coefficients for the second-generation group in the regression models indicate, immigrant students often lag behind their native peers even when they were born in the receiving country. This indicates that time alone cannot be expected to resolve the challenges associated with an immigrant status. Instead, targeted support measures seem necessary to help immigrant students succeed at school (see Chapter 5).

DIFFERENCES BETWEEN IMMIGRANT AND NATIVE STUDENTS WITHIN AND BETWEEN SCHOOLS

The next part of this chapter analyses the situation of immigrant students at the school level. First, it describes the extent to which performance differences between immigrant students and students from native families occur within schools or between schools. In addition, it examines the extent to which immigrant students attend schools with high proportions of students whose families have immigrated as well. Subsequently, this section provides information on resource and climate characteristics in the schools that immigrant and non-immigrant students attend. Again, in interpreting the findings, it is important to keep in mind that the results of the school-level analyses reflect the structures of the different school systems. In tracked systems, low achieving immigrant students will typically attend schools within the lower tracks. As a result, it is inherent in the systems of these countries that schools will show variations in immigrant students' performance levels. Such a pattern does not necessarily imply that the lower performance of immigrant students is caused by their concentration in certain schools, although this may be the case under some conditions. It is not possible to identify the effects of selection processes (such as tracking or residential segregation) and the effects of student body composition based on the PISA data (at least not without longitudinal data or alternative estimates of students' prior knowledge (Baumert, Stanat and Watermann, 2006; Schümer, 2004; Stanat, 2004, 2006). Keeping this in mind, however, it is useful to consider where the disadvantages of immigrant students are located within a school system, as this may provide some guidance for policy makers and practitioners in identifying target points for interventions.

Figure 3.6 displays the extent to which performance differences between immigrant students and non-immigrant students occur between schools or within schools. The length of the bars to the left of the central line shows the differences between schools that are attributable to students' immigrant status. The length of the bars to the right of the central line shows the differences within schools that are attributable to students' immigrant status. In addition, the columns to the left and

Background characteristics, mathematics performance and learning environments of immigrant students

Figure 3.6 ■ **Variance in student performance in mathematics explained by immigrant status between schools and within schools**

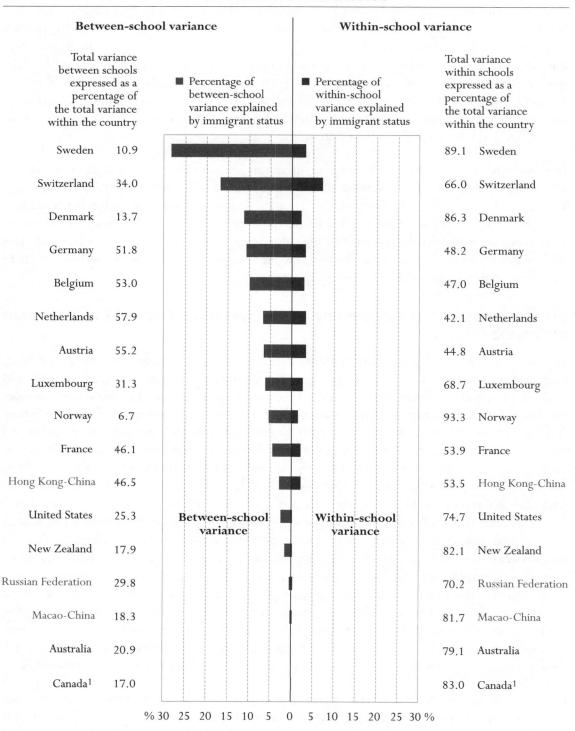

Between-school variance		Within-school variance
Total variance between schools expressed as a percentage of the total variance within the country	■ Percentage of between-school variance explained by immigrant status ■ Percentage of within-school variance explained by immigrant status	Total variance within schools expressed as a percentage of the total variance within the country
Sweden 10.9		89.1 Sweden
Switzerland 34.0		66.0 Switzerland
Denmark 13.7		86.3 Denmark
Germany 51.8		48.2 Germany
Belgium 53.0		47.0 Belgium
Netherlands 57.9		42.1 Netherlands
Austria 55.2		44.8 Austria
Luxembourg 31.3		68.7 Luxembourg
Norway 6.7		93.3 Norway
France 46.1		53.9 France
Hong Kong-China 46.5		53.5 Hong Kong-China
United States 25.3	Between-school variance Within-school variance	74.7 United States
New Zealand 17.9		82.1 New Zealand
Russian Federation 29.8		70.2 Russian Federation
Macao-China 18.3		81.7 Macao-China
Australia 20.9		79.1 Australia
Canada[1] 17.0		83.0 Canada[1]

% 30 25 20 15 10 5 0 5 10 15 20 25 30 %

1. Accounting for immigrant student status slightly increases the school-level variance in Canada, resulting in a negative estimate for explained between-school variance.
Source: OECD PISA 2003 database, Table 3.6.

© OECD 2006   Where immigrant students succeed - A comparative review of performance and engagement in PISA 2003

to the right of the graph indicate the degree to which student performance varies between schools and within schools overall. In the Netherlands, for example, 58% of the total variation in student performance is between schools and 42% within schools. Of the 58% variation between schools, approximately 7% is attributable to students' immigrant status, and of the 42% variation within schools, approximately 3% is attributable to immigrant status.

Overall, the results in Figure 3.6 indicate that students' immigrant status explains only a small proportion of the total variation in student performance. Within schools, it is below 4% in all countries except Switzerland where immigrant status accounts for 7% of the performance variation. The extent to which schools differ in terms of disparities between immigrant and native students varies across countries, however. The between-school variation due to students' immigrant background is comparatively high in some of the tracked education systems, including Switzerland (17%), Germany (11%) and Belgium (10%). This reflects the comparatively lower performance of immigrant students in these countries and the fact that low performing students are grouped in schools within the lower tracks. Yet, the proportion of between-school variation associated with students' immigrant status is also quite high in some comprehensive school systems. This is most notable in Sweden where more than 28% of the between-school variation is explained by students' immigrant status, followed by Denmark with 11%. At the same time, however, the overall variation in student performance between schools is much lower in these countries, with 11% in Sweden and 14% in Denmark, compared to more than 50% in the tracked education systems of Belgium and Germany and 34% in Switzerland. In absolute terms, therefore, the proportion of between-school variation in student performance in mathematics explained by immigrant status has different meanings in these two groups of countries. For example, in Sweden, immigrant status accounts for about 3% of the total variation in students' mathematics performance, while in Germany the proportion is 5.5% (see last two columns in Table 3.6).

The extent to which immigrant status explains variation within and between schools depends on the overall size of the performance differences between students from immigrant and native families and on the level of segregation in terms of the schools the two student groups attend. Chapter 2 and the previous section of this chapter described the size of the performance differences in detail. Figure 3.7 provides information on the degree to which immigrant students are grouped together within schools. More specifically, the bars in the first panel represent the percentages of second-generation students and the bars in the second panel represent the percentages of first-generation students in schools that are attended by varying proportions of immigrant students overall (both first-generation and second-generation). For both panels of Figure 3.7 the length of the bars to the left of the central line represents the percentage of students attending schools where less than half of the student population has an immigrant status. The length of the bar to the right of the central line shows the percentage of students in schools where at least half of the student population has an immigrant status. The findings indicate that, in several countries, many immigrant students attend schools with high proportions of first-generation or second-generation students. The most pronounced clustering occurs in Macao-China where almost all second-generation students and first-generation students attend schools with an immigrant student population of 50% or higher.[8] Due to the relatively large immigrant population in Macao-China, however, the majority of native students also attend schools with 50% or more immigrant students (see Table 3.7c). In Austria, Canada and the Netherlands, more than 40% of second-generation students are in schools where at least half of the students are immigrants and more than 30% of second-generation students in

Background characteristics, mathematics performance and learning environments of immigrant students

Figure 3.7 ■ **Percentages of second-generation and first-generation students attending schools with different proportions of immigrant students**

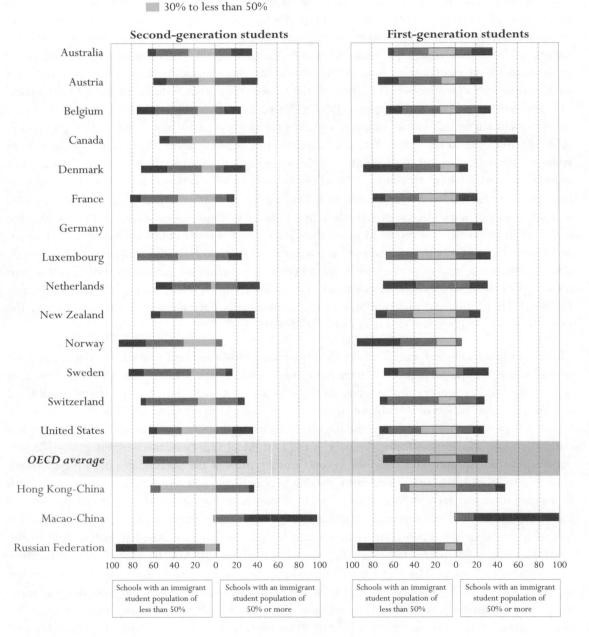

Percentage of students attending schools with an immigrant student population
(first- and second-generation students combined) of:

■ Less than 10% ▨ 50% to less than 70%
▨ 10% to less than 30% ■ 70% or more
▨ 30% to less than 50%

Source: OECD PISA 2003 database, Tables 3.7a and 3.7b.

© OECD 2006 *Where immigrant students succeed - A comparative review of performance and engagement in PISA 2003*

Box 3.1 ■ Do high levels of immigration impair integration?

People often assume that high levels of immigration will impair integration processes. In terms of student performance, however, this does not necessarily seem to be the case. Figure 3.8 shows the relationship between the proportion of immigrant students overall (second-generation and first-generation) within each country and the extent to which these students perform less well in mathematics compared to their native peers. If anything, this association is negative (OECD countries only: r = -.48, p = .086).[1] That is, the performance gap tends to be smaller in countries with higher proportions of immigrants. This pattern is likely to be due to a number of factors, such as between-country differences in the composition of immigrant populations. Some of the countries with high levels of immigration also have extensive support measures for immigrant students in place (see Chapter 5) which may contribute to the relative success of this group.

Figure 3.8 ■ **Differences in mathematics performance between native and immigrant students and percentage of immigrant students within countries**

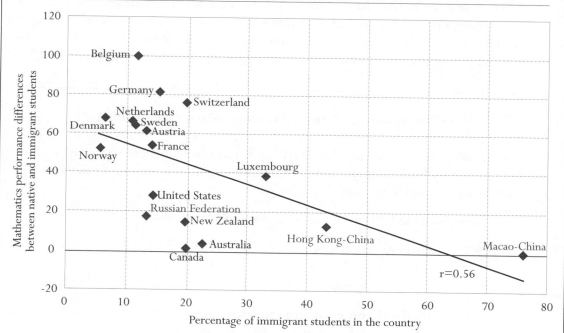

Source: OECD PISA 2003 database, Table 3.8.

1. The equivalent figure for all countries within this report is r = -.56, p = .020.

Australia, Germany, New Zealand, the United States and Hong Kong-China. Among first-generation students, the level of clustering is less pronounced. Nevertheless, more than 30% of first-generation students attend schools where at least half of the student population has an immigrant background in Australia, Belgium, Canada, Luxembourg, the Netherlands, Sweden, Hong Kong-China and Macao-China.

The pattern of findings for the extent to which immigrant students are grouped together within schools suggests that uneven distributions are not necessarily associated with lower relative performance levels for this group. In fact, some systems with high degrees of clustering have comparatively small performance differences between immigrant and native students. These include Australia, Canada and Macao-China. Accordingly, there is no significant relationship at the country level between the proportion of first-generation or second-generation students attending schools with 50% or more immigrant students and the size of the performance differences for these groups compared to their native peers (first-generation students, OECD countries: $r = .33$, $p = .256$; second-generation students, OECD countries: $r = .16$, $p = .583$).[9] Therefore, the distribution of immigrant students across schools does not seem to account for international variations in performance gaps between immigrant and native students. Within countries, however, high proportions of immigrants in schools may be related to performance levels, although the evidence on such contextual effects is not consistent (*e.g.* Coradi Vellacott *et al.*, 2003; Rüesch, 1998; Portes and Hao, 2004; Stanat, 2006; Westerbeek, 1999).

Characteristics of schools attended by immigrant and native students

The final set of analyses in this chapter explores differences between characteristics of schools attended by immigrant students and native students (the school-level variables selected for this analysis are presented in Box 3.2 and full descriptions are included in Annex A1). Figure 3.9 shows the mean index of economic, social and cultural status (ESCS) of students within schools. Clearly

---

Box 3.2 ■ **Measures of selected school characteristics in PISA**

Chapter 3 presents information on selected school characteristics that were collected in PISA 2003 either directly from the students or from the school principals. Annex A1 includes full descriptions for each of the measures listed below:

Mean economic, social and cultural status of students within schools

Human resources
Teacher/student ratio
Teacher shortage

Physical and educational resources
Quality of the school's physical infrastructure
Quality of the school's educational resources

Students' perceptions of classroom climate
Teacher support
Disciplinary climate

Principals' perceptions of school climate
Student-related factors affecting school climate
Teacher-related factors affecting school climate
Teacher morale and commitment

© OECD 2006   Where immigrant students succeed - A comparative review of performance and engagement in PISA 2003

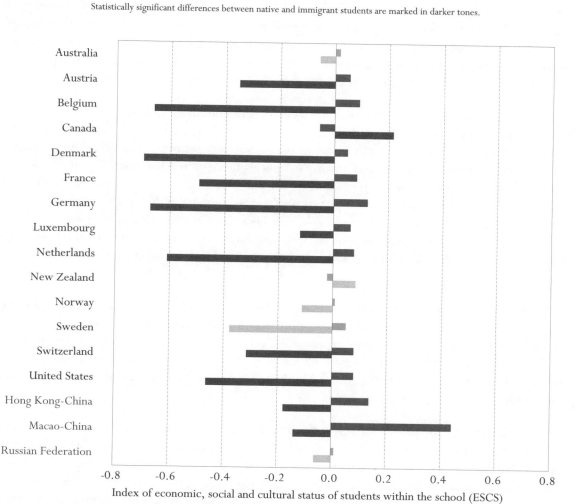

Mean economic, social and cultural status (ESCS) for:

■ ■ Native students
■ ■ Immigrant students

Statistically significant differences between native and immigrant students are marked in darker tones.

Index of economic, social and cultural status of students within the school (ESCS)

Source: OECD PISA 2003 database, Table 3.9.

immigrant students in most countries attend schools with less socio-economically advantaged student populations. The differences between the two student groups are significant in all countries except Australia, New Zealand, Norway, Sweden and the Russian Federation. In several European countries, such as Belgium, Denmark, France, Germany and the Netherlands, the differences are large. In some of these countries (Belgium, Germany and the Netherlands), the pattern probably reflects tracking effects within the education system. In Canada, the difference between the two student groups is also significant, but in the opposite direction. Therefore, immigrant students in Canada seem to attend schools with relatively advantaged student populations.

In terms of human, physical and educational resources, the differences between schools attended by immigrant and native students are smaller (see Table 3.9). For the student-teacher ratio, for example, there are only a few countries with significant differences. In three of the five countries where there are differences, immigrant students are in a less favourable position than native students. Compared to their native peers, immigrant students in Luxembourg, New Zealand and the United States tend to be in schools with higher numbers of students per teacher. In contrast, the student-teacher ratio in Belgium and (to a lesser extent) in Macao-China tends to be more favourable for immigrant students. This may reflect an attempt to improve performance by providing schools with high proportions of immigrant students with additional teachers. At the same time, however, immigrant students in Belgium are more likely than native students to attend schools where the principals perceive shortages of qualified and experienced teachers to be a problem (see Table 3.9).

Differences in the quality of physical infrastructure and educational resources between schools attended by immigrant and native students tend to be small (see Table 3.9). Similarly, Table 3.9 shows that there are only a few differences in the various aspects of teacher behaviour (students' perceptions of teacher support and principals' perceptions of teacher-related factors affecting school climate and teacher morale). In Luxembourg and Macao-China, immigrant students tend to experience more favourable conditions in terms of teacher support in their mathematics lessons. In addition, teacher morale in Luxembourg is relatively high in schools attended by immigrant students. In Belgium, however, the opposite is true. Here, immigrant students tend to attend schools with lower teacher morale and with less positive teacher-related factors affecting school climate (see Table 3.9).

With regard to student-perceived disciplinary climate in mathematics classes and principal-perceived student behaviour affecting school climate, a different picture emerges (see Table 3.9). In several countries, immigrant students experience less favourable school environments compared to native students. The differences are significant for both disciplinary climate and student behaviour in Austria, Belgium and Luxembourg; for student behaviour in the Netherlands and Sweden; and for disciplinary climate in Germany.

Overall, the findings for school characteristics indicate that immigrant and native students typically attend schools with similar resources. In Luxembourg, New Zealand and the United States, however, the number of students per teacher seems to be higher in the schools attended by immigrant students. The opposite is true for Belgium where schools attended by immigrant students tend to have lower student-teacher ratios. Yet, in terms of teacher shortage, teacher morale and commitment, student-related factors affecting school climate and disciplinary climate, the school environment in Belgium seems to be less favourable for immigrant students than for non-immigrant students.

In most countries, immigrant students often attend schools with relatively disadvantaged student populations in terms of economic, social and cultural background. The only exceptions are three of the settlement countries, Australia, Canada and New Zealand, as well as the two Nordic countries Norway and Sweden. Here, immigrant students and native students attend schools with comparable socio-economic compositions. Finally, in several European countries, the school environment for immigrant students compared to native students is less favourable in terms of school or disciplinary climate. This is true for immigrant students in Austria, Belgium and Luxembourg and, to a lesser extent, Germany, the Netherlands and Sweden.

SUMMARY AND CONCLUSIONS

The first part of this chapter described background characteristics of second-generation and first-generation students and examined their relationship with performance. The analyses provided estimates for the extent to which performance differences between immigrant and non-immigrant students persist after accounting for aspects of their families' economic, social and cultural status. The chapter also explored characteristics specifically related to students' immigrant status, including the role of students' and parents' country of birth, the language spoken at home and the age of students at the time of immigration.

The second part of the chapter focused on schools. It analysed the extent to which differences between immigrant and native students occur within and between schools and described the schools that the two student groups attend within the countries. A number of key findings emerged:

(a) **In the majority of countries, parents of immigrant students have completed fewer years of schooling and show lower levels of economic, social and cultural status than parents of native students. At the same time, there are a few countries where the two student groups do not differ substantially in terms of these background characteristics.** The disadvantages of first-generation families in terms of educational and socio-economic background are pronounced in most of the European countries as well as in the United States and in Hong Kong-China. The largest and most consistent differences occur in Germany. By contrast, in three of the settlement countries, Australia, Canada and New Zealand, the differences between immigrant and non-immigrant populations in terms of parental education and socio-economic status are small or non-significant. A similar pattern emerges for Macao-China and the Russian Federation.

(b) **At the country level, there is a relationship between the relative mathematics performance of immigrant students and their relative educational and socio-economic background. However, performance differences remain between immigrant and non-immigrant students in many countries after accounting for these background characteristics. This suggests that the relative performance levels of immigrant students cannot solely be attributed to the composition of immigrant populations in terms of their human capital potential.** Countries differ with regard to their immigration policies and practices and the background characteristics of their immigrant populations. To explore the effectiveness of integration policies and practices within the countries in this report, it would be necessary to control for background characteristics of immigrants at the time they entered the respective country. PISA does not collect this information. Yet, assuming that the educational and socio-economic status of first-generation students' families reflects their situation at the time of immigration, accounting for these characteristics provides a rough estimate for the extent to which the lower performance of immigrant students can be attributed to the human capital potential of countries' immigrant populations. The findings indicate that in most countries with large performance gaps between immigrant and native students, these differences remain significant after accounting for parents' educational and occupational status.

(c) **In several countries, students who do not speak the language of instruction at home perform significantly less well in mathematics than students who do. This suggests that some immigrant students in these countries may not have sufficient**

opportunity to learn the language of instruction. After accounting for parents' educational and occupational status, the performance gap associated with the language spoken at home is significant in Belgium, Canada, Germany, the United States, Hong Kong-China, Macao-China and the Russian Federation. Countries with a strong relationship between the language students speak at home and their performance in mathematics may want to consider strengthening language support measures in schools.

(d) **The proportion of variation in mathematics performance within and between schools that is due to students' immigrant status is relatively small. In some countries, the difference between immigrant and non-immigrant students is mainly found between schools.** Countries with larger proportions of between-school variation due to immigrant status include three countries with tracked school systems, Belgium, Germany and Switzerland, as well as two countries with comprehensive school systems, Denmark and Sweden.

(e) **In several countries, many immigrant students attend schools with relatively high proportions of students whose families have also immigrated.** Higher levels of grouping – with more than 30 to 40% of first-generation or second-generation students attending schools where at least half of the student population has an immigrant background – occur in Australia, Austria, Belgium, Canada, Germany, Luxembourg, the Netherlands, New Zealand, Sweden, the United States, Hong Kong-China and Macao-China. The degree of clustering within a country, however, does not seem to be related to the size of the performance gap between immigrant and native students.

(f) **Within the OECD countries, the size of the immigrant student population is not significantly associated with the size of the performance differences between immigrant and native students.** In fact, there seems to be a tendency for the performance gap to be smaller in countries with higher proportions of immigrant students. This finding contradicts the assumption that high levels of immigration will necessarily hinder integration.

(g) **Immigrant students in most countries often attend schools with relatively disadvantaged student populations in terms of economic, social and cultural background. In terms of resource and climate characteristics of schools, the pattern varies across countries.** In three of the settlement countries, Australia, Canada and New Zealand, the characteristics of schools attended by immigrant students and non-immigrant students are similar. In Belgium, immigrant students are likely to attend schools with less favourable characteristics, although the number of students per teacher tends to be lower in their schools. A higher student-teacher ratio for immigrant students compared to native students occurs in Luxembourg, New Zealand and the United States. In addition to the economic, social and cultural background of student populations, the group differences are largest and most consistent for student factors related to school climate and disciplinary climate. Immigrant students attend schools with less favourable conditions for at least one of these factors in Austria, Belgium, Germany, Luxembourg, the Netherlands, Sweden and Macao-China.

Overall, the findings in this chapter confirm the need to provide immigrant students with targeted support in a number of countries. Chapter 5 describes countries' current policies and practices to help immigrant students learn the language of instruction. Before moving on to this description, however, Chapter 4 analyses central learning prerequisites of immigrant students that form a foundation for success at school.

1   For qualifications of this general assumption see Borjas, 1987.

2   In fact, it is generally not admissible to generalise relationships at the aggregate level to the individual level or vice versa (King, 1997; Klieme and Stanat, 2002; Robinson, 1950).

3   The pattern of findings does not change substantially in any of the countries if gender is included as an additional variable in the regression analyses.

4   As pointed out in Chapter 1, a common approach to dealing with the problem of missing values is to create a complete dataset by way of multiple imputation. Because this approach could not be employed within the OECD-PISA context, the mean substitution method suggested by Cohen and Cohen (1983) was initially used for the regression analyses. These analyses yielded findings that were almost identical to those with listwise deletion, however. Therefore, mean substitution was only used for students' age of immigration as the proportion of missing values is particularly high for this variable (see Table 3.5).

5   It should be noted, however, that all variables included in the model are measured with error. To the extent that the indicators of parents' educational and occupational status are imprecise, the results of the regression analyses should underestimate their contribution.

6   In Canada and Hong Kong-China, significant differences are also present for second-generation students but in the opposite direction, thus indicating a performance advantage for this group after accounting for the student background characteristics included in the model.

7   Due to the high proportion of missing values on this variable in many countries, they were replaced by within-country means. In addition, a dummy-variable representing whether or not the variable is missing was included in the model. Yet, the pattern of results for this analysis does not deviate substantially from the same analysis using listwise deletion.

8   It should be noted that the number of schools is quite small within the samples for Luxembourg ($N = 29$) and Macao-China ($N = 39$).

9   The equivalent figures including all countries within this report are first-generation students: $r = .36, p = .146$ and second-generation students: $r = .28, p = .267$.

4

Immigrant students' approaches to learning

INTRODUCTION[1]

While previous chapters have focused on student performance and its relationship with student background, it is also important to examine how well education systems are serving immigrant students in other aspects of learning. School systems not only need to provide students with essential literacy skills, but also with other fundamental skills and dispositions necessary to manage their own learning. These include interest in learning, motivation and confidence (OECD, 2004a). Positive attitudes towards school help foster these learning fundamentals (Blum and Libbey, 2004). Students who feel alienated from school are at risk of performing poorly in school as well as later on in life (OECD, 2003c). Adolescents with a positive attitude to learning are more likely to leave school with a better chance of successfully adapting and acquiring new skills throughout their lives.

Educational studies have stressed the importance of motivation and attitude in relation to achievement and success in school and work (*e.g.* OECD, 2003b; OECD, 2003c; Eccles, Wigfield and Schiefele, 1998; Zimmerman, 2000). Motivation is essential for learning throughout life, both in professional contexts and in less directed learning environments (OECD, 2003b). In addition, Willms (in OECD 2003c) links engagement in school with student achievement and points to several studies on child development indicating that children who feel detached from school not only compromise their potential levels of achievement, but also tend to behave badly in school, risk dropping out of school and developing poor physical and mental health (Coie and Jacobs, 1993; Hawkins, Doueck and Lishner, 1988; Power, Manor and Fox, 1991; Pulkkinen and Tremblay, 1992; Rodgers, 1990; Rumberger, 1995; Yoshikawa, 1994).

Overall previous research suggests that desirable "non-achievement outcomes of schooling" such as strong motivation, positive self-perception and a good level of school engagement are critical for students' potential for lifelong learning, as well as their future financial success and general well-being and should therefore be considered along with academic achievement as key schooling outcomes (OECD, 2003b; OECD, 2003c). Despite the importance of these factors, however, there is very little research focusing on immigrant students' motivation and perceptions of school from an international perspective. In turn, this chapter seeks to examine these learning dispositions as part of considering immigrant students' success in school.

Previous chapters indicate that in many countries, immigrant students tend to lag behind their native peers in the subject areas assessed by PISA. This, however, may not be the case for motivation and perception of school. Some research suggests that the willingness and initiative of a family to emigrate may be associated with immigrant students and their parents being optimistic about the future and highly motivated to take advantage of new opportunities in their new home (Suárez-Orozco and Suárez-Orozco, 1995). The desire to succeed may cause students to have a relatively positive attitude towards schooling. First-generation students should have more of a tendency to have these attitudes, as they themselves have experienced immigration and the hope that may be associated with it.

At the same time, however, immigrant students often perform poorly. This can dampen their initial motivation over time. Similarly, children from immigrant families may perceive their new and unfamiliar school environments as hostile, which could lead to less engagement in school. For example, studies of immigrants in the United States indicate that length of residency in the country appears to be associated with lower levels of achievement, motivation, aspirations and health (Conchas, 2001; Portes and Rumbaut, 2001; Rumbaut, 1995; Steinberg, 1996; Suárez-Orozco, 2001; Suárez-Orozco and Suárez-Orozco, 1995; Waters, 1999). It is therefore possible that second-generation students show lower levels of motivation and less positive attitudes towards school than first-generation students.

This chapter seeks to explore these non-achievement outcomes of learning to provide new insights into how immigrant students' motivational orientations and attitudes related to learning and school compare to those of their peers from native families and how these relationships differ across countries. PISA provides a unique opportunity to examine these characteristics, which are essential for learning throughout life, by exploring broader learning profiles of immigrant and non-immigrant students at age 15. This includes information on students' motivation, engagement and confidence. Since mathematics was the focus of PISA 2003, many of the questions are analysed in relationship to this domain. This chapter first reviews the measures available and then presents the results of analyses organised around the four categories below (for a more in-depth description of these categories see Figure 4.1):

- *Students' interest and motivation in mathematics.* Subject motivation is frequently viewed as the essential force for learning and is related to both students' interest and enjoyment in the subject along with external incentives for learning.

- *Students' beliefs about themselves.* Students' views about their competence and ability to learn influence the way they set goals, whether or not they use effective learning strategies and how well they perform.

- *Students' anxiety about mathematics.* Students often experience fear associated with mathematics which tends to negatively affect performance.

- *Students' engagement and perceptions of school.* Students' attitudes towards school and sense of belonging are closely associated with performance, as well as long-term outcomes ranging from economic success to health.

While including analyses of the relationship between these characteristics and performance, this chapter emphasises motivation, self-perception and engagement as critical non-achievement outcomes of schooling for immigrant and non-immigrant students. These are all qualities in students which can be improved and could be targeted by parents, teachers and policy makers.

Previous research suggests that immigrants tend to be optimistic and may therefore possess more positive learning characteristics. These characteristics may be especially strong for first-generation students, who themselves experience immigration. They may be less strong among second-generation students, as the challenges of succeeding in the host country might be more apparent to parents and students who have been in the country longer. Furthermore, assimilation tendencies may also lead second-generation students to show characteristics more similar to native students than to first-generation students. To the extent that immigrant students show more positive learning characteristics, educators may be able to use these to improve achievement scores. For example, schools could make better use of the motivational characteristics of immigrant students to encourage them to engage in additional activities aimed at improving language skills or lessening achievement differences.

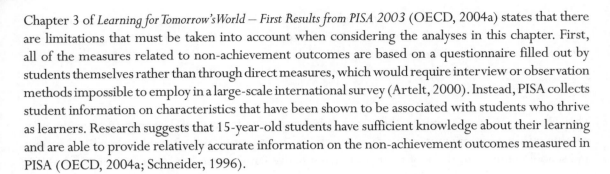

Chapter 3 of *Learning for Tomorrow's World – First Results from PISA 2003* (OECD, 2004a) states that there are limitations that must be taken into account when considering the analyses in this chapter. First, all of the measures related to non-achievement outcomes are based on a questionnaire filled out by students themselves rather than through direct measures, which would require interview or observation methods impossible to employ in a large-scale international survey (Artelt, 2000). Instead, PISA collects student information on characteristics that have been shown to be associated with students who thrive as learners. Research suggests that 15-year-old students have sufficient knowledge about their learning and are able to provide relatively accurate information on the non-achievement outcomes measured in PISA (OECD, 2004a; Schneider, 1996).

A second limitation is that students in the various countries may interpret the survey questions on school-related motivations and attitudes differently. These questions require subjective judgments, which may be shaped by students' cultural backgrounds. In fact, focusing on immigrant children brings another level of cultural complexity to the analyses, which may further influence these students' responses. However, analyses of PISA 2000 and 2003 data indicate that for most characteristics, including self-related beliefs and sense of belonging, valid cross-country comparisons can be made, as analyses of PISA 2003 data confirmed comparability and found similar relationships between self-reported characteristics and student performance both within and across countries (OECD, 2004a). For other characteristics, such as motivation, cross-country comparisons of country averages should be interpreted with caution. More importantly for this chapter, it is possible to make valid comparisons among sub-groups within countries for all characteristics (OECD, 2004a). Therefore, this chapter mainly compares immigrant sub-groups within countries and makes cross-national comparisons with caution, especially for more problematic variables, such as motivation.

A further limitation is that PISA is a cross-sectional survey (*i.e.* data are collected at one moment in time as opposed to over time), which does not allow for the examination of causal relationships. For example, previous research shows that academic performance and motivation are related and that the two factors are mutually reinforcing (Marsh, Trautwein, Lüdtke, Köller and Baumert, 2005). While this type of analysis cannot be carried out with the PISA data, it is possible to use PISA data to examine learning characteristics of students that are associated with better performance in school (OECD, 2004a).

PISA investigated characteristics that indicate whether or not students are likely to have positive feelings and attitudes related to learning and school. Students who participated in PISA responded to a series of questions about each of these characteristics. The focus of PISA 2003 was mathematics and consequently most of these questions were placed in the context of learning mathematics. These characteristics represent four broad categories namely motivation, self-related beliefs, emotions and student attitudes towards and perceptions of school. Figure 4.1 provides an overview of the characteristics included in each category, a brief description of the reason for its inclusion and example questions that students answered. Box 4.1 explains the indices used to represent these characteristics. Each index is scaled with the average score across all OECD countries set at 0 with a standard deviation of 1 (*i.e.* two-thirds of the students score between 1 and -1). The full set of questions can be found in Annex A1 of *Learning for Tomorrow's World – First Results from PISA 2003* (OECD, 2004a). These categories, scales and specific survey questions form the basis for the analysis in this chapter.

Figure 4.1 ■ **Characteristics and attitudes of students as learners of mathematics**

Category of characteristics and rationale for inclusion	Student characteristics used to report results
A. Motivational factors Motivation is often considered the driving force behind learning. There are internally generated motives, such as interest in a particular subject area; there are also external motives deriving from external rewards for good performance, such as praise or future prospects (Deci and Ryan, 1985).	*1. Interest and enjoyment of mathematics.* Students were asked about their interest in mathematics as a subject as well as their enjoyment of learning mathematics. Interest and enjoyment of a subject is an orientation that affects the intensity and continuity of engagement in learning situations, as well as the selection of learning strategies. *2. Instrumental motivation in mathematics.* Students were asked to what extent they are encouraged to learn by external rewards such as good job prospects. Studies carried out over time indicate that motivation influences both what students study and how they perform (Wigfield, Eccles and Rodriguez, 1998).
B. Self-related beliefs in mathematics Learners form views about their own abilities and learning characteristics. These influence the way they set goals, their strategies and their achievement (Zimmerman, 1999). Two ways of defining these beliefs are: self-efficacy - how well students think they can handle even difficult tasks (Bandura, 1994); and self concept – students beliefs in their own abilities (Marsh, 1993). Each of these closely associated characteristics is critical for independent learning. Self-related beliefs are sometimes referred to in terms of self-confidence, indicating that such beliefs are positive. In both cases, confidence in itself has important benefits for motivation and the way in which students approach learning tasks.	*3. Self-efficacy in mathematics.* Students were asked to what extent they believe in their own ability to handle learning situations and overcome difficulties in mathematics effectively. This affects students' willingness to take on challenging tasks and persist in tackling them. In turn, this has significant implications for motivation (Bandura, 1994). *4. Self-concept in mathematics.* Students were asked about their beliefs in their own competence in mathematics. Belief in one's own abilities is highly relevant to successful learning, as well as being a goal in its own right (Marsh, 1986).
C. Emotional dispositions in mathematics Students' avoidance of mathematics due to emotional stress is reported to be widespread in many countries. It is often associated with achievement and choice of study (Meece, Wigfield, and Eccles, 1990).	*5. Anxiety in mathematics.* Students were asked to what extent they feel helpless and under emotional stress when dealing with mathematics.
D. Student attitudes and perceptions of schools Students' engagement in school is seen as a disposition towards learning, cooperating with others and having the ability to successfully function in a social institution (OECD, 2003c). It has relevant implications for learning both in school and beyond.	*6. Attitudes toward school.* Students were asked to think about what they had learned at school in relation to how the school had prepared them for adult life, given them confidence to make decisions, taught them things that could be useful in their job or a waste of time. *7. Sense of belonging at school.* Students were asked to express their perceptions about whether their school was a place where they felt like an outsider, made friends easily, felt like they belonged, felt awkward and out of place or felt lonely.

Adapted from Figure 3.1 OECD, 2004a, p.115 and OECD, 2003b, p. 13-14).

Box 4.1 ■ Interpreting the PISA indices

The measures are presented as indices that summarise student responses to a series of related questions constructed on the basis of previous research (Annex A1). The validity of comparisons across countries was explored using structural equation modelling. In describing students in terms of each characteristic (*e.g.* interest in mathematics), scales were constructed on which the average OECD student (*i.e.* the student with an average level of interest) was given an index value of zero, and about two-thirds of the OECD student population are between values of -1 and 1 (*i.e.* the index has a standard deviation of 1). Negative values on an index do not necessarily imply that students responded negatively to the underlying questions. Rather, a student with a negative score replied less positively than the OECD average. Likewise, a student with positive scores responded more positively than the OECD average. As each indicator is introduced below, a diagram shows more precisely which scores are associated with a particular response with an emphasis on the three sub-groups of this report: first-generation, second-generation and native students.

In this report, the OECD average is the average across the OECD countries included in this study; however, the scaling described above is used based on all OECD countries which participated in PISA 2003.

From Box 3.2 OECD, 2004a, p. 117.

STUDENTS' INTEREST AND MOTIVATION IN MATHEMATICS

This section examines interest and motivational characteristics related to learning and how these may differ between immigrant and non-immigrant students. Interest and motivation are two main forces driving learning. These characteristics often affect students' satisfaction with life in adolescence and have particular bearing on their educational and work pursuits (OECD, 2004a; OECD, 2003b). As mathematical literacy and the ability to gain new skills are critical for students' future success in work and life, educators need to ensure that students possess both the interest and motivation to continue learning mathematics when they leave school. These dispositions are of particular importance for immigrant students, as many lag behind their native peers in performance. It is therefore likely that they will have an even greater need to continue learning beyond school.

Students' interest in and enjoyment of mathematics

The first characteristic explored in this area investigates students' intrinsic motivation – their interest in and enjoyment of a subject domain. Intrinsic motivation affects the level of engagement in learning and the level of understanding. In addition, interest and motivation in a particular subject have been shown to function independently of motivation to learn in general (OECD, 2004a). As a result, it is necessary to consider students' interest in and enjoyment of mathematics separately from their general motivation. Analyses of these factors can indicate whether education systems are successful in encouraging intrinsic motivation in mathematics among different groups of students, in this case immigrant and non-immigrant students.

Across the OECD countries in this study, 38% of native, 43% of second-generation and 48% of first-generation students report that they do mathematics because they enjoy it (see the first panel of Figure 4.2). This indicates that a higher percentage of immigrant students enjoy mathematics with the percentage being even higher among first-generation students than among second-generation students. Similarly, 52% of native students, 59% of second-generation students and 64% of first-generations students agree or strongly agree with the statement that they are interested in what they learn in mathematics. The index variable summarising the answers to these questions also indicates that first-generation and second-generation students display significantly higher levels of interest in and enjoyment of mathematics.

While the OECD average provides a useful glimpse at differences in interest in and enjoyment of mathematics among first-generation, second-generation and native students across the case countries, it does not reveal whether this pattern holds in each of the countries. The second panel of Figure 4.2 shows both the level of interest in and enjoyment of mathematics for each sub-group in the case countries. The large bar represents the averages for native students, while the triangle and square represent the average level for first-generation and second-generation students respectively. If there are significant differences between first-generation and native students, the triangle is shaded in a darker tone. Similarly, significant differences between second-generation and native students are indicated by a square shaded in a darker tone. The same type of figure is used throughout the chapter to show significant differences between immigrant and non-immigrant students.

Based on the patterns of responses to the survey questions described above, in the majority of countries, there are significant differences between immigrant and non-immigrant students. The second panel of Figure 4.2 indicates that in all OECD countries and Macao-China, first-generation students report a significantly higher interest in and enjoyment of mathematics. Although the differences between native and second-generation students tend to be somewhat smaller than between native and first-generation students, in 10 out of 17 countries – Australia, Belgium, Canada, Germany, Luxembourg, the Netherlands, New Zealand, Norway, the United States and Hong Kong-China – second-generation students show greater interest in and enjoyment of mathematics than native students. Even after accounting for socio-economic background, both first-generation and second-generation students still tend to show significantly higher levels of motivation than their native peers in most of the countries (see Table 4.1). Furthermore, after accounting for students' mathematics performance, the level of motivation tends to be even higher for both immigrant sub-groups compared to their native peers (see Table 4.1). In none of the countries do first-generation or second-generation students show significantly lower levels of intrinsic motivation than their native peers.

To illustrate the extent of the differences, it is useful to consider students' responses to individual questions related to interest in and enjoyment of mathematics displayed in the first panel of Figure 4.2. In 12 of the 17 countries in this report, the percentage of students who agree or strongly agree that they are interested in the things they learn in mathematics is at least 10 percentage points higher in the first-generation group than in the native group. In Sweden, the figure for first-generation students is even 20 percentage points higher. For second-generation students, the level of agreement is at least ten percentage points higher compared to native students in Belgium, Germany, the Netherlands, New Zealand and Norway. Again, these findings show that immigrant students tend to report more often that they have an interest in the things they learn in mathematics than native students.

Immigrant students' approaches to learning

Figure 4.2 ■ Students' interest in and enjoyment of mathematics by immigrant status

Percentage of students agreeing or strongly agreeing with the following statements:

Index of interest in and enjoyment of mathematics

- Native students
- Second-generation students
- First-generation students

Statistically significant differences from native students are marked in darker tones

Index points

Change in mathematics score per unit change in the index of interest in and enjoyment of mathematics

- Native students
- Second-generation students
- First-generation students

Statistically significant changes are marked in darker tones

Score point differences

		I enjoy reading about mathematics.	I look forward to my mathematics lessons.	I do mathematics because I enjoy it.	I am interested in the things I learn in mathematics.	Percentage of explained variance in student performance
Australia	Native	25	34	33	48	4.2
	Second-generation	37	46	45	57	2.3
	First-generation	43	49	49	61	1.7
Austria	Native	18	30	27	40	2.2
	Second-generation	26	35	33	44	0.4
	First-generation	28	34	29	48	0.2
Belgium	Native	22	22	33	52	4.0
	Second-generation	31	33	36	63	0.1
	First-generation	36	33	44	67	1.1
Canada	Native	28	30	34	49	6.7
	Second-generation	37	40	39	53	8.2
	First-generation	51	56	53	68	3.6
Denmark	Native	47	46	58	65	11.1
	Second-generation	56	65	64	67	0.1
	First-generation	56	58	63	67	1.0
France	Native	31	23	47	67	5.6
	Second-generation	30	28	44	70	3.9
	First-generation	45	28	55	75	6.1
Germany	Native	19	39	42	53	2.8
	Second-generation	32	46	49	66	6.7
	First-generation	29	45	49	63	0.5
Luxembourg	Native	18	29	31	39	2.5
	Second-generation	24	28	35	48	0.7
	First-generation	30	36	42	57	0.1
Netherlands	Native	17	17	34	44	4.6
	Second-generation	40	38	45	61	0.1
	First-generation	44	46	46	59	0.8
New Zealand	Native	30	38	36	53	2.1
	Second-generation	50	52	47	64	0.1
	First-generation	56	59	56	68	0.7
Norway	Native	26	28	33	49	18.5
	Second-generation	37	49	43	60	17.6
	First-generation	37	44	46	63	4.0
Sweden	Native	48	29	35	52	11.7
	Second-generation	56	38	35	59	8.6
	First-generation	59	47	45	72	1.3
Switzerland	Native	22	40	51	58	3.8
	Second-generation	25	42	52	61	0.1
	First-generation	38	52	61	71	0.5
United States	Native	30	38	33	50	1.2
	Second-generation	40	53	43	58	2.1
	First-generation	45	59	47	65	0.1
OECD average	*Native*	*28*	*31*	*38*	*52*	*4.8*
	Second-generation	*35*	*40*	*43*	*59*	*1.7*
	First-generation	*41*	*47*	*48*	*64*	*1.3*
Hong Kong-China	Native	35	43	51	50	9.9
	Second-generation	38	49	56	53	10.8
	First-generation	39	46	51	52	7.8
Macao-China	Native	31	32	44	38	1.7
	Second-generation	35	34	44	43	6.8
	First-generation	38	42	49	48	2.0
Russian Federation	Native	27	42	41	69	1.7
	Second-generation	28	36	36	68	0.1
	First-generation	29	43	41	68	0.7

Source: OECD PISA 2003 database, Table 4.1.

© OECD 2006   Where immigrant students succeed - A comparative review of performance and engagement in PISA 2003

The initial PISA 2003 results indicate that within each country, students with higher levels of interest in and enjoyment of mathematics tend to show higher levels of performance than students with relatively lower levels of interest and enjoyment (OECD, 2004a). These results also indicate that the strength of this relationship varies across countries. When considering the association separately for native, first-generation and second-generation students, a different pattern emerges. The third panel of Figure 4.2 displays the association between interest in and enjoyment of mathematics and performance in mathematics for each of the three sub-groups. The length of each bar indicates the increase in mathematics scores associated with each unit increase in the index of interest in and enjoyment of mathematics (in this case one OECD standard deviation). In addition, the values to the right of the panel indicate the percentage of variation in the mathematics performance scores explained by the interest and enjoyment index.

These findings indicate that in only three of the case countries, Australia, Canada and Hong Kong-China is there a significant positive relationship between interest in and enjoyment of mathematics and mathematics performance for first-generation students. In seven OECD countries, Australia, Canada, France, Germany, Norway, Sweden, the United States, as well as Hong Kong-China and Macao-China there is a significant positive relationship for second-generation students. In comparison, native students in all of the countries, except Macao-China, show a strong positive relationship ranging from about 10 score points per unit increase on the index of interest in and enjoyment of mathematics in the United States to over 30 score points in Denmark, Norway, Sweden and Hong Kong-China. This result may partially be attributable to the smaller sample size (and therefore larger standard errors for immigrant students), but the sizes of the coefficients, while generally positive, also tend to be smaller. Furthermore, in most countries, the percentage of variation in student performance that is explained by students' interest in and enjoyment of mathematics is also substantially lower for first-generation and second-generation students compared to native students (see fourth panel of Figure 4.2).

These findings seem to indicate that although immigrant students display higher levels of interest in and enjoyment of mathematics, this does not necessarily mean they perform better. This may indicate that motivation is not related to performance for these students. This may be the case especially amongst first-generation students, who experience challenges related to academic success, such as language problems or lack of familiarity with the school system. The relationship between interest and enjoyment in a subject and performance is clearly complex and cannot be determined through these analyses (OECD, 2004a). The findings do indicate, however, that first-generation and second-generation students show higher levels of interest in and enjoyment of mathematics, with first-generation students showing the highest levels of intrinsic motivation. This is also the case in countries where both groups of immigrants perform relatively poorly in the mathematics assessment (see Figure 2.1a). The findings therefore point to immigrant students' potential in terms of their positive attitude to mathematics learning that could perhaps be better exploited to improve these students' performance.

Instrumental motivation and future expectations

In addition to interest and enjoyment as components of intrinsic motivation, external factors can also be important driving forces for learning and school success. Individuals with higher levels of instrumental motivation (motivation related to external factors) tend to show higher levels of performance (OECD, 2003b). Furthermore, instrumental motivation is a significant predictor of important non-achievement schooling outcomes, including course selection and career choices

(Wigfield *et al.*, 1998). Across the OECD countries in this report, the vast majority of students report that mathematics is highly relevant for their future lives – at least 60% of students in all sub-groups agree or strongly agree with questions related to the importance of mathematics for school and work. This tends to be particularly the case for immigrant students. Compared to native students, higher percentages of first-generation and second-generation 15-year-olds agree or strongly agree with statements about the importance of mathematics in their future lives. The level of agreement is especially high among first-generation students. For example, across the OECD countries in this report, 79% of first-generation students, 76% of second-generation students and 74% of native students agree or strongly agree that making an effort in mathematics is valuable because it will help them in the work they want to do later. The same trend can be seen across all of the questions related to students' instrumental motivation in mathematics (see first panel of Figure 4.3a).

The index of instrumental motivation in mathematics summarises the responses to the four questions related to external motivation and reflects the findings described above. Among most of the OECD countries in this report, both first-generation and second-generation students show significantly higher levels of instrumental motivation than native students. First-generation students display slightly higher instrumental motivation than second-generation students. This pattern of first-generation and second-generation students reporting similar or higher levels of instrumental motivation compared to their native peers holds in every country included this study. In fact instrumental motivation is usually higher for first-generation students – only in Denmark, Norway, Macao-China and the Russian Federation do first-generation students display similar instrumental motivation to native students. In the other 13 case countries, first-generation students report significantly higher levels of instrumental motivation. Moreover, in 10 of the 17 countries – Australia, Belgium, Canada, France, Germany, Luxembourg, the Netherlands, New Zealand, Sweden and Switzerland – second-generation students report significantly more instrumental motivation than native students.

Although first-generation and second-generation students show equivalent or higher instrumental motivation in each country, there are substantial differences among countries in the degree to which students report having instrumental motivation. For example, students in Austria and Luxembourg demonstrate the lowest levels of instrumental motivation among the countries in this report (OECD, 2004a). Within these two countries first-generation and second-generation immigrant students also display higher instrumental motivation than native students, yet their results are still relatively low compared to first-generation and second-generation students in countries with relatively high levels of motivation, such as Denmark or New Zealand. In other words, while immigrant students within each country generally appear to show greater or similar motivation compared to their native peers, immigrant students' results appear to reflect the level of motivation among native students.

Like intrinsic motivation, the association between instrumental motivation and performance is weaker for first-generation and second-generation students than for native students across the OECD case countries, with first-generation students showing the weakest association (see the third panel of Figure 4.3a). Not surprisingly, the OECD averages mask variations among the case countries. In Australia, Canada, New Zealand, Norway, the United States and Hong Kong-China, there is a significant positive relationship between instrumental motivation and performance for first-generation students. Within these countries, the association among first-generation students ranges from an increase of 13 score points per unit (*i.e.* standard deviation) of instrumental motivation in New Zealand to almost 31 score points in Norway.

Figure 4.3a ■ **Students' instrumental motivation in mathematics by immigrant status**

		Percentage of students agreeing or strongly agreeing with the following statements:				Percentage of explained variance in student performance
		Making an effort in mathematics is worth it because it will help me in the work that I want to do later.	Learning mathematics is worthwhile for me because it will improve my career prospects.	Mathematics is an important subject for me because I need it for what I want to study later on.	I will learn many things in mathematics that will help me get a job.	
Australia	Native	82	86	72	79	3.3
	Second-generation	85	88	78	81	3.1
	First-generation	85	89	79	80	2.5
Austria	Native	64	50	34	54	0.0
	Second-generation	64	58	44	63	0.5
	First-generation	70	55	47	63	0.8
Belgium	Native	65	64	55	56	2.4
	Second-generation	71	71	60	63	0.2
	First-generation	73	72	66	68	0.2
Canada	Native	78	86	71	78	6.1
	Second-generation	83	89	76	82	4.7
	First-generation	87	90	83	84	3.4
Denmark	Native	91	88	75	83	5.0
	Second-generation	84	8	72	77	2.7
	First-generation	90	92	75	81	0.5
France	Native	73	73	64	61	3.2
	Second-generation	73	77	67	65	1.9
	First-generation	78	78	74	77	2.1
Germany	Native	73	79	46	71	0.2
	Second-generation	72	78	57	75	0.3
	First-generation	75	82	60	77	0.0
Luxembourg	Native	48	56	47	49	0.8
	Second-generation	55	66	51	57	0.5
	First-generation	67	74	65	69	0.6
Netherlands	Native	69	70	62	58	1.0
	Second-generation	81	80	76	81	0.1
	First-generation	73	71	70	69	1.8
New Zealand	Native	84	88	75	81	3.1
	Second-generation	87	92	84	86	0.1
	First-generation	89	91	84	85	1.3
Norway	Native	82	82	75	73	10.5
	Second-generation	84	82	81	78	12.1
	First-generation	84	82	77	73	12.1
Sweden	Native	69	86	66	73	7.3
	Second-generation	78	89	76	76	8.8
	First-generation	81	91	80	77	0.5
Switzerland	Native	75	73	50	64	0.1
	Second-generation	81	80	56	72	0.6
	First-generation	79	83	63	74	1.7
United States	Native	81	82	72	82	2.2
	Second-generation	84	84	77	88	3.4
	First-generation	83	85	79	85	2.2
OECD average	*Native*	*74*	*76*	*62*	*69*	*1.9*
	Second-generation	*76*	*80*	*67*	*73*	*1.1*
	First-generation	*79*	*81*	*71*	*76*	*0.7*
Hong Kong-China	Native	72	80	69	60	6.2
	Second-generation	72	81	70	61	6.6
	First-generation	84	88	75	73	3.4
Macao-China	Native	76	84	65	61	0.8
	Second-generation	79	86	71	65	1.2
	First-generation	81	86	76	69	0.5
Russian Federation	Native	77	70	68	72	2.1
	Second-generation	76	70	68	71	2.2
	First-generation	77	70	70	73	0.6

Source: OECD PISA 2003 database, Table 4.2.

As noted earlier, instrumental motivation is an important educational outcome because it is not just associated with academic achievement. Students with strong instrumental motivation often choose more challenging courses and have higher educational and career aspirations (Wigfield, *et al.*, 1998). While it is not possible to examine these choices based on the PISA 2003 assessment, the 15-year-old students who took the PISA test were asked about the education level they expect to attain. Figure 4.3b shows that in most countries, instrumental motivation is higher among students expecting to complete at least a secondary programme (ISCED Levels 3A and 4) that will give them access to a tertiary education programme compared to students expecting to complete lower secondary programmes (ISCED Level 2). It is even higher among students who expect to complete a university-level programme (ISCED Levels 5A and 6) (see Figure 4.3b and Table 4.3). This general trend can be seen for native, first-generation and second-generation students. Once more, however, there are exceptions to this trend. In Figure 4.3b, countries in which there is no clear association between students' instrumental motivation in mathematics and their expected level of education are

Figure 4.3b ■ **Students' instrumental motivation in mathematics and their educational expectations by immigrant status**

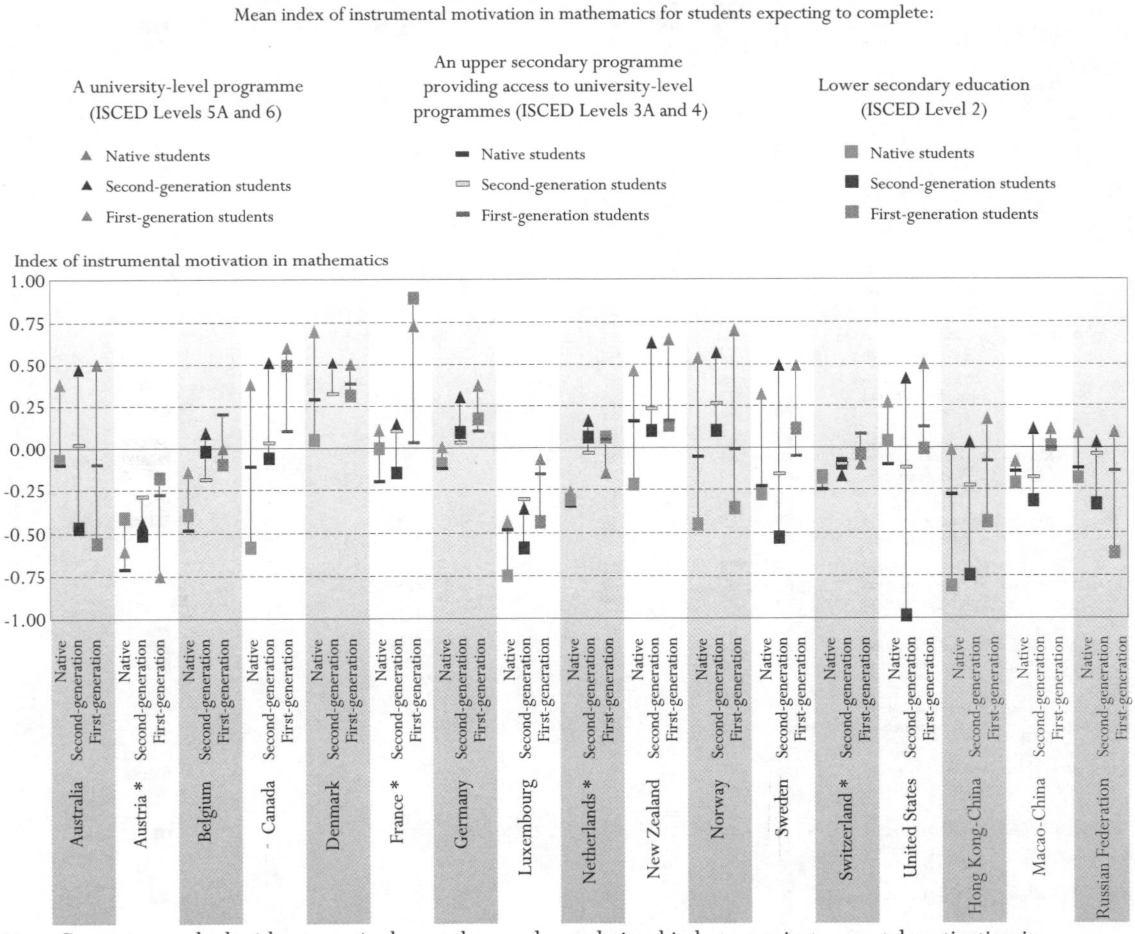

Mean index of instrumental motivation in mathematics for students expecting to complete:

A university-level programme
(ISCED Levels 5A and 6)

▲ Native students
▲ Second-generation students
▲ First-generation students

An upper secondary programme providing access to university-level programmes (ISCED Levels 3A and 4)

▬ Native students
▭ Second-generation students
▬ First-generation students

Lower secondary education
(ISCED Level 2)

■ Native students
■ Second-generation students
■ First-generation students

Index of instrumental motivation in mathematics

Note: Countries marked with an asterix do not show a clear relationship between instrumental motivation in mathematics and students' expected level of education (OECDa, 2004, p.124). In other countries where there is a clear relationship at the country level this relationship may not exist for some of the subgroups by immigrant background.
Source: OECD PISA 2003 database, Table 4.3.

© OECD 2006   *Where immigrant students succeed - A comparative review of performance and engagement in PISA 2003*

noted with an asterisk. They include Austria, France, the Netherlands and Switzerland. There are also countries where the immigrant sub-groups do not follow the expected trend. This is the case for first-generation students in Belgium, Canada, Germany and Sweden and for second-generation students in Belgium, Denmark, Germany and Luxembourg. In these countries and for these sub-groups, there is no definitive positive association between instrumental motivation and expected educational attainment.

In most countries, immigrant and non-immigrant students with higher educational expectations appear also to have higher levels of motivation, yet remarkable differences emerge among the three sub-groups when examining students' expected educational level alone. These analyses compare native students with first-generation and second-generation students in terms of the likelihood that they report expecting to complete a tertiary level education programme. The statistical method employed here is logistic regression (see Box 4.2). This allows for a comparison of the occurrence of certain traits in different groups, in this case the level of education immigrant and non-immigrant students expect to complete.

Box 4.2 ■ **Logistic Regression and Odds Ratios**

Multiple regression is appropriate when the outcome variables are continuous, such as the measures of reading, mathematics and science performance used in PISA. However, when the outcome variable is dichotomous, such as whether or not a child repeated a grade at school, a variant of multiple regression called logistic regression is appropriate. It is useful to policy research, because of frequent interest in binomial traits, such as expecting to finish a university degree. The policy analyst is interested in the likelihood of the student having the trait and how various characteristics of the child, such as age, immigrant status or family income, influence that likelihood. The regression coefficients from a logistic regression can be easily transformed to odds ratios, which can be interpreted simply for policy purposes.

An odds ratio is the ratio of the odds for two different sets of circumstances. For example, if an event has a 75% chance of occurring, then the odds of it occurring are [0.75/(1-0.75)], which is 3.0. An event with the odds of 1.0 has an equal chance of occurring or not. For example, the odds of an event occurring for girls and for boys could be assessed, and the ratio of the odds could be calculated. Odds ratios are interpreted in a similar way to multiple regression coefficients: they stand for the ratio of the odds of an event occurring after a one-unit change in the independent variable, compared to what it was previously, given all other independent variables in the model are held constant. (Adapted from OECD, 2003c, p. 36).

The upper panel of Figure 4.3c displays the odds ratios of first-generation and second-generation students compared to native students expecting to complete a university-level programme in the future (see Table 4.4 also). Statistically significant differences from native students are marked using darker tones. An event with an odds ratio of 1.0 has an equal chance of occurring or not within the sub-groups. For example, the results indicate that in the Netherlands, the odds of first-generation students expecting to complete a university-level programme (ISCED Levels 5a and 6) are 0.97 relative to native students. This is close to 1.0 and not statistically

Figure 4.3c ■ Educational expectations by immigrant status before and after accounting for students' economic, social and cultural status (ESCS) and mathematics performance

■ ▨ Second-generation students   ■ ▨ First-generation students

Statistically significant differences from native students are marked in darker tones

Educational expectations by immigrant status BEFORE accounting for ESCS and mathematics performance

Note: Odds of 1 indicate that all students are equally likely to expect to complete a university-level (ISCED 5A/6) programme. Odds of 2 indicate that immigrant students are 2.0 more times likely to expect to complete a university-level (ISCED 5A/6) programme than are native students.

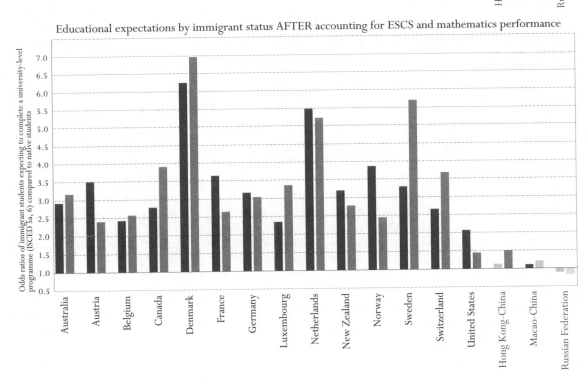

Educational expectations by immigrant status AFTER accounting for ESCS and mathematics performance

Source: OECD PISA 2003 database, Table 4.4.

significant, indicating that first-generation and native students in the Netherlands are equally likely to expect to complete a university-level education programme. In contrast, the odds ratio for first-generation students in Australia is 2.39, indicating that the odds of a first-generation student expecting to complete a tertiary education programme are 2.39 times higher than the odds for native students.

In examining the results, compared to native students, immigrant students in the majority of the 17 countries in this report have similar or somewhat lower odds of reporting that they expect to complete a tertiary programme. There are a few countries, however, where first-generation and second-generation students are significantly more likely to expect to complete a tertiary programme than their native peers. In Australia, Canada, Denmark, New Zealand and Sweden, the odds that first-generation students expect to complete their education at the tertiary level range from 1.93 in Sweden to 3.22 in Canada. In these same countries and in Norway, second-generation students also have higher odds of expecting to complete a university-level programme, yet the odds for this subgroup are somewhat smaller ranging from 1.7 in Sweden to 2.29 in Canada.

These results shift considerably when accounting for students' level of performance and socio-economic background. Based on Chapters 2 and 3, it is clear that immigrants tend to have both lower levels of performance and also come from less advantaged families, which may make it less likely for immigrant students to have high educational expectations. This does not seem to be the case, however. The second panel of Figure 4.3c shows the odds ratios of first-generation and second-generation students after accounting for their mathematics performance and socio-economic background. In all of the countries, except Hong Kong-China, Macao-China and the Russian Federation, first-generation and second-generation students have significantly higher odds of expecting to complete university programmes than native students with comparable performance levels and socio-economic backgrounds. For first-generation students, the odds range from 1.43 in the United States to 6.96 in Denmark. For second-generation students, the odds range from 2.05 in the United States to 6.23 in Denmark.

Based on these results, it is clear that immigrant students have much higher educational aspirations than their native counterparts, especially after accounting for performance and socio-economic background. One might suggest that first-generation and second-generation students possibly have unrealistic expectations, perhaps because they only have a limited understanding of the education systems in the receiving countries. Nevertheless, these results confirm that immigrant students tend to be optimistic about their future educational prospects. Although some immigrant students may experience long-term disappointment if they do not meet their goals, high expectations are likely to be positive in terms of their motivation and willingness to make an effort at school. Furthermore, findings in this section suggest that first-generation and second-generation students generally have relatively high intrinsic and instrumental motivation, with first-generation students in many countries showing the most motivation. These characteristics should help support their learning throughout their adolescent and adult lives.

STUDENTS' SELF-RELATED BELIEFS

Students' beliefs about themselves play a critical role in their ability to learn independently. In order to be able to engage in effective learning, students need to have a pragmatic understanding of the difficulty of a task and the ability to adopt effective strategies to complete it. Independent learning skills are essential for successfully tackling the various challenges adults encounter throughout their lives. Through school and life experiences, students develop views about their ability and learning characteristics. Previous research shows that these beliefs substantially influence students' goal setting and engagement in effective learning strategies (Zimmerman, 1999). They are also related to students' performance (OECD, 2004a). Two types of beliefs are often distinguished: *self-concept* – the belief in one's own academic abilities and *self-efficacy* – the belief in one's ability to handle tasks effectively and overcome challenges. PISA 2003 asked questions related to both aspects in the area of mathematics. This section examines immigrant students' beliefs about themselves compared to those of their native peers, as well as the associations between these beliefs and performance.

Students' self-concept in mathematics

Students' academic self-concept is often associated with student success. It is also a valuable outcome of education in itself, as individuals with higher self-concept believe in their ability and are more likely to look for learning opportunities. In addition, belief in one's ability is vital to successful learning (Marsh, 1986). Self-concept is also significantly related to overall well-being and personality development – outcomes shown to be especially significant for less advantaged students (*e.g.* Becker and Luthar, 2002).

One might expect immigrant students to develop lower levels of self-concept in mathematics, as they tend to be less successful academically than non-immigrant students. However, this does not appear to be the case when examining how immigrant students across the OECD case countries responded to questions related to their self-concept in mathematics. One illustration of this is that 61% of first-generation students, 55% of second-generation students and 54% of native students agree or strongly agree that they learn mathematics quickly (see first panel of Figure 4.4). Also, 44% of first-generation, 37% of second-generation and 35% of native students in the OECD case countries agree or strongly agree that they believe mathematics is one of their best subjects. This may partially reflect that immigrant students feel they do relatively better in mathematics compared to reading where they may struggle more with a foreign language (Marsh, 1986; Shajek, Lüdtke and Stanat, forthcoming). In line with this idea, first-generation students have significantly higher levels of self-concept in mathematics compared to their native peers across the OECD case countries. There is no significant difference between second-generation and native students however (see the second panel of Figure 4.4).

When looking at the index which summarises the questions related to students' self-concept in mathematics, country variations in the differences between immigrant and non-immigrant students emerge (see Figure 4.4). The self-concept of first-generation and second-generation students tends to be similar or slightly higher than that of their native peers. Only in Denmark do second-generation students score significantly lower than native students. In seven case countries – Australia, Canada, Germany, Luxembourg, New Zealand, Switzerland and Macao-China – first-generation students show significantly higher levels of self-concept than native students. In Australia and Macao-China second-generation students also have higher scores than their native peers.

After accounting for students' socio-economic background, immigrant students tend to have similar or more positive reported self-concepts than native students. Specifically, first-generation students show significantly higher levels of self-concept than their native peers in 11 countries: Australia, Belgium, Canada, France, Germany, Luxembourg, New Zealand, Sweden, Switzerland, the

Figure 4.4 ■ **Self-concept in mathematics by immigrant status**

		Percentage of students agreeing or strongly agreeing with the following statements:					Index of self-concept in mathematics	Change in mathematics score per unit change in the index of self-concept in mathematics	Percentage of explained variance in student performance
		I am just not good at mathematics.	I get good marks in mathematics.	I learn mathematics quickly.	I have always believed that mathematics is one of my best subjects.	In my mathematics class, I understand even the most difficult work.			
Australia	Native	33	64	55	36	37			18.1
	Second-generation	28	67	60	44	42			14.5
	First-generation	28	69	62	47	44			11.5
Austria	Native	35	60	54	32	39			11.2
	Second-generation	38	59	60	38	37			6.5
	First-generation	38	53	59	38	37			1.9
Belgium	Native	38	62	50	30	27			6.2
	Second-generation	38	60	52	31	36			0.5
	First-generation	36	61	59	36	35			2.3
Canada	Native	35	63	57	39	42			20.5
	Second-generation	35	61	57	39	41			24.2
	First-generation	29	70	67	55	53			16.0
Denmark	Native	29	71	60	49	35			29.1
	Second-generation	40	57	52	41	25			10.2
	First-generation	34	63	64	45	29			15.1
France	Native	39	49	47	26	28			11.3
	Second-generation	38	42	45	24	29			8.2
	First-generation	40	57	58	38	35			12.5
Germany	Native	37	58	56	35	41			8.6
	Second-generation	33	62	58	37	40			15.9
	First-generation	33	64	63	42	43			9.3
Luxembourg	Native	40	59	54	34	37			6.8
	Second-generation	36	64	53	33	34			5.4
	First-generation	33	66	58	39	38			5.2
Netherlands	Native	38	62	54	33	29			7.2
	Second-generation	37	63	52	30	31			2.0
	First-generation	35	60	54	38	30			7.3
New Zealand	Native	34	70	54	37	37			17.8
	Second-generation	39	67	56	43	39			15.5
	First-generation	24	75	67	53	48			15.9
Norway	Native	45	49	47	30	30			33.6
	Second-generation	44	47	52	40	43			33.9
	First-generation	51	42	45	33	32			16.5
Sweden	Native	34	59	60	31	44			27.9
	Second-generation	34	61	57	30	44			27.9
	First-generation	31	64	65	37	49			11.2
Switzerland	Native	33	61	56	36	40			9.7
	Second-generation	37	59	57	38	32			1.8
	First-generation	34	65	63	45	43			4.7
United States	Native	36	73	58	44	44			15.0
	Second-generation	32	69	60	48	45			20.1
	First-generation	38	75	60	48	48			10.7
OECD average	*Native*	*36*	*61*	*54*	*35*	*36*			*14.1*
	Second-generation	*35*	*61*	*55*	*37*	*37*			*9.8*
	First-generation	*33*	*65*	*61*	*44*	*42*			*9.1*
Hong Kong-China	Native	57	25	45	32	30			14.0
	Second-generation	56	27	47	33	32			14.5
	First-generation	55	23	42	29	28			6.3
Macao-China	Native	56	24	40	21	19			9.9
	Second-generation	51	31	46	27	31			13.8
	First-generation	42	33	52	27	32			10.2
Russian Federation	Native	37	51	46	42	42			11.6
	Second-generation	43	42	45	39	41			2.9
	First-generation	41	45	44	42	44			5.6

Legend — Index of self-concept in mathematics:
- ■ Native students
- ■ Second-generation students
- ▶ First-generation students

Statistically significant differences from native students are marked in darker tones

Index points: -1.0   -0.5   0.0   0.5   1.0

Legend — Change in mathematics score per unit change in the index of self-concept in mathematics:
- ■ ■ Native students
- ■ ■ Second-generation students
- ■ ■ First-generation students

Statistically significant changes are marked in darker tones

Score point differences: -60 -40 -20   0   20 40 60

Source: OECD PISA 2003 database, Table 4.5.

United States and Macao-China (see Table 4.5). In Australia, Belgium, Norway and Macao-China, second-generation students have significantly higher self-concept in mathematics after accounting for socio-economic background. In many countries, immigrant students come from relatively less advantaged backgrounds and after accounting for this, first-generation students show higher levels of self concept.

After taking student performance in PISA 2003 into account, both first-generation and second-generation students tend to have substantively more positive self-concept (see Table 4.5). Specifically, first-generation students show significantly higher self-concept in every country, except the Russian Federation. This same result occurs for second-generation students in all of the case countries, except Canada, Denmark, Hong Kong-China and the Russian Federation. One may argue that these students have unrealistic self-concepts or that they might have relatively higher self-concepts in this subject which is less language intensive (Marsh, 1986). Nevertheless, this should be viewed as a positive sign as it indicates that immigrant students have this essential prerequisite for learning. Despite the challenges that immigrant students face, such as lower socio-economic status or lower mathematics achievement, they generally do not appear to have lower levels of self-concept. In fact, first-generation immigrant students often have higher levels of self-concept than their native peers.

Despite immigrant students' similar or even more positive self-concept, they tend to lag behind their native peers in performance. The results indicate, however, that there is still a significant association between self-concept and performance for both first-generation and second-generation students (see the third panel of Figure 4.4). Across the OECD case countries, the relationship is more than 30 score points per unit of self-concept. With only a few exceptions, there is a significant positive relationship between self-concept in mathematics and performance within all student subgroups and countries. A one unit (or standard deviation) increase in self-concept in mathematics is associated with a significant increase in mathematics performance ranging from 16 score points in Belgium to nearly 45 score points in New Zealand for first-generation students and from more than 12 score points in Switzerland to almost 55 score points in Sweden for second-generation students.

More research is needed to better understand how to channel this positive self-concept to lessen differences between immigrant and non-immigrant student performance. While it may be encouraging that many immigrant students report similar or even higher levels of self-concept compared to their native peers, it may also be true that immigrant students are in situations where there are lower expectations or where they feel relatively better about themselves in mathematics than in reading and in turn show comparatively high levels of self-concept.

Students' self-efficacy in mathematics

A second key aspect of students' beliefs about themselves as learners is self-efficacy. Students not only need to feel able to pursue specific learning objectives, they must also have confidence in their ability to overcome the challenges that they may face in trying to reach their goal. Students who lack this confidence are at risk of failing both in school and in their adult lives (OECD, 2004a). Self-efficacy has been linked to improved learning, which helps students acquire new knowledge and skills in school and throughout their lives. Furthermore, increases in self-efficacy are associated with improvements in student performance (Bandura, 1994; OECD, 2004a). In PISA 2003, the questions related to self-efficacy examine students' confidence in their ability to master a number of specific mathematics tasks.

The PISA 2003 survey asked students to answer a series of questions about their confidence in being able to solve various mathematics problems. The index of self-efficacy summarises students' answers to these questions. As for the other indices, the scale is defined so that the average score across all OECD countries is 0 with a standard deviation of 1, *i.e.* two thirds of the students score between 1 and -1. Figure 4.5 (second panel) indicates the average level of self-efficacy by immigrant sub-group. Across the OECD countries, there is no significant difference between the self-efficacy reported by first-generation and native students, yet second-generation students report significantly lower levels of self-efficacy than their native peers. Substantively, however, this difference is fairly small, at about 0.07 of a standard deviation.

Considering differences in the level of self-efficacy reported by non-immigrant and immigrant students in an international context reveals a substantial amount of variation among countries. First-generation students in Austria, Belgium, Germany, Luxembourg, Switzerland and Hong Kong-China, report significantly lower levels of self-efficacy compared to their native peers. In contrast, first-generation students in Australia, Canada and New Zealand report significantly higher levels of self-efficacy. For the remaining eight countries, the differences between first-generation and native students are not significant. A similar pattern emerges when comparing differences between second-generation and native students. Second-generation students report lower levels of self-efficacy than their native peers in Austria, Denmark, France, Germany, Luxembourg and Switzerland. Only in Australia does the opposite pattern emerge with reported self-efficacy being higher among second-generation students than among native students.

In over half of the countries in this report, first-generation and second-generation students report similar or higher levels of self-efficacy. At the same time, however, there is a group of countries where immigrant students report lower levels of confidence in tackling mathematics tasks, even though they show similar levels of self-concept in mathematics. In other words, relative to their native peers, immigrant students in many countries believe in their ability in mathematics, but when it comes to completing specific and potentially challenging tasks, they tend to lack confidence. It is useful to point out that after accounting for the socio-economic background of students, the differences between immigrant and non-immigrant students disappear in most countries (see Table 4.6). This may indicate that self-efficacy is generally lower among disadvantaged students. These findings point to a need for schools and educators to consider how they may work to bolster self-efficacy among immigrant students and disadvantaged children more generally. One potentially positive sign is that after accounting for mathematics performance, first-generation students and second-generation students in the majority of the case countries have significantly higher levels of self-efficacy than their native peers (Table 4.6).

The school and policy implications are reinforced when considering the association between self-efficacy and mathematics performance. The third panel of Figure 4.5 indicates that there is an even stronger relationship between self-efficacy and mathematics performance than there was with self-concept. Self-efficacy is one of the strongest predictors of student performance. Across the OECD case countries it explains 25% of the variation in mathematics performance for native students, 24% for second-generation students and 24% for first-generation students. Furthermore, analyses in *Learning for Tomorrow's World – First Results from PISA 2003* (OECD 2004a) indicate that even when considering other learning characteristics simultaneously, self-efficacy continues to have a strong and positive relationship with student performance.

Immigrant students' approaches to learning

Figure 4.5 ■ Students' self-efficacy in mathematics by immigrant status

Percentage of students agreeing or strongly agreeing with the following statements:

Index of self-efficacy in mathematics

Change in mathematics score per unit change in the index of self-efficacy in mathematics

Index of self-efficacy in mathematics:
- Native students
- Second-generation students
- First-generation students

Change in mathematics:
- Native students
- Second-generation students
- First-generation students

Statistically significant differences from native students are marked in darker tones — Index points

Statistically significant changes are marked in darker tones — Score point differences

		Using a train timetable, how long it would take to get from Zedtown to Zedtown.	Calculating how much cheaper a TV would be after a 30 per cent discount.	Calculating how many square metres of tiles you need to cover a floor.	Understanding graphs presented in newspapers.	Solving an equation like 3x +5=17.	Finding the actual distance between two places on a map with a 1:10,000 scale.	Solving an equation like 2(x+3)=(x²+3)(x-3).	Calculating the petrol consumption rate of a car.	Percentage of explained variance in student performance
Australia	Native	90	78	76	89	82	58	66	60	27.4
	Second-generation	92	83	74	90	88	59	74	63	24.2
	First-generation	87	84	76	85	90	62	76	63	29.2
Austria	Native	87	83	77	76	84	55	77	57	26.6
	Second-generation	82	75	61	66	77	47	73	48	18.8
	First-generation	78	72	76	68	81	48	76	55	9.3
Belgium	Native	81	79	66	74	82	66	65	54	19.5
	Second-generation	72	77	66	70	78	70	69	58	15.9
	First-generation	70	64	63	64	71	66	59	54	12.9
Canada	Native	81	80	78	87	91	61	80	60	28.4
	Second-generation	83	83	72	84	94	60	83	53	33.9
	First-generation	85	85	79	87	93	69	87	61	30.3
Denmark	Native	86	78	69	87	75	63	47	61	28.6
	Second-generation	76	78	54	76	75	62	51	65	15.3
	First-generation	83	88	68	81	71	72	50	66	14.8
France	Native	74	75	64	82	85	50	68	58	25.8
	Second-generation	69	73	56	76	84	47	67	56	22.7
	First-generation	65	73	59	75	86	46	71	55	31.0
Germany	Native	85	78	76	81	87	55	73	58	26.5
	Second-generation	74	76	65	62	79	48	71	60	23.8
	First-generation	76	74	74	70	81	51	70	57	26.1
Luxembourg	Native	83	75	70	76	91	61	80	55	20.6
	Second-generation	76	70	56	66	88	54	77	55	20.4
	First-generation	73	69	58	66	85	57	74	60	25.3
Netherlands	Native	80	87	72	84	73	64	54	63	22.4
	Second-generation	72	90	65	82	75	55	58	66	11.7
	First-generation	80	81	66	84	74	66	60	60	21.1
New Zealand	Native	86	79	75	90	83	53	59	53	28.4
	Second-generation	86	81	72	87	81	45	65	48	28.7
	First-generation	85	87	78	85	89	61	77	61	22.9
Norway	Native	85	83	60	71	74	44	47	61	30.9
	Second-generation	80	80	58	65	75	74	51	57	36.7
	First-generation	74	85	51	65	73	63	53	57	20.8
Sweden	Native	89	82	69	91	74	60	49	63	35.0
	Second-generation	92	86	65	90	79	66	57	67	29.6
	First-generation	79	82	64	82	74	67	55	58	22.0
Switzerland	Native	91	86	82	78	87	64	76	66	31.5
	Second-generation	82	85	70	69	85	59	72	64	21.8
	First-generation	81	83	75	67	81	65	72	70	24.3
United States	Native	72	82	80	89	91	62	81	75	27.2
	Second-generation	69	78	76	85	93	61	82	70	37.7
	First-generation	77	77	80	85	90	63	83	76	22.6
OECD average	Native	83	80	74	83	85	60	70	60	25.1
	Second-generation	81	80	69	79	86	58	72	59	24.0
	First-generation	80	80	72	77	85	62	74	62	24.1
Hong Kong-China	Native	76	91	79	75	92	65	77	45	31.5
	Second-generation	79	93	81	77	92	67	79	45	31.3
	First-generation	75	91	73	66	93	65	68	43	25.3
Macao-China	Native	69	92	70	60	95	56	85	33	16.9
	Second-generation	72	94	73	61	98	58	86	34	19.3
	First-generation	70	95	77	69	98	65	86	38	22.8
Russian Federation	Native	67	72	68	66	91	57	80	63	20.5
	Second-generation	66	68	69	56	90	57	75	64	8.1
	First-generation	67	71	67	57	90	58	72	69	13.3

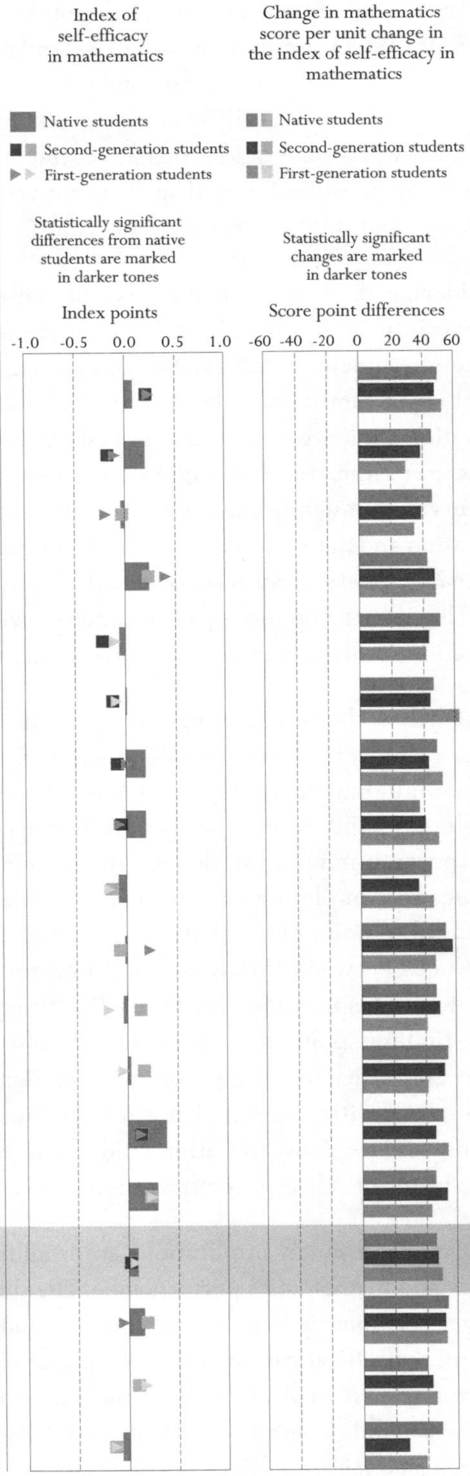

Source: OECD PISA 2003 database, Table 4.6.

© OECD 2006 Where immigrant students succeed - A comparative review of performance and engagement in PISA 2003

The findings indicate that an increase of one index point (or one standard deviation) on the scale of self-efficacy in mathematics across the OECD case countries corresponds to 46 score points in mathematics performance for native students, 50 score points for first-generation students and 47 score points for second-generation students. This is equivalent to almost one mathematics proficiency level. Improving self-efficacy is therefore an area where teachers and policy makers may want to place additional emphasis, in an effort to reduce differences between immigrant and non-immigrant students. Furthermore, increasing immigrant students' confidence in their ability to overcome learning obstacles should be a goal alongside improving performance, as this characteristic is essential for long-term independent learning and closely related to students' motivation and the use of effective learning strategies (Bandura, 1994).

EMOTIONAL DISPOSITIONS IN MATHEMATICS

PISA 2003 also collected information on students' negative attitudes to mathematics. Many students experience emotional stress or anxiety in relation to school mathematics. It has been shown that these negative dispositions are associated with lower levels of mathematics achievement, lower grades in mathematics, course enrolment (e.g. choosing lower level mathematics courses or not enrolling in mathematics courses at all) and choice of academic speciality (Wigfield et al., 1998; Pajares and Miller, 1994, 1995; Ramirez and Dockweiler, 1987; Schwarzer, Seipp and Schwarzer, 1989; Wigfield and Meece, 1988). The initial results from PISA 2003 indicate that a large percentage of 15-year-old students experience negative dispositions towards mathematics. For example, more than 50% of students in OECD countries report that they often worry that mathematics classes will be difficult and that they will get poor marks in these classes (OECD, 2004a). This section explores whether immigrant students report similar levels of anxiety compared to native students and how the patterns differ across case countries.

In the OECD countries in this report, 54% of first-generation students and 57% of second-generation students report concern about mathematics classes being difficult for them (see first panel of Figure 4.6). This compares to 48% of native students. Also across the OECD case countries, 58% of first-generation students and 62% of second-generation students report that they worry about receiving poor marks in mathematics. This compares to 52% of native students. Among all three immigrant subgroups, there is generally less concern about mathematics homework or doing mathematics problems. Yet, for each of these questions immigrant students also report more anxiety related to mathematics than native students.

Considering the overall index of anxiety in mathematics for the OECD case countries, immigrant students report significantly higher levels of anxiety compared to their native peers. At the same time, there is substantial variation across countries (see the second panel of Figure 4.6). For example, students in France, Hong Kong-China and Macao-China report the highest levels of anxiety related to mathematics, and students in Denmark, the Netherlands and Sweden report the least. While immigrant students may show significant differences compared to native students within these countries, the level of anxiety tends to mirror the degree of anxiety in overall country results (except for Macao-China). For example, in France, both native students and immigrant students report high levels of anxiety in mathematics. The opposite is true for native and immigrant students in the Netherlands and Sweden.

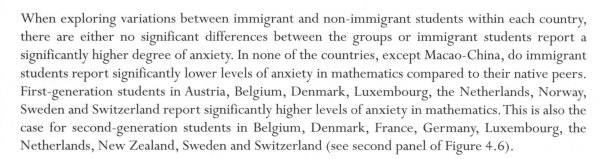

When exploring variations between immigrant and non-immigrant students within each country, there are either no significant differences between the groups or immigrant students report a significantly higher degree of anxiety. In none of the countries, except Macao-China, do immigrant students report significantly lower levels of anxiety in mathematics compared to their native peers. First-generation students in Austria, Belgium, Denmark, Luxembourg, the Netherlands, Norway, Sweden and Switzerland report significantly higher levels of anxiety in mathematics. This is also the case for second-generation students in Belgium, Denmark, France, Germany, Luxembourg, the Netherlands, New Zealand, Sweden and Switzerland (see second panel of Figure 4.6).

When the socio-economic background of students is taken into account, first-generation students in Austria, Belgium, the Netherlands, Sweden, Switzerland and Macao-China still show significantly higher levels of anxiety in mathematics than their native counterparts. For second-generation students, this is the case in Belgium, Denmark, France, Luxembourg, the Netherlands, New Zealand, Sweden, Switzerland and Macao-China. In countries where immigrant students report significantly higher levels of anxiety than native students, educators and administrators may need to pay particular attention to factors that may lead to this (see Table 4.7).

Not surprisingly, higher levels of anxiety in mathematics are generally associated with significantly lower scores in mathematics (see third panel in Figure 4.6). Among first-generation students, for every one unit (one standard deviation) increase in anxiety in mathematics the associated decline in student scores ranges from 18 score points in Austria to almost 49 score points in New Zealand. For second-generation students, the decrease ranges from just under 17 score points in Belgium to more than 50 score points in New Zealand. The strong association between anxiety in mathematics and performance coupled with the relatively high level of anxiety in mathematics among students in general, and the even higher levels experienced by immigrant students in a substantial number of countries, indicate a need for more policy focus in this area.

STUDENTS' ATTITUDES TOWARDS AND PERCEPTIONS OF SCHOOLS

This section moves beyond examining students' interests, beliefs and dispositions related to mathematics to a broader view of students' attitudes and perceptions of schools and examines whether these differ among immigrant and non-immigrant students. Students' *attitudes towards school* – the extent to which students perceive school as preparing them for life – will be explored in the first part of the section. Students with positive attitudes towards schooling are more likely to pursue their education beyond secondary school (OECD, 2003c). The second part of the section explores *students' sense of belonging at school*. A strong sense of belonging at school is a vital part of students' well-being during adolescence, as it is central to their daily experiences. Students who do not feel connected to school are at risk of a series of negative social and health outcomes, including school dropout, disruptive behaviour, school violence, substance use and emotional distress (Catalano, *et al.* 2004; Lonczak, *et al.* 2002). By exploring immigrant students' attitudes towards school and their sense of belonging it is possible to develop a broader understanding of how these non-academic school outcomes may differ across countries and among immigrant students within countries. In turn, the findings of the analyses will indicate whether it may be useful to pay particular attention to how immigrant students perceive their school experiences to help ensure their long-term success.

Figure 4.6 ■ **Students' anxiety in mathematics by immigrant status**

		Percentage of students agreeing or strongly agreeing with the following statements:					Index of anxiety in mathematics	Change in mathematics score per unit change in the index of anxiety in mathematics	Percentage of explained variance in student performance
		I often worry that it will be difficult for me in mathematics classes.	I get very tense when I have to do mathematics homework.	I get very nervous doing mathematics problems.	I feel helpless when doing a mathematics problem.	I worry that I will get poor marks in mathematics.	Index points	Score point differences	
Australia	Native	53	29	21	20	57			12.9
	Second-generation	52	24	22	18	62			9.6
	First-generation	51	24	24	22	59			10.6
Austria	Native	56	29	22	23	42			10.0
	Second-generation	59	31	21	23	49			10.5
	First-generation	59	34	28	25	53			4.8
Belgium	Native	56	26	31	28	68			5.2
	Second-generation	67	42	40	36	72			2.6
	First-generation	59	36	36	34	70			7.5
Canada	Native	54	33	25	24	58			15.8
	Second-generation	57	32	33	23	60			17.2
	First-generation	49	30	30	21	56			16.8
Denmark	Native	33	25	14	16	39			26.6
	Second-generation	50	41	27	29	61			11.7
	First-generation	42	32	20	22	52			22.4
France	Native	60	52	38	36	74			5.8
	Second-generation	67	58	45	42	80			5.0
	First-generation	66	54	42	44	76			14.9
Germany	Native	52	29	23	22	46			10.7
	Second-generation	58	35	36	26	52			15.1
	First-generation	57	31	29	22	53			19.9
Luxembourg	Native	57	24	31	30	59			10.0
	Second-generation	60	42	36	35	67			9.0
	First-generation	59	37	35	30	65			9.1
Netherlands	Native	35	6	14	16	42			4.3
	Second-generation	48	9	25	19	58			2.6
	First-generation	46	16	33	27	53			7.8
New Zealand	Native	52	24	20	21	55			18.1
	Second-generation	61	27	30	29	63			22.1
	First-generation	48	23	22	23	55			21.9
Norway	Native	46	37	19	31	57			25.3
	Second-generation	49	44	22	30	60			16.5
	First-generation	57	46	38	36	72			26.8
Sweden	Native	30	13	10	16	45			19.6
	Second-generation	41	23	16	24	57			18.8
	First-generation	53	22	17	21	53			24.1
Switzerland	Native	46	25	17	24	45			9.3
	Second-generation	53	32	25	30	55			4.6
	First-generation	54	32	29	28	53			13.8
United States	Native	55	34	26	22	46			14.7
	Second-generation	57	27	26	22	51			20.5
	First-generation	59	35	30	30	55			17.7
OECD average	*Native*	*48*	*28*	*22*	*23*	*52*			*12.0*
	Second-generation	*57*	*34*	*30*	*28*	*62*			*9.7*
	First-generation	*54*	*31*	*29*	*26*	*58*			*12.9*
Hong Kong-China	Native	68	30	34	35	73			7.8
	Second-generation	68	30	32	35	71			1.1
	First-generation	69	26	32	33	71			5.9
Macao-China	Native	78	37	44	48	69			9.0
	Second-generation	66	32	40	36	63			12.7
	First-generation	60	23	30	26	56			4.8
Russian Federation	Native	57	38	32	24	72			15.7
	Second-generation	60	39	32	23	70			4.3
	First-generation	61	43	31	27	76			7.8

Index of anxiety in mathematics:
- Native students
- Second-generation students
- First-generation students

Statistically significant differences from native students are marked in darker tones

Change in mathematics score per unit change in the index of anxiety in mathematics:
- Native students
- Second-generation students
- First-generation students

Statistically significant changes are marked in darker tones

Index points scale: -1.0 -0.5 0.0 0.5 1.0
Score point differences scale: -60 -40 -20 0 20 40 60

Source: OECD PISA 2003 database, Table 4.7.

Immigrant students' approaches to learning

Students' attitudes towards school

Education systems generally seek to provide children and adolescents not only with a strong foundation in terms of subject-related knowledge and skills, but also with a grounding for a smooth transition to adult life. As Figure 4.7 shows, the majority of students, including first-generation and second-generation students, report quite positive attitudes towards school. The index of attitudes towards school summarises the questions presented in the first panel of Figure 4.7. Across the OECD case countries, both first-generation and second-generation students report significantly higher levels of positive school perceptions compared to their native peers.

In examining sub-group differences at an international level, first-generation students in most of the OECD case countries report having more positive attitudes towards school. Only in a handful of case countries – Australia, Denmark, the United States, Hong Kong-China, Macao-China and the Russian Federation – are there no significant differences between first-generation and native students. In none of the 17 countries do first-generation or second-generation students have significantly less positive attitudes towards school. The number of countries where second-generation students report a significantly more positive attitude towards school than native students is smaller than when first-generation and native students are compared. More specifically in Australia, Belgium, Canada, France, Germany, Luxembourg, the Netherlands and New Zealand, second-generation students perceive school much more favourably. First-generation students report more positive attitudes towards school in all of the case countries except Australia, Denmark, New Zealand and the three partner countries. As with many other variables discussed in this chapter, first-generation students tend to have an even more positive attitude towards school than second-generation students (although, due to the relatively small sample sizes, the differences between first-generation and second-generation students are rarely statistically significant).

While it generally appears that immigrant students have similar or more positive attitudes towards school compared to their native peers, there is still a significant minority of students who report negative attitudes. There do not seem to be clear overall differences however in the percentage of immigrant and non-immigrant students reporting negative feelings towards school. For example, across OECD countries 33% of first-generation students agree or strongly agree with the statement "school has done little to prepare me for adult life when I leave school." This compares to 29% of second-generation students and 30% of native students. There is also a small but significant minority of students that agree that school has been a waste of time. This includes 8% of first-generation, 7% of second-generation and 9% of native students in the OECD case countries. While clear group differences between immigrant and non-immigrant students do not emerge, the small percentage of students who have strong negative perceptions of school should be of concern. These students may be at risk of other negative outcomes, including participating less in school activities, skipping class or dropping out. They may therefore need special attention to ensure that they will successfully complete school (OECD, 2003c). While there is no particular strong association between attitudes towards school and performance (see Figure 4.7), ensuring that students have a positive attitude towards school is valuable as it is closely related to dispositions necessary for lifelong learning (OECD, 2004a).

Sense of belonging at school

Another critical aspect of schooling is for students to feel that they belong at school. This can foster academic success by reducing barriers to learning as well as health and safety problems

Figure 4.7 ■ **Students' attitudes towards school by immigrant status**

Percentage of students agreeing or strongly agreeing with the following statements:

Index of attitudes towards school

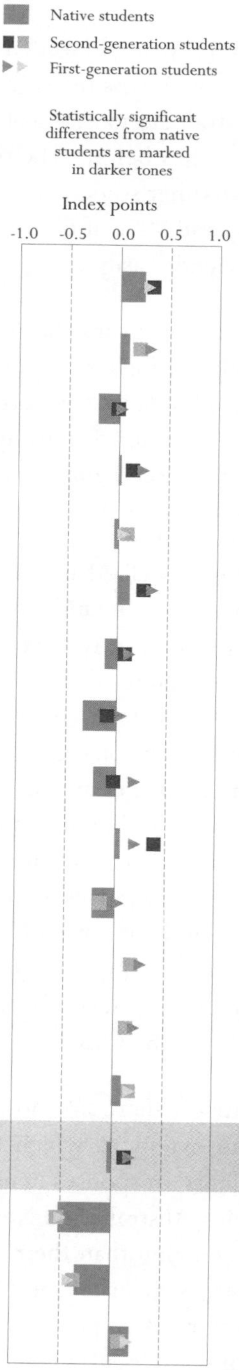

Change in mathematics score per unit change in the index of attitudes towards school

Native students
Second-generation students
First-generation students

Native students
Second-generation students
First-generation students

Statistically significant differences from native students are marked in darker tones

Statistically significant changes are marked in darker tones

Index points

Score point differences

		School has done little to prepare me for adult life when I leave school.	School has been a waste of time.	School helped give me confidence to make decisions.	School has taught me things which could be useful in a job.	Index points (-1.0 to 1.0)	Score point differences (-60 to 60)	Percentage of explained variance in student performance
Australia	Native	22	7	84	92			3.1
	Second-generation	21	4	85	93			0.3
	First-generation	28	7	86	93			1.4
Austria	Native	29	7	63	85			0.0
	Second-generation	30	8	66	88			4.8
	First-generation	26	10	71	89			1.7
Belgium	Native	31	11	62	90			0.0
	Second-generation	36	11	71	92			0.4
	First-generation	38	11	73	92			0.0
Canada	Native	26	9	72	89			1.0
	Second-generation	25	6	79	92			1.8
	First-generation	26	5	82	90			0.1
Denmark	Native	31	6	72	86			0.8
	Second-generation	27	2	79	85			1.4
	First-generation	35	11	77	91			2.4
France	Native	25	8	68	93			1.2
	Second-generation	23	4	67	95			0.0
	First-generation	27	11	72	98			2.4
Germany	Native	44	7	55	89			0.3
	Second-generation	44	9	65	88			0.7
	First-generation	44	5	60	92			4.1
Luxembourg	Native	52	10	48	86			0.3
	Second-generation	41	9	62	90			1.1
	First-generation	40	9	68	92			1.6
Netherlands	Native	23	11	65	92			0.6
	Second-generation	24	4	66	94			0.2
	First-generation	26	7	73	94			1.1
New Zealand	Native	30	8	79	90			3.1
	Second-generation	24	6	85	94			0.2
	First-generation	32	7	85	91			1.9
Norway	Native	38	10	63	85			3.2
	Second-generation	40	24	74	86			2.3
	First-generation	34	14	81	86			4.1
Sweden	Native	31	7	65	92			3.3
	Second-generation	28	4	71	93			0.2
	First-generation	31	8	76	93			3.4
Switzerland	Native	36	9	64	88			0.4
	Second-generation	37	6	70	90			1.3
	First-generation	39	8	73	89			0.2
United States	Native	30	10	79	91			0.4
	Second-generation	33	6	82	91			0.0
	First-generation	40	10	86	93			2.8
OECD average	*Native*	*30*	*9*	*70*	*89*			*0.6*
	Second-generation	*29*	*7*	*75*	*91*			*0.0*
	First-generation	*33*	*8*	*77*	*91*			*0.0*
Hong Kong-China	Native	53	13	64	83			0.8
	Second-generation	55	13	64	82			2.6
	First-generation	52	13	72	86			1.0
Macao-China	Native	46	6	71	90			0.2
	Second-generation	47	10	70	86			0.0
	First-generation	47	12	67	86			0.3
Russian Federation	Native	18	4	86	90			0.3
	Second-generation	21	6	83	89			0.1
	First-generation	21	7	88	93			0.1

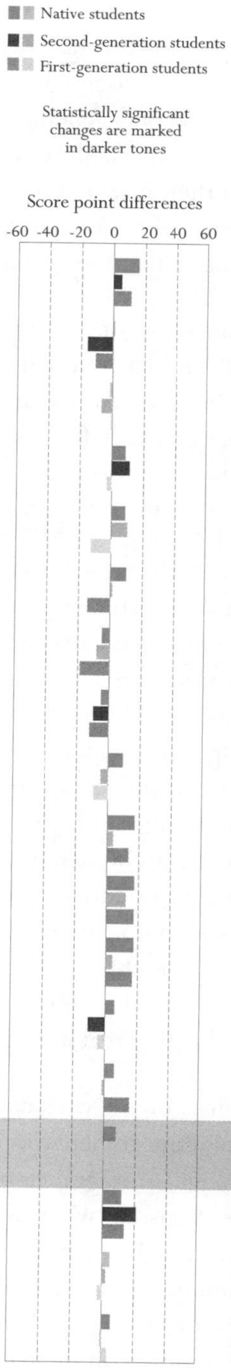

Source: OECD PISA 2003 database, Table 4.8.

(Catalano *et al.*, 2004; Libbey, 2004; OECD, 2003c). This section explores immigrant and non-immigrant students' sense of belonging and how it compares to their native peers. One might expect this to be an area of particular concern for immigrant students, as first-generation students and second-generation students come from different cultural backgrounds and may therefore find it more challenging to feel like they belong in the schools of the receiving country.

In PISA 2003 the majority of 15-year-old students responded positively to a series of questions related to sense of belonging at school. Across the OECD case countries, 78% of first-generation students, 77% of second-generation students and 79% of native students agree or strongly agree that they feel their school is a place where they belong. The percentages are even higher when students are asked about their interactions with other students. For example, 89% of first-generation students, 91% of second-generation students and 90% of native students agree or strongly agree with the statement indicating that they make friends easily.

At the same time, however, it appears that there is a substantial minority of students who feel lonely and left out and a slightly higher percentage of first-generation students who report having such feelings. For example, 11% of first-generation students and 8% of second-generation students report that they feel like an outsider or left out of things, while only 7% of native students report having these feelings. A similar trend appears in students' responses to feeling awkward and out of place (see the first panel of Figure 4.8).

As with the other variables described in this chapter, an index of sense of belonging at school summarises students' responses to the individual questions. Across the OECD case countries, first-generation students report significantly lower levels of sense of belonging than their native peers. This difference is substantively quite small, just over one-tenth of a standard deviation. There are no significant differences between second-generation and first-generation students. Across countries, first-generation and second-generation students' responses tend to be similar to the sense of belonging of native students in the individual countries *i.e.* if native students' sense of belonging is relatively high, immigrant students' sense of belonging is also relatively high. For example, in countries like Austria and Sweden, where native students tend to report relatively high levels of sense of belonging in comparison to the other case countries, first-generation and second-generation students also tend to have comparatively high levels of sense of belonging. Luxembourg is an exception to this trend. Native students in Luxembourg report a sense of belonging that is a quarter of a standard deviation higher than the OECD average, yet second-generation and first-generation students report feelings of belonging that are similar to the OECD averages for these groups.

In most of the case countries, there are no significant differences between immigrant and non-immigrant students in the extent to which they report feeling a sense of belonging at school, although immigrant students' responses tend to be less positive. There are, however, notable exceptions. In two countries, Australia and New Zealand, second-generation students report having a much higher sense of belonging than their native peers. In contrast, first-generation students in Luxembourg, New Zealand, Switzerland and Hong Kong-China report having a significantly lower sense of belonging than their native peers. This is also the case for second-generation students in Luxembourg. In these countries, focusing on helping immigrant students feel more like they belong at school may help indirectly to reduce the learning differences and also reduce possible behavioural problems (OECD, 2003c; OECD, 2004a). Furthermore, in countries where sense of belonging is

Figure 4.8 ■ Students' sense of belonging at school by immigrant status

		Percentage of students agreeing or strongly agreeing with the following statements:						Index of sense of belonging at school	Change in mathematics score per unit change in the index of sense of belonging at school	Percentage of explained variance in student performance
		I feel like an outsider (or left out of things).	I make friends easily.	I feel like I belong.	I feel awkward and out of place.	Other students seem to like me.	I feel lonely.	Index points	Score point differences	
Australia	Native	8	91	88	9	95	6			0.2
	Second-generation	6	94	90	6	97	5			0.4
	First-generation	9	90	87	11	94	8			0.2
Austria	Native	6	90	89	8	79	7			0.0
	Second-generation	10	87	84	12	74	11			0.2
	First-generation	7	90	89	13	75	8			0.1
Belgium	Native	7	89	57	15	92	6			0.2
	Second-generation	12	92	53	18	93	6			0.3
	First-generation	14	91	44	23	84	11			0.8
Canada	Native	8	90	81	11	94	8			0.0
	Second-generation	8	90	84	11	95	7			0.1
	First-generation	11	89	81	13	93	9			0.8
Denmark	Native	5	88	70	12	92	6			0.1
	Second-generation	4	87	62	8	91	6			0.1
	First-generation	6	83	59	13	91	8			0.6
France	Native	7	92	45	12	93	7			0.1
	Second-generation	11	94	44	14	92	6			0.4
	First-generation	17	90	54	15	90	10			0.4
Germany	Native	6	87	87	11	70	6			0.0
	Second-generation	7	85	89	11	77	8			0.1
	First-generation	8	86	82	14	64	10			0.2
Luxembourg	Native	6	89	77	9	92	7			0.2
	Second-generation	10	89	62	12	89	7			0.2
	First-generation	11	90	65	13	89	9			0.1
Netherlands	Native	4	91	78	7	93	3			0.6
	Second-generation	6	93	76	12	89	4			0.3
	First-generation	9	93	72	13	93	7			0.2
New Zealand	Native	7	91	86	10	94	6			0.1
	Second-generation	7	93	88	10	92	8			0.5
	First-generation	13	89	82	13	91	8			1.5
Norway	Native	5	90	86	9	91	7			0.0
	Second-generation	11	82	85	20	87	11			1.1
	First-generation	10	87	78	10	87	12			0.1
Sweden	Native	5	88	82	5	91	7			0.0
	Second-generation	7	91	75	8	91	7			0.1
	First-generation	8	88	77	7	88	6			3.2
Switzerland	Native	6	88	82	11	78	6			0.6
	Second-generation	8	90	76	14	82	4			0.0
	First-generation	17	88	83	15	82	13			2.3
United States	Native	m	m	m	m	m	m			m
	Second-generation	m	m	m	m	m	m			m
	First-generation	m	m	m	m	m	m			m
OECD average	Native	7	90	79	10	90	7			0.0
	Second-generation	8	91	77	11	91	6			0.0
	First-generation	11	89	78	13	88	9			0.0
Hong Kong-China	Native	17	88	68	10	77	11			0.8
	Second-generation	18	88	70	11	78	12			1.2
	First-generation	19	86	66	11	75	12			1.7
Macao-China	Native	18	81	68	13	75	16			1.2
	Second-generation	15	86	65	13	73	13			0.6
	First-generation	14	79	59	15	69	20			0.6
Russian Federation	Native	6	88	92	15	51	8			1.2
	Second-generation	7	87	92	14	42	11			0.3
	First-generation	8	87	91	17	56	9			0.9

Index of sense of belonging at school: Native students / Second-generation students / First-generation students. Statistically significant differences from native students are marked in darker tones. Index points scale: -1.0, -0.5, 0.0, 0.5, 1.0

Change in mathematics score per unit change in the index of sense of belonging at school: Native students / Second-generation students / First-generation students. Statistically significant changes are marked in darker tones. Score point differences scale: -60, -40, -20, 0, 20, 40, 60

Source: OECD PISA 2003 database, Table 4.9.

low across all immigrant sub-groups, special attention should be paid to raising all students' sense of belonging at school. While there may be only limited direct associations between sense of belonging and mathematics performance (see Figure 4.8), feeling connected to school is essential for students' long-term well-being and an important disposition for successful learning (OECD, 2003c).

SUMMARY OF DIFFERENCES BETWEEN IMMIGRANT AND NON-IMMIGRANT STUDENTS IN LEARNING CHARACTERISTICS

This section summarises the differences in learning characteristics between immigrant and non-immigrant students. Figure 4.9 and Table 4.10 show the results for each variable presented in this chapter. All results are expressed as effect sizes (*i.e.* estimates to the degree to which student groups differ) so that the results may be compared across the available measures and countries. As in other

Figure 4.9 ■ **Summary of main differences in learner characteristics by immigrant status**

Characteristics (based on index variable for each characteristic)	Number of OECD countries with significant differences between immigrant and native students for each variable	Average effect size across OECD countries[1]
Interest in mathematics	Second-generation *stronger* in 9 countries	**0.16**
	First-generation *stronger* in 14 countries	**0.32**
Instrumental motivation	Second-generation *stronger* in 10 countries	0.14
	First-generation *stronger* in 12 countries	**0.25**
Self-concept in mathematics	Second-generation *stronger* in 1 country and *weaker* in 1 country	0.01
	First-generation *stronger* in 6 countries	**0.16**
Self-efficacy in mathematics	Second-generation *stronger* in 1 country and *weaker* in 6 countries	**-0.06**
	First-generation *stronger* in 3 countries and *weaker* in 5 countries	-0.01
Anxiety related to mathematics	Second-generation *weaker* in 9 countries	**-0.24**
	First-generation *weaker* in 8 countries	**-0.11**
Attitudes towards school	Second-generation *stronger* in 8 countries	**0.17**
	First-generation *stronger* in 11 countries	**0.23**
Sense of belonging at school	Second-generation *stronger* in 2 countries and *weaker* in 1 country	-0.02
	First-generation *weaker* in 3 countries	**-0.09**

1. Positive scores = immigrant students higher; negative scores = native students higher. Graph based on Figure 4.5 in OECD 2003b. Native students are considered stronger on the anxiety measure, because they report less anxiety than immigrant students on average across the OECD case countries. Numbers in bold indicate significant differences between native students and the immigrant subgroup across OECD countries. As noted earlier, for the effect size to be meaningful it must be greater than 0.20.
Source: OECD PISA 2003 database, Table 4.10.

PISA reports, an effect size of 0.20 is used as a benchmark to indicate differences that may be considered important for policy makers. A striking finding is that in many countries immigrant students report having similar or even more positive learning characteristics. This trend is very different from the one that emerges when examining performance (see Chapters 2 and 3), where significant gaps between immigrant and non-immigrant students are found in almost every country.

Figure 4.9 indicates that of the three sub-groups, first-generation students tend to report the highest levels of non-achievement learning outcomes. Considering the 14 OECD countries in this report, first-generation students report higher levels of interest in mathematics in all 14 countries, higher levels of instrumental motivation in 12 countries, and higher levels of self-concept in 6 countries. First-generation students also report more positive attitudes towards school than their native peers in 11 countries. The average effect size across the OECD countries is greater than 0.20 for all of the variables noted above, except self-concept in mathematics. These findings suggest that first-generation students report at least similar if not stronger learning dispositions than their native peers in the majority of non-achievement outcomes measured in PISA 2003.

Second-generation students also tend to show stronger dispositions towards learning compared to native students, but these differences are smaller than those between first-generation and native students. Furthermore, there are fewer countries where the differences between second-generation and native students are significant. Again, considering the 14 OECD countries in this report, second-generation students in 9 countries report higher levels of interest in mathematics, in 10 countries they report higher levels of instrumental motivation and in 8 countries they report more positive attitudes towards school. The results are very different for self-concept and sense of belonging: second-generation students report higher levels in one and two OECD countries respectively and native students report higher levels in one OECD country. The average effect size across countries does not reach 0.20 for any of the variables, although this masks variation across countries. In many countries, the effect sizes for second-generation students on several variables is greater than 0.20. For example, the effect size for interest in mathematics is at least 0.20 in Australia, Belgium, Canada, Germany, the Netherlands, New Zealand, Norway and the United States (see Table 4.10). These findings indicate that in many countries second-generation students also report stronger non-achievement outcomes, but that these students are more similar to their native peers than first-generation students. The overall results seem to support hypotheses related to immigrant optimism and assimilation with first-generation students reporting the highest levels of interest and motivation. Among second-generation students, the levels of interest and motivation are lower and more similar to levels reported by native students.

There are two learning characteristics that do not fit this trend: self-efficacy in mathematics and anxiety related to mathematics. These two variables are also more strongly associated with performance than the other learning characteristics presented in the chapter (see Figures 4.5 and 4.6). Immigrant students in a considerable number of the OECD case countries report less positive values on these two characteristics (*i.e.* lower values for self-efficacy and higher values for anxiety). In the case of self-efficacy (as measured by questions about specific mathematics problems), this is of a less relative nature than some of the other measures. The intra-class correlation of these measures indicates that while there are only very low levels of variation between schools for most of the measures, self-efficacy does vary greatly between schools, and especially in the more differentiated school systems (see Table 3.15, p. 381 in OECD, 2004a).

This may mean that in school systems where immigrant students tend to be in the lower level school tracks, they may have less exposure to the mathematics curriculum necessary to feel confident about particular mathematics problems.

Native students report higher levels of self-efficacy than first-generation students in five of the OECD case countries and higher levels than second-generation students in six OECD countries. The average effect size across the OECD case countries is small, but this once again masks a pattern of country results where the effect size may be of concern to educators and policy makers. Among first-generation students, the effect size in absolute terms is greater than 0.20 in Austria, Luxembourg and Switzerland. This indicates that first-generation students have substantively lower levels of self-efficacy than native students in these countries. Second-generation students in Austria, Germany, Luxembourg and Switzerland also report substantively lower levels of self-efficacy than their native peers (see Table 4.10). These are the countries with some of the largest gaps in mathematics performance. While these immigrant students report high levels of motivation and interest in mathematics, in terms of confidence in their ability to solve mathematics tasks (and in their performance on the mathematics assessment) they fall short of their native peers.

First-generation and second-generation students also tend to report more anxiety in mathematics than their native peers. First-generation students report higher levels of anxiety in eight of the OECD case countries and second-generation students report higher levels in nine OECD countries. The average effect size across the OECD countries is 0.11 for first-generation students and greater than 0.20 for second-generation students. Among first-generation students the effect sizes are greater than 0.20 in Denmark, the Netherlands, Norway, Sweden and Switzerland. For second-generation students, this is the case in Belgium, Denmark, France, Luxembourg, the Netherlands, New Zealand, Sweden and Switzerland. Again, this may indicate that additional attention needs to be paid to lessening the anxiety that immigrant students experience in these countries. This may be beneficial for students' learning of mathematics in the long-term and for reducing the gap in achievement differences.

Furthermore, of the three sub-groups, second-generation students tend to report the lowest levels of self-efficacy and the highest levels of anxiety. These findings may support previous research indicating that second-generation students may have less positive non-achievement outcomes than first-generation students. These results indicate that schools and educators may need to pay special attention to raising second-generation students' self-efficacy in mathematics or reducing their mathematics anxiety, as this may lead to more positive outcomes for these students. This is especially the case in countries where second-generation students have substantively poorer outcomes in these areas. Further research could provide additional insight as to why these students report lower levels of non-achievement outcomes, as well as offer specific suggestions on ways of raising their levels.

It is also useful to move beyond individual characteristics to explore how first-generation and second-generation students compare to native students across the range of learning characteristics. Figure 4.10 summarises the results in each country related to significant differences between immigrant and native students on the seven learning and attitudinal characteristics included in this chapter. A general trend emerges across all of the case countries included in this study – there is not a single country where native students have higher scores than first-generation students on a majority of learning and school perception characteristics. This is also the case when second-generation and

Figure 4.10 ■ **Differences in learning characteristics between immigrant and native students by country**

Significant differences in seven reported learning characteristics compared to native students

	First-generation students			Second-generation students	
	Significantly HIGHER scores	Significantly LOWER scores		Significantly HIGHER scores	Significantly LOWER scores
Canada	5	0	Australia	6	0
New Zealand	5	1	New Zealand	5	0
Luxembourg	5	2	Belgium	4	0
Switzerland	5	2	Netherlands	4	0
Australia	4	0	Germany	4	1
Germany	4	1	Luxembourg	4	2
Netherlands	4	0	Canada	3	0
Sweden	4	0	France	3	1
Austria	4	1	Sweden	2	0
Belgium	4	1	Switzerland	2	1
France	3	0	Macao-China	1	1
Norway	3	0	Norway	1	0
Macao-China	2	1	United States	1	0
United States	2	0	Hong Kong-China	1	0
Denmark	2	0	Denmark	1	2
Hong Kong-China	1	2	Austria	0	1
Russian Federation	0	0	Russian Federation	0	0

Note: Countries are ranked in descending order of significantly higher scores on learning characteristics for first-generation and second-generation students.
Source: OECD PISA 2003 database, Table 4.10.

native students are compared. Given the relative differences in performance, it is encouraging to see that immigrant students generally do not report weaker learning characteristics than their native peers and in many cases may even report stronger learning characteristics.

In addition, distinctive patterns for each immigrant sub-group emerge. The left panel of Figure 4.10 shows that first-generation students in 10 OECD countries – Australia, Austria, Belgium, Canada, Germany, Luxembourg, New Zealand, the Netherlands, Sweden and Switzerland – report stronger dispositions for at least four of the seven characteristics. As with many areas explored in this report, first-generation students in the three settlement countries of Australia, Canada and New Zealand show very strong learning characteristics. More surprisingly though, in some of the countries with relatively large performance differences – Germany, Luxembourg and Switzerland – first-generation students also report higher levels for the majority of learning characteristics. In these countries, schools may want to consider focusing on programmes that build on these students' strong learning dispositions while trying to lessen the negative differences (such as high levels of anxiety in mathematics).

In six of the case countries – Australia, Belgium, Germany, Luxembourg, the Netherlands and New Zealand – second-generation students show more positive learning dispositions for a majority of the characteristics. Overall there appear to be fewer significant differences between second-generation and native students than between first-generation and native students. Yet when there are differences, second-generation students tend to show more positive dispositions than native students. For example, second-generation students report significantly more positive levels for at least three of seven learning characteristics in half of the OECD case countries. As was the case for first-generation students, even in countries where there are large performance gaps between second-generation and native students, these gaps are not mirrored in other learning characteristics.

CONCLUSIONS

This chapter examined differences among first-generation, second-generation and native students on non-achievement learning outcomes. A series of findings emerged that may be of particular relevance to schools and policy makers:

(a) **First-generation and second-generation students generally report similar or higher levels of non-achievement outcomes compared to their native peers. Among the three sub-groups, first-generation students tend to report the strongest learning dispositions.** These findings strikingly contrast the previous chapters related to performance outcomes. First-generation and second-generation students generally report higher levels of interest and motivation in mathematics and more positive attitudes towards schooling. Furthermore, immigrant students also have very high educational expectations. First-generation students report the strongest learning characteristics which may reflect optimism associated with immigration. Second-generation students appear to have assimilated to some extent, but still often report more positive learning characteristics than their native peers.

(b) **First-generation and second-generation students are much more likely than native students to report that they expect to complete a university programme, especially after accounting for student background and performance.** Immigrant students have high expectations for themselves, which corresponds with the high levels of interest and motivation described in (a). Despite the challenges of being in a new country and education system, these students report that they are motivated and expect to succeed.

(c) **In many countries, first-generation and second-generation students report much lower levels of self-efficacy in mathematics and higher levels of anxiety in mathematics. Of the three sub-groups, second-generation students report the lowest levels of self-efficacy and the highest levels of anxiety.** Self-efficacy and anxiety do not follow the general pattern described in (a) and (b). More negative outcomes for these two characteristics tend to occur in countries with relatively large performance gaps between immigrant and non-immigrant students. Furthermore, while immigrant students in these countries may have high levels of motivation and interest, they do not have as much confidence in their ability to solve mathematics tasks and experience more anxiety when performing mathematics tasks. This may indicate that although immigrant students tend to be interested and motivated in mathematics, they realistically assess that they have problems in the subject and in turn report lower levels of confidence and higher levels of anxiety in mathematics.

Based on the results in this chapter, a comparatively positive picture emerges for the situation of first-generation and second-generation students in terms of their learning characteristics and attitudes towards schooling. Despite often facing many challenges, such as coming from more disadvantaged backgrounds, speaking a different language in school than at home or being in an unfamiliar school environment, immigrant students do not generally report lower levels of positive learning characteristics. In fact, they often reported more positive learning characteristics than those of their native peers. These findings may point to areas where schools and policy makers could develop additional programmes to seek to reduce achievement gaps by making use of immigrant students' enthusiasm to learn. In some countries where first-generation and second-generation students' self-reports are comparatively less favourable for specific characteristics, such as lower levels of self-efficacy in mathematics, weaker sense of belonging at school or higher levels of anxiety in mathematics, schools and teachers may need to pay additional attention to reducing differences in these essential non-achievement outcomes. This could prove beneficial not only for immigrant students' potential to learn throughout life, but also for helping to increase their level of achievement.

Notes

———

1   The authors would like to thank Cordula Artelt for her advice in developing this chapter. In addition, we used the OECD report *Learners for Life: Student Approaches to Learning: Results from PISA 2000* by Artelt, Baumert, McElvany, and Peschar (OECD, 2003b) and Chapter 3 of *Learning for Tomorrow's World* (OECD, 2004a) as a framework for exploring relationships among immigrant status, motivation and achievement.

Policies and practices to help immigrant students attain proficiency in the language of instruction

INTRODUCTION

In order to contextualise the findings from Chapters 2 to 4 which focused on immigrant students' school performance and engagement, Chapter 1 provided background information on immigration policies and immigrant populations in the case countries. The present chapter complements this information by examining countries' approaches to integration. The integration process is a major concern for immigrant receiving countries worldwide. Schools and other educational institutions play a central role in this process. While much has been written about immigration policies and labour market integration in different countries (*e.g.* Castles, 1995; Freeman, 1995), international comparative analyses of integration policies related to schooling are rare. One exception is a publication by Pitkänen, Kalekin-Fishman and Verma (2002) that describes educational responses to immigration in five countries: Finland, France, Germany, Greece and Israel. It provides an account of general approaches to integration and is relatively broad.

The information network on education in Europe *Eurydice* (Eurydice, 2004) carried out a survey on support measures for immigrant students in pre-primary, primary and compulsory secondary education. This survey employs an open approach asking countries to describe their policies related to immigrant students in response to general questions. The resulting report covers a wide range of support measures implemented in participating countries (provision of interpreters, measures supporting students' cultural and religious backgrounds *e.g.* adaptations of food served in school cafeterias). Because the survey was carried out within the European Union, however, some of the OECD countries with high levels of immigration are not included in the publication.

Using the Eurydice project as a starting point, the authors of this report performed a supplementary survey within PISA on countries' approaches to supporting immigrant students' school success. The survey focuses on selected aspects of school-related integration policies using structured questions and response formats. This chapter starts with a brief overview of the survey, describing its content and the process of data collection. Subsequently, it provides a summary of the survey results. Based on this summary, the chapter concludes with a discussion of policy implications that emerge from the findings.

PISA 2003 SUPPLEMENTARY SURVEY ON NATIONAL POLICIES AND PRACTICES TO HELP IMMIGRANT STUDENTS ATTAIN PROFICIENCY IN THE LANGUAGE OF INSTRUCTION

Starting with the assumption that proficiency in the receiving countries' official languages is a key prerequisite for the integration of immigrants, the PISA supplementary survey focuses on approaches to supporting immigrant students' acquisition of the language of instruction. The goal of the survey is to capture policies and practices addressing the needs of students with limited proficiency in the language of instruction whose parents or grandparents have immigrated to the respective country. Programmes for children from native families who are fluent in one of the country's official languages and set out to learn another official language are not considered. The members of the PISA Governing Board nominated experts on the education of immigrant students within their country to complete the survey.

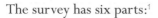

The survey has six parts:[1]

i. Policies and practices designed to help newly arrived immigrant adults attain proficiency in the country's official language(s)[2]

ii. Policies and practices in pre-primary education (ISCED 0)

iii. Policies and practices in primary education (ISCED 1)

iv. Policies and practices in lower secondary education (ISCED 2)

v. Additional school resources

vi. Supplementary classes to improve proficiency in immigrant students' native languages

Within each of these sections, the survey asks about the kinds of measures implemented in the countries, the intensity of their implementation (*e.g.* hours per week) and the target group coverage (*e.g.* approximate proportion of immigrant students receiving the respective support measure). Several questions request country experts to indicate which type of language support measure students typically receive at different levels of the education system. These questions focus on six general approaches distinguished in the literature, as defined in Box 5.1 (*e.g.* Hakuta, 1999; Reich, Roth *et al.*, 2002). Throughout the chapter, the abbreviation "L1" is used for students' native (first) languages and "L2" for students' non-native (second) languages or the language of instruction.

The survey instructions ask respondents to focus on the three largest groups of second-language immigrants in their country and, if necessary, to differentiate their answers for these groups. In most countries with federal structures it was necessary to carry out the survey at the level of sub-national entities and to focus on a selection of regions. In these cases, countries chose regions with relatively high proportions of immigrant students and well established approaches to helping these students attain proficiency in the language of instruction. In addition, the survey instructions request respondents to focus on current policies and practices and to indicate whether a given measure has been introduced relatively recently (within the last ten years).

The survey process involved four steps. First, the country experts completed the questionnaire. Second, the authors of the thematic report summarised the survey data, indicating information gaps and open questions. This draft summary was sent back to the country experts with requests for clarification and additional information. Third, based on experts' feedback, the authors revised the summary and finalised it for inclusion in the thematic report. Finally, countries could request additional changes in the descriptions as they reviewed the complete report.

All countries participating in PISA were invited to take part in the supplementary survey, regardless of whether or not they could be included in the empirical chapters of this report. Of the 17 countries represented in the previous chapters, 13 completed the questionnaire: Australia, Austria, Belgium (French community), Canada, Denmark, Germany, Luxembourg, Netherlands, Norway, Sweden, Switzerland, Hong Kong-China and Macao-China. In addition, England, Finland and Spain participated in the survey. Four countries with federal structures provided information for two or three sub-national entities including Australia (New South Wales, Queensland and Victoria), Austria (Vienna and Vorarlberg), Canada (British Columbia and Ontario) and Switzerland (Berne, Geneva and Zurich).

Policies and practices to help immigrant students attain proficiency in the language of instruction

Box 5.1 ■ **General approaches to educating immigrant students in the language of instruction**[1]

A.   Submersion/Immersion:

Students with limited proficiency in the language of instruction are taught in a regular class-room. Language skills in L2 develop as students participate in mainstream instruction. No systematic language support specifically targeted at immigrant students is provided.

B.   Immersion with systematic language support in L2:

Students with limited proficiency in the language of instruction are taught in a regular class-room. In addition, they receive specified periods of instruction aimed at the development of language skills in L2, with primary focus on grammar, vocabulary, and communication rather than academic content areas. Academic content is addressed through mainstream instruction.

C.   Immersion with an L2 monolingual preparatory phase:

Before transferring to regular classrooms, students with limited proficiency in the language of instruction participate in a preparatory programme designed to develop language skills in L2. The goal is to make the transition to mainstream instruction as rapidly as possible.

D.   Transitional bilingual education:

Most students in the programme have limited proficiency in L2. They initially receive some instruction through their native language, but there is a gradual shift toward instruction in L2 only. The goal of the programme is to make the transition to mainstream classrooms as rapidly as possible.

E.   Maintenance bilingual education:

Most students in the programme are from the same language background and have limited proficiency in L2. They receive significant amounts of instruction in their native language. These programmes aim to develop proficiency in both L2 and the native language (L1).

1. Based on Hakuta, 1999, p. 36.

The following sections of Chapter 5 summarise the results from the supplementary survey. In interpreting the findings, it is important to keep in mind that the authors did not design the survey to provide a comprehensive account of immigrant education in each of the countries. Instead, the instrument focuses on selected aspects in order to provide comparative information on general approaches to help immigrants attain proficiency in the case countries' official language(s). Accordingly, the information applies to the most prevalent language support measures that large proportions of immigrant students within a country receive.

POLICIES AND PRACTICES DESIGNED TO HELP NEWLY ARRIVED IMMIGRANT ADULTS ATTAIN PROFICIENCY IN THE CASE COUNTRIES' OFFICIAL LANGUAGE(S)

The first part of the survey asks about the measures countries take to help newly arrived immigrant adults attain proficiency in the respective country's official language(s). The inclusion of questions on language programmes for adults relies on the assumption that parents' ability to communicate in the receiving country's official language is likely to affect their children's chances of succeeding in school. The questions relate to requirements of language proficiency tests and to the provision of compulsory and optional language classes. Tables 5.1a and 5.1b summarise the information the countries provided.

Table 5.1a

Policies and practices designed to help newly arrived immigrant adults attain proficiency in the country's official language(s): obligatory language proficiency tests and mandatory classes

Country	Sub-national entity	Are recently immigrated adults who do not speak the receiving country's official language(s) required to take a **language proficiency test**?		Mandatory classes						
				Does the state offer **mandatory** language classes for recently immigrated adults who do not speak the receiving country's official language(s)?		Is there a **minimal participation requirement** for the mandatory language classes?		May participants **leave the programme early**?		What happens if a person **fails to participate** in the mandatory language programme? Please explain.
		Yes or No	Notes	Yes or No	Notes	Yes or No	Number of hours	Yes or No	Conditions	General consequences/penalties
Australia		No	Only if they are eligible for and wish to access fee-free English language tuition under the Federal Government's *Adult Migrant English Program*.	No		a		a		a
Austria	Vienna and Voralberg	Yes	Since 2004	Yes	Since 2004	Yes	100	No		Residency/Status penalty: Individuals who fail to fulfill the requirements of the language programme within four years after entering the country run the risk of not having their residency permits renewed. Ultimately, they might be forced to leave the country.
Belgium	French Community	No		No		a		a		a
Canada	British Columbia	No	Only if they wish to enrol in *Language Instruction for Newcomers to Canada* (LINC) or *Cours de langue pour les immigrants au Canada* (CLIC) classes.	No		a		a		a
	Ontario	No	Only if they wish to enrol in *Language Instruction for Newcomers to Canada* (LINC) or *Cours de langue pour les immigrants au Canada* (CLIC) classes.	No		a		a		a
Denmark		No		Yes	Since 1999	No		Yes		Financial penalty: Failure to participate in the language programme may result in economical consequences, such as reductions in social benefits. Residency/status penalty: Consequences for the attainment of permanent residence status and Danish citizenship.
England		No		No		a		a		a
Finland		No		Yes		No		Yes	Pregnancy, illness and if the level of the course is inadequate.	Individuals will be referred to other programmes. Financial penalty: The individual may lose an integration subsidy.

OECD countries

Policies and practices to help immigrant students attain proficiency in the language of instruction

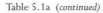

Table 5.1a (*continued*)

Policies and practices designed to help newly arrived immigrant adults attain proficiency in the country's official language(s): obligatory language proficiency tests and mandatory classes

Country	Sub-national entity	Are recently immigrated adults who do not speak the receiving country's official language(s) required to take a **language proficiency test**?		Mandatory classes						
				Does the state offer **mandatory** language classes for recently immigrated adults who do not speak the receiving country's official language(s)?		Is there a **minimal participation requirement** for the mandatory language classes?		May participants **leave the programme early**?		What happens if a person **fails to participate** in the mandatory language programme? Please explain.
		Yes or No	Notes	Yes or No	Notes	Yes or No	Number of hours	Yes or No	Conditions	General consequences/penalties
OECD countries										
Germany		No	Only if they are required to participate in integration classes (since 2005).	Yes	Since 2005	Yes	Up to 630 (depending on the level of proficiency)	Yes	*e.g.* if "sufficient knowledge in German" is reached earlier	The process of naturalisation may be delayed. Financial penalty: Social security payments may be reduced by 10%. Residency/status penalty: A permit to take up residence is only issued if the applicant has attained a sufficient level of proficiency in German and basic knowledge of the legal and social order of Germany.
Luxembourg		No		No		a		a		a
Netherlands		Yes	Since 1998	Yes	Since 1998	Yes	600	No		Financial penalty: If a newcomer who is entitled to national assistance fails in any way to meet his or her obligations defined in the *Integration of Newcomer Act*, an executive fine is imposed. Municipalities are required to attune the measures or the amount of the fine to the degree of culpability, the seriousness of the offence and the personal circumstances of the newcomer.
Norway		Yes	Since 2005 municipalities may require new immigrants to take a language proficiency test.	Yes	Since 2005	Yes	225 (300 lessons of 45 minutes)	Yes	If participants have achieved sufficient language skills	Residency/status penalty: Individuals failing to participate in the programme will not obtain a permanent settlement permit or Norwegian citizenship unless they are able to prove that they have achieved language skills in other ways.
Spain		No		No		a		a		a
Sweden		No		No		a		a		a
Switzerland	Canton Berne	No		No		a		a		a
	Canton Geneva	No		No		a		a		a
	Canton Zurich	No		No		a		a		a
Partner countries										
Hong Kong China		No		No		a		a		a
Macao-China		No		No		a		a		a

© OECD 2006   *Where immigrant students succeed - A comparative review of performance and engagement in PISA 2003*

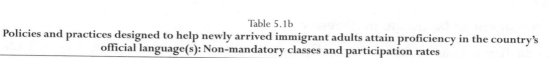

Table 5.1b

Policies and practices designed to help newly arrived immigrant adults attain proficiency in the country's official language(s): Non-mandatory classes and participation rates

Country	Sub-national entity	Non-mandatory classes				Participation rates	
		Does the state offer non-mandatory language classes for recently immigrated adults who do not speak the receiving country's official language(s)?		If non-mandatory language classes are offered: Are they free of charge?		If language classes are offered by the state: Approximately what proportion of newly arrived immigrants who do not speak the receiving country's official language(s) participated in these classes during the last five years?	
		Yes or No	Notes	Yes or No	Notes	Percentage in mandatory classes	Percentage in non-mandatory classes
OECD countries							
Australia		Yes	In addition to the Federal Government's *Adult Migrant English Program*, there is a variety of other English language training programmes, funded by both Federal and State/Territory governments.	Yes		a	m (33% of <u>ALL</u> new immigrants, including those not requiring English language tuition)
Austria	Vienna and Voralberg	No		a		a (programme was introduced in 2004)	a
Belgium	French Community	Yes		Yes and No		a	m
Canada	British Columbia	Yes	Language training for eligible individuals is up to 3 years for a total of 900 hours depending on their level of assessed proficiency.	Yes		a	Approx. 80% (over the last 3 years)
	Ontario	Yes		Yes	*Language Instruction for Newcomers to Canada* (LINC) and Ontario provincially funded language classes are free. Some of Ontario's provincially funded programmes may have a small materials fee.	a	m
Denmark		Yes	Yes, but with some restriction in terms of target groups.	Yes		m	m
England		Yes		Yes	Subject to availability of funds, *e.g.* from the EU for refugees or asylum seekers.	a	m
Finland		Yes		Yes		30%	80%
Germany		Yes		No	There is a small fee for most classes. A remission of charges is possible in individual cases.	a (programme was introduced in 2005)	m
Luxembourg		Yes		No		a	m
Netherlands		Yes		No		90%	m
Norway		Yes	Available to individuals who immigrated before the introduction of mandatory classes in 2005.	Yes	This does not apply to Nordic citizens or persons holding an EEA-/EFTA-permit (European Economic Area and European Free Trade Association). Similarly, migrant workers and their families who arrived in Norway after 1 January 2003 will not benefit from free training.	a (programme was introduced in 2005; a system to collect these data has been launched)	m
Spain		Yes		Yes		a	m
Sweden		Yes		Yes		a	33%
Switzerland	Canton Berne	Yes		No		a	m
	Canton Geneva	Yes		No		a	m
	Canton Zurich	Yes	Offered by vocational schools, communes and private providers.	No	Usually not free but often subsidised by the *canton* (sub-national entity).	a	m
Partner countries							
Hong Kong-China		Yes		Yes		a	m
Macao-China		No		No		a	a

Assessment of language proficiency

As the first column in Table 5.1a shows, a few countries require recently immigrated adults who do not speak the official language(s) to take language proficiency tests. This requirement seems to be most comprehensive in Austria and the Netherlands. It has been in place in the Netherlands since 1998 when the *Integration of Newcomers Act* (*Wet inburgering nieuwkomers – WIN*) was introduced. In Austria, it is part of a recently established integration policy package (*Integrationsvereinbarung*) introduced in 2004. A similar development is under way in Germany where a 2005 immigration law (*Zuwanderungsgesetz*) requires new immigrants unable to communicate in German to attend integration classes that involve mandatory language proficiency tests. Norway also introduced a new law in 2005 whereby municipalities may require new immigrants to complete language assessments.

Australia and Canada require some new immigrants to take language proficiency tests as an obligation tied to their participation in certain language programmes. In both countries, the federal government offers language classes to eligible immigrants and humanitarian entrants with limited proficiency in the official language(s). In Australia they are part of the *Adult Migrant English Program*. In Canada they are known as *Language Instruction for Newcomers to Canada* (LINC) and *Cours de langue pour les immigrants au Canada* (CLIC). Eligible adults who wish to attend these programmes have to participate in a language assessment. Yet in Canada, additional language programmes exist that do not involve a standard requirement of proficiency testing (*e.g.* Ontario's provincially funded language classes).

Mandatory and non-mandatory language classes

All countries and sub-national entities except Macao-China indicate that they offer language classes to recently immigrated adults. There seems therefore to be a broad consensus on the importance of assisting immigrants to attain proficiency in the official language(s) of the receiving country. In four countries that generally require language assessments for some groups of immigrants – Austria, Germany, the Netherlands and Norway – participation in language courses is mandatory. Again, while this requirement has been in place in the Netherlands since 1998, Austria, Germany and Norway have introduced it very recently, within the past two years. Finland also provides mandatory language classes. Since 1999, Denmark requires newly arrived refugees and family-reunion immigrants with residency to attend language classes while other newcomers to the country are entitled but not obliged to take the classes.

With the exception of Denmark and Finland, the countries offering mandatory language courses specify a participation requirement of 100 hours in Austria, 630 hours in Germany, 600 hours in the Netherlands and 300 lessons of 45 minutes in Norway. In Norway, participants have to attend a minimum of 300 lessons to obtain a special permit for settlement and citizenship. Those who need additional support may apply to take up to 2700 lessons. Failure to comply with the stipulations for participation in mandatory language classes may result in sanctions in all six countries providing such programmes. These sanctions can apply to the individual's residence status or financial benefits.

Almost all countries indicate that they provide voluntary language classes for recently immigrated adults including those offering compulsory programmes. One exception is Austria where the state supplies compulsory courses only. Similarly, Norway no longer offers voluntary classes since the introduction of the compulsory programme. Macao-China does not provide language classes for adults at all. In more than half of the countries with voluntary courses, they are free of charge.

The adult language courses available in the various countries vary widely in terms of content and scope. Given this report focuses on students in schools, the various approaches will not be described. However, Box 5.2 provides an example of structured language support for immigrant adults, by presenting a brief description of the Canadian LINC programme.

Although some of the countries that participated in the survey invest considerable resources in language classes for immigrant adults, very few of them know what proportion of their immigrant populations participate in these programmes. Only Australia, the Canadian province of British Columbia, Finland, the Netherlands and Sweden are able to provide figures for participation rates. According to these numbers, about 90% of new immigrants in the Netherlands participated in the mandatory language programme during the last five years. In Finland, the attendance rates are 30% and 80% for the voluntary and compulsory classes respectively. For the voluntary classes in the Canadian province of British Columbia, the participation rate has been approximately 80% over the last three years. In Australia and Sweden, about 33% of newly arrived immigrants attended the voluntary programmes. It should be noted, however, that the estimate for Australia covers

---

Box 5.2 ■ **An example of structured language support for immigrant adults** – *Language Instruction for Newcomers to Canada* **(LINC)**

The objective of the LINC programme is to provide language training in one of Canada's official languages (English or French) to adult immigrants. In addition, the LINC curriculum includes information that helps to orient newcomers to the Canadian way of life. These measures aim at facilitating the social, cultural, economic and political integration of immigrants to Canada.

To be eligible for the LINC programme, a person must be

- an adult immigrant (older than legal school-leaving age) and

- either a permanent resident or a newcomer who has been allowed to remain in Canada, to whom Citizenship and Immigration Canada (CIC) intends to grant permanent resident status and who has not yet acquired Canadian citizenship.

Eligible individuals may participate in LINC training, whether they are destined for the labour market or not, for up to three years. While attending the LINC programme, participants may continue to receive benefits such as employment insurance, *Adjustment Assistance Program* benefits or social assistance. Before training starts, both part-time and full-time students must have written approval from a Human Resources Development Centre to continue receiving benefits while in training.

LINC may provide additional funding to assist in the supervision of dependent children. This assistance can only be provided to participants who show that it will make a difference as to whether they can attend classes. Transportation costs may also be paid for participants who have no other way of attending training. In some circumstances (such as school holidays or when clients must attend weekend or evening classes), LINC funds may also cover transportation costs for children who must accompany parents to classes.

Before language training can be provided, participants' level of language proficiency must be rated with the *Canadian Language Benchmarks Assessment* (CLBA). It involves a set of task-based descriptors of English language ability, distinguishing four benchmark levels for speaking, listening, reading and writing. The CLBA provides an indication of the amount of training that may be required for participants to achieve the LINC programme outcome competency level. CLBA results are provided to both participants and language training providers. Only a person who is trained in the use of the CLBA may implement it.

LINC strives to achieve a uniform quality of language training across the country. All LINC providers are expected to be in a position to teach CLBA stage 1 of listening, speaking, reading and writing skills. Where enrolment numbers permit, all students in a LINC class will typically be working at the same level. The LINC curriculum is required to meet provincial standards.

A LINC graduate is a participant who has completed LINC training and has reached the LINC programme outcome competency level. The amount of training clients need varies according to their background, circumstances and abilities. The progress of each participant is charted and assessed against the CLBA.

A variety of institutions including businesses, non-governmental organisations, individuals, educational institutions or municipal governments may apply to become LINC service providers. They have to meet a number of requirements specified by the Federal Government (Citizenship and Immigration Canada) and are subject to quality control measures.

(Cited from the *LINC Handbook for Service Providers* by Citizenship and Immigration Canada: *http://www.cic.gc.ca/english/newcomer/linc-1e.html*)

For additional information on LINC see:

http://www.cic.gc.ca/english/newcomer/welcome/wel-22e.html

http://www.cic.gc.ca/english/newcomer/linc-1e.html#overview

http://www.tbs-sct.gc.ca/rma/eppi-ibdrp/hrdb-rhbd/linc-clic/description_e.asp

all newcomers to the country, not only those eligible for or requiring English language tuition. Significant proportions of immigrants in Australia come from English-speaking countries or must demonstrate a functional level of English-language proficiency to meet visa requirements if they enter under the skilled worker category.

Table 5.2

Assessment of language proficiency in pre-primary (ISCED 0) and primary (ISCED 1) education

| | | Is children's proficiency in the language of instruction **generally assessed** before and/or during pre-primary education (ISCED 0)? (Please note that this question refers to **all children**, not only students with immigrant backgrounds.) | | Are **immigrant children** specifically required to participate in a language assessment before and/or during pre-primary education (ISCED 0)? | | Is children's proficiency in the language of instruction **generally assessed** shortly before or immediately after they enter first grade? (Please note that this question refers to **all children**, not only students with immigrant backgrounds.) | | Are **immigrant students** specifically required to participate in a language assessment shortly before/immediately after they enter first grade? | |
Country	Sub-national entity	Yes or No	Notes	Yes or No	Notes	Yes or No	Notes	Yes or No	Notes
Australia	New South Wales	Yes	Teachers conduct a general language and literacy assessment of all students to plan programs which meet students' individual learning needs.	No		Yes	Since 2000. The assessment is conducted within the first 10 weeks of enrolment. Teachers are assisted in performing these assessments through the provision of syllabuses and curriculum documents which outline literacy outcomes expected to be achieved at key stages of primary schooling.	Yes	Since 2005. For students whose first language is not English, teachers are required to use the *English as a Second Language* scales. Following the initial assessment in the first 10 weeks, immigrant students are expected to be assessed twice a year in order for parents to be advised on their childrens' English language development.
	Queensland	No		No		Yes		Yes	Where possible, immigrant students entering first grade are assessed by an *English as a Second Language* teacher to determine the level of support required.
	Victoria	Yes		No		Yes		No	While not mandatory, on-going assessment of immigrant children is encouraged to determine progress made and level of support required.
Austria	Vienna	Yes		No		Yes		Yes	Immigrant students are specifically required to participate in the general assessment, but there is no special assessment component for this group.
	Vorarlberg	Yes		No		Yes		No	
Belgium	French Community	Yes		No		No	An assessment is common but not mandatory. Most often, there is an assessment at the end of pre-primary school, just before first grade.	No	
Canada	British Columbia	Yes	The kindergarten teacher assesses all children for language delays, developmental delays and gifted abilities.	Yes	It is mandated by provincial policy that immigrant children participate in the assessment if their language proficiency is sufficient to do so.	Yes	Children's proficiency is assessed by the classroom teacher.	Yes	A standardised assessment is either done at the school or assessment centre depending on the date of arrival in British Columbia. Immigrant children have to participate in the assessment if their language proficiency is sufficient to do so.
	Ontario	No	School boards may choose to assess language proficiency, but it is not general policy or practice.	No	School boards may choose to assess language proficiency, but it is not general policy or practice.	No	School boards may choose to assess language proficiency, but it is not general policy or practice.	Recommended	There is no policy for assessing immigrant students' proficiency in English. Yet, a Grade 1-8 *English as a Second Language* (ESL/ELD) resource document is in place which makes recommendations for best practice that boards may choose to follow. The document recommends language assessment for immigrant students when they enter school.

OECD countries

Policies and practices to help immigrant students attain proficiency in the language of instruction

Table 5.2 (*continued*)

Assessment of language proficiency in pre-primary (ISCED 0) and primary (ISCED 1) education

Country	Sub-national entity	Is children's proficiency in the language of instruction **generally assessed** before and/or during pre-primary education (ISCED 0)? (Please note that this question refers to **all children**, not only students with immigrant backgrounds.)		Are **immigrant children** specifically required to participate in a language assessment before and/or during pre-primary education (ISCED 0)?		Is children's proficiency in the language of instruction **generally assessed** shortly before or immediately after they enter first grade? (Please note that this question refers to **all children**, not only students with immigrant backgrounds.)		Are **immigrant students** specifically required to participate in a language assessment shortly before/immediately after they enter first grade?	
		Yes or No	Notes	Yes or No	Notes	Yes or No	Notes	Yes or No	Notes
OECD countries									
Denmark		No		Yes	Every bilingual child is assessed at age three. Depending on the results, the child may have to participate in a language stimulation programme.	No		Yes	Every bilingual child is assessed upon admission to school. Depending on the results, the child may receive instruction in *Danish as a Second Language.*
England		Yes	By means of the *Foundation Stage Profile.*	No	Where possible, children are assessed in their home language.	Yes		No	
Finland		No		No		Yes		Yes	
Germany		No		Yes	Recently introduced in some of the *Länder* (sub-national entities).	No	No, but language assessments are being used increasingly in the *Länder* (sub-national entities).	No	No, but language assessments are being used increasingly in the *Länder* (sub-national entities).
Luxembourg		No		No		Yes		No	
Netherlands		No		No		No		No	
Norway		Yes		No		No		Yes	There is no national assessment system for language proficiency. Instead, assessments are conducted by the teachers and are based on their own professional considerations.
Spain		No		No		No		No	
Sweden		No		No		No		No	
Switzerland	Canton Berne	No		No		No		Yes	
	Canton Geneva	Yes		No		Yes		Yes	
	Canton Zurich	No		No		No		No	
Partner countries									
Hong Kong-China		No		No		No		No	
Macao-China		No		No		No		Yes	

ASSESSMENT OF LANGUAGE PROFICIENCY IN PRE-PRIMARY (ISCED 0) AND PRIMARY (ISCED 1) EDUCATION

Four questions in the survey asked countries about language assessments in pre-primary (ISCED 0) and primary (ISCED 1) education. Table 5.2 summarises the results for these questions. The findings indicate that nine countries or sub-national entities have a general assessment in place before or during pre-primary education that involves all children. Of these, the Canadian province of British Columbia specifically requires immigrant children to participate in the assessment if their language proficiency is sufficient to do so. In addition, Denmark and some *Länder* of Germany have special testing requirements for immigrant students that are not embedded in a general assessment.

Ten countries or sub-national entities generally assess children's language proficiency shortly before or immediately after they enter first grade (ISCED 1). In six of these, a special assessment requirement for immigrant students is in place: Australia (New South Wales and Queensland), Austria (Vienna), Canada (British Columbia), Finland and Switzerland (Geneva). In Australia (New South Wales and Queensland), teachers of *English as a Second Language* (ESL) assess immigrant students entering first grade to determine the level of ESL support they require. Language proficiency tests shortly before or during primary education are also compulsory for immigrant students in four countries or sub-national entities that do not have a general assessment involving all children: Denmark, Norway, Switzerland (Berne) and Macao-China. Similarly, the Canadian province of Ontario encourages school boards to assess immigrant students' level of language proficiency when they enter school.

Taken together, most countries or sub-national entities collect information on immigrant students' language skills at some point during pre-primary (ISCED 0) or primary (ISCED 1) education. For the most part, this occurs as part of a general assessment, involving all children. Some of the countries or sub-national entities with general language assessments specifically require immigrant students to participate or employ a special assessment component for immigrant students. Strictly specific approaches that are particularly aimed at immigrant children and not embedded in general assessments are reported for Denmark (ISCED 0 and ISCED 1), Germany (ISCED 0), Norway (ISCED 1), the Swiss Canton of Berne and (ISCED 1) and Macao-China (ISCED 1). In addition, the Canadian province of Ontario advises school boards to follow a specific approach in primary schools (ISCED 1). In contrast, five countries or sub-national entities do not employ any general or specific language assessments during pre-primary or primary education: the Netherlands, Spain, Sweden, the Swiss Canton of Zurich and Hong Kong-China.

LANGUAGE SUPPORT FOR IMMIGRANT STUDENTS IN PRE-PRIMARY EDUCATION (ISCED 0)

Table 5.3 summarises countries' responses to questions on language support measures for immigrant students in pre-primary education (ISCED 0). In five countries or sub-national entities, it is mandatory for all children to attend pre-primary education. In addition, Denmark, some German *Länder* and Norway specifically require children with limited proficiency in the language of instruction to participate in pre-primary programmes. Among the twelve countries or sub-national entities that could provide this information, the proportion of immigrant children attending pre-primary education ranges between less than 5% in Macao-China to more than 80% in Austria, England, Luxembourg, the Netherlands, Spain and the Swiss Cantons of Geneva and Zurich.

Very few countries offer language support based on an explicit national or regional curriculum to immigrant children in pre-primary education. Therefore, to the extent that countries expect pre-primary education programmes to improve immigrant children's language skills, they seem to rely mainly on implicit language learning. The only exceptions are the Canadian province of British Columbia and the Netherlands where explicit curricula are in place. These programmes involve five to eight hours of systematic language support per week in British Columbia and one-and-a-half hours in the Netherlands. Similarly, a handbook provided to kindergarten teachers in the Swiss Canton of Zurich earmarks one to two hours per week of language support for immigrant children with limited proficiency in the language of instruction.

Policies and practices to help immigrant students attain proficiency in the language of instruction

Table 5.3
General approaches to supporting immigrant students with limited proficiency in the language of instruction: Pre-primary education (ISCED 0)

Country	Sub-national entity	Are **all children** regardless of their language proficiency and immigration background required to attend pre-primary education (ISCED 0)?		Are children with limited proficiency in the language of instruction **specifically required** to attend pre-primary education (ISCED 0) before entering primary education (ISCED 1)?		Approximately what proportion of **immigrant students** attends general pre-primary education (ISCED 0) programmes?	Do children with limited proficiency in the language of instruction generally receive language support in L2 **based on an explicit curriculum** as part of their pre-primary education (ISCED 0)?		If yes: With what intensity? (approximate number of hours per week)
		Yes or No	Notes	Yes or No	Notes	Percentage	Yes or No	Notes	Hours per week
Australia	New South Wales	No		No		m	No		a
	Queensland	No		No		m	No		a
	Victoria	No		No		m	No		a
Austria	Vienna and Voralberg	No		No		>80	No		a
Belgium	French Community	Yes		No		m	No		a
Canada	British Columbia	No		No		50-64	Yes	It is part of the kindergarten curriculum.	5-8
	Ontario	No		No		m	No		a
Denmark		No		Yes		35-49	No		a
England		Yes	They are required from the term of their fifth birthday but may start to attend funded pre-school education from age three.	No	No, but they are encouraged to do so and given priority in some local education authorities and maintained settings.	>80	No		a
Finland		No		No		m	No		a
Germany		No		Yes	Recently introduced in some of the *Länder* (sub-national entities).	65-80	No		a
Luxembourg		Yes		No		>80	No	Support is available by individuals speaking Luxembourgish for 2-3 hours/week.	a
Netherlands		Yes		No		>80	Yes		1.5
Norway		No		Yes		35-49	No		a
Spain		No		No		>80	No		a
Sweden		No		No		m	No		a
Switzerland	Canton Berne	No		No		m	No		a
	Canton Geneva	No		No		>80	No		a
	Canton Zurich	Yes		No		>80	No	A handbook for kindergarten teachers provides a basis for language support.	1-2
Hong Kong-China		No		No		m	No	Schools may choose to design a school-based language curriculum according to the needs of the students.	a
Macao-China		No		No		<5	No		a

OECD countries / Partner countries

LANGUAGE SUPPORT FOR IMMIGRANT STUDENTS IN PRIMARY EDUCATION (ISCED 1) AND LOWER SECONDARY EDUCATION (ISCED 2)

In terms of general approaches to supporting immigrant students with limited proficiency in the language of instruction, a surprisingly homogeneous picture emerges (see Tables 5.4a and 5.4b). Although all types of programmes are likely to be found in one form or another in many of the countries, the most prominent approach is clearly immersion with systematic language support. This is particularly the case within primary education. In 14 countries or sub-national entities, more than 50% of primary students with limited proficiency in the language of instruction participate in such a programme; in two other countries or sub-national entities, the proportion lies between 35 and 49%. These students attend regular classes and receive additional periods of instruction aimed at developing second language skills. The primary focus of the lessons is on grammar, vocabulary and communication rather than on academic content, which is delivered in mainstream instruction.

A less common programme type in primary schools is submersion/immersion. In these programmes, students with limited proficiency in the language of instruction also attend regular classes, yet they

Table 5.4a
General approaches to supporting immigrant students with limited proficiency in the language of instruction: Primary education (ISCED 1)

			Submersion / immersion	Immersion with systematic language support in the language of instruction		Immersion with a preparatory phase in the language of instruction		Transitional bilingual education	Maintenance bilingual education
	Country	Sub-national entity	Percentage of students	Percentage of students	Approximate hours per week	Percentage of students	Approximate number of months	Percentage of students	Percentage of students
OECD countries	Australia	New South Wales	5-19	>80	1-4	n	n	n	n
		Queensland	5-19	>80	0.5-1	<5	m	<5	<5
		Victoria	n	35-49	5-10	50-64	6-9	n	n
	Austria	Vienna	n	>80	6	n	n	n	<5
		Voralberg	m	m	0.18-0.5 per student	n	n	n	n
	Belgium	French Community	>80	n	n	<5	1 week - 12 months	n	n
	Canada	British Columbia	m	35-49	6	m	m	n	n
		Ontario	n	65-80 (rough estimate)	m	n	n	n	n
	Denmark		n	>80	1.5	<5	Up to 24	n	n
	England		n	>80	Depends on school resources and pupils' needs	n	n	n	n
	Finland		n	50-64	2-4	20-34	6-9	n	n
	Germany		5-19	50-80	1-2	<5	6-18	<5	n
	Luxembourg		65-80	20-34	2	<5	n	<5	n
	Netherlands		n	>80	1.5	n	n	n	n
	Norway		<5	>80	2-4	<5	6	<5	n
	Spain		>80	n	n	n	n	n	n
	Sweden		n	50-64	m	35-49	6-12	n	n
	Switzerland	Canton Berne	m	m	2	<5	12		
		Canton Geneva	n	>80	3-20	n	n	n	n
		Canton Zurich	20-34	20-34 (newly immigrated students in the first year after immigration: approximately 50 percent)	8	<5	10-12	n	n
Partner countries	Hong Kong-China		n	>80	m	<5	6	n	n
	Macao-China		n	>80	m	<5	9	n	n

Table 5.4b

General approaches to supporting immigrant students with limited proficiency in the language of instruction: Lower secondary education (ISCED 2)

Country	Sub-national entity	Submersion / immersion — Percentage of students	Immersion with systematic language support in the language of instruction — Percentage of students	Immersion with systematic language support in the language of instruction — Approximate hours per week	Immersion with a preparatory phase in the language of instruction — Percentage of students	Immersion with a preparatory phase in the language of instruction — Approximate number of months	Transitional bilingual education — Percentage of students	Maintenance bilingual education — Percentage of students	Other — Percentage of students
Australia	New South Wales[1]	n / 35-49	n / 50-64	1-4	>80 / n	9-12	n	n	n
	Queensland[1]	<5 / >80	65-80 / n	1-1.5	20-34 / n	m	n	n	n
	Victoria[2]	n	20-34	5-10	65-80	6-9	n	n	n
Austria	Vienna[1]	m	5-19 / 5-19	6-12	n	n	n	n	n
	Voralberg[1]	m	5-19 / 5-19	0.18-0.5 per student	n	n	n	n	n
Belgium	French Community[2]	>80	n	n	<5	1 week - 12 months	<5	n	n
Canada	British Columbia[2]	m	m	m	50-64	36	n	n	n
	Ontario[2]	n	65-80 (rough estimation)	5-6	n	n	n	n	n
Denmark[1]		n / m	>80 / m	1.5	<5 / m	Up to 24	n	n	n
England[2]		n	>80	Depends on school resources and pupil's needs	n	n	n	n	n
Finland[2]		n	50-64	2-4	20-34	6-9	n	n	<5
Germany[2]		>80	5-19	1-2	<5	6-18	n	n	n
Luxembourg[1]		>80 / >80	5-19 / <5	4-9	5-19 / <5	10	n	n	n
Netherlands[2]		<5	5-19	m	>80	24	<5	<5	<5
Norway[2]		<5	>80	2-4	<5	6	<5	n	n
Spain[1]		m	>80 / n	4	n	n	n	n	n
Sweden[2]		n	35-49	m	35-49	6-12	n	n	n
Switzerland	Canton Berne[2]	m	m	2	m	12	n	n	n
	Canton Geneva[1]	<5 / m	65-80 / m	m	<5 / m	8-15	n	n	n
	Canton Zurich[1]	n / 65-80	35-49 / 20-34	10-12	50-64 / n	10-12	n	n	n
Hong Kong-China[2]		n	>80	m	<5	6	n	n	n
Macao-China[1]		n	>80 / >80	m	<5	9	n	n	n

1. Two participation rate estimates are provided for lower secondary education: The first (before the /) refers to newly immigrated students and the second (after the /) to immigrant students who have completed primary school in the respective country but continue to lack proficiency in the language of instruction.

2. One participation rate estimate is provided for lower secondary education, and the reference group is not completely clear (*e.g.* newly immigrated students or all student who lack proficiency in the language of instruction).

do not receive systematic support specifically targeted at second language learning. This is the modal approach in the French community of Belgium, Luxembourg and Spain.

Immersion with a preparatory phase that aims at developing second language skills before immigrant students transfer to mainstream instruction plays a substantial role in primary education within the Australian state of Victoria, Finland and Sweden where 50 to 64%, 20 to 34% and 35 to 49% of eligible students participate in such a programme.

Bilingual approaches involving both students' native language and the language of instruction are not very common in primary schools of any of the countries or sub-national entities that responded to the survey. Although some school systems offer supplementary classes designed to sustain and improve students' proficiency in their native languages (see Table 5.6), programmes that provide instruction in various school subjects using students' natives languages are rare. Most countries therefore rely on monolingual approaches to supporting immigrant students with limited proficiency in the language of instruction.

For the most part, the pattern is quite similar for lower secondary education (ISCED 2), although the proportions of students receiving different types of support tend to shift slightly from immersion with systematic language support to either immersion with a preparatory phase or submersion/ immersion (see Table 5.4b). However, one difficulty associated with participation rate estimates is that they are sometimes based on all immigrant students living in the country and sometimes only on newly arrived immigrant students. This is particularly the case for immersion with a preparatory phase. Therefore, the entries that do not distinguish between newly immigrated students and students who completed primary school in the receiving country but continue to lack proficiency in the language of instruction (see footnotes below Table 5.4b) should be interpreted with caution. Nevertheless, the figures indicate that, at least for newly immigrated students, immersion programmes with a preparatory phase present the modal approach in five countries or sub-national entities: Australia (New South Wales and Victoria), Canada (British Columbia), the Netherlands and Switzerland (Zurich). In addition, more than 20% of newly arrived immigrant students attend such programmes in Australia (Queensland), Finland and Sweden. In most other countries or sub-national entities, immigrant students with limited language proficiency attend immersion programmes with

Table 5.5

Existence of an explicit curriculum for the most common language support programmes

Country	Sub-national entity	Primary education (ISCED 1)		Lower secondary education (ISCED 2)	
		Immersion with systematic language support in the language of instruction	Immersion with a preparatory phase in the language of instruction	Immersion with systematic language support in the language of instruction	Immersion with a preparatory phase in the language of instruction
Australia	New South Wales	Yes	a	Yes	Yes
	Queensland	No	No	No	No
	Victoria	Yes	Yes	Yes	Yes
Austria	Vienna	Depends on the school	a	Depends on the school	a
	Vorarlberg	Depends on the school	a	Depends on the school	a
Belgium	French Community	a	No	a	No
Canada	British Columbia	No	a	a	Yes
	Ontario	No	a	Yes	a
Denmark		Yes	Yes	Yes	Yes
England		No	a	No	a
Finland		No	No	No	No
Germany		Yes, in some *Länder* (sub-national entities)	No	No	No
Luxembourg		No	No	No	Yes
Netherlands		Yes	a	No	No
Norway		Yes	m	Yes	m
Spain		a	a	No	a
Sweden[1]		Yes	No	Yes	No
Switzerland	Canton Berne	No	No	No	No
	Canton Geneva	No	a	No	No
	Canton Zurich	No	No	No	No
Hong Kong-China		No (guidelines only)	No (guidelines only)	No (guidelines only)	No (guidelines only)
Macao-China		Yes	m	Yes	m

1. A curriculum exists for the school subject *Swedish as a Second Language* which may be implemented in different types of programmes.

OECD countries | Partner countries (left margin labels)

Policies and practices to help immigrant students attain proficiency in the language of instruction (right margin)

systematic language support. Yet the proportion of students in submersion/immersion programmes without special support is also quite high in several countries, most notably in Belgium (French Community), Germany and Luxembourg. Bilingual programmes continue to play a minor role in lower secondary education in all countries participating in the survey.

For the two most commonly implemented language support programmes – immersion with systematic languages support and immersion with a preparatory phase – the survey asked countries to indicate whether an explicit curriculum exists. Less than half of the countries or sub-national entities using immersion with systematic language support have an explicit curriculum. The proportion is even lower for immersion with a preparatory phase (see Table 5.5). Moreover, the types of curricula implemented in the case countries differ in terms of content, level of detail and scope (see the country descriptions below).

Despite the striking similarities among countries in terms of their general approaches to supporting immigrant students with limited proficiency in the language of instruction, the specific programmes vary considerably, even if they can be listed under the same label. Although it is beyond the scope of this report to describe the various measures in detail, the next section presents brief summaries in order to provide a general idea of the types of support implemented in each country. Where feasible, the summaries use the exact wording from the survey responses. The country descriptions focus on the two most common approaches, namely immersion with systematic language support and immersion with a preparatory phase.

COUNTRY DESCRIPTIONS OF LANGUAGE SUPPORT MEASURES IN PRIMARY (ISCED 1) AND LOWER SECONDARY (ISCED 2) EDUCATION

Australia – New South Wales (NSW): Focus on immersion with systematic language support and on immersion with a preparatory phase for newly immigrated students in lower secondary education (ISCED 2).

In primary schools of NSW, specialised *English as a Second Language* (ESL) teachers provide ESL programmes for newly arrived immigrant students as well as Australian-born ESL learners. In most schools, ESL students are integrated into mainstream classes and receive support from an ESL teacher working in a team with the class teacher. Some schools establish separate groups or classes for a short term in order to provide intensive ESL tuition to newly arrived students for all or part of the day.

In secondary education, newly arrived immigrant students in the Sydney metropolitan area enrol in an *Intensive English Centre* (IEC) or the *Intensive English High School* (IEHS). The IECs/IEHS provide full-time English language tuition, in the context of the secondary curriculum areas, in order to prepare students for study in a NSW high school. IECs and the IEHS also offer student orientation and welfare programmes with support from migrant counsellors and bilingual support staff. The class size and length of time students spend in an IEC/IEHS depends on their classification as 'regular' or 'special needs' students. Regular students have typically received continuous schooling prior to immigration. Special needs students often come from disadvantaged backgrounds and are behind in English because of learning problems, physical disabilities, previous refugee status or other educational disruptions. Regular students are placed in classes with a maximum size of 18 and may stay for up to 9 months. Special needs students are placed in classes with a maximum size of ten and stay for up to one year. The English language programmes in IECs/IEHS use the *Intensive English Programs (IEP) Curriculum Framework*. It addresses both ESL and key learning area requirements of the NSW school curriculum. When students transfer from an IEC/IEHS to a high school, they receive support from specialised ESL teachers.

In rural and regional areas of NSW where there are no IECs/IEHS, secondary school aged immigrant students enrol directly in a mainstream high school and receive support from an ESL teacher. Primary and secondary schools without current ESL programmes receive funding to hire ESL teachers to tutor students three hours a week for up to nine months.

In both primary and secondary schools, the emphasis is on students acquiring English in the context of the mainstream curriculum, with ESL teachers working in co-operation with class teachers. This integrated approach is designed to support students in learning the subject-specific language as well as the grammatical structures and features of English. At the same time, ESL teachers help students develop an understanding of the cultural contexts of the school and the wider community in which they live and of the social conventions that govern the appropriate use of language. Three broad types of delivery for ESL teaching are distinguished: (1) *Direct ESL teaching modes* involve the provision of ESL instruction to groups of ESL students separately from their class for a limited part of the teaching day; (2) *Collaborative ESL teaching modes* or 'team teaching' involve ESL teachers and class teachers sharing responsibility for planning, programming, teaching, assessment and evaluation; (3) *Resource ESL teaching modes* involve using ESL teachers' expertise as a professional development resource for individual teachers or the whole school staff.

Both primary and secondary schools use *ESL Scales* in assessing the English language proficiency of the students. This assessment tool examines the areas of *Oral Interaction, Reading and Responding* and *Writing. ESL Steps: ESL Curriculum Framework K-6* provides the framework for teaching ESL in primary schools while high schools use the *English 7-10* syllabus.

Schools are allocated ESL teachers, in addition to normal staffing entitlements, based on the number of ESL students and their level of English language proficiency. For staffing purposes, schools report students' English language proficiency each year in terms of three broad phases of ESL learning – phases one, two or three. Formulae determine the weightings for each of the phases. As a general guide, ESL learners remain in phase one for up to nine months, in phase two from nine months to three years and in phase three from three to seven years.

ESL teachers typically have special training. Approximately 30% have completed a special teacher training programme/specialisation during their initial studies, 28% have completed their initial studies in other subject areas and received in-service training (with the duration of courses varying between 18 and 300 hours), 17% have completed a post-graduate degree specialising in *Teaching English to Speakers of Other Languages* (TESOL) or equivalent since beginning their teaching and another 14% have a range of other qualifications such as adult TESOL teacher training or qualifications gained in other countries.

For further information see:
http://www.det.nsw.edu.au

Australia – Queensland: Focus on immersion with systematic language support.

Additional support for immigrant students is typically provided by an *Advisory Visiting Teacher* who works in a number of schools each week, offering specialist advice to the classroom teacher and the school community on the educational needs of *English as a Second Language* (ESL) students. The amount of time allocated to any one school depends on the number of eligible ESL students with allocation models developed and implemented locally. *ESL Teacher Aides* may provide further support under the guidance of an ESL teacher. Teacher Aide support is common in schools with low levels of ESL enrolments which have infrequent *Advisory Visiting Teacher* service. On average, students in primary schools receive half an hour to one hour of ESL support per week for three years after entering the first grade or from the date of their arrival in Australia. Students in lower secondary schools receive one to one-and-a-half hours of ESL support per week for five years. There is no explicit ESL curriculum. ESL teachers are typically experienced teachers who undertake further study to acquire *Teaching English to Speakers of Other Languages* (TESOL) qualifications and are employed specifically for the delivery of the ESL programme. *ESL Teacher Aides* typically receive targeted in-service training.

For further information see:

http://education.qld.gov.au/curriculum/advocacy/access/equity/students/inclusion/cultural/index.html

Australia – Victoria: Focus on immersion with a preparatory phase and on immersion with systematic language support.

Two approaches are commonly employed to support immigrant students' proficiency in the language of instruction. Newly arrived immigrant students participate in intensive full-time English language programmes or targeted support delivered by special purpose English language schools and centres. The curriculum for these programmes is determined at the local level, but is based on centrally developed key curriculum documents. These documents are comprehensive and provide advice on programme development and delivery, assessment and reporting as well as expected student outcomes for key stages of English language development. Students in both primary and lower secondary school typically stay in the preparatory programme for approximately six to nine months.

Upon completion of the preparatory programme, second language learners receive *English as a Second Language* (ESL) support within their schools for up to five years after their arrival in Australia. This support varies according to the age and needs of students. They may be withdrawn from the mainstream classroom for certain times during the week to receive intensive ESL instruction, or they may receive assistance within the regular classroom. Again, the programmes are based on centrally developed key curriculum documents for ESL. On average, students receive five to ten hours of ESL support per week in both primary and lower secondary schools. A whole-school approach is encouraged to ensure that the varying needs of the range of ESL students are met.

Teachers in English language schools and centres are required to have specialist tertiary ESL qualifications. Of the teachers working in ESL programmes in regular schools, about 15% in primary schools and more than 80% in secondary schools have specialised ESL qualifications. Also, professional development activities are available to enhance teachers' expertise in working with second language learners.

For further information see:
http://www.sofweb.vic.edu.au/lem/esl/index.htm

Austria – Vienna: Focus on immersion with systematic language support.

Language support measures for immigrant students aim at teaching the general curriculum, but they allow for the use of students' first languages, extra time for covering the curriculum and smaller learning groups. Teachers with special qualifications in students' native languages serve as adjunct (*i.e.* supplementary) teachers. They have completed additional training of 120 curriculum hours during their primary studies or as in-service training. The adjunct teachers provide their support within the regular classroom along with the classroom teacher ("integrated"), or they teach a subgroup of students separately either in a different classroom ("parallel") or at a different time ("additive"). In addition to teaching the general curriculum, the parallel and additive support may at times focus on basic German language skills. Students are generally entitled to six adjunct-teacher hours a week. In the lower track of secondary school (*Hauptschule*), newly arrived immigrant students with practically no German skills may receive 12 hours of adjunct-teacher instruction. The level of support depends on the resources of the individual school in a given year.

For further information see:

http://www.bmbwk.gv.at/fremdsprachig/en/schools/schools1.htm4701.xml#1 (some information in English)

Austria – Vorarlberg: Focus on immersion with systematic language support.

Two programmes are provided for students with limited proficiency in the language of instruction depending on their residence and language proficiency status. The first programme offers children with "extraordinary student status" intensive language support during the first and second years after entering school (second year only if necessary). The intensity of the support depends on the group size, with a factor of 0.5 hours per student per week (*e.g.* if five students are in the group, the lessons would involve 5*0.5 = 2.5 hours per week). "Extraordinary student status" is a designation that applies to students who are likely to have severe difficulty understanding the teacher. It can be assigned to a student for a maximum of two years. Initially, principals make the determination, but they may revise their decision at the suggestion of classroom teachers. Under the second programme, children with "regular student status" may also receive support in *German as a Second Language* (GSL), with a factor of 0.18 hours per student per week. No explicit language curricula exist for these classes, as they are based on the general curriculum (see information for Vienna above). Recently, a course on teaching GSL has become mandatory in teacher training, and students may choose a specialisation in this domain.

For further information see:

http://www.bmbwk.gv.at/fremdsprachig/en/schools/schools1.htm4701.xml#1 (some information in English)

Belgium – French Community: Focus on submersion/immersion and on immersion with a preparatory phase for some newly immigrated students.

Most immigrant students with limited proficiency in the language of instruction attend regular classes without systematic support in the language of instruction. Schools may choose either to organise a course on learning French as a foreign language, or to organise separate classes as a part of the total amount of hours paid by the Ministry of Education. Some schools hire teachers who followed specific training to teach French as a foreign language as part of their initial training. However, such courses are a relatively recent component of teachers' initial training. In some cases, however, non-European pupils who have recently arrived in Belgium may participate in preparatory classes for one week to a year. Schools need to apply to set up these classes. If permission is granted, additional teacher hours are allocated, usually amounting to 30 periods for a school year for this class. Schools are free to use these additional resources as they wish. There is no explicit curriculum for the preparatory classes, yet they are required to include a minimum number of hours of intensive French-language tuition (15 periods per week). Teachers who work in transitional classes receive in-service training, *e.g. soutenir l'apprentissage du français chez les primo-arrivants dans les classes passerelles*. The training is designed to help teachers: a) Understand current research on learning French as a second language; b) Identify specific difficulties in learning French as a second language; c) Implement specific learning tools for pupils who have recently arrived in Belgium.

For further information see:
http://www.enseignement.be (general information French Community Education System); http://www.ifc.cfwb.be (in-service training); and http://www.cdadoc.cfwb.be/cdadocrep/pdf/2001/20010614s25914.pdf (legal basis for the organisation of preparatory classes).

Canada – British Columbia: Focus on immersion with systematic language support in primary education (ISCED 1) and on immersion with a preparatory phase in lower secondary education (ISCED 2).

Immigrant students in primary school participate in the standard curriculum but may receive additional support that is not based on an explicit curriculum. The Ministry of Education provides the funds for additional language support if a series of criteria is met: a) A recent English language assessment must confirm that the student lacks proficiency and will not achieve the expected learning outcomes of the standard curriculum without additional support; b) The school must have a current annual instruction plan in place that meets the identified needs of the student; c) A teaching specialist must participate in the development of the instruction plan and in regular reviews of that plan; d) The school must provide additional services for the students including pull-out instruction and in-class language assistance, as well as specialised support for teachers to deal with the special language needs of their students. In grades one to three the specialised support focuses on language acquisition. In grades three to four it focuses on writing; e) The school must document the additional services, detailing the amount of direct support provided by an *English as a Second Language* (ESL)/specialist teacher; and f) The student's progress must be recorded. If parents decline additional language support for their children, they are usually asked to sign a form indicating their refusal and agreeing to abstain from holding the school liable for their child's progress or lack thereof. On average, students receive up to six hours per week of additional support.

Depending on the school board or school, teachers providing pull-out services may or may not have specialised qualifications. In general, teachers without specialised qualifications have participated in targeted in-service training or professional development. Data on the proportion of teachers with different types of training backgrounds are not available.

In lower secondary school, immigrant students with limited proficiency in English participate in a preparatory programme that involves three phases:

(1) In the *reception* phase, students require extensive assistance. They may stay at this level for several years. The programme is organised in eight blocks, involving four to five blocks of specialised ESL courses (ESL reading, ESL writing, ESL conversation, ESL social studies, ESL science) and

three to four blocks of grade level content courses: mathematics, physical education, art, band, chorus and keyboarding. Students are not required to take additional foreign languages.

(2) In the *transition* phase, the relative emphasis of the schedule shifts from ESL classes to standard grade level content courses. Students typically take six blocks of content classes (*e.g.* mathematics, science, social studies, physical education) and two blocks of language support classes (ESL English or language arts and/or ESL social studies or ESL science).

(3) The *integration* phase, finally, involves seven blocks of content courses and one language support block. Students only receive course credit for content classes, not for ESL classes.

Students typically stay in the ESL system for up to 36 months. Ministries and Departments of Education provide curriculum guidelines for ESL instruction. The latter define the principles that schools and school boards are to follow in curriculum development. ESL teachers typically receive specialist training through various means, including additional qualification courses offered by the faculties of education, in-service training or professional development.

Canada – Ontario: Focus on immersion with systematic language support.

A recommendation stipulates that immigrant students with limited proficiency in English should receive systematic language support either from a classroom teacher or an *English as a Second Language* (ESL) teacher. This recommendation is specified in a resource guide (*Ontario Curriculum 1-8, English as a Second Language and English Literacy Development*, 2001) that describes teaching strategies specifically designed to support English language learners. However, ESL support is not a policy requirement, and it is therefore not always provided. As there is no requirement or curriculum for ESL in primary schools, it is impossible to estimate the number of hours per week students typically receive additional language training. If provided by the regular classroom teacher, he or she will typically implement a range of language-support strategies throughout the day. For lower secondary schools, however, an explicit ESL curriculum is available. ESL courses typically involve 5-6 hours of instruction per week when implemented.

Denmark: Focus on immersion with systematic language support and on immersion with a preparatory phase for newly immigrated students.

Schools refer newly arrived immigrant students to reception classes if they are incapable of participating in mainstream instruction due to language barriers. Students in reception classes receive as many hours of instruction as students in mainstream classes at the same grade level. The classes provide basic instruction in *Danish as a Second Language* (DSL). The goal is for students to make the transition to mainstream instruction as quickly as possible; they may stay in the reception classes for a maximum of 24 months. However, data on the actual length of time students remain in the classes are not available.

Students who attend standard classes and have limited proficiency in Danish are entitled to receive special language support upon admission to school. They may receive this support either as an integrated part of the standard class instruction or in separate lessons during or after school hours. Results from an evaluation of DSL indicate that schools do not always implement the support measures as required. On average, students receive 1.5 hours of instruction in DSL per week in both primary and lower secondary school.

An explicit curriculum specifying the objectives for DSL sets target levels of proficiency for students in both the reception classes and in mainstream classes. The *Folkskole* act requires teachers providing support to have special training. Teacher training colleges offer DSL as a subject and as part of the curriculum for Danish. Additional courses are available for in-service training. Information on the proportions of teachers with special language qualifications is not available.

For further information see:
http://www.retsinfo.dk/_GETDOCM_/ACCN/B19980006305-REGL
http://www.faellesmaal.uvm.dk/fag/Dansksomandetsprog/formaal.html (websites in Danish)

England: Focus on immersion with systematic language support.

Support for pupils whose first language is not English depends on the background of students within a school and on the available resources. The language of instruction in all schools is English. Pupils generally attend mainstream classes and are not withdrawn for any significant period of time on the basis of language proficiency. There is no separate curriculum for language minority students.

Schools can use a range of approaches to help pupils access the curriculum and gain proficiency in English. This may include use of their first languages to help them grasp key vocabulary in English and concepts in the national curriculum. The extent to which first languages are used depends on the school's resources, the languages spoken by teachers and support staff and the profile of the student population. While use of first languages is encouraged as a means to improving attainment and English language proficiency, there is no statutory right to instruction in any language other than English.

Additional funding is allocated to local education authorities and schools to support activities that contribute to raising the achievement of ethnic minority pupils and pupils whose first language is not English. Authorities can retain up to 15% of the grant for centrally provided services. The grant can only be used for activities directly related to raising the achievement of ethnic minority pupils and pupils whose first language is not English.

For further information see:
http://www.standards.dfes.gov.uk/ethnicminorities/

Finland: Focus on immersion with systematic language support and on immersion with a preparatory phase, which may involve transitional bilingual components.

Immigrant students may be taught *Finnish/Swedish as a Second Language* (F/SSL) in primary, lower secondary and general upper secondary education if their Finnish/Swedish language skills are poorer than those of native speakers in all areas of language proficiency. However, in the curriculum, F/SSL is not a separate school subject. Instead, Finnish/Swedish is taught as one of the subjects within the "mother tongue and literature" subject. If a school does not offer instruction in F/SSL, tuition in the regular Finnish/Swedish mother tongue and literature classes is modified to meet the needs of each individual student. Some schools may offer instruction in students' first languages. Teaching of Finnish/Swedish is not limited to language classes; all education offered at school is expected to support it.

In addition, bodies authorised to provide education may arrange preparatory instruction for pupils with an immigrant background who lack the Finnish/Swedish language skills that are necessary for studying in a mainstream classroom. Preparatory classes involve at least 450 hours of instruction

© OECD 2006   Where immigrant students succeed - A comparative review of performance and engagement in PISA 2003

for children aged 6 to 10 and at least 500 hours for children older than 10. The objective of the preparatory programme is to promote pupils' balanced development and integration into Finnish society, and to foster the skills necessary for transferring to general education. Pupils receive instruction in F/SSL, and may well also receive instruction in their native languages in order to strengthen their multicultural identity and to create a foundation for functional bilingualism. In preparatory classrooms, students receive instruction in basic education subjects as specified more precisely in their individual study programmes. For all pupils, the preparatory instruction emphasises the study of F/SSL. In the course of the preparatory phase, pupils are integrated into mainstream education groups according to their individual study programmes.

Germany: Focus on immersion with systematic language support in primary education (ISCED 1) and on submersion/immersion in lower secondary education (ISCED 2).

Schools receive additional teacher hours for special support of immigrant children with limited proficiency in the language of instruction. However the type of support implemented varies considerably across schools, as schools decide for themselves how to use the additional teacher hours. Common approaches include splitting up classes into smaller groups during some lessons, providing additional lessons covering the curriculum and providing lessons in *German as a Second Language* (GSL). In some *Länder*, there is an explicit curriculum for GSL. On average, students will receive one to two hours per week of additional language support. Some teachers providing the language support have received special training during their initial studies or as in-service training, but estimates of the proportions are not available.

For new immigrants, some *Länder* also offer immersion programmes with a preparatory phase. In the preparatory classes, instruction starts with GSL and mathematics tuition. Students may stay in these classes for 6 to 18 months before transferring to mainstream instruction, although there is a tendency to limit the duration to one year. Since at present, few newly arrived immigrants enter the school system, the proportion of students attending preparatory classes is relatively low. Immigrant students in lower secondary school who have completed primary education in Germany but continue to have limited proficiency in German do not generally receive systematic language support, although this varies across *Länder*.

Luxembourg: Focus on submersion/immersion and immersion with systematic language support in primary education (ISCED 1) and on submersion/immersion in lower secondary education (ISCED 2).

Most immigrant students with limited proficiency in the language of instruction attend standard classes according to the submersion/immersion approach. Yet, in primary schools, up to about one third of the students receive special language support. This support involves an average of approximately two hours per week, and it is not based on an explicit curriculum. Some of the teachers in pre-primary education (ISCED 0) have special training, but estimates of the proportions are not available.

In lower secondary education, three types of approaches are commonly employed, including submersion/immersion, submersion with systematic language support and immersion with a preparatory phase. Submersion with systematic language support classes (*classes d'insertion*) are mainly attended by students who have lived in Luxembourg for at least one year. It is geared towards the needs of students with a solid schooling background from their countries of origin but with limited knowledge of Luxembourg's languages of instruction. They receive intensive training in either French or German as well as instruction in other subjects.

Preparatory classes (*classes d'accueil* – welcome classes) are offered in one of the school types (technical secondary education) to students aged 12 to 15 who have recently immigrated. In the preparatory classes, students typically receive language instruction in Luxembourgish and in at least one other language of instruction (French and/or German). Only in exceptional cases will students stay in the preparatory class for more than a year. On average, they transfer to the mainstream class after ten months. An explicit curriculum exists for the transition classes, and almost all teachers in these classes have completed special teacher training.

The programme CASNA (*cellule d'accueil scolaire pour élèves nouveaux arrivants*) provides newly arrived immigrant students with information on Luxembourg's school system and helps assign them to an appropriate school. Special classes with language support are also available for students who are 16 years or older at the time of arrival in Luxembourg (*classes d'insertion pour jeunes adults* or *classes d'insertion préprofessionnelles*).

For further information see:
http://www.men.lu/edu/fre/enseignement/etrangers/

Netherlands: Focus on immersion with systematic language support in primary education (ISCED 1) and on immersion with a preparatory phase in lower secondary education (ISCED 2).

In primary schools, the majority of immigrant students with limited proficiency in Dutch receive systematic language support, although not all schools offer such programmes. These language classes have an explicit curriculum. On average, primary school students receive one-and-a-half hours per week of additional language support. The majority of teachers providing this support have completed special training programmes, but this is not mandatory. The training programmes are offered by institutions of higher professional education and involve a total of 680 hours.

In lower secondary education, recently immigrated students typically attend a preparatory programme before transferring to a standard class. There is no explicit curriculum for the preparatory classes, these are rather adapted to individual students' needs. These classes involve 16 hours of instruction in *Dutch as a Second Language*, 3.2 hours in arithmetic, 2.1 hours in physical education and 1.4 hours in computer science per week. Students are often grouped according to their language proficiency and cognitive skills. Each group has its own teacher. After two years in the preparatory programme, students typically transfer to a mainstream class. Teachers in the transition classes do not have special training, other than a general teaching qualification. However, specific courses do exist for teachers who need to work with different methods.

Norway: Focus on immersion with systematic language support which may involve a preparatory phase as well as transitional bilingual components.

Immigrant students with limited proficiency in the language of instruction typically receive systematic support based on an explicit curriculum. Parents must agree with the choice of this curriculum for their children. On average, the additional language support involves two to four hours of instruction per week. In some schools, it may entail a preparatory phase of approximately six months and some bilingual support. The municipalities decide on the curriculum for these

© OECD 2006   Where immigrant students succeed - A comparative review of performance and engagement in PISA 2003

support measures. Some teachers providing instruction in *Norwegian as a Second Language* have special qualifications, but this is not compulsory. Precise estimates of the proportion of teachers with special training are not available, but the relevant data are currently being collected.

Spain: Focus on submersion/immersion in primary education (ISCED 1) and on immersion with systematic language support in lower secondary education (ISCED 2).

In primary education, the majority of immigrant students with limited proficiency in the language of instruction attend a standard class right away without systematic language support. In lower secondary education, special support measures are available for newly immigrated students. These measures involve teaching the mainstream curriculum while taking into account students' level of language proficiency. Most secondary schools with immigrant students offer special support.

Sweden: Focus on immersion with systematic language support and on immersion with a preparatory phase for newly immigrated students.

Students whose first language is not Swedish may study *Swedish as a Second Language* (SSL) as a subject. The goal of SSL is to help students develop daily communication skills and to ensure that they will attain the proficiency required to study other school subjects in Swedish. An explicit curriculum for SSL is in place. Achievement levels and proficiency requirements for SSL students are similar to those for native students studying Swedish. SSL, however, aims at developing the prerequisites for students to express complicated thoughts in speech and writing, without placing high demands on formal language correctness. The right and opportunity to study SSL applies to both compulsory and upper secondary school. As a subject, SSL is equivalent to Swedish (as a first language) with respect to eligibility for admission to university or other post-secondary study. The guaranteed number of instruction hours for SSL is the same as for Swedish (as a first language). Teachers of SSL are supposed to have completed a special teacher training programme/specialisation, but there is a shortage of teachers with this specialisation.

Students who have recently immigrated to Sweden may attend a preparatory programme as an introduction to the Swedish school system before transferring to a mainstream class. There is no national steering document that regulates the organisation or content of this preparatory phase. The programmes vary across municipalities and schools, and the time spent in the preparatory phase depends on students' individual progress. Typically, they stay in the programme for six months to a year.

Switzerland – Berne: Focus on submersion/immersion, immersion with systematic language support and on immersion with a preparatory phase for newly immigrated students.

The type of support immigrant students with limited proficiency in the language of instruction receive depends on the communities and schools. In small villages, the most common approach is submersion/immersion without targeted language support. In larger villages and towns children may receive additional instruction in small groups. As a rule, the lessons are provided for two years, although the period of time may be extended under special circumstances. The additional support involves two hours per week on average. An explicit curriculum does not exist. Whether or not systematic support measures are offered depends on the size of the school and the number of students with limited proficiency in the language of instruction. Reliable estimates for the proportion of immigrant students receiving additional support are not available.

Students who have recently immigrated may attend a preparatory programme before transferring to a standard class. These programmes are available in towns and larger villages to children in second grade (seven-year-olds) and higher. The focus of the preparatory programme, which is not based on an explicit curriculum, is on language learning. As a rule, students do not stay in the programme for more than a year.

Teachers providing special language support to immigrant students within the standard classes or the preparatory programme have typically received in-service training to prepare them for their task.

For further information, see:
http://www.erz.be.ch/site/biev-schulung-fremdsprachiger-grundsaetze.pdf (website in German)

Switzerland – Geneva: Focus on immersion with systematic language support and on immersion with a preparatory phase for newly immigrated students in lower secondary education (ISCED 2).

In primary schools, the majority of immigrant students with limited proficiency in French receive systematic support in the language of instruction. On average, the additional support involves 3 to 20 hours of instruction per week.

In lower secondary education, recently immigrated students typically attend a preparatory programme before transferring to a regular classroom. The programme consists of about 32 lessons per week and covers the subjects French, German, English, Sports and Social Studies. After 8 to 15 months in the preparatory programme, students typically transfer to a standard class.

The language support measures in elementary and lower secondary schools are provided by fully trained school teachers who have completed special in-service modules (elementary school teachers: thirty-six two-hour modules; secondary school teachers: twenty four-hour modules). The modules include *French as a Foreign Language*, problems of foreign language teaching and intercultural aspects. An explicit curriculum for the programmes does not exist.

Switzerland – Zurich: Focus on submersion/immersion, immersion with systematic language support and on immersion with a preparatory phase for newly immigrated students in lower secondary education (ISCED 2).

Immigrant students with limited proficiency in the language of instruction often receive special language support. An explicit curriculum does not exist for the support measures, although a textbook for *German as a Second Language* (GSL) is available. Language instruction takes place in small groups. On average, it involves approximately 8 lessons per week in primary school and 10 to 12 hours per week in lower secondary school. The teachers providing the additional language support are qualified as primary or lower secondary school teachers. At present, in-service training for teaching GSL is only recommended, but such training will probably be made compulsory in the future.

Students who have recently immigrated may attend a preparatory programme before transferring to a standard class. Apart from additional lessons in German, the programme follows the general curriculum at its own pace. The transfer process is often gradual and is generally completed within a year.

© OECD 2006 Where immigrant students succeed - A comparative review of performance and engagement in PISA 2003

Hong Kong-China: Focus on immersion with systematic language support and on immersion with a preparatory phase for newly immigrated students.

The *School-Based Support Scheme Grant* for schools with immigrant children regulates support measures for students with limited proficiency in the language of instruction. The regulation has been in effect since 1997 for newly arrived students from mainland China and was extended to non-Chinese speaking immigrant children in 2000. Public sector schools may receive a grant upon application. Schools are required to keep a separate account recording all the income and expenditure chargeable to the grant, but the grants offer a great degree of flexibility to schools in terms of how they provide support for newly arrived immigrants. Services may include supplementary lessons in Chinese or English as well as other subjects, the implementation of a school-based curriculum or a remedial programme designed to address the needs of immigrant children, teaching aids and resource materials, orientation or guidance programmes and extra-curricular activities. All schools approved for the grant are required to offer a language support programme. The programme is not based on an explicit curriculum, but guidelines exist for curriculum development in schools. The number of hours of instruction per week that students receive special language support varies. Teachers providing the support are not required to complete a special teacher training programme. Information on the number of teachers who have received in-service training related to second-language support is not available.

Since 2000, newly arrived students from mainland China may choose to attend a preparatory programme before transferring to mainstream schools. In 2002, the service was extended to include non-Chinese speaking immigrant children. Schools receive a grant to operate the programme and may use the funds to design the curriculum and support measures. The programme includes academic and non-academic elements designed to integrate students in the local education system and community. Again, the programme is not based on an explicit curriculum, but there are curriculum guidelines for schools. Students stay in the preparatory programme for six months.

Macao-China: Focus on immersion with systematic language support.

Special classes in the main languages of instruction, Cantonese and English, are offered after school to newly-immigrated children from mainland China. Students attend the classes during the school year as well as during the summer holidays. There is an explicit curriculum for the classes. In addition, for a small fee, immigrant children and adults may take a number of other language courses in their spare time.

SUPPLEMENTARY CLASSES TO IMPROVE PROFICIENCY IN IMMIGRANT STUDENTS' NATIVE LANGUAGES

The relationship between the first language that immigrant students learn and use at home and the receiving country's language of instruction in schools has been a matter of considerable controversy among researchers as well as policy makers. For a long time, the interdependence hypothesis proposed by Cummins (1979a; 1979b; 1981) dominated the discussion suggesting that students will only be able to become proficient in a second language if they already have a good command of their first language. Although few people today agree with the strict version of this hypothesis, the assumption that proficiency in the first language presents a crucial prerequisite for second language acquisition is still widespread. The empirical support for this assumption, however, is weak, and it

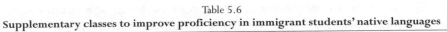

Table 5.6
Supplementary classes to improve proficiency in immigrant students' native languages

Country	Sub-national entity	Do **primary schools** (ISCED 1) attended by immigrant students typically offer native language classes for the most common minority languages?		Do **lower secondary schools** (ISCED 2) attended by immigrant students typically offer native language classes for the most common minority languages?		General comments
		Yes or No	Proportion of immigrant students taking the classes	Yes or No	Proportion of immigrant students taking the classes	
Australia	New South Wales	Depends on the school (in 2003, approximately 10% of schools offered heritage language classes).	13% of total primary enrolment (31% of students taking the classes were native speakers of the language)	Depends on the school	6% of native speakers	Schools offer supplementary classes in approximately 23 heritage languages as a curriculum option. In addition, the NSW government provides funding to assist immigrant community organisations to run heritage language classes for school-aged children on weekends and evenings.
	Queensland	No	a	No	a	
	Victoria	Depends on the school	m	Depends on the school	m	
Austria	Vienna	Depends on the school	39%	Depends on the school	30% across compulsory schooling (including primary schools)	
	Voralberg	Depends on the school	33%	Depends on the school	30% across compulsory schooling (including primary schools)	
Belgium	French Community	Depends on the school	m	Depends on the school	m	The Charter about language and culture of origin concerns immigrant children from Italy, Greece, Portugal, Turkey and Morocco. In addition to the mandatory curriculum, courses in the native languages with at least two periods of 50 minutes are provided.
Canada	British Columbia	No	a	No	a	Immigrant families often send their children to *Saturday school* where they learn and maintain their first language. It is not under the control of the school board or ministry of education.
	Ontario	No	a	No	a	Some schools in the province may choose to offer heritage language classes to students, but this is not general practice.
Denmark		Depends on the municipality	m	Depends on the municipality	m	Since 2002, municipalities are no longer obliged to offer native language teaching to all bilingual children, only to citizens from the European Union, Norway, Liechtenstein, Iceland, Greenland and the Faroe Islands. Municipalities now choose to offer native language teaching for immigrants of their own accord. The Danish Ministry of Education does not have information on the extent to which municipalities and schools offer such courses.
England		Depends on the school	m	Depends on the school	m	
Finland		Depends on the municipality	m	Depends on the municipality	m	Approximately 75% of immigrant students receive mother tongue instruction, but the proportion of in-school programmes is not known.
Germany		No	a	No	a	Heritage language classes are offered by embassies, consulates and immigrant organisations.
Luxembourg		No	a	No	a	
Netherlands		No	a	No	a	
Norway		Depends on the school	m	Depends on the school	m	

© OECD 2006 Where immigrant students succeed - A comparative review of performance and engagement in PISA 2003

Table 5.6 *(continued)*

Supplementary classes to improve proficiency in immigrant students' native languages

Country	Sub-national entity	Do **primary schools** (ISCED 1) attended by immigrant students typically offer native language classes for the most common minority languages?		Do **lower secondary schools** (ISCED 2) attended by immigrant students typically offer native language classes for the most common minority languages?		General comments
		Yes or No	Proportion of immigrant students taking the classes	Yes or No	Proportion of immigrant students taking the classes	
Spain		No	a	No	a	
Sweden		Yes	50-59%	Yes	50-59%	Most schools offer native language classes independent of the proportion of immigrant students (if there are five or more students with the same native language in the municipality).
Switzerland	Canton Berne	No	a	No	a	
	Canton Geneva	Yes	20-30%	Yes	m	
	Canton Zurich	Depends on the school	40-49%	Depends on the school	40-49%	Heritage language classes are offered by embassies, consulates and parent organisations (presently 15 languages, 2-4 lessons per week). The co-operation between providers of such courses and schools is regulated. There is a general curriculum for matters of second language acquisition, multiculturalism, integration etc.
Hong Kong-China		No	a	No	a	Hindi and Urdu are offered only in 1-2 government primary schools admitting a larger number of non-Chinese speaking students.
Macao-China		Depends on the school	m	Depends on the school	m	

(Left margin labels: OECD countries / Partner countries)

is unclear whether bilingual approaches are more effective than monolingual approaches in helping immigrant children attain proficiency in the language of instruction (*e.g.* Greene, 1997; Limbird and Stanat, 2006; Rossell and Baker, 1996; Slavin and Cheung, 2003; Willig, 1985). Accordingly, few countries seem to have programmes in place that systematically involve language support in students' first languages as a means of promoting learning a second language (see above).

Although the value of first language instruction for the acquisition of second language skills is unclear, helping immigrant students maintain and develop their bilingualism may be viewed as worthwhile in its own right (*e.g.* Portes and Hao, 1998). Being able to communicate proficiently in more than one language may present a resource that could potentially have valuable returns. Multilingualism could conceivably open up additional opportunities for students' educational and professional development and could improve their chances on the job market, although the evidence supporting this assumption is unclear (Pendakur and Pendakur, 2002). Keeping up their native language may also increase students' social capital by helping to preserve and intensify their social ties with members of the immigrant community and with residents in the sending country (*e.g.* Bankston and Zhou, 1995). Therefore, the survey also asked about the provision of classes that aim at improving immigrant students' proficiency in their native languages.

As Table 5.6 indicates, very few countries consistently offer native language classes in their schools. One exception is Sweden where primary and lower secondary schools generally provide such classes if at least five students with the same native language live in the municipality. In fact, immigrant

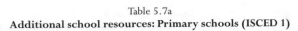

Table 5.7a
Additional school resources: Primary schools (ISCED 1)

Country	Sub-national entity	Additional teachers without special training in second language acquisition	Additional teachers with special training in second language acquisition	Additional financial resources	Smaller classes	Other (please specify)
		Do **primary schools** (ISCED 1) with high proportions of immigrant students receive the following special resources?				
Australia	New South Wales	No	Yes	Yes (funds are provided to educational regions which allocate *English as a Second Language* teachers, teacher aides etc. to schools)	No	Schools with a minimum of 10 refugee students receive small grants to assist in buying uniforms, textbooks, school excursions, etc. Bilingual teachers aides are provided in schools with significant enrolments of refugee students. Schools are supported by regional Multicultural/*English as a Second Language* consultants who provide teaching resources and professional development for teachers and Community Information Officers who support communication between schools and parents/community members. Schools receive funding to conduct cultural transition courses to assist immigrants in adjusting to life in Australia.
	Queensland	No	Yes	No (funds are provided to educational regions which allocate *English as a Second Language* teachers, teacher aides, etc. to schools)	No	
	Victoria	No	Yes	Yes	*English as a Second Language* classes are usually smaller depending on the needs of the students. Average class size for intensive new arrivals programme is 13.	Multicultural education aides are provided in many schools to assist *English as a Second Language* students in the classroom and with communication between parents, guardians and schools. Schools also have access to support and advice including materials specifically developed for ESL learners.
Austria	Vienna	No	Yes	No	No	Teaching materials and school books in their native language for students with non-German native languages and teachers with non-German mother tongue.
	Voralberg	No	No	Yes	Yes	
Belgium	French Community	m	m	m	m	
Canada	British Columbia	Depends on the school	Depends on the school	Yes	Depends on the school	
	Ontario	No	No	Yes	Depends on the school	
Denmark		Depends on the school	Depends on the school	Yes, for *Danish as a Second Language* instruction	No	
England		Yes	Yes	Yes	No	Additional support varies across schools and depends on the needs, resources and priorities of the schools and local education authorities. Schools receiving additional funding have the autonomy to decide how to use it.
Finland		Yes	Yes	Yes	No	Additional teachers only in bigger cities.
Germany		Yes (predominantly)	Yes (less often)	No	No	There is a variety of possible support, such as homework support, courses in the language of instruction for mothers, social workers, and first language teachers. In some areas there are local support centres providing teacher training, language courses, teaching material, translation services and advice.

OECD countries

Policies and practices to help immigrant students attain proficiency in the language of instruction

Table 5.7a (*continued*)
Additional school resources: Primary schools (ISCED 1)

Country	Sub-national entity	Do **primary schools** (ISCED 1) with high proportions of immigrant students receive the following special resources?				
		Additional teachers without special training in second language acquisition	Additional teachers with special training in second language acquisition	Additional financial resources	Smaller classes	Other (please specify)

OECD countries

Country	Sub-national entity	Additional teachers without special training	Additional teachers with special training	Additional financial resources	Smaller classes	Other (please specify)
Luxembourg		Yes	Yes	No	No	Intercultural mediators speaking Serbo-Croatian, Albanian, Russian, Portuguese, Cape Verdean or Chinese come to schools on request of teachers, parents, or the school authority to assist immigrant children or young asylum seekers or refugees.
Netherlands		No	Yes	Yes	Yes	
Norway		Depends on the municipality	Depends on the municipality	Yes	Depends on the school	Each municipality applies for extra resources on the basis of the amount of pupils evaluated in proficiency in the language of instruction, and the number of different languages concerned.
Spain		No	Yes	No	Yes	
Sweden		Depends on the school	Depends on the school	Depends on the school	Depends on the school	Approaches vary - decisions are made at the local level. Normally, the schools receive additional financial resources and additional teachers who should have special training.
Switzerland	Canton Berne	Depends on the school	No	Yes	Yes	
	Canton Geneva	No	Yes	No	No	
	Canton Zurich	No	Yes	Yes	Yes	

Partner countries

Country	Sub-national entity	Additional teachers without special training	Additional teachers with special training	Additional financial resources	Smaller classes	Other (please specify)
Hong Kong-China		No	No	Yes	Yes	
Macao-China		No	No	Yes, for extra language courses	No	Schools can apply for special funding from the Education and Youth Affairs Bureau to organise extra language courses outside the normal curriculum for immigrant students to facilitate their learning in school.

Policies and practices to help immigrant students attain proficiency in the language of instruction

Table 5.7b

Additional school resources: Lower secondary schools (ISCED 2)

Policies and practices to help immigrant students attain proficiency in the language of instruction

OECD countries

Country	Sub-national entity	Do **lower secondary schools** (ISCED 2) with high proportions of immigrant students receive the following special resources?				
		Additional teachers without special training in second language acquisition	Additional teachers with special training in second language acquisition	Additional financial resources	Smaller classes	Other (please specify)
Australia	New South Wales	No	Yes	Yes (funds are provided to educational regions which allocate *English as a Second Language* teachers, teacher aides, etc. to schools)	Yes	Schools with a minimum of ten refugee students receive small grants to assist in buying uniforms, textbooks, school excursions, etc. Bilingual teachers aides are provided in schools with significant enrolments of refugee students. Schools are supported by regional Multicultural/*English as a Second Language* consultants who provide teaching resources and professional development for teachers and Community Information Officers who support communication between schools and parents/ community members. Schools receive funding to conduct cultural transition courses to assist immigrants in adjusting to life in Australia.
	Queensland	No	Yes	No (funds are provided to educational regions which allocate *English as a Second Language* teachers, teacher aides, etc. to schools)	No	
	Victoria	No	Yes	Yes	*English as a Second Language* classes are usually smaller depending on the needs of the students. Average class size for intensive new arrivals programme is 13.	Multicultural education aides are also provided in many schools to assist *English as a Second Language* (ESL) students in the classroom and to assist with communication between parents and guardians and schools. Schools also have access to support and advice including materials specifically developed for ESL learners.
Austria	Vienna	No	Yes	No	No	Teaching materials and school books in native language of students with non-German native language.
	Voralberg	No	No	Yes	No	
Belgium	French Community	m	m	m	m	
Canada	British Columbia	Yes	Yes	Yes	Yes	
	Ontario	Depends on school	Depends on the school	Yes	Depends on the school	
Denmark		Depends on the school	Depends on the school	Yes, for *Danish as a Second Language* instruction	No	
England		Yes	Yes	Yes	No	Additional support varies across schools and depends on the needs, resources and priorities of the schools and local education authorities. Schools receiving additional funding have the autonomy to decide how to use it.
Finland		Yes	Yes	Yes	No	There are special posts for teachers of *Finnish as a Second Language* in the largest municipalities.
Germany		Yes (predominantly)	Yes (less often)	No	No	

© OECD 2006 Where immigrant students succeed - A comparative review of performance and engagement in PISA 2003

Table 5.7b
Additional school resources: Lower secondary schools (ISCED 2)

Country	Sub-national entity	Do **lower secondary schools** (ISCED 2) with high proportions of immigrant students receive the following special resources?				
		Additional teachers without special training in second language acquisition	Additional teachers with special training in second language acquisition	Additional financial resources	Smaller classes	Other (please specify)
OECD countries						
Luxembourg		Yes	Yes	No	No	Intercultural mediators speaking Serbo-Croatian, Albanian, Russian, Portuguese, Cape Verdean or Chinese come to schools on request of teachers, parents or the school authority to assist immigrant children or young asylum seekers or refugees.
Netherlands		Yes	No	Yes	No	
Norway		m	m	Yes	m	Each municipality applies for extra resources on the basis of the number of pupils with limited proficiency in the language of instruction and the number of different languages involved.
Spain		No	Yes	No	Yes	
Sweden		Depends on the school	Depends on the school	Depends on the school	Depends on the school	Approaches vary - decisions are made at local level. Normally, the schools receive additional financial resources and additional teachers who should have special training.
Switzerland	Canton Berne	Yes	No	Yes	Yes	
	Canton Geneva	No	Yes	No	Yes	
	Canton Zurich	No	Yes	Yes	Yes	
Partner countries						
Hong Kong-China		No	No	Yes	No	Additional teachers will be provided to schools to address the learning diversity of students.
Macao-China		No	No	Yes, for extra language courses	No	Schools can apply for special funding from the Education and Youth Affairs Bureau to organise extra language courses outside the normal curriculum for immigrant students to facilitate their learning in school.

Policies and practices to help immigrant students attain proficiency in the language of instruction

Policies and practices to help immigrant students attain proficiency in the language of instruction

Table 5.7c
Additional school resources: Allocation criteria

Country	Sub-national entity	What are the allocation criteria for special ressources?
OECD countries		
Australia	New South Wales	Schools are allocated *English as a Second Language* (ESL) teachers, in addition to normal staffing entitlements, according to the relative numbers of ESL students and their level of English language proficiency in terms of three broad phases of ESL learning – phase 1, 2 or 3. A formula is used to apply weightings to the phases. Intensive English Centres (IECs) receive 0.5 bilingual teacher's aide per class. Primary schools receive 0.5 bilingual teacher's aide for 10 newly arrived refugee students. Class sizes: IECs maximum 10 (special needs) or 18 (regular). Primary and high schools may choose to create smaller groups using existing resources. A minimum of 10 refugee students for receving small grants.
	Queensland	Financial resources relating to immigrant students are provided to the educational region which allocates *English as a Second Language* teachers, teacher aides and resources across that region for use in schools. Commencing in 2005, additional financial resources are being allocated for the support of refugee students.
	Victoria	m
Austria	Vienna	The allocation of additional (teaching) resources depends on the number of students with non-German native language in the schools.
	Voralberg	Only primary schools: Students with a non-German native language are counted as 1.4 children, resulting in smaller classes. Thus, classes with immigrant students are smaller. Primary and secondary schools: The amount of additional funds for language programmes depends on the number of students with a non-German native language.
Belgium	French Community	Special resources are allocated based on the policy of positive discrimination, which takes into account the socio-economic context in which the students grow up and the number of immigrant students in the school.
Canada	British Columbia	Allocation is based on a per capita formula: For each immigrant student, the school receives the base rate plus $1100 annually for a maximum of 5 years.
	Ontario	The Ministry of Education provides extra funding for *English as a Second Language* students. Allocation is based on a formula that is linked to the number of immigrant students identified in the most recent census data. How the money is used is up to the individual school boards with no accountability measures currently in place and no data available to indicate how the money is actually being used.
Denmark		With an amendment to an Act introduced in 1996, the municipalities became obliged to offer instruction in *Danish as a Second Language* to bilingual students in pre-school classes and in grades 1-10. Municipalities receive compensation for these programmes.
England		Additional funding through the *Standards Fund Ethnic Minority Achievement Grant* (EMAG) is allocated to local education authorities based on a formula that includes the number of minority ethnic pupils from nationally underachieving ethnic groups and the number of pupils whose first language is not English with a weigthing for eligibility for free school meals (as a proxy indicator for relative deprivation). There is no distinction in funding terms made between pupils from minority ethnic backgrounds in terms of the length of time they have spent in the country. In addition, the *Standards Fund Vulnerable Children Grant* (VCG) may provide additional support for children from Gypsy, Roma and Traveller backgrounds and children of refugees and asylum seekers. The VCG became part of the new *Children's Service Grant* from April 2006.
Finland		Municipalities may receive special resources for: (1) curriculum support for pupils who have arrived in Finland within the last four years (1 lesson per week per school and 0.5 lessons per week per student); (2) mother tongue instruction if there are at least 4 pupils in the school speaking the same language (2 hours per week); (3) a preparatory phase if municipalities provide the minimum number of hours of instruction (450 hours to children aged 6-10, 500 hours to children older than 10).
Germany		Until recently, the only criterion was the number of immigrant students. Increasingly, the *Länder* (sub-national entities) move towards the use of other criteria, such as proficiency in German, socio-economic background, and the development of specific support programmes for the respective school.
Luxembourg		m
Netherlands		m
Norway		m
Spain		m
Sweden		m
Switzerland	Canton Berne	Allocation decided by school inspectors.
	Canton Geneva	m
	Canton Zurich	From 2006, allocation of teaching staff is based on a social index involving the following criteria: unemployment rate, immigration rate, housing situation, population fluctuation (proportion of families moving to/out of a commune). The number of lessons to improve proficiency in the language of instruction depends on the demand. Additional financial resources are provided to schools with a proportion of immigrant students of more than 40%. (This approach to funding allocation is currently being tested in a project involving 20 schools.)
Partner countries		
Hong Kong-China		Schools can apply for a block grant to provide support services for newly arrived immigrant children. Schools may receive additional funding for their *School-based Support and Learning Programmes* organised for disadvantaged immigrant children.
Macao-China		m

© OECD 2006 *Where immigrant students succeed - A comparative review of performance and engagement in PISA 2003*

children in Sweden have a legal right to native language tuition. Accordingly, 50 to 59% of students in primary and lower secondary schools take classes in their first language. Similarly, the Swiss Canton of Geneva indicated that primary and secondary schools typically offer native language classes for the most common minority languages. The approximate participation rate for immigrant students is 20% to 30%.

In eleven other countries or sub-national entities, heritage language classes may also be available, yet whether or not they are offered depends on the municipality or the individual school. In most cases, it is unclear how many students attend these classes. In fact, only 6 of the 22 countries or sub-national entities were able to provide any data on participation rates.

Finally, nine of the school systems that participated in the survey do not offer any classes in immigrant students' native languages. However, this does not necessarily mean that no first language tuition is available at all. For example, in the Canadian province of British Columbia, Germany and the Swiss Canton of Zurich non-school institutions such as embassies, consulates or immigrant organisations offer heritage language courses. Thus, in these countries or sub-national entities, it is left to families or community groups to organise native language instruction for immigrant children.

ADDITIONAL SCHOOL RESOURCES

All countries participating in the survey indicated that they provide some special resources to schools with high proportions of immigrant students. The most prevalent approaches are to allocate additional financial resources or teachers to schools. Particularly in the Australian state of Queensland and a few European countries and sub-national entities: Austria (Vienna), Germany, Luxembourg, Spain and Switzerland (Geneva) the focus is on the provision of teachers rather than on financial recourses. The additional teachers typically have some kind of special training in second language acquisition (see Tables 5.7a, 5.7b and 5.7c for details on additional resources in primary schools (ISCED 1), lower secondary schools (ISCED 2) and allocation criteria).

SUMMARY AND CONCLUSIONS

This chapter presented information on countries' approaches to help immigrant students attain proficiency in the language of instruction. The information stems from a supplementary survey carried out by the authors of this report. Of the 17 case countries included in the previous chapters of the report, 13 completed the questionnaire: Australia, Austria, Belgium (French community), Canada, Denmark, Germany, Luxembourg, the Netherlands, Norway, Sweden, Switzerland, Hong Kong-China and Macao-China. In addition, England, Finland and Spain responded to the survey questions. The following patterns emerge from the survey results:

(a) **Almost all of the countries that completed the questionnaire offer language classes to recently immigrated adults. In a few European countries, participation in language classes is mandatory and the failure to attend these programmes may result in sanctions.** The majority of countries provide voluntary language classes to immigrant adults. An example is the Canadian LINC programme that is based on a comprehensive curriculum that involves specified benchmark levels for speaking, listening, reading and writing. Austria, Denmark, Finland, Germany, the Netherlands and Norway have mandatory programmes in

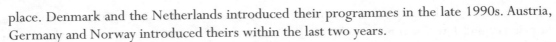

place. Denmark and the Netherlands introduced their programmes in the late 1990s. Austria, Germany and Norway introduced theirs within the last two years.

(b) Most countries collect information on immigrant students' language skills during pre-primary (ISCED 0) or primary (ISECD 1) education. Typically, this occurs as part of a general assessment involving all children. In some countries, the general assessment involves a special participation requirement or assessment component for immigrant students. Denmark, Germany, Norway, the Swiss Canton of Berne and Macao-China have language assessments for immigrant students in place that are not embedded in a general test programme.

(c) Very few countries provide systematic language support based on an explicit curriculum in pre-primary education (ISCED 0). The countries that have an explicit curriculum in place include the Canadian province of British Columbia and the Netherlands.

(d) The most widespread approach to supporting immigrant students with limited proficiency in the language of instruction is immersion with systematic language support in both primary (ISCED 1) and lower secondary (ISCED 2) education. In these programmes, students attend standard classes and receive specified periods of instruction aimed at the development of skills in the language of instruction. The content, organisation and scope of these programmes vary considerably across countries.

(e) Several countries offer immersion programmes with a preparatory phase for newly-immigrated students. This approach is adopted more in lower secondary education (ISCED 2) than in primary education (ISCED 1). In immersion with a preparatory phase, students with limited proficiency in the language of instruction participate in a programme designed to develop skills in the language of instruction before they transfer to a mainstream classroom. Substantial proportions of immigrant students attend preparatory programmes during primary education in Australia (Victoria), Finland and Sweden and during lower secondary education in Australia, Canada (British Columbia), Finland, Luxembourg, the Netherlands, Sweden and Switzerland (Zurich).

(f) Bilingual language support programmes involving both students' native language and the language of instruction are relatively uncommon. In England, Finland and Norway immersion with systematic language support may include some bilingual components. Transitional bilingual programmes with initial instruction in students' native language and a gradual shift towards instruction in their second language, however, do not play a substantial role in any of the countries involved in the survey.

(g) Several countries or sub-national entities have explicit curricula or curriculum framework documents in place for second language support. These include Australia (New South Wales and Victoria), Denmark and the Netherlands (for primary education only) for both immersion with systematic language support and immersion with a preparatory phase; Canada (Ontario), some *Länder* of Germany, Norway, Sweden and Macao-China for immersion with systematic language support; and Canada (British Columbia) and Luxembourg for immersion with a preparatory phase. However, the curricula vary considerably in terms of content, level of specificity and scope.

(h) Very few countries generally offer supplementary classes to improve students' native languages in their schools. In Sweden, students have a legal right to native language tuition, and schools typically provide such classes if at least five students with the same native language live in the municipality. Schools in the Swiss Canton of Geneva also offer native language classes for the most common minority languages. In eleven other countries or sub-national entities, the provision of native language tuition depends on the municipality or the individual school. The remaining nine school systems generally leave it to the families or community groups to arrange native language instruction for their children. These include Australia (Queensland), Canada (British Columbia), Germany, Luxembourg, the Netherlands, Spain, Switzerland (Berne) and Hong Kong-China.

(i) **All countries participating in the survey provide special resources to schools with high proportions of immigrants.** The most common approaches are to provide additional financial resources or additional teachers who will typically have special training in second language acquisition.

Overall, countries' approaches to help immigrants attain proficiency in the language of instruction have key characteristics in common. This includes the emphasis on immersion with systematic language support in many countries. In addition, several countries offer immersion programmes with a preparatory phase to newly immigrated students. Bilingual programmes, in contrast, seem to play a minor role in most school systems. Despite these similarities, however, the specific measures countries or sub-national entities implement vary considerably with regard to such aspects as the existence of explicit curricula and standards, the focus of the support (*e.g.* general curriculum versus language development) or the organisation of the support (*e.g.* within mainstream instruction versus in separate classes or language support as a specific school subject).

It is not possible to establish the extent to which the different language support programmes contribute to the relative achievement levels of immigrant students in the case countries on the basis of the analyses presented in the present report. The survey information does indicate, however, that in some countries with relatively small achievement gaps between immigrant and native students, or smaller gaps for second-generation students compared to first-generation students (see Chapter 2), long-standing language support programmes exist with relatively clearly defined goals and standards (*e.g.* Australia, Canada and Sweden). In contrast, in some countries where immigrant students perform at significantly lower levels than their native peers, language support tends to be less systematic. This situation seems to be changing, however. In the past two to six years, several countries have introduced new programmes that aim to support immigrant students' learning. These developments may help to reduce the achievement gap between immigrant students and their native peers.

Notes

1 The survey instrument is available on the OECD's PISA homepage (*www.pisa.oecd.org*). NB The survey included a seventh section on out-of-school programmes. However countries did not respond sufficiently for the information to be presented in the report.

2 The extent to which parents are able to communicate in the receiving country's official language is likely to affect immigrant students' school experiences. Therefore, the survey also includes questions on language courses for adults.

References

Alba, R. and Nee, V. (1997), "Rethinking assimilation theory for a new era of immigration. *International Migration Review*", Vol. 31, pp. 826-874.

Abedi, J. (2003), *Impact of Student Language Background on Content Based Performance: Analyses of Extant Data*, CRESST/University of California, Los Angeles, CA.

Artelt, C. (2000), *Strategisches Lernen*, Waxmann, Münster.

Bandura, A. (1994), *Self Efficacy: The Exercise of Control*, Freeman, New York, NY.

Bankston, C. and Zhou, M. (1995), "Effects of minority-language literacy on the academic achievement of Vietnamese youth In New Orleans", *Sociology of Education*, Vol. 68, pp. 1-17.

Bauer, T., Lofstrom, M. and Zimmermann, K. F. (2000), "Immigration policy, assimilation of immigrants, and natives' sentiments toward immigrants: Evidence from 12 OECD countries", *Swedish Economic Policy Rewiew*, Vol. 7, pp. 11-53.

Baumert, J. and Schümer, G. (2001), "Familiäre Lebensverhältnisse, Bildungsbeteiligung und Kompetenzerwerb", in Baumert J, *et al., PISA 2000: Basiskompetenzen von Schülerinnen und Schülern im internationalen Vergleich*, pp. 159-200, Leske and Budrich, Opladen.

Baumert, J., Stanat, P. and Watermann, R. (eds.), (2006), *Herkunftsbedingte Disparitäten im Bildungswesen: Differenzielle Bildungsprozesse und Probleme der Verteilungsgerechtigkeit*, VS Verlag für Sozialwissenschaften, Wiesbaden.

Becker, B. E. and Luthar, S. S. (2002), "Social-emotional factors affecting achievement outcomes among disadvantaged students: Closing the achievement gap", *Educational Psychologist*, Vol. 37(4), pp. 197-214.

Berry, J. W. (1992), "Acculturation and adaptation in a new society", *International Migration Review*, Vol. 30, pp. 69-85.

Betts, J. R. and Lofstrom, M. (2000), "The educational attainment of immigrants: Trends and implications", in G. J. Borjas (ed.), *Issues in the Economics of Immigration*, pp. 51-115, The University of Chicago Press, Chicago, IL.

Bialystok, E. (2001), *Bilingualism in development. Language, literacy & cognition*, Cambridge: University Press.

Blum, R. W. and Libbey, H. P. (2004), "School connectedness. Strengthening health and educational outcomes for teens: Executive summary", *Journal of School Health*, Vol. 74(7), pp. 231-233.

Borjas, G. J. (1987), "Self-selection and the earnings of immigrants", *American Economic Review*, Vol. 77(4), pp. 531-553.

Borjas, G. J. (1999), *Heaven's Door: Immigration Policy and the American Economy*, Princeton University Press, Princeton.

Bourhis, R. Y., *et al.,* (1997), "Towards an interactive acculturation model: A social psychological approach", *International Journal of Psychology*, Vol. 32, pp. 369-386.

Buchmann, C. and Parrado, E. (2006), "Educational achievement of immigrant-origin and native students: A comparative analysis informed by institutional theory", in D. P. Baker and A. W. Wiseman (eds.)", *The Impact of Comparative Education Research on Institutional Theory*, Oxford, UK, Elsevier Science, forthcoming.

Burgers, J. (1998), "In the margin of the welfare state: Labour market position and housing conditions of undocumented immigrants in Rotterdam", *Urban Studies,* Vol. 35(10), pp. 1855-1868.

Castles, S. (1995), "How nation-states respond to immigration and ethnic diversity", *New community,* Vol. 21(3), pp. 293-308.

Castles, S. (2000), "International migration at the beginning of the twenty-first century: Global trends and issues", *International Social Science Journal,* Vol. 52(165), pp. 269-281.

Castles, S. and Miller, M. J. (1993), *The Age of Migration: International Population Movements in the Modern World*, Palgrave Macmillan, Houndmills, UK.

Castles, S. and Miller, M. J. (2003), *The Age of Migration: International Population Movements in the Modern World* (3rd ed.), Guildford, New York, NY.

Catalano, R., *et al.* (2004), "The importance of bonding to school for healthy development: Findings from the Social Development Research Group", *Journal of School Health,* Vol. 74(7), pp. 252-261.

Chiquiar, D. and Hanson, G. H. (2005), "International migration, self-selection, and the distribution of wages: Evidence from Mexico and the United States", *Journal of Political Economy,* Vol. 113, pp. 239-281.

Chiswick, B. (1999), "Are immigrants favourably self-selected?" *American Economic Review, Papers and Proceedings,* Vol. 82(2), pp. 181-185.

Chiswick, B. R. (2000), "Are Immigrants Favorably Self-Selected? An Economic Analysis", *IZA Discussion Paper No. 131*, Institute for the Study of Labor (IZA), Bonn.

Chiswick, B. R. and Miller, P. W. (2003), "The complementarity of language and other human capital: Immigrant earnings in Canada", *Economics of Education Review,* Vol. 22, pp. 469-480.

Christensen, G. (2004), "What Matters for Immigrant Achievement Cross-Nationally? A Comparative Approach Examining Immigrant and Non-Immigrant Student Achievement", Unpublished Dissertation, Stanford University, Stanford, CA.

Cohen, J. and Cohen, P. (1983), *Applied Multiple Regression / Correlation Analysis for the Behavioral Sciences* (2nd ed.), Hillsdale, Erlbaum, New Jersey.

Coie, J. D. and Jacobs, M. R. (1993), "The role of social context in the prevention of conduct disorder", *Development and Psychopathology,* Vol. 5, pp. 263-275.

Conchas, G. (2001), "Structuring failure and success: Understanding the variability in Latino school engagement", *Harvard Educational Review,* Vol. 71(3), pp. 475-504.

Coradi Vellacott, *et al.* (2003), *Soziale Integration und Leistungsförderung. Thematischer Bericht der Erhebung PISA 2000*, Bundesamt für Statistik (BFS) / Schweizerische Konferenz der kantonalen Erziehungs direktoren (EDK), Neuchâtel.

Cummins, J. (1979a), "Cognitive / Academic language proficiency, linguistic interdependence, the optimum age question and some other matters", *Working Papers on Bilingualism,* Vol. 19, pp. 121-129.

Cummins, J. (1979b), "Linguistic interdependence and the educational development of bilingual children", *Review of Educational Research*, Vol. 49, pp. 222-251.

Cummins, J. (1981), "The role of primary language development in promoting educational success for language minority students", in Office of Bilingual Bicultural Education (eds.), *Schooling and language minority students: A theoretical framework*, pp. 3-49, California State Department of Education, Los Angeles, CA.

Deci, E. L. and Ryan, R. M. (1985), *Instrinic Motivation and Self-Determination in Human Behavior*. Plenum Press, New York, NY.

Eccles, J. S. Wigfield, A. and Schiefele, U. (1998), "Motivation to succeed", in W. Damon and N. Eisenberg (eds.), *Handbook of child psychology* (Vol. 3, pp. 1017-1095), Wiley, New York, NY.

Entorf, H. and Minoiu, N. (2004), "PISA results: What a difference immigration law makes", *IZA Discussion Paper No. 1021*, Institute for the Study of Labor (IZA), Bonn.

Esser, H. (2001), "Integration und ethnische Schichtung", *Arbeitspapiere des Mannheimer Zentrums für Europäische Sozialforschung*, Vol. 40, MZES, Mannheim.

Eurydice (2004), *Integrating Immigrant Children into Schools in Europe*, Eurydice, Brussels.

Fase, W. (1994), *Ethnic Divisions in Western European Education*, Waxmann, Münster.

Freeman, G. P. (1995), "Modes of immigration politics in liberal democratic states", *International Migration Review*, Vol. 29, pp. 881-902.

Freeman, G. and Ögelman, N. (1998), "Homeland citizenship policies and the status of third country nationals in the European Union", *Journal of Ethnic and Migration Studies*, Vol. 24(4), pp. 769-789.

Freeman, G. and Ögelman, N. (2000), "State regulatory regimes and immigrant informal economic activity", in J. Rath (eds.), *Immigrant Businesses: The Economic, Political and Social Environment* pp. 107-123, Palgrave Macmillan, Houndmills, UK.

Freeman, G. P. (2004), "Immigrant incorporation in Western democracies", *International Migration Review*, Vol. 38(3), pp. 945-969.

Fuligni, A. J. (1997), "The academic achievement of adolescents from immigrant families: The roles of family background, attitudes, and behaviour", *Child Development*, Vol. 68(2), pp. 351-363.

Ganzeboom, H. B. G., De Graaf P. M. and Treiman D. J. (1992), "A standard international socio-economic index of occupational status", *Social Science Research*, Vol. 21(1), Elsevier Ltd., pp. 1-56.

Gibson, M. A. and Ogbu, J. U. (1991), *Minority Status and Schooling: A Comparative Study of Immigrant and Involuntary Minorities*, Garland, New York, NY.

Glenn, C. L. and de Jong, E. J. (1996), *Educating Immigrant Children: Schools and Language Minorities in Twelve Nations*, Garland, New York, NY.

Gomolla, M. and Radtke, F. O. (2002), *Institutionelle Diskriminierung. Die Herstellung ethnischer Differenz in der Schule*, Leske and Budrich, Opladen.

Gonzalez, G. C. (2002), "Family Background, Ethnicity, and Immigration Status: Predicting School Success for Asian and Latino Students", Unpublished Dissertation, Harvard University, Cambridge, MA.

Greene, J. P. (1997), "A meta-analysis of the Rossell and Baker review of bilingual education research", *Bilingual Research Journal*, Vol. 21, pp. 103-122.

Hakuta, K. (1999), "The debate on bilingual education", *Developmental and Behavioral Pediatrics*, Vol. 20, pp. 36–37.

Hawkins, J. D., Doueck, H. J. and Lishner, D. M. (1988), "Changing teaching practices in mainstream classrooms to improve bonding and behavior of low achievers", *American Educational Research Journal*, Vol. 25(1), pp. 31-50.

Jones, F. E. (1987), "Age at immigration and education: Further explorations", *International Migration Review*, Vol. 21(1), pp. 70-85.

Joppke, C. and Morawska, E. (2003), "Integrating immigrants in liberal nation-states: Policies and practices," in C. Joppke and E. Morawska (eds.), *Toward assimilation and citizenship: Immigrants in liberal nation-states* pp. 1-36, Palgrave Macmillan, Houndmills, UK.

Jungbluth, P. (1999), "Lehrererwartungen und Ethnizität: Innerschulische Chancendeterminanten bei Migrantenkindern in den Niederlanden" (Teacher expectations and ethnicity: Within-school determinants of migrant students' chances in the Netherlands), *Zeitschrift für Pädagogik*, Vol. 40(1), pp. 113-125.

Kao, G and Tienda, M. (1995), "Optimism and achievement: The educational performance of immigrant youth", *Social Science Quarterly*, Vol. 76(1), pp. 1-19.

Kao, G., Tienda, M. and Schneider, B. (1996), "Racial and ethnic variation in academic performance research", *Sociology of Education and Socialization*, Vol. 11, pp. 263-297.

Kennedy, E. and Park, H. (1994), "Home language as a predictor of academic achievement: A comparative study of Mexican- and Asian-American youth", *Journal of Research and Development in Education*, Vol. 27, pp. 188-194.

King, G. (1997), *A Solution to the Ecological Inference Problem*, Princeton University Press, Princeton, NJ.

Klieme, E. and Stanat, P. (2002), "Zur Aussagekraft internationaler Schulleistungsvergleiche: Befunde und Erklärungsansätze am Beispiel von PISA" (The meaning of international comparisons of student performance: Findings and explanations using PISA as an example), *Bildung und Erziehung*, Vol. 55, pp. 25-44.

Libbey, H. P. (2004), "Measuring student relationship to school: Attachment, bonding, connectedness, and engagement", *Journal of School Health*, Vol. 74(7), pp. 274-283.

Liebig, T. and Sousa-Poza, A. (2004), "Migration, self-selection and income inequality: An international analysis", *KYKLOS*, Vol. 57, pp. 125-146.

Limbird, C. and Stanat, P. (2006), "Sprachförderung bei Schülerinnen und Schülern mit Migrationshintergrund: Ansätze und ihre Wirksamkeit", in J. Baumert, P. Stanat and R. Watermann (eds.), *Herkunftsbedingte Disparitäten im Bildungswesen: Differenzielle Bildungsprozesse und Probleme der Verteilungsgerechtigkeit* pp. 257-308. Wiesbaden: VS Verlag für Sozialwissenschaften.

Lonczak, H. S., *et al.* (2002), "The effects of the Seattle Social Development Project: Behavior, pregnancy, birth, and sexually transmitted disease outcomes by age 21", *Archives of Pediatric Adolescent Health*, Vol. 156, pp. 438-447.

Losen, D. and Orfield, G. (eds.) (2002), *Minority Issues in Special Education*, The Civil Rights Project at Harvard University and Harvard Education Press, Cambridge, MA.

Marsh, H. W. (1986), "Verbal and math self-concepts: An internal/external frame of reference model", *American Educational Research Journal,* Vol. 23(1), pp. 129-149.

Marsh, H.W. (1993), "The multidimensional structure of academic self-concept: Invariance over gender and age", *American Educational Research Journal,* Vol. 30(4), pp. 841-860.

Marsh, H.W., *et al.* (2005), "Academic self-concept, interest, grades and standardized test scores: Reciprocal effects models of causal ordering", *Child Development,* Vol. 76, pp. 397-416.

Massey, D. S., *et al.* (1993), "Theories of international migration: A review and appraisal", *Population and Development Review,* Vol. 19(3), pp. 341-466.

Meece, J. L., Wigfield, A. and Eccles, J. S. (1990), Predictors of math anxiety and its influence on young adolescents' course enrolment intentions and performance in mathematics, *Journal of Educational Psychology,* Vol. 82(1), pp. 60-70.

Meyers, E. (2004), *International Immigration Policy: A Theoretical and Comparative Analysis.* Palgrave Macmillan, Houndmills, UK.

Müller, A. G. and Stanat, P. (2006), "Schulischer Erfolg von Schülerinnen und Schülern mit Migrationshintergrund: Analysen zur Situation von Zuwanderern aus der ehemaligen Sowjetunion und aus der Türkei", in J. Baumert, P. Stanat and R. Watermann (eds.), *Herkunftsbedingte Disparitäten im Bildungswesen: Differenzielle Bildungsprozesse und Probleme der Verteilungsgerechtigkeit*, VS Verlag für Sozialwissenschaften, Wiesbaden, forthcoming.

OECD (1999), *Classifying Educational Programmes: Manual for ISCED-97 Implementation in OECD Countries*, OECD, Paris.

OECD (2001a), *Trends in International Migration: SOPEMI 2000 Edition,* OECD, Paris.

OECD (2001b), *Knowledge and Skills for Life: First Results from the OECD Programme for International Student Assessment (PISA) 2000*, OECD, Paris.

OECD (2002), *PISA 2000 Technical Report*, OECD, Paris.

OECD (2003a), *The PISA 2003 Assessment Framework - Mathematics, Reading, Science and Problem Solving Knowledge and Skills*, OECD, Paris.

OECD (2003b), *Learners for Life: Student Approaches to Learning: Results from PISA 2000*, OECD, Paris.

OECD (2003c), *Student Engagement in School: A Sense of Belonging and Participation. Results from PISA 2000*, OECD, Paris.

OECD (2004a), *Learning for Tomorrow's World: First Results from PISA 2003*, OECD, Paris.

OECD (2004b), *Recent Trends in Migration Movements and Policies in Hong Kong, China*, OECD, Paris.

OECD (2005a), *Trends in International Migration: SOPEMI 2004 Edition*, OECD, Paris.

OECD (2005b), *PISA 2003 Technical Report*, OECD, Paris.

Pajares, F. and Miller, M. D. (1994), "The role of self-efficacy and self-concept beliefs in mathematical problem-solving: A path analysis", *Journal of Educational Psychology,* Vol. 86, pp. 193-203.

Pajares, F. and Miller, M. D. (1995), "Mathematics self-efficacy and mathematics outcomes: The need for specificity of assessment", *Journal of Counseling Psychology,* Vol. 42, pp. 190-198.

Passel, J., Capps, R. and Fix, M. (2004), *Undocumented Immigrants: Facts and Figures.* The Urban Institute, Washington, DC.

Pendakur, K. and Pendakur R. (2002), "Language knowledge as human capital and ethnicity", International Migration Review, Vol. 36(1).

Pitkänen, P., Kalekin-Fishman and Verma, G. K. (2002), *Education and Immigration. Settlement Policies and Current Challenges*, Routledge Falmer, London.

Portes, A. and Hao, L. (1998), "E pluribus unum: Bilingualism and loss of language in the second generation", *Sociology of Education,* Vol. 71, pp. 269-94.

Portes, A. and Hao, L. (2004). "The Schooling of Children of Immigrants: Contextual Effects on the Educational Attainment of the Second Generation." *Proceeding of National Academy of Science* Vol. 101(33) pp. 11920-27.

Portes, A. and Rumbaut, R. (2001), *Legacies. The Story of the Second Generation*, University of California Press, Berkeley, CA.

Power, C., Manor, O. and Fox, J. (1991), *Health and Class: The Early Years*, Chapman and Hall, London.

Pulkkinen, L. and Tremblay, R. E. (1992), "Adult life-styles and their precursors in the social behaviour of children and adolescents", *European Journal of Personality,* Vol. 4(3), pp. 237-251.

Ramirez, O. M. and Dockweiler, C. J. (1987), "Mathematics anxiety: A systematic review, in R. Schwarzer and H. M. van der Ploeg and C. D. Spielberger (eds.), *Advances in Test Anxiety Research,* Vol. 5, pp. 157-175, Swets North America, Berwyn, PA.

Reich, H. H., *et al.* (2002), *Spracherwerb zweisprachig aufwachsender Kinder und Jugendlicher: Ein Überblick über den Stand der nationalen und internationalen Forschung*, Behörde für Bildung und Sport, Amt für Schule (BSJB), Hamburg.

Rivera-Batiz, F. L. (1999), "Undocumented workers in the labor market: An analysis of the earnings of legal and illegal Mexican immigrants in the United States", *Journal of Population Economics,* Vol. 12(1), pp. 91-116.

Robinson, W. S. (1950), "Ecological correlations and the behavior of individuals", *American Sociological Review,* Vol. 15(3), pp. 351-357.

Rodgers, B. (1990), "Behavior and personality in childhood as predictors of adult psychiatric disorder", *Journal of Child Psychology and Psychiatry,* Vol. 31(3), pp. 393-414.

Rossell, C. H. and Baker, K. (1996), "The educational effectiveness of bilingual education", *Research in the Teaching of English,* Vol. 30, pp. 7-74.

Rüesch, P. (1998), *Spielt die Schule eine Rolle? Schulische Bedingungen ungleicher Bildungschancen von Immigrantenkindern. Eine Mehrebenenanalyse*, Lang, Bern.

Rumbaut, R. (1995), "The new Californians: Comparative research findings on the educational progress of immigrant children", in R. Rumbaut and W. Cornelius (eds.), *California's Immigrant Children* (pp. 17-69), Center for U.S.-Mexican Studies, La Jolla, CA.

Rumberger, R. W. (1995), "Dropping out of middle school: A multi-level analysis of students and schools", *American Educational Research Journal,* Vol. 32(3), pp. 583-625.

Schmid, C. L. (2001), "Educational achievement, language-minority students, and the new second generation", *Sociology of Education (Extra Issue)*, pp. 71-87.

Schneider, W. (1996), "Zum Zusammenhang zwischen Metakognition und Motivation bei Lern- und Gedächtnisvorgängen", in C. Spiel, U. Kastner-Koller and P. Deimann (eds.), *Motivation und Lernen aus der Perspektive lebenslanger Entwicklung,* pp. 121-133, Waxmann, Münster.

Schnepf, S. V. (2005), "How different are immigrants? A cross-country and cross-survey analysis of educational achievement", in C. Parsons and T. Smeeding (eds.), *Immigration and the Transformation of Europe,* Cambridge University Press, Cambridge, UK.

Schümer, G. (2004), "Zur doppelten Benachteiligung von Schülern aus unterpriveligierten Gesellschaftsschichten im deutschen Schulwesen", in G. Schümer, K. J. Tillmann and M. Weiß (eds.), *Die Institution Schule und die Lebenswelt der Schüler: Vertiefende Analysen der PISA-2000-Daten zum Kontext von Schülerleistungen,* pp. 73-114, VS Verlag für Sozialwissenschaften, Wiesbaden.

Schwarzer, R., Seipp, B. and Schwarzer, C. (1989), "Mathematics performance and anxiety: A meta-analysis", in R. Schwarzer, H. M. van der Ploeg and C. D. Spielberger (eds.), *Advances in Test Anxiety Research,* Vol. 6, pp. 105-119, Swets North America, Berwyn, PA.

Schwippert, K., Bos, W. and Lankes, E. M. (2003), "Heterogenität und Chancengleicheit am Ende der vierten Jahrgangsstufe im internationalen Vergleich", in W. Bos *et al.* (eds.), *Erste Ergebnisse aus IGLU* pp. 265-302, Waxmann, Münster.

Shajek, A., Lüdtke, O. and Stanat, P. (2006), "Akademische Selbstkonzepte bei Jugendlichen mit Migrationshintergrund", *Unterrichtswissenschaft,* forthcoming.

Shavit, Y. and Blossfeld, H.-P. (1993), *Persistent inequality: Changing educational stratification in thirteen countries,* Boulder.

Skeldon, R. (1997), *Migration and Development: A Global Perspective,* Longman, London.

Skolverket (2005), *Reading literacy and students with a foreign background: Further analyses from the PISA 2000 results,* English summary of report p. 227, Skolverket, Stockholm.

Slavin, R. E. and Cheung, A. (2003), *Effective reading programs for English language learners. A best-evidence synthesis,* Johns Hopkins University, Baltimore.

Stanat, P. (2004), "The role of migration background for student performance: An international comparison", paper presented at the Annual Meeting of the American Educational Research Association (AERA), San Diego, USA.

Stanat, P. (2006), "Schulleistungen von Jugendlichen mit Migrationshintergrund: Die Rolle der Zusammensetzung der Schülerschaft", in J. Baumert, P. Stanat and R. Watermann (eds), *Herkunftsbedingte Disparitäten im Bildungswesen: Differenzielle Bildungsprozesse und Probleme der Verteilungsgerechtigkeit,* VS Verlag für Sozialwissenschaften, Wiesbaden.

Steinberg, L. (1996), *Beyond the classroom: Why school reform has failed and what parents need to do,* Simon and Shuster, New York, NY.

Stevenson, H. W., Chen, C. and Lee, S.-Y. (1993), "Mathematics achievement of Chinese, Japanese, and American children: Ten years later", *Science,* Vol. 259(1), pp. 53-58.

References

Stevenson, H. W. and Stigler, J. (1992), *The Learning Gap: Why our schools are failing and what we can learn from Japanese and Chinese education*, Summit Books, New York, NY.

Suárez-Orozco, M. M. (2001), "Globalization, immigration, and education: The research agenda", *Harvard Educational Review*, Vol. 71(3), pp. 345-365.

Suárez-Orozco, M. M. and Suárez-Orozco, C. (1995), *Transformations: Migration, Family Life, and Achievement Motivation Among Latino Adolescents*, Stanford University Press, Stanford, CA.

Warm, T.A. (1985), "Weighted maximum likelihood estimation of ability in Item Response Theory with tests of finite length", *Technical Report CGI-TR-85-08,* U.S. Coast Guard Institute, Oklahoma City.

Waters, M. (1999), *Black Identities: West Indian Immigrant Dreams and American Realities*, Harvard University Press, Cambridge, MA.

Westerbeek, K. (1999), *The colours of my classroom. A study into the effects of the ethnic composition of classrooms on the achievement of pupils from different ethnic backgrounds,* European University Institute, Florence.

Wigfield, A., Eccles, J. S. and Rodriguez, D. (1998), "The development of children's motivation in school contexts", *Review of Research in Education*, Vol. 23, pp. 73-118.

Wigfield, A., and Meece, J. L. (1988), "Math anxiety in elementary and secondary students", *Journal of Educational Psychology*, Vol. 80, pp. 210-216.

Willig, A. C. (1985), "A meta-analysis of selected studies on the effectiveness of bilingual education", *Review of Educational Research,* Vol. 55, pp. 269-317.

Yeung, A. S. and McInerney, D. M. (1999, February), "Students' perceived support from teachers: Impacts on academic achievement, interest in schoolwork, attendance, and self-esteem", paper presented at the International Conference on Teacher Education at the Hong Kong Institute of Education, Hong Kong, China.

Yoshikawa, H. (1994), "Prevention as cumulative protection: Effects of early family support and education on chronic delinquency and risks", *Psychological Bulletin,* Vol. 115(1), pp. 28-54.

Zimmerman, B. J. (1999), "Commentary: Toward a cyclically interactive view of self-regulated learning", *International Journal of Educational Research,* Vol. 31(6), pp. 545-551.

Zimmerman, B. J. (2000), "Self-efficacy: An essential motive to learn", *Contemporary Educational Psychology,* Vol. 25, pp. 82-91.

Annex **A**

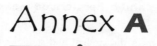

TECHNICAL NOTES

Annex A1:   Technical Background

Annex A2:   Summary descriptions of the five levels of reading proficiency.

Annex A1. Construction of indices and other derived measures from the student and school context questionnaires

This section explains the indices derived from the student and school context questionnaires that are used in this report.

Several of PISA's measures reflect indices that summarise responses from students or school representatives (typically principals) to a series of related questions. The questions were selected from larger constructs on the basis of theoretical considerations and previous research. Structural equation modelling was used to confirm the theoretically expected behaviour of the indices and to validate their comparability across countries. For this purpose, a model was estimated separately for each country and collectively for all OECD countries.

For a detailed description of other PISA indices and details on the methods see the *PISA 2000 Technical Report* (OECD, 2002) or the *PISA 2003 Technical Report* (OECD 2005b).

Unless otherwise indicated, where an index involves multiple questions and student responses, the index was scaled using a weighted maximum likelihood estimate (WLE) (see Warm, 1985), using a one-parameter item response model, which in the case of items with more than two categories was the Partial Credit Model. The scaling was done in three stages:

- The item parameters were estimated from equal-sized sub-samples of students from each OECD country.

- The estimates were computed for all students and all schools by anchoring the item parameters obtained in the preceding step.

- The indices were then standardised so that the mean of the index value for the OECD student population was zero and the standard deviation was one (countries being given equal weight in the standardisation process).

To illustrate the meaning of the international scores on the index, item maps were constructed that relate the index value to typical student responses to the questions asked. These item maps can be found on the website *www.pisa.oecd.org*. The vertical lines on the maps indicate for each of the index scores at the top of the figure which response a student is most likely to give, with zero representing the average student response across OECD countries.

It is important to note that negative values for an index do not necessarily imply that students responded negatively to the underlying questions. A negative value merely indicates that a group of students (or all students, collectively, in a single country) or principals responded less positively than all students or principals did on average across OECD countries. Likewise, a positive value on an index indicates that a group of students or principals responded more favourably, or more positively, than students or principals did, on average, in OECD countries.

Terms enclosed in brackets < > in the following descriptions were replaced in the national versions of the student and school questionnaires by the appropriate national equivalent. For example, the term <qualification at ISCED level 5A> was translated in the United States into "Bachelor's degree, post-graduate certificate program, Master's degree program or first professional degree program". Similarly the term <classes in the language of assessment> in Luxembourg was translated into "German classes" or "French classes" depending on whether students received the German or French version of the assessment instruments.

For additional information on how these indices were constructed, see the *PISA 2000 Technical Report* (OECD, 2002) or the *PISA 2003 Technical Report* (OECD, 2005b).

© OECD 2006 *Where immigrant students succeed - A comparative review of performance and engagement in PISA 2003*

Student level variables

Student background

Family structure

Students were asked to report who usually lived at home with them. The response categories were then grouped into four categories: *i) single-parent family* (students who reported living with one of the following: mother, father, female guardian or male guardian); *ii) nuclear family* (students who reported living with a mother and a father); *iii) mixed family* (students who reported living with a mother and a guardian, a father and a guardian, or two guardians); and *iv) other response combinations*. Non responses are maintained as missing.

Parental occupations

Students were asked to report their mothers' and fathers' occupations, and to state whether each parent was in full-time paid work; part-time paid work; not working but looking for a paid job; or "other". The open-ended responses for occupations were then coded in accordance with the International Standard Classification of Occupations (ISCO 1988).

The PISA *international socio-economic index of occupational status* (ISEI) was derived from students' responses on parental occupation. The index captured the attributes of occupations that convert parents' education into income. The index was derived by the optimal scaling of occupation groups to maximise the indirect effect of education on income through occupation and to minimise the direct effect of education on income, net of occupation (both effects being net of age). For more information on the methodology, see Ganzeboom *et al.* (1992). The *highest international socio-economic index of occupational status* (HISEI) corresponds to the highest ISEI of either the father or the mother.

Index of economic, social and cultural status

The index of economic, social and cultural status was created to capture wider aspects of a student's family and home background in addition to occupational status and is a variation of the index used in PISA 2000. It was derived from the following variables: i) the highest international socio-economic index of occupational status of the father or mother; ii) the highest level of education of the father or mother converted into years of schooling (for the conversion of levels of education into years of schooling see Table A1.1); and iii) the number of books at home as well as access to home educational and cultural resources, obtained by asking students whether they had at their home: a desk to study at, a room of their own, a quiet place to study, a computer they can use for school work, educational software, a link to the Internet, their own calculator, classic literature, books of poetry, works of art (*e.g.* paintings), books to help with their school work, and a dictionary. The rationale for the choice of these variables was that socio-economic status is usually seen as being determined by occupational status, education and wealth. As no direct measure on parental wealth was available from PISA, access to relevant household items was used as a proxy. The student scores on the index are factor scores derived from a Principal Component Analysis which are standardised to have an OECD mean of zero and a standard deviation of one.

The Principal Component Analysis was also performed for each participating country to determine to what extent the components of the index operate in similar ways across countries. The analysis revealed that patterns of factor loadings were very similar across countries, with all three components contributing to a similar extent to the index. For the occupational component, the average factor loading was 0.81, ranging from 0.72 to 0.86 across countries. For the educational component, the average factor loading was 0.80, ranging from 0.70 to 0.87 across countries. For the wealth component, the average factor loading was 0.76, ranging from 0.65 to 0.80 across countries. The reliability of the index ranged from 0.56 to 0.77. These results support the cross-national validity of the index of economic, social and cultural status.

The correlation between the average value on the index and the Gross Domestic Product of countries is 0.62 (increasing to 0.69 when Luxembourg is removed).

The index used in PISA 2000 (OECD, 2001b) was similar to the one used for PISA 2003. However, some adjustments were made. First of all, only 11 questions on home educational resources were common to both surveys. Second, for the question on parental levels of education no distinction had been made in PISA 2000 between university-level and non-university tertiary education. Where comparisons between 2000 and 2003 data are made, the index for PISA 2000 was recomputed on the basis of a common methodology used for both assessments. Results may therefore differ slightly from those reported in PISA 2000. This being said, the correlation between the PISA 2000 and PISA 2003 indices is very high (R of 0.96). This shows that different methods of computation of the indices did not have a major impact on the results. For more information on this index see the *PISA 2003 Technical Report* (OECD, 2005b).

Table A1.1

Levels of parental education converted into years of schooling

	Did not go to school	Completed ISCED Level 1 (primary education)	Completed ISCED Level 2 (lower secondary education)	Completed ISCED Levels 3B or 3C (upper secondary education providing direct access to the labour market or to ISCED 5B programmes)	Completed ISCED Level 3A (upper secondary education providing access to ISCED 5A and 5B programmes)	Completed ISCED Level 5A (university level tertiary education)	Completed ISCED Level 5B (non-university tertiary education)
Australia	0.0	6.5	10.0	11.0	12.0	15.0	14.0
Austria	0.0	4.0	8.0	9.0	13.0	17.0	15.0
Belgium	0.0	6.0	8.0	12.0	12.0	16.0	15.0
Canada	0.0	6.0	9.0	12.0	12.0	17.0	15.0
Denmark	0.0	6.0	9.0	12.0	12.0	15.0	14.0
France	0.0	5.0	9.0	11.0	12.0	14.0	14.0
Germany	0.0	4.0	10.0	11.0	12.0	17.0	15.0
Luxembourg	0.0	6.0	9.0	12.0	13.0	17.0	17.0
Netherlands	0.0	6.0	8.0	12.0	13.0	15.0	13.0
New Zealand	0.0	6.0	10.0	12.0	13.0	16.0	16.0
Norway	0.0	7.0	10.0	13.0	13.0	16.0	14.0
Sweden	0.0	6.0	9.0	12.0	12.0	15.0	13.5
Switzerland	0.0	6.0	9.0	11.0	12.0	15.0	14.0
United States	0.0	6.0	9.0	a	12.0	15.0	14.0
Hong Kong-China	0.0	6.0	9.0	11.0	13.0	17.0	16.0
Russian Federation	0.0	4.0	9.0	11.0	11.0	15.0	13.0

OECD countries (Australia through Switzerland) / *Partner countries* (United States through Russian Federation)

Educational level of parents

Parental education is a family background variable that is often used in the analysis of educational outcomes. Indices were constructed using information on the *educational level of the father*, the *educational level of the mother*, and the highest level of education between the two parents, referred to as the *highest educational level of parents*. Students were asked to identify the highest level of education of their mother and father on the basis of national qualifications, which were then coded in accordance with the International Standard Classification of Education (ISCED 1997, see OECD, 1999) in order to obtain internationally comparable categories of educational attainment. The resulting categories were: (0) for no education; (1) for the completion of <ISCED Level 1> (primary education); (2) for completion of <ISCED Level 2> (lower secondary education); (3) for the completion of <ISCED Level 3B or 3C> (vocational/pre-vocational upper secondary education, aimed in most countries at providing direct entry into the labour market); (4) for completion of <ISCED Level 3A> (upper secondary education, aimed in most countries at gaining entry into tertiary-type A (university level) education) and/or <ISCED Level 4> (non-tertiary post-secondary); (5) for qualifications in <ISCED 5B> (vocational tertiary); and (6) for completion of<ISCED Level 5A, 6> (tertiary-type A and advanced research programmes).

As noted above, the highest level of educational attainment of the parents was also converted into *years of schooling* using the conversion coefficients shown in **Table A1.1**.

Immigration background

The index on **immigrant background** was derived from students' responses to questions about whether or not their mother and their father were born in the country of assessment or in another country. The response categories were then grouped into three categories: i) "native" students (those students born in the country of assessment or who had at least one parent born in that country); ii) "second-generation" students (those born in the country of assessment but whose parents were born in another country); and iii) "first-generation" students (those born outside the country of assessment and whose parents were also born in another country). For some comparisons, first-generation and second-generation students were grouped together.

Language used at home

Students were asked if the language spoken at home most of the time or always was the language of assessment, another official national language, other national dialect or language, or another language. The index on **language spoken at home** distinguishes between students who report using the language of assessment, another official national language, a national dialect or another national language always or most of the time at home and those who report using another language always or most of the time at home.

In most countries, the languages were individually identified and were coded internationally to allow for further research and analysis in this area.

School climate (students' views)

Attitudes towards school

The PISA index of **attitudes towards school** was derived from students' reported agreement with the following statements: i) school has done little to prepare me for adult life when I leave school; ii) school has been a waste of time; iii) school helped give me confidence to make decisions; and iv) school has taught me things which could be useful in a job. A four-point scale with the response categories "strongly agree" (=1), "agree" (=2), "disagree" (=3) and "strongly disagree" (=4) was used. As items iii) and iv) were inverted for scaling, positive values on this index indicate positive attitudes towards school. Scale construction was done using IRT scaling.

Sense of belonging at school

The PISA index of **sense of belonging at school** was derived from students' reported agreement that school is a place where: i) I feel like an outsider (or left out of things); ii) I make friends easily; iii) I feel like I belong; iv) I feel awkward and out of place; v) other students seem to like me; and vi) I feel lonely. A four-point scale with the response categories "strongly agree", "agree", "disagree" and "strongly disagree" was used. Items ii), iii), and v) are inverted for scaling and positive values indicate positive feelings about the students' school. This index was constructed using IRT scaling.

Self-related cognitions in mathematics

Interest in and enjoyment of mathematics

The PISA index of **interest in and enjoyment of mathematics** was derived from students' reported agreement with the following statements: i) I enjoy reading about mathematics; ii) I look forward to my mathematics lessons; iii) I do mathematics because I enjoy it; and iv) I am interested in the things I learn in mathematics. A four-point scale with the response categories "strongly agree", "agree", "disagree" and "strongly disagree" was used. All items were inverted for IRT scaling and positive values on this index indicate higher levels of interest in and enjoyment of mathematics. This index was constructed using IRT scaling.

Instrumental motivation in mathematics

The PISA index of **instrumental motivation in mathematics** was derived from students' reported agreement with the following statements: i) making an effort in mathematics is worth it because it will help me in the work that I want to do later on; ii) learning mathematics is important because it will help me with the subjects that I want to study further on in school; iii) mathematics is an important subject for me because I need it for what I want to study later on; and iv) I will learn many things in mathematics that will help me get a job. A four-point scale with the response categories "strongly agree", "agree", "disagree" and "strongly disagree" was used. All items were inverted for scaling and positive values on this index indicate higher levels of instrumental motivation to learn mathematics. This index was constructed using IRT scaling.

Self-efficacy in mathematics

The PISA index of *self-efficacy in mathematics* was derived from students' reported level of confidence with the following calculations: *i)* using a <train timetable>, how long it would take to get from Zedville to Zedtown; *ii)* calculating how much cheaper a TV would be after a 30 per cent discount; *iii)* calculating how many square metres of tiles you need to cover a floor; *iv)* understanding graphs presented in newspapers; solving an equation like $3x + 5 = 17$; *v)* finding the actual distance between two places on a map with a 1:10,000 scale; *vi)* solving an equation like $2(x+3) = (x + 3)(x - 3)$; and *vii)* calculating the petrol consumption rate of a car. A four-point scale with the response categories "very confident", "confident", "not very confident", "not at all confident" was used. All items were inverted for scaling and positive values on this index indicate higher levels of self-efficacy in mathematics. This index was constructed using IRT scaling.

Anxiety in mathematics

The PISA index of *anxiety in mathematics* was derived from students' reported agreement with the following statements: *i)* I often worry that it will be difficult for me in mathematics classes; *ii)* I get very tense when I have to do mathematics homework; *iii)* I get very nervous doing mathematics problems; *iv)* I feel helpless when doing a mathematics problem; and *v)* I worry that I will get poor <marks> in mathematics. A four-point scale with the response categories "strongly agree", "agree", "disagree" and "strongly disagree" was used. All items were inverted for scaling and positive values on this index indicate higher levels of mathematics anxiety. This index was constructed using IRT scaling.

Self-concept in mathematics

The PISA index of self-concept in mathematics was derived from students' level of agreement with the following statements: *i)* I am just not good at mathematics; *ii)* I get good <marks> in mathematics; *iii)* I learn mathematics quickly; *iv)* I have always believed that mathematics is one of my best subjects; and *v)* in my mathematics class, I understand even the most difficult work. A four-point scale with the response categories "strongly agree", "agree", "disagree" and "strongly disagree" was used. Items *ii)*, *iii)*, *iv)*, and *v)* were inverted for scaling and positive values on this index indicate a positive self-concept in mathematics. This index was constructed using IRT scaling.

Expected educational level

In PISA 2003 students were asked about their educational aspirations. Educational levels were classified according to International Standard Classification of Education (OECD, 1999).

An index on the *expected educational level* was developed with the following categories: *i)* did not go to school; *ii)* completed ISCED Level 1 (primary education); *iii)* completed ISCED Level 2 (lower secondary education); *iv)* completed ISCED Levels 3B or 3C (upper secondary education providing direct access to the labour market or to ISCED 5B programmes); *v)* completed ISCED Level 3A (upper secondary education providing access to ISCED 5A and 5B programmes); *vi)* completed ISCED Level 5A (university level tertiary education); and *vii)* completed ISCED Level 5B (non-university level education).

Classroom climate

Teacher support

The PISA index of *teacher support* was derived from students' reports on the frequency with which: *i)* the teacher shows an interest in every student's learning; *ii)* the teacher gives extra help when students need it; *iii)* the teacher helps students with their learning; *iv)* the teacher continues teaching until the students understand; and *v)* the teacher gives students an opportunity to express opinions. A four-point scale with the response categories "every lesson", "most lessons", "some lessons' and "never or hardly ever" was used. All items were inverted for scaling and positive values on this PISA 2003 index indicate perceptions of higher levels of teacher support. This index was constructed using IRT scaling.

Disciplinary climate

The PISA index of *disciplinary climate* was derived from students' reports on the frequency with which, in their mathematics lessons: *i)* students don't listen to what the teacher says; *ii)* there is noise and disorder; *iii)* the teacher has to wait a long time for students to <quieten down>; *iv)* students cannot work well; and *v)* students don't start working for a long time after the lesson begins. A four-point scale with the response categories "every lesson", "most lessons", "some lessons", and "never or hardly ever" was used. Positive values on this PISA 2000/2003 index indicate perceptions of a more positive disciplinary climate whereas low values indicate a more negative disciplinary climate. This index was constructed using IRT scaling.

School level variables

Indicators of school resources

Quantity of teaching staff at school

School principals reported the number of full-time and part-time teachers in total, of full-time and part-time teachers fully certified by <the appropriate authority>, of full-time and part-time teachers with an <ISCED 5A> qualification in <pedagogy>. From this an index of *total student-teacher* ratio is obtained by dividing the school size by the total number of teachers. The number of part-time teachers contributes 0.5 and the number of full-time teachers contributes 1.0 to the total number of teachers.

School resources

Quality of the school's physical infrastructure

The PISA index of the *quality of the school's physical infrastructure* was derived from three items measuring the school principals' perceptions of potential factors hindering instruction at school: *i)* school buildings and grounds; *ii)* heating/cooling and lighting systems; and *iii)* instructional space (*e.g.* classrooms). A four-point scale with the response categories "not at all", "very little", "to some extent", and "a lot" was used. All items were inverted for scaling and positive values indicate positive evaluations of this aspect. This index was constructed using IRT scaling.

Quality of the school's educational resources

The PISA index of the *quality of the school's educational resources* was derived from seven items measuring the school principals' perceptions of potential factors hindering instruction at school: *i)* instructional materials (*e.g.* textbooks); *ii)* computers for instruction; *iii)* computer software for instruction; *iv)* calculators for instruction; *v)* library materials; *vi)* audio-visual resources; and *vii)* science laboratory equipment and materials. A four-point scale with the response categories "not at all", "very little", "to some extent", and "a lot" was used. All items were inverted for scaling and positive values indicate positive evaluations of this aspect. This index was constructed using IRT scaling.

Teacher shortage

The PISA index on *teacher shortage* was derived from items measuring the school principal's perceptions of potential factors hindering instruction at school. These factors are a shortage or inadequacy of: *i)* qualified mathematics teachers; *ii)* qualified science teachers; *iii)* qualified <test language> teachers; *iv)* qualified foreign language teachers; and *v)* experienced teachers. For PISA 2003 these items were administered together with the items on the quality of physical environment and educational resources. A four-point scale with the response categories "not at all", "very little", "to some extent" and "a lot" is used. The items were not inverted for scaling and positive values indicate school principal's reports of teacher shortage at a school. This index was constructed using IRT scaling.

School climate (school principals' views)

School principals' perceptions of teacher morale and commitment

The PISA index of *teacher morale and commitment* was derived from items measuring the school principals' perceptions of teachers with the following statements: *i)* the morale of teachers in this school is high; *ii)* teachers work with enthusiasm; *iii)* teachers take pride in this school; and *iv)* teachers value academic achievement. A four-point scale with the response categories "strongly agree", "agree", "disagree" and "strongly disagree" was used. All items were inverted for scaling and the categories "disagree" and "strongly disagree" were combined into one category. Positive values indicate principals' reports of higher levels of teacher morale and commitment. This index was constructed using IRT scaling.

School principals' perceptions of teacher-related factors affecting school climate

The index of *teacher-related factors affecting school climate* was derived from items measuring the school principals' reports of potential factors hindering the learning of students at school with the following statements: *i)* teachers' low expectations of students; *ii)* poor student-teacher relations; *iii)* teachers not meeting individual students' needs; *iv)*

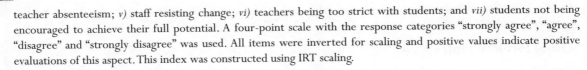

teacher absenteeism; *v)* staff resisting change; *vi)* teachers being too strict with students; and *vii)* students not being encouraged to achieve their full potential. A four-point scale with the response categories "strongly agree", "agree", "disagree" and "strongly disagree" was used. All items were inverted for scaling and positive values indicate positive evaluations of this aspect. This index was constructed using IRT scaling.

School principals' perceptions of student-related factors affecting school climate

The index of *student-related factors affecting school climate* was derived from items measuring the school principals' perceptions of potential factors hindering the learning of students at school with the following statements: *i)* student absenteeism; *ii)* disruption of classes by students; *iii)* students skipping classes; *iv)* students lacking respect for teachers; *v)* students' use of alcohol or illegal drugs; and *vi)* students intimidating or bullying other students. A four-point scale with the response categories "strongly agree", "agree", "disagree" and "strongly disagree" was used. All items were inverted for Iscaling and positive values indicate positive evaluations of this aspect. This index was constructed using IRT scaling.

ANNEX A2. Summary descriptions of the five levels of reading proficiency

Figure A2.1 ■ Combined Reading Literacy Scale

Level	Distinguishing features of tasks at each level:
Level 5	The reader must: sequence or combine several pieces of deeply embedded information, possibly drawing on information from outside the main body of the text; construe the meaning of linguistic nuances in a section of text; or make evaluative judgements or hypotheses, drawing on specialised knowledge. The reader is generally required to demonstrate a full, detailed understanding of a dense, complex or unfamiliar text, in content or form, or one that involves concepts that are contrary to expectations. The reader will often have to make inferences to determine which information in the text is relevant, and to deal with prominent or extensive competing information.
Level 4	The reader must: locate, sequence or combine several pieces of embedded information; infer the meaning of a section of text by considering the text as a whole; understand and apply categories in an unfamiliar context; or hypothesise about or critically evaluate a text, using formal or public knowledge. The reader must draw on an accurate understanding of long or complex texts in which competing information may take the form of ideas that are ambiguous, contrary to expectation, or negatively worded.
Level 3	The reader must: recognise the links between pieces of information that have to meet multiple criteria; integrate several parts of a text to identify a main idea, understand a relationship or construe the meaning of a word or phrase; make connections and comparisons; or explain or evaluate a textual feature. The reader must take into account many features when comparing, contrasting or categorising. Often the required information is not prominent but implicit in the text or obscured by similar information.
Level 2	The reader must: locate one or more pieces of information that may be needed to meet multiple criteria; identify the main idea, understand relationships or construe meaning within a limited part of the text by making low-level inferences; form or apply simple categories to explain something in a text by drawing on personal experience and attitudes; or make connections or comparisons between the text and everyday outside knowledge. The reader must often deal with competing information.
Level 1	The reader must: locate one or more independent pieces of explicitly stated information according to a single criterion; identify the main theme or author's purpose in a text about a familiar topic; or make a simple connection between information in the text and common, everyday knowledge. Typically, the requisite information is prominent and there is little, if any, competing information. The reader is explicitly directed to consider relevant factors in the task and in the text.
Below Level 1	There is insufficient information to describe features of tasks at this level.

Scale values: 625.6, 552.9, 480.2, 407.5, 334.8

Annex B

DATA TABLES FOR CHAPTERS 1, 2, 3 AND 4

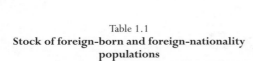

Table 1.1
Stock of foreign-born and foreign-nationality populations

	Percentage of total population that:	
	Is foreign-born	Has foreign nationality
Australia	23.0	7.4
Austria	12.5	8.8
Belgium	10.7	8.2
Canada	19.3	5.3
Denmark	6.8	5.0
France	10.0	5.6
Germany	12.5	8.9
Luxembourg	32.6	36.9
Netherlands	10.1	4.2
New Zealand	19.5	m
Norway	7.3	4.3
Sweden	12.0	5.3
Switzerland	22.4	20.5
United States	12.3	6.6

Source: Census data except for foreign nationality data for Germany (register of foreigners, 2002) and the United Kingdom (Labour force survey).

Table 1.2
Distribution of permanent or long-term immigration flows into selected OECD countries in 2002, by main immigration categories[1]

	Percentage of permanent or long-term immigration flows in immigration category:		
	Workers	Family reunification	Refugees
Australia[2]	54.5	35.3	10.2
Canada	25.8	63.1	11.1
Denmark	23.0	57.5	19.4
France[3]	16.2	75.1	8.7
Norway[4]	8.2	68.4	23.3
Sweden[5]	1.3	57.7	41.0
Switzerland	45.4	52.4	2.2
United States[6]	18.0	69.1	12.9

1. For Australia, Canada, Norway, Sweden and the United States, data concern acceptances for settlement. For Denmark, France and Switzerland, entries correspond to residence permits usually delivered for longer than one year. For Australia, category "Workers" includes accompanying dependents who are included in the category "Family reunification" for all other countries.
2. Data refer to fiscal year (July 2001 to June 2002). Category "Workers" includes accompanying dependents. Citizens from New Zealand do not need a visa to enter the country. They are therefore excluded.
3. Entries of EU family members are estimated. Visitors are excluded. Among those who benefited from the regularisation programme, only those who received a permit under the family reunification procedure are counted. The "Family" category also includes spouses of French citizens and scientists, parents of French children and those with family relationships who received the permit "*vie privée et familiale*".
4. Category "Workers" includes specialists and other permits that constitute grounds for permanent residence in Norway. Non-renewable permits are not included. Category "Refugees" includes refugees and individuals granted residence permits on humanitarian grounds on a permanent basis.
5. Excluding Nordic and EEA citizens.
6. Data refer to fiscal year (October 2001 to September 2002). Immigrants who obtained a permanent residence permit following the 1986 Immigration Reform and Control Act (IRCA) are excluded.
Sources: National Statistical Offices, OECD calculations.

Table 1.3
Distribution of native- and foreign-born populations (aged 15 years and older) by level of education in selected OECD countries (circa 2000)

	Below upper secondary education (ISCED 0/1/2)		Upper secondary and post-secondary non-tertiary education (ISCED 3/4)		Tertiary education (ISCED 5A/5B/6)	
	Native-born population	Foreign-born population	Native-born population	Foreign-born population	Native-born population	Foreign-born population
Australia	45,8	38,3	15,7	18,8	38,6	42,9
Austria	33,4	49,4	55,7	39,3	10,9	11,3
Belgium	46,8	54,2	30,3	24,2	22,9	21,6
Canada	31,6	30,1	36,9	31,9	31,5	38,0
Denmark	41,0	48,6	40,2	31,9	18,8	19,5
France	45,8	54,8	37,4	27,2	16,9	18,1
Germany	23,6	43,4	57,0	41,0	19,4	15,7
Luxembourg	28,7	36,7	58,6	41,6	12,8	21,7
Netherlands	40,7	53,0	39,8	29,4	19,5	17,6
New Zealand	30,1	18,7	42,7	50,4	27,2	31,0
Norway	21,2	18,3	55,6	50,6	23,2	31,1
Sweden	25,0	29,6	52,2	46,2	22,8	24,2
Switzerland	25,6	41,6	56,3	34,7	18,1	23,7
United States	21,9	39,8	51,2	34,3	26,9	25,9

Note: Data are from the 2000 round of censuses.
Source: OECD (2005), *Trends in International Migration* (SOPEMI 2004), OECD, Paris.

Table 1.4
Unemployment rates among national and foreign-nationality or native-born and foreign-born individuals in selected OECD countries[1]

	Unemployment rate (%) by immigrant background															
	National				Foreign-nationality				Native-born				Foreign-born			
	1993	1995	2000	2003	1993	1995	2000	2003	1993	1995	2000	2003	1993	1995	2000	2003
Australia	a	a	a	a	a	a	a	a	10.4	8.1	6.2	6.0	12.9	10.2	6.7	6.5
Austria	m	4.1	4.3	4.4	m	6.8	8.8	8.3	m	4.1	4.3	4.2	m	6.9	8.0	8.3
Belgium	7.1	8.2	5.8	6.9	19.4	23.5	15.6	18.2	7.3	8.4	5.6	6.4	16.0	19.5	15.8	17.8
Canada	a	a	a	a	a	a	a	a	9.2	8.4	5.6	6.0	8.9	10.6	6.8	8.0
Denmark	10.9	7.5	4.0	4.1	30.9	24.2	10.6	9.2	m	7.3	3.9	4.0	m	20.6	9.5	8.7
France	10.8	11.3	9.6	8.5	20.7	21.7	20.9	18.8	10.8	11.2	9.4	8.2	16.4	17.6	16.7	15.8
Germany	7.2	7.5	7.5	9.2	12.5	15.1	12.9	16.7	m	m	7.4	9.1	m	m	12.6	15.7
Luxembourg	2.0	2.5	1.6	2.4	2.9	3.6	3.4	5.2	2.0	2.6	2.0	2.9	2.9	3.4	2.9	4.8
Netherlands	5.8	6.5	2.6	3.4	19.7	23.6	7.2	9.5	5.5	6.0	2.3	2.9	16.2	19.6	6.3	8.9
Norway	m	m	3.4	4.1	m	m	m	10.1	m	m	3.3	3.9	m	m	6.1	9.0
Sweden	m	7.7	5.1	5.3	m	19.7	14.6	13.2	m	7.3	4.7	4.8	m	21.7	11.6	11.1
Switzerland	m	m	1.9	2.9	m	m	5.6	8.8	m	m	m	2.9	m	m	m	8.0
United States	a	a	a	a	a	a	a	a	m	5.8	4.4	6.4	m	8.0	4.9	7.5

1. The categories *national* and *foreign-nationality* are defined on the basis of nationality; the categories *native-born* and *foreign-born* are defined on the basis of country of birth.
Source: OECD (2005), *Trends in International Migration* (SOPEMI 2004), OECD, Paris.

Table 1.5

Number and weighted percentage of participating students in PISA 2003, by immigrant status

	Native students		Second-generation students		First-generation students		Students with missing values on immigrant status variable	
	Number of participating students	Percentage of all participating students	Number of participating students	Percentage of all participating students	Number of participating students	Percentage of all participating students	Number of participating students	Percentage of all participating students
Australia	9 682	75.5	1 342	11.5	1 258	10.8	269	2.2
Austria	3 966	85.7	174	4.1	403	9.1	54	1.2
Belgium	7 584	85.8	486	6.2	497	5.3	229	2.7
Canada	23 481	70.8	1 365	8.2	1 411	9.6	1696	11.4
Denmark	3 891	92.0	137	3.4	126	3.0	64	1.6
France	3 639	84.0	442	10.6	133	3.4	86	2.1
Germany	3 685	77.3	281	6.3	349	7.8	345	8.7
Luxembourg	2 554	64.9	600	15.4	658	16.9	111	2.8
Netherlands	3 434	85.0	265	6.8	147	3.7	146	4.6
New Zealand	3 534	78.5	284	6.4	602	13.0	91	2.1
Norway	3 773	92.9	95	2.2	133	3.3	63	1.6
Sweden	4 048	87.2	241	5.6	271	5.8	64	1.5
Switzerland	6 477	78.9	787	8.8	1 034	10.9	122	1.4
United States	4 523	82.9	442	8.1	319	5.9	172	3.2
Hong Kong-China	2 507	55.6	1 038	22.5	848	20.0	85	2.0
Macao-China	300	23.5	700	57.1	231	17.9	19	1.5
Russian Federation	5 093	85.2	367	6.3	417	6.9	97	1.5
Belgium (Flemish Community)	4 572	90.4	185	3.7	141	2.8	161	3.0
Belgium (French Community)	2 377	79.8	282	9.5	239	8.4	60	2.3

OECD countries / *Partner countries*

Source: OECD PISA 2003 database.

Table 1.6

Average age of first-generation students in PISA 2003 at the time of immigration

	Average age at immigration
Australia	6.8
Austria	5.1
Belgium	7.9
Canada	7.2
Denmark	6.0
France	6.3
Germany	5.7
Luxembourg	5.2
Netherlands	6.1
New Zealand	9.1
Norway	6.1
Sweden	5.2
Switzerland	5.3
United States	6.0
OECD average	*6.1*
Hong Kong-China	8.5
Macao-China	8.2
Russian Federation	5.8
Belgium (Flemish Community)	8.1
Belgium (French Community)	7.8

OECD countries / *Partner countries*

Source: OECD PISA 2003 database.

© OECD 2006 Where immigrant students succeed - A comparative review of performance and engagement in PISA 2003

Table 1.7

Comparison of percentage of immigrant students in PISA 2003 with data on total immigrant populations

| | | Immigrant students in PISA 2003 | | Total immigrant populations[1] | |
		Number of immigrant students	Percentage of immigrant students	Percentage foreign-born	Percentage foreign nationalilty
OECD countries	Australia	2 600	22.2	23.0	7.4
	Austria	577	13.1	12.5	8.8
	Belgium	983	11.5	10.7	8.2
	Canada	2 776	17.8	19.3	5.3
	Denmark	263	6.4	6.8	5.0
	France	575	14.0	10.0	5.6
	Germany	630	14.1	12.5	8.9[2]
	Luxembourg	1 258	32.3	32.6	36.9
	Netherlands	412	10.5	10.1	4.2
	New Zealand	886	19.4	19.5	m
	Norway	228	5.5	7.3	4.3
	Sweden	512	11.4	12.0	5.3
	Switzerland	1 821	19.7	22.4	20.5
	United States	761	14.0	12.3	6.6
Partner countries	Hong Kong-China	1 886	42.4	m	m
	Macao-China	931	75.0	m	m
	Russian Federation	784	13.2	m	m
	Belgium (Flemish Community)	326	6.6	m	m
	Belgium (French Community)	521	17.9	m	m

1. *Source*: OECD (2005), *Trends in International Migration* (SOPEMI 2004), OECD, Paris.
2. Data for Germany from 2002.

Table 1.8

Comparison of the three most frequent countries of origin for immigrant students in PISA 2003 and for total immigrant populations

	Three most frequent countries of origin (mother's country of birth) for immigrant students in PISA 2003	Three most frequent countries of origin for total foreign-born population (SOPEMI)	Immigrant students in PISA 2003		Stock of foreign-born population by country of birth in SOPEMI 2004 (reference year: 2002)[1]	
			Number of immigrant students	Percentage of immigrant students	Number of immigrants (thousands)	Percentage of total immigrant population[2]
OECD countries						
Australia	1. England and Scotland[2]	1. United Kingdom	419	13.9	1 123.9	24.6
	2. New Zealand	2. New Zealand	189	7.0	413.7	9.1
	3. China		130	5.0	164.9	3.6
		3. Italy	68	2.8	235.2	5.2
Austria	1. Former Yugoslavia[2,3]	1. Former Yugoslavia[2,4]	276	47.2	330.4	35.7
	2. Turkey	2. Turkey	141	25.9	127.3	13.7
	3. Romania		19	3.6	39.9	4.3
		3. Germany	m	m	120.9	13.1
Belgium	1. France	2. France	184	16.3	113.0	13.3
	2. Turkey		140	14.8	42.6	5.0
	3. Netherlands	3. Netherlands	54	5.8	96.6	11.4
		1. Italy	m	m	187.0	22.0
Canada		1. United Kingdom	m	m	606.0	11.1
	m	2. China	m	m	332.8	6.1
		3. Italy	m	m	315.5	5.8
Denmark	1. Turkey	1. Turkey	53	32.1	30.9	9.1
	2. Pakistan		31	11.6	10.7	3.2
	3. Former Yugoslavia	2. Former Yugoslavia[2,5]	23	9.4	30.5	9.0
		3. Germany	m	m	22.5	6.7
France		1. Portugal	m	m	553.7	17.0
	m	2. Morocco	m	m	504.1	15.4
		3. Algeria	m	m	477.5	14.6
Germany	1. Turkey	1. Turkey	197	32.1	1 912.2	26.1
	2. Former Soviet Republic		180	28.3	m	m
	3. Poland		100	16.1	317.6	4.3
	Former Yugoslavia[2,6]	2. Former Yugoslavia[2,7]	45	7.0	986.3	13.4
		3. Italy	27	4.1	609.8	8.3
Luxembourg	1. Portugal	1. Portugal	595	47.3	41.7	28.8
	2. Italy	3. Italy	99	7.9	12.3	8.5
	3. Former Yugoslavia		92	7.3	m	m
		2. France	m	m	18.8	13.0
Netherlands		1. Turkey	m	m	190.5	11.1
	m	2. Suriname	m	m	189.0	11.0
		3. Morocco	m	m	163.4	9.5
New Zealand	1. Samoa	2. Samoa	124	14.6	47.1	6.7
	2. United Kingdom	1. United Kingdom	103	11.2	218.4	31.3
	3. China		76	8.4	38.9	5.6
		3. Australia	18	2.1	56.3	8.1
Norway		1. Sweden	m	m	33.0	9.9
	m	2. Denmark	m	m	22.3	6.7
		3. Pakistan	m	m	14.6	4.4
Sweden		1. Finland	m	m	189.3	17.6
	m	2. Former Yugoslavia[2,8]	m	m	139.0	12.9
		3. Iraq	m	m	67.6	6.3
Switzerland	1. Former Yugoslavia	1. Former Yugoslavia[2,9]	408	23.0	347.3	24.0
	2. Albania/Kosovo		257	16.2	m	m
	3. Italy	2. Italy	245	11.7	308.3	21.3
		3. Portugal	200	8.1	141.1	9.7
United States		1. Mexico	m	m	10 237.2	29.6
	m	2. Philippines	m	m	1 457.5	4.2
		3. India	m	m	1 183.6	3.4
Partner countries						
Hong Kong-China	m	m	m	m	m	m
Macao-China	m	m	m	m	m	m
Russian Federation	m	m	m	m	m	m
Belgium (Flemish Community)	1. Turkey		87	27.6	m	m
	2. Netherlands		54	18.0	m	m
Belgium (French Community)	1. France		113	23.6	m	m
	2. Turkey		49	8.7	m	m

Note: Data for the stock of foreign-born population are by: country of birth in Canada, Luxembourg and New Zealand (2001) and in Australia, Austria, the Netherlands and Norway (2002); place of birth in the United States (2003); and nationality in Belgium (2002), France (1999), Germany (2002) and Switzerland (2003).

1. *Source*: OECD (2005), *Trends in International Migration* (SOPEMI 2004), OECD, Paris.
2. Authors' calculation.
3. Yugoslavia and Slovenia.
4. Bosnia-Herzegovina, Slovenia, Croatia and the former Yugoslavia (other).
5. Refers to persons who immigrated before the dissolution of the former Yugoslavia and persons from Bosnia-Herzegovina.
6. Montenegro, Serbia, Bosnia-Herzegovina, Croatia and Macedonia.
7. Serbia/Montenegro, Bosnia-Herzegovina and Croatia.
8. Serbia/Montenegro and Bosnia-Herzegovina.
9. Serbia/Montenegro, the former Yugoslav Republic of Macedonia, Bosnia-Herzegovina and Croatia.

© OECD 2006 Where immigrant students succeed - A comparative review of performance and engagement in PISA 2003

Table 1.9

Number and weighted percentage of students participating in PISA 2003 who speak a different language at home from the language of instruction

		Students who speak a different language at home from the language of instruction		Students with missing values on the "language spoken at home" variable	
		Number of students	Percentage of students	Number of students	Percentage of students
OECD countries	Australia	968	8.7	299	2.3
	Austria	376	8.7	156	3.3
	Belgium	399	4.2	1009	11.5
	Canada	1 688	10.0	1693	11.2
	Denmark	156	3.8	138	3.4
	France	228	5.9	160	3.9
	Germany	296	6.7	544	13.0
	Luxembourg	920	23.7	212	5.4
	Netherlands	166	4.2	275	7.7
	New Zealand	405	8.9	54	1.2
	Norway	178	4.4	134	3.4
	Sweden	288	6.5	285	6.0
	Switzerland	873	8.8	607	7.6
	United States	480	8.6	207	4.1
Partner countries	Hong Kong-China	183	4.3	150	3.5
	Macao-China	54	4.5	35	2.2
	Russian Federation	289	5.4	77	1.2
	Belgium (Flemish Community)	159	3.1	558	11.0
	Belgium (French Community)	168	5.6	337	12.0

Source: OECD PISA 2003 database.

Table 1.10

Number and weighted percentage of students who speak a different language at home from the language of instruction in PISA 2003, by immigrant status

		Native students		Second-generation students		First-generation students		Immigrant students (first- and second-generation combined)	
		Number of students	Percentage of students	Number of students	Percentage of students	Number of students	Percentage of students	Number of students	Percentage of students
OECD countries	Australia	70	0.7	333	27.5	539	45.1	872	36.1
	Austria	30	0.8	92	63.0	248	74.7	340	71.0
	Belgium	129	1.4	146	40.1	117	32.2	263	36.3
	Canada	318	1.2	414	30.4	892	66.9	1 306	50.2
	Denmark	53	1.4	43	39.6	57	51.0	100	45.0
	France	25	0.8	140	35.7	58	52.7	198	39.6
	Germany	14	0.5	94	44.8	151	49.0	245	47.2
	Luxembourg	38	1.6	352	64.3	511	83.0	863	74.1
	Netherlands	14	0.4	76	31.3	68	56.4	144	40.0
	New Zealand	9	0.2	77	27.6	77	52.8	385	44.4
	Norway	32	0.9	40	50.7	40	83.8	142	71.5
	Sweden	23	0.7	85	42.3	176	77.1	261	59.9
	Switzerland	47	0.5	196	33.8	615	64.0	811	50.9
	United States	53	1.1	195	46.9	210	71.0	405	57.2
Partner countries	Hong Kong-China	103	4.3	30	3.0	43	5.9	73	4.4
	Macao-China	16	6.4	21	3.9	16	4.9	37	4.2
	Russian Federation	219	4.9	17	5.5	43	10.6	60	8.1
	Belgium (Flemish Community)	28	0.7	76	61.6	52	46.9	128	54.2
	Belgium (French Community)	47	2.2	68	30.7	49	25.7	117	28.4

Source: OECD PISA 2003 database.

Table 1.11

Number and weighted percentage of most common languages spoken at home, as reported by immigrant students in PISA 2003

		Test language or other national language		Languages other than the language of instruction								
				First most common language			Second most common language			Third most common language		
	Language[1]	Number of students	Percentage of students	Language[1]	Number of students	Percentage of students	Language[1]	Number of students	Percentage of students	Language[1]	Number of students	Percentage of students
OECD countries												
Australia	English	11258	89.0	Cantonese	87	0.8	Arabic	78	0.8	Vietnamese	71	0.7
	Indigenous Australian language	26	0.1									
Austria	German	4065	88.0	Serbo-Croat	166	3.7	Turkish	104	2.5	Albanian	20	0.4
Belgium	Dutch	3468	40.0	Turkish	98	1.2	Wallon	76	0.3	Arabic	58	0.7
	French	2625	35.9									
	German	482	0.6									
	Flemish dialect	813	8.7									
Canada	English	20951	60.0	Other languages	1688	10.0						
	French	3621	18.9									
Denmark	Danish	3924	92.8	Arabic	26	0.6	Turkish	19	0.5	Serbo-Croatian	12	0.3
France	French	3886	89.7	Other languages	228	5.9						
	Other national dialects or languages	26	0.6									
Germany	German	3820	80.3	Russian	81	1.8	Turkish	71	1.7	Polish	26	0.6
Luxembourg	Luxembourgian	2460	62.4	Portuguese	518	13.3	Italian	89	2.3	Yugoslavian and others	71	2.0
	French	260	6.7									
	German	71	1.8									
Netherlands	Dutch	3173	78.9	Foreign languages	166	4.2						
	Dutch regional languages or dialects	378	9.2									
New Zealand	English	4043	89.6	Samoan	58	1.4	Cantonese	58	1.2	Mandarin	42	0.8
	Te Reo Maori	9	0.2									
Norway	Norwegian	3726	91.7	Other languages	162	4	Swedish	10	0.3	Danish	6	0.1
	Sami	26	0.6									
Sweden	Swedish	4022	86.9	Foreign languages	288	6.8						
	Finnish, Yiddish, Romanian and others	29	0.7									
Switzerland	Swiss German	3995	60.3	Albanian	237	2.4	Portuguese	125	1.1	Turkish	66	0.8
	French	2014	17.9									
	Italian	672	3.5									
	Swiss Italian	170	0.6									
	German	72	0.9									
	Romance	17	0.3									
United States	English	4769	87.3	Spanish	327	5.9						
Hong Kong-China	Cantonese	3961	87.9	Other languages	183	3.8						
	English	25	0.5									
	Oth. nat. dial. or lang.	159	3.8									
Macao-China	Cantonese	1090	87.4	Other languages	53	4.5						
	Portuguese	1	0.0									
	Other national dialects	68	5.8									
Russian Federation	Russian	5608	93.5	Other languages	289	5.3						
Belgium (Flemish Community)	Dutch	3431	38.8	Turkish	70	0.8	Arabic	22	0.2	English	13	0.1
	French	95	1.0									
	German	3	0.0									
	Flemish dialect	813	8.7									
Belgium (French Community)	French	2506	34.9	Arabic	35	0.5	Turkish	28	0.4	Wallon	25	0.3
	Dutch	30	0.2									
	German	15	0.2									

1. Language categories in questionnaire were chosen by participating countries.
Source: OECD PISA 2003 database.

© OECD 2006 Where immigrant students succeed - A comparative review of performance and engagement in PISA 2003

Table 2.1a
Differences in mathematics performance by immigrant status

| | Performance on the mathematics scale | | | | | | Difference in the mathematics score | | | | | |
| | Native students | | Second-generation students | | First-generation students | | Second-generation students minus native students | | First-generation students minus native students | | First-generation students minus second-generation students | |
	Mean score	S.E.	Mean score	S.E.	Mean score	S.E.	Difference	S.E.	Difference	S.E.	Difference	S.E.
OECD countries												
Australia	527	(2.1)	522	(4.7)	525	(4.9)	-5	(4.7)	-2	(4.9)	3	(4.8)
Austria	515	(3.3)	459	(8.8)	452	(6.0)	**-56**	(9.3)	**-63**	(6.0)	-7	(9.5)
Belgium	546	(2.5)	454	(7.5)	437	(10.8)	**-92**	(7.6)	**-109**	(10.9)	-17	(12.4)
Canada	537	(1.6)	543	(4.3)	530	(4.7)	6	(4.4)	-7	(4.8)	**-13**	(5.1)
Denmark	520	(2.5)	449	(11.2)	455	(10.1)	**-70**	(11.1)	**-65**	(9.8)	5	(13.5)
France	520	(2.4)	472	(6.1)	448	(15.0)	**-48**	(6.6)	**-72**	(15.0)	-25	(15.5)
Germany	525	(3.5)	432	(9.1)	454	(7.5)	**-93**	(9.6)	**-71**	(7.9)	22	(11.2)
Luxembourg	507	(1.3)	476	(3.3)	462	(3.7)	**-31**	(3.7)	**-45**	(4.1)	**-14**	(5.6)
Netherlands	551	(3.0)	492	(10.3)	472	(8.4)	**-59**	(11.1)	**-79**	(8.8)	-19	(10.8)
New Zealand	528	(2.6)	496	(8.4)	523	(4.9)	**-32**	(9.1)	-5	(5.6)	27	(8.0)
Norway	499	(2.3)	460	(11.7)	438	(9.3)	**-39**	(11.3)	**-61**	(9.4)	-22	(13.8)
Sweden	517	(2.2)	483	(9.8)	425	(9.6)	**-34**	(9.1)	**-92**	(9.7)	**-58**	(10.9)
Switzerland	543	(3.3)	484	(5.0)	453	(6.1)	**-59**	(4.9)	**-89**	(6.0)	**-31**	(6.4)
United States	490	(2.8)	468	(7.6)	453	(7.5)	**-22**	(7.2)	**-36**	(7.5)	-14	(7.4)
OECD average	*523*	*(0.7)*	*483*	*(2.1)*	*475*	*(1.9)*	*-40*	*(2.0)*	*-48*	*(2.1)*	*-8*	*(2.4)*
Partner countries												
Hong Kong-China	557	(4.5)	570	(4.6)	516	(5.3)	13	(4.3)	-41	(4.5)	-54	(5.2)
Macao-China	528	(5.9)	532	(4.1)	517	(9.2)	4	(7.9)	-11	(10.4)	-15	(10.4)
Russian Federation	472	(4.4)	457	(7.2)	452	(5.9)	-14	(7.2)	-20	(5.4)	-6	(8.3)
Belgium (Flemish Community)	567	(2.9)	445	(10.7)	472	(10.0)	**-122**	(11.3)	**-95**	(9.9)	27	(13.5)
Belgium (French Community)	514	(4.3)	458	(9.6)	419	(14.4)	**-56**	(9.3)	**-94**	(14.4)	**-39**	(15.2)

Note: Differences that are statistically significant are indicated in bold.

Table 2.1b
Differences in reading performance by immigrant status

| | Performance on the reading scale | | | | | | Difference in the reading score | | | | | |
| | Native students | | Second-generation students | | First-generation students | | Second-generation students minus native students | | First-generation students minus native students | | First-generation students minus second-generation students | |
	Mean score	S.E.	Mean score	S.E.	Mean score	S.E.	Difference	S.E.	Difference	S.E.	Difference	S.E.
OECD countries												
Australia	529	(2.2)	525	(4.6)	517	(5.0)	-4	(4.7)	-12	(4.9)	-8	(5.6)
Austria	501	(3.8)	428	(13.5)	425	(8.0)	**-73**	(13.8)	**-77**	(8.5)	-3	(12.9)
Belgium	523	(2.7)	439	(7.5)	407	(11.9)	**-84**	(7.2)	**-117**	(11.9)	-33	(12.8)
Canada	534	(1.6)	543	(4.2)	515	(4.7)	10	(4.2)	-19	(4.8)	**-28**	(4.8)
Denmark	497	(2.7)	440	(13.8)	454	(9.5)	**-57**	(13.8)	**-42**	(9.6)	15	(15.5)
France	505	(2.6)	458	(6.9)	426	(15.3)	**-48**	(7.4)	**-79**	(15.5)	-32	(15.2)
Germany	517	(3.5)	420	(9.9)	431	(8.9)	**-96**	(10.5)	**-86**	(9.0)	10	(12.8)
Luxembourg	500	(1.8)	454	(4.0)	431	(4.4)	**-47**	(4.3)	**-69**	(4.9)	**-22**	(6.3)
Netherlands	524	(2.9)	475	(8.2)	463	(8.1)	**-50**	(8.7)	**-61**	(8.8)	-11	(9.8)
New Zealand	528	(2.9)	506	(8.3)	503	(5.3)	**-22**	(9.0)	-25	(6.1)	**-3**	(8.0)
Norway	505	(2.7)	446	(11.1)	436	(11.5)	**-59**	(11.0)	**-68**	(11.3)	-10	(14.8)
Sweden	522	(2.2)	502	(8.7)	433	(11.3)	**-20**	(8.2)	**-89**	(11.6)	**-69**	(12.2)
Switzerland	515	(3.2)	462	(5.2)	422	(6.3)	**-53**	(5.1)	**-93**	(6.0)	**-40**	(6.7)
United States	503	(3.1)	481	(8.7)	453	(8.3)	**-22**	(8.3)	**-50**	(8.4)	-28	(8.5)
OECD average	*514*	*(0.8)*	*475*	*(2.1)*	*456*	*(2.1)*	*-39*	*(2.1)*	*-58*	*(2.3)*	*-19*	*(2.7)*
Partner countries												
Hong Kong-China	513	(3.7)	522	(3.8)	494	(4.9)	9	(3.5)	-19	(4.1)	-28	(4.8)
Macao-China	499	(5.1)	497	(2.9)	499	(7.1)	-2	(5.7)	0	(9.2)	2	(8.4)
Russian Federation	446	(4.0)	426	(6.9)	413	(7.6)	-20	(6.6)	-34	(6.8)	-13	(9.7)
Belgium (Flemish Community)	543	(3.0)	440	(10.2)	450	(10.6)	**-103**	(11.0)	**-93**	(10.8)	10	(14.1)
Belgium (French Community)	494	(4.8)	439	(10.4)	385	(15.8)	**-55**	(9.4)	**-109**	(15.6)	**-54**	(16.6)

Note: Differences that are statistically significant are indicated in bold.

Table 2.1c
Differences in science performance by immigrant status

	Performance on the science scale						Difference in the science score					
	Native students		Second-generation students		First-generation students		Second-generation students minus native students		First-generation students minus native students		First-generation students minus second-generation students	
	Mean score	S.E.	Mean score	S.E.	Mean score	S.E.	Difference	S.E.	Difference	S.E.	Difference	S.E.
Australia	529	(2.1)	520	(4.7)	515	(5.5)	-10	(4.8)	-15	(5.4)	-5	(5.7)
Austria	502	(3.4)	434	(9.6)	422	(6.4)	**-68**	(10.1)	**-80**	(6.4)	-13	(11.0)
Belgium	524	(2.6)	435	(7.7)	416	(10.5)	**-89**	(7.5)	**-108**	(10.4)	-18	(11.7)
Canada	527	(1.9)	519	(5.0)	501	(5.1)	-8	(5.2)	-26	(5.4)	**-18**	(5.6)
Denmark	481	(2.8)	396	(13.7)	422	(11.0)	**-86**	(13.8)	**-59**	(10.9)	27	(16.4)
France	521	(3.0)	465	(7.0)	433	(17.1)	**-56**	(8.0)	**-88**	(17.3)	-32	(16.7)
Germany	529	(3.7)	412	(9.6)	444	(8.8)	**-117**	(10.0)	**-85**	(8.9)	32	(12.4)
Luxembourg	500	(1.7)	464	(3.9)	441	(4.4)	**-35**	(4.3)	**-59**	(4.5)	**-23**	(6.0)
Netherlands	538	(3.2)	465	(10.3)	457	(10.6)	**-72**	(10.8)	**-80**	(11.1)	-8	(13.0)
New Zealand	528	(2.7)	485	(8.8)	511	(5.3)	**-44**	(9.3)	-17	(5.9)	27	(8.5)
Norway	490	(2.7)	427	(13.3)	399	(11.9)	**-63**	(12.9)	**-91**	(11.9)	-28	(17.7)
Sweden	516	(2.6)	466	(9.7)	409	(10.9)	**-50**	(9.4)	**-107**	(11.3)	**-57**	(12.0)
Switzerland	531	(3.5)	462	(6.0)	429	(6.8)	**-69**	(5.8)	**-102**	(6.6)	**-33**	(7.0)
United States	499	(2.9)	466	(8.9)	462	(8.3)	**-33**	(8.7)	**-37**	(8.1)	-4	(9.1)
OECD average	*515*	*(0.9)*	*467*	*(2.2)*	*456*	*(2.2)*	*-48*	*(2.0)*	*-59*	*(2.3)*	*-11*	*(2.5)*
Hong Kong-China	545	(4.3)	557	(4.3)	511	(5.4)	12	(4.1)	**-34**	(4.5)	**-47**	(5.3)
Macao-China	526	(6.9)	524	(4.3)	529	(8.3)	-2	(9.0)	3	(9.9)	5	(9.8)
Russian Federation	493	(4.2)	463	(7.6)	478	(6.9)	**-30**	(7.3)	-15	(6.4)	14	(10.0)
Belgium (Flemish Community)	540	(2.8)	425	(11.2)	448	(10.0)	**-115**	(11.9)	**-92**	(9.8)	23	(13.8)
Belgium (French Community)	500	(4.5)	440	(9.8)	401	(14.2)	**-60**	(9.0)	**-99**	(14.1)	**-39**	(15.9)

Note: Differences that are statistically significant are indicated in bold.

Table 2.1d
Differences in problem-solving performance by immigrant status

	Performance on the problem-solving scale						Difference in the problem-solving score					
	Native students		Second-generation students		First-generation students		Second-generation students minus native students		First-generation students minus native students		First-generation students minus second-generation students	
	Mean score	S.E.	Mean score	S.E.	Mean score	S.E.	Difference	S.E.	Difference	S.E.	Difference	S.E.
Australia	534	(2.1)	521	(4.0)	523	(4.8)	**-14**	(4.3)	**-12**	(4.7)	2	(5.1)
Austria	515	(3.2)	465	(9.9)	453	(5.9)	**-50**	(10.2)	**-62**	(5.8)	-12	(9.7)
Belgium	540	(2.5)	445	(7.5)	447	(8.5)	**-95**	(7.5)	**-93**	(8.8)	2	(10.1)
Canada	535	(1.6)	532	(4.0)	533	(4.7)	-3	(4.2)	-2	(4.7)	1	(4.9)
Denmark	522	(2.4)	443	(10.5)	464	(8.8)	**-79**	(10.5)	**-58**	(8.7)	21	(13.0)
France	529	(2.5)	482	(6.2)	445	(14.8)	**-47**	(6.5)	**-84**	(14.9)	-37	(14.3)
Germany	534	(3.4)	443	(9.3)	461	(7.4)	**-90**	(9.6)	**-73**	(7.8)	18	(11.6)
Luxembourg	507	(1.8)	475	(3.7)	463	(3.9)	**-33**	(4.2)	**-44**	(4.4)	**-11**	(5.6)
Netherlands	532	(3.1)	463	(9.7)	462	(8.8)	**-69**	(10.4)	**-70**	(9.5)	-1	(10.5)
New Zealand	537	(2.5)	500	(7.5)	534	(4.6)	**-38**	(8.1)	-3	(5.3)	**35**	(7.7)
Norway	494	(2.6)	452	(11.7)	417	(10.3)	**-43**	(11.5)	**-78**	(10.7)	-35	(14.9)
Sweden	516	(2.2)	483	(8.9)	434	(10.1)	**-33**	(8.3)	**-82**	(10.4)	**-49**	(11.5)
Switzerland	538	(3.0)	480	(4.8)	447	(5.8)	**-58**	(4.7)	**-91**	(5.9)	**-33**	(6.2)
United States	483	(2.9)	464	(8.5)	446	(8.3)	**-19**	(8.1)	**-37**	(8.1)	-18	(8.4)
OECD average	*522*	*(0.8)*	*480*	*(2.0)*	*476*	*(1.9)*	*-42*	*(2.0)*	*-46*	*(2.1)*	*-4*	*(2.3)*
Hong Kong-China	556	(4.1)	572	(4.0)	505	(5.0)	17	(3.8)	**-51**	(4.4)	**-68**	(5.0)
Macao-China	536	(5.1)	533	(3.3)	531	(8.9)	-4	(6.5)	-6	(10.0)	-2	(9.6)
Russian Federation	482	(4.7)	473	(6.7)	451	(7.4)	-9	(6.9)	**-31**	(6.2)	-22	(9.4)
Belgium (Flemish Community)	559	(2.8)	436	(10.8)	475	(10.4)	**-123**	(11.4)	**-84**	(10.5)	39	(14.4)
Belgium (French Community)	512	(4.1)	449	(9.7)	433	(11.3)	**-63**	(9.3)	**-79**	(11.5)	-16	(12.4)

Note: Differences that are statistically significant are indicated in bold.

© OECD 2006 *Where immigrant students succeed - A comparative review of performance and engagement in PISA 2003*

Table 2.2

Correlations between mathematics, reading, science and problem-solving performance, by immigrant status

Native students

Correlation between the performance in:

	Mathematics and reading		Mathematics and science		Mathematics and problem-solving		Reading and science		Reading and problem-solving		Science and problem-solving	
	Coef.	S.E.	Coef.	S.E.	Coef.	S.E.	Coef.	S.E.	Coef.	S.E.	Coef.	S.E.
Australia	0.77	(0.01)	0.84	(0.01)	0.89	(0.00)	0.84	(0.00)	0.82	(0.01)	0.83	(0.01)
Austria	0.78	(0.01)	0.87	(0.01)	0.90	(0.01)	0.85	(0.01)	0.81	(0.01)	0.84	(0.01)
Belgium	0.79	(0.01)	0.84	(0.01)	0.90	(0.00)	0.84	(0.01)	0.83	(0.01)	0.82	(0.01)
Canada	0.77	(0.01)	0.83	(0.01)	0.88	(0.00)	0.85	(0.00)	0.85	(0.00)	0.82	(0.00)
Denmark	0.71	(0.01)	0.79	(0.01)	0.89	(0.00)	0.78	(0.01)	0.77	(0.01)	0.78	(0.01)
France	0.74	(0.01)	0.80	(0.01)	0.86	(0.01)	0.84	(0.01)	0.84	(0.01)	0.77	(0.01)
Germany	0.76	(0.01)	0.86	(0.01)	0.90	(0.01)	0.83	(0.01)	0.83	(0.01)	0.84	(0.01)
Luxembourg	0.76	(0.01)	0.84	(0.01)	0.88	(0.01)	0.85	(0.01)	0.82	(0.01)	0.83	(0.01)
Netherlands	0.86	(0.01)	0.89	(0.01)	0.93	(0.00)	0.88	(0.01)	0.87	(0.01)	0.87	(0.01)
New Zealand	0.82	(0.01)	0.88	(0.01)	0.90	(0.00)	0.85	(0.01)	0.86	(0.01)	0.83	(0.01)
Norway	0.74	(0.01)	0.81	(0.01)	0.88	(0.01)	0.79	(0.01)	0.83	(0.01)	0.74	(0.01)
Sweden	0.73	(0.01)	0.78	(0.01)	0.84	(0.01)	0.84	(0.01)	0.79	(0.01)	0.73	(0.01)
Switzerland	0.73	(0.01)	0.82	(0.01)	0.87	(0.01)	0.79	(0.01)	0.79	(0.01)	0.79	(0.01)
United States	0.84	(0.01)	0.86	(0.01)	0.92	(0.00)	0.87	(0.01)	0.86	(0.01)	0.84	(0.01)
OECD average	*0.77*	*(0.00)*	*0.83*	*(0.00)*	*0.89*	*(0.00)*	*0.83*	*(0.00)*	*0.82*	*(0.00)*	*0.80*	*(0.00)*
Hong Kong-China	0.81	(0.01)	0.86	(0.01)	0.91	(0.01)	0.83	(0.01)	0.85	(0.01)	0.84	(0.01)
Macao-China	0.58	(0.05)	0.71	(0.04)	0.82	(0.02)	0.73	(0.04)	0.66	(0.05)	0.69	(0.05)
Russian Federation	0.61	(0.02)	0.69	(0.01)	0.79	(0.01)	0.74	(0.01)	0.74	(0.01)	0.62	(0.02)
Belgium (Flemish community)	0.76	(0.02)	0.82	(0.01)	0.94	(0.01)	0.86	(0.02)	0.91	(0.02)	0.89	(0.02)
Belgium (French community)	0.79	(0.02)	0.84	(0.01)	0.92	(0.01)	0.8	(0.02)	0.81	(0.02)	0.82	(0.02)

Second-generation students

Correlation between the performance in:

	Mathematics and reading		Mathematics and science		Mathematics and problem-solving		Reading and science		Reading and problem-solving		Science and problem-solving	
	Coef.	S.E.	Coef.	S.E.	Coef.	S.E.	Coef.	S.E.	Coef.	S.E.	Coef.	S.E.
Australia	0.79	(0.02)	0.85	(0.01)	0.90	(0.01)	0.86	(0.01)	0.83	(0.01)	0.84	(0.01)
Austria	0.75	(0.04)	0.83	(0.03)	0.87	(0.02)	0.76	(0.06)	0.82	(0.04)	0.81	(0.04)
Belgium	0.80	(0.02)	0.85	(0.02)	0.90	(0.01)	0.85	(0.02)	0.84	(0.02)	0.84	(0.02)
Canada	0.76	(0.02)	0.82	(0.01)	0.87	(0.01)	0.85	(0.01)	0.84	(0.02)	0.82	(0.01)
Denmark	0.70	(0.05)	0.78	(0.04)	0.85	(0.03)	0.80	(0.04)	0.78	(0.04)	0.76	(0.04)
France	0.73	(0.04)	0.78	(0.03)	0.83	(0.02)	0.83	(0.02)	0.82	(0.02)	0.74	(0.03)
Germany	0.79	(0.03)	0.88	(0.02)	0.91	(0.02)	0.84	(0.02)	0.85	(0.02)	0.86	(0.03)
Luxembourg	0.78	(0.02)	0.85	(0.02)	0.88	(0.01)	0.87	(0.01)	0.85	(0.02)	0.84	(0.02)
Netherlands	0.83	(0.02)	0.86	(0.03)	0.92	(0.01)	0.88	(0.02)	0.85	(0.02)	0.85	(0.03)
New Zealand	0.84	(0.03)	0.89	(0.01)	0.92	(0.01)	0.87	(0.02)	0.87	(0.02)	0.85	(0.02)
Norway	0.77	(0.05)	0.83	(0.04)	0.90	(0.02)	0.83	(0.03)	0.85	(0.03)	0.78	(0.04)
Sweden	0.73	(0.05)	0.79	(0.04)	0.84	(0.03)	0.82	(0.03)	0.78	(0.03)	0.72	(0.06)
Switzerland	0.77	(0.02)	0.84	(0.02)	0.88	(0.02)	0.81	(0.02)	0.81	(0.02)	0.81	(0.02)
United States	0.85	(0.04)	0.87	(0.02)	0.92	(0.01)	0.87	(0.02)	0.86	(0.02)	0.85	(0.02)
OECD average	*0.79*	*(0.01)*	*0.85*	*(0.01)*	*0.89*	*(0.00)*	*0.85*	*(0.01)*	*0.84*	*(0.01)*	*0.83*	*(0.01)*
Hong Kong-China	0.82	(0.02)	0.86	(0.01)	0.90	(0.01)	0.83	(0.02)	0.86	(0.01)	0.83	(0.01)
Macao-China	0.61	(0.04)	0.71	(0.04)	0.81	(0.02)	0.75	(0.02)	0.67	(0.03)	0.67	(0.03)
Russian Federation	0.55	(0.05)	0.58	(0.06)	0.75	(0.03)	0.72	(0.03)	0.72	(0.04)	0.52	(0.05)
Belgium (Flemish community)	0.73	(0.05)	0.82	(0.06)	0.90	(0.05)	0.91	(0.05)	0.95	(0.06)	0.87	(0.06)
Belgium (French community)	0.82	(0.06)	0.86	(0.05)	0.91	(0.05)	0.82	(0.07)	0.83	(0.06)	0.86	(0.07)

First-generation students

Correlation between the performance in:

	Mathematics and reading		Mathematics and science		Mathematics and problem-solving		Reading and science		Reading and problem-solving		Science and problem-solving	
	Coef.	S.E.	Coef.	S.E.	Coef.	S.E.	Coef.	S.E.	Coef.	S.E.	Coef.	S.E.
Australia	0.81	(0.02)	0.86	(0.02)	0.91	(0.01)	0.87	(0.01)	0.84	(0.02)	0.85	(0.02)
Austria	0.79	(0.02)	0.86	(0.01)	0.88	(0.01)	0.83	(0.02)	0.80	(0.02)	0.82	(0.02)
Belgium	0.84	(0.03)	0.88	(0.02)	0.89	(0.01)	0.88	(0.02)	0.85	(0.02)	0.84	(0.02)
Canada	0.79	(0.02)	0.83	(0.02)	0.89	(0.01)	0.87	(0.01)	0.85	(0.02)	0.83	(0.02)
Denmark	0.74	(0.05)	0.80	(0.05)	0.89	(0.03)	0.80	(0.04)	0.79	(0.04)	0.76	(0.06)
France	0.81	(0.04)	0.83	(0.03)	0.89	(0.02)	0.86	(0.03)	0.86	(0.03)	0.80	(0.03)
Germany	0.81	(0.02)	0.88	(0.01)	0.92	(0.01)	0.86	(0.02)	0.86	(0.02)	0.86	(0.02)
Luxembourg	0.82	(0.02)	0.87	(0.01)	0.91	(0.01)	0.88	(0.01)	0.86	(0.01)	0.86	(0.01)
Netherlands	0.82	(0.04)	0.85	(0.03)	0.93	(0.01)	0.88	(0.02)	0.83	(0.04)	0.84	(0.04)
New Zealand	0.80	(0.02)	0.87	(0.01)	0.91	(0.01)	0.87	(0.01)	0.85	(0.02)	0.84	(0.02)
Norway	0.77	(0.04)	0.82	(0.05)	0.86	(0.03)	0.80	(0.03)	0.82	(0.04)	0.74	(0.06)
Sweden	0.78	(0.04)	0.79	(0.03)	0.85	(0.03)	0.88	(0.02)	0.81	(0.03)	0.76	(0.04)
Switzerland	0.81	(0.03)	0.85	(0.02)	0.90	(0.01)	0.83	(0.02)	0.83	(0.02)	0.83	(0.02)
United States	0.85	(0.02)	0.87	(0.02)	0.93	(0.01)	0.88	(0.02)	0.86	(0.02)	0.86	(0.02)
OECD average	*0.82*	*(0.01)*	*0.87*	*(0.00)*	*0.91*	*(0.00)*	*0.87*	*(0.00)*	*0.85*	*(0.00)*	*0.85*	*(0.01)*
Hong Kong-China	0.80	(0.02)	0.85	(0.02)	0.90	(0.01)	0.82	(0.02)	0.84	(0.02)	0.83	(0.02)
Macao-China	0.63	(0.06)	0.70	(0.05)	0.82	(0.03)	0.75	(0.03)	0.72	(0.05)	0.69	(0.05)
Russian Federation	0.60	(0.04)	0.68	(0.04)	0.81	(0.03)	0.75	(0.03)	0.75	(0.04)	0.62	(0.04)
Belgium (Flemish community)	0.79	(0.04)	0.89	(0.04)	0.97	(0.06)	0.95	(0.06)	1.00	(0.06)	0.92	(0.07)
Belgium (French community)	0.72	(0.05)	0.79	(0.06)	0.87	(0.04)	0.89	(0.06)	0.92	(0.07)	0.87	(0.09)

OECD countries / Partner countries

Table2.3a

Distribution of student performance on the mathematics scale by immigrant status

Native students

	Mean score		5th		25th		75th		95th	
	Mean	S.E.	Score	S.E.	Score	S.E.	Score	S.E.	Score	S.E.
Australia	527	(2.1)	371	(3.3)	463	(2.5)	592	(2.3)	675	(2.5)
Austria	515	(3.3)	366	(4.2)	451	(4.1)	579	(3.7)	664	(4.4)
Belgium	546	(2.5)	369	(5.3)	477	(3.4)	620	(2.4)	698	(2.1)
Canada	537	(1.6)	390	(2.7)	478	(1.9)	598	(2.0)	676	(2.5)
Denmark	520	(2.5)	369	(4.2)	460	(3.0)	582	(3.0)	665	(3.8)
France	520	(2.4)	369	(5.1)	460	(3.4)	582	(2.8)	660	(3.6)
Germany	525	(3.5)	371	(4.9)	462	(4.5)	590	(3.5)	669	(3.6)
Luxembourg	507	(1.3)	361	(3.2)	449	(2.0)	566	(1.9)	644	(2.8)
Netherlands	551	(3.0)	408	(4.5)	487	(4.7)	617	(3.2)	688	(3.4)
New Zealand	528	(2.6)	367	(4.6)	461	(3.3)	596	(2.6)	684	(2.9)
Norway	499	(2.3)	348	(3.5)	437	(2.5)	563	(3.1)	647	(3.2)
Sweden	517	(2.2)	368	(3.3)	455	(2.6)	581	(2.8)	666	(4.3)
Switzerland	543	(3.3)	388	(4.2)	482	(3.4)	605	(4.4)	690	(6.3)
United States	490	(2.8)	333	(4.0)	427	(3.3)	555	(3.1)	642	(4.0)
OECD average	*523*	*(0.7)*	*368*	*(1.3)*	*459*	*(1.0)*	*589*	*(0.8)*	*672*	*(0.9)*
Hong Kong-China	557	(4.5)	384	(10.8)	494	(6.6)	627	(3.8)	702	(4.9)
Macao-China	528	(5.9)	393	(12.7)	468	(9.8)	584	(8.0)	664	(7.5)
Russian Federation	472	(4.4)	321	(5.2)	408	(5.2)	534	(4.5)	626	(6.0)
Belgium (Flemish Community)	567	(2.9)	399	(7.8)	503	(4.0)	637	(2.5)	709	(2.2)
Belgium (French Community)	514	(4.3)	339	(7.6)	448	(5.3)	586	(4.7)	672	(6.2)

Second-generation students

	Mean score		5th		25th		75th		95th	
	Mean	S.E.	Score	S.E.	Score	S.E.	Score	S.E.	Score	S.E.
Australia	522	(4.7)	360	(8.1)	455	(5.0)	590	(5.7)	676	(9.7)
Austria	459	(8.8)	317	(21.9)	397	(12.1)	521	(12.0)	593	(12.1)
Belgium	454	(7.5)	286	(12.1)	383	(7.7)	525	(9.8)	630	(11.1)
Canada	543	(4.3)	404	(7.6)	484	(4.2)	601	(5.7)	684	(6.8)
Denmark	449	(11.2)	c	c	388	(13.7)	500	(11.2)	c	c
France	472	(6.1)	322	(9.8)	412	(7.5)	531	(6.2)	612	(9.6)
Germany	432	(9.1)	280	(19.1)	361	(11.4)	497	(11.0)	603	(11.9)
Luxembourg	476	(3.3)	324	(6.7)	415	(3.8)	534	(4.3)	633	(7.3)
Netherlands	492	(10.3)	361	(11.0)	431	(12.0)	552	(11.5)	634	(14.3)
New Zealand	496	(8.4)	335	(13.9)	423	(10.0)	567	(10.6)	664	(13.1)
Norway	460	(11.7)	281	(18.8)	386	(13.0)	535	(18.6)	c	c
Sweden	483	(9.8)	321	(17.7)	421	(10.3)	547	(14.6)	645	(17.9)
Switzerland	484	(5.0)	328	(7.7)	417	(5.5)	549	(6.6)	648	(8.1)
United States	468	(7.6)	318	(11.1)	398	(9.1)	535	(9.6)	623	(14.1)
OECD average	*483*	*(2.1)*	*324*	*(3.4)*	*416*	*(2.2)*	*549*	*(2.8)*	*645*	*(3.1)*
Hong Kong-China	570	(4.6)	388	(10.4)	514	(7.8)	636	(4.2)	706	(5.3)
Macao-China	532	(4.1)	384	(7.4)	473	(5.1)	591	(5.4)	669	(10.9)
Russian Federation	457	(7.2)	318	(13.3)	403	(7.5)	509	(9.6)	594	(12.6)
Belgium (Flemish Community)	445	(10.7)	276	(23.1)	374	(12.5)	511	(15.6)	637	(22.3)
Belgium (French Community)	458	(9.6)	289	(16.6)	387	(10.8)	532	(11.5)	626	(12.0)

First-generation students

	Mean score		5th		25th		75th		95th	
	Mean	S.E.	Score	S.E.	Score	S.E.	Score	S.E.	Score	S.E.
Australia	525	(4.9)	357	(9.3)	455	(6.8)	596	(5.8)	687	(10.1)
Austria	452	(6.0)	321	(7.7)	391	(7.2)	506	(8.8)	608	(13.4)
Belgium	437	(10.8)	245	(19.9)	357	(19.7)	513	(8.7)	625	(10.4)
Canada	530	(4.7)	377	(7.8)	468	(6.2)	596	(6.1)	674	(7.5)
Denmark	455	(10.1)	296	(33.6)	396	(12.9)	516	(12.6)	c	c
France	448	(15.0)	283	(21.6)	367	(16.7)	526	(23.6)	621	(18.1)
Germany	454	(7.5)	297	(9.8)	379	(8.5)	528	(9.1)	609	(9.5)
Luxembourg	462	(3.7)	302	(6.3)	391	(5.0)	532	(5.6)	632	(8.0)
Netherlands	472	(8.4)	344	(16.6)	415	(9.1)	526	(11.6)	611	(24.4)
New Zealand	523	(4.9)	351	(11.5)	455	(7.4)	595	(5.5)	677	(6.9)
Norway	438	(9.3)	292	(25.2)	370	(9.2)	499	(10.2)	599	(19.7)
Sweden	425	(9.6)	253	(19.6)	361	(12.6)	492	(9.5)	587	(15.5)
Switzerland	453	(6.1)	297	(8.7)	380	(6.9)	514	(6.4)	634	(13.5)
United States	453	(7.5)	287	(12.4)	374	(11.5)	527	(7.8)	619	(9.9)
OECD average	*475*	*(1.9)*	*306*	*(3.4)*	*401*	*(2.5)*	*547*	*(2.6)*	*647*	*(2.8)*
Hong Kong-China	516	(5.3)	355	(10.9)	457	(6.1)	583	(4.9)	662	(7.1)
Macao-China	517	(9.2)	367	(13.5)	452	(11.1)	575	(12.6)	672	(14.5)
Russian Federation	452	(5.9)	302	(11.2)	394	(7.1)	507	(7.8)	606	(12.0)
Belgium (Flemish Community)	472	(10.0)	c	c	406	(16.8)	537	(9.4)	630	(20.7)
Belgium (French Community)	419	(14.4)	233	(20.5)	332	(25.0)	496	(11.6)	622	(12.6)

© OECD 2006 Where immigrant students succeed - A comparative review of performance and engagement in PISA 2003

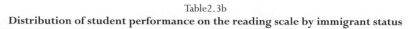

Table2.3b

Distribution of student performance on the reading scale by immigrant status

Native students

| | | Mean score | | Percentiles of the reading performance distribution | | | | | | | |
| | | | | 5th | | 25th | | 75th | | 95th | |
		Mean	S.E.	Score	S.E.	Score	S.E.	Score	S.E.	Score	S.E.
OECD countries	Australia	529	(2.2)	358	(4.1)	469	(3.0)	595	(2.0)	673	(2.5)
	Austria	501	(3.8)	331	(6.0)	437	(4.8)	572	(3.7)	651	(4.1)
	Belgium	523	(2.7)	341	(7.8)	462	(3.8)	595	(1.9)	666	(2.1)
	Canada	534	(1.6)	380	(3.0)	479	(2.0)	595	(1.6)	666	(2.1)
	Denmark	497	(2.7)	347	(5.7)	443	(3.1)	556	(2.7)	628	(3.0)
	France	505	(2.6)	339	(7.5)	446	(3.3)	572	(2.5)	644	(3.2)
	Germany	517	(3.5)	353	(5.9)	455	(4.8)	584	(3.3)	659	(3.1)
	Luxembourg	500	(1.8)	340	(3.9)	444	(2.2)	564	(2.1)	635	(2.9)
	Netherlands	524	(2.9)	390	(5.0)	468	(4.2)	583	(2.7)	649	(2.9)
	New Zealand	528	(2.9)	350	(6.4)	462	(3.9)	600	(2.6)	683	(2.8)
	Norway	505	(2.7)	330	(4.4)	441	(3.3)	574	(3.0)	658	(3.7)
	Sweden	522	(2.2)	365	(4.4)	462	(2.6)	586	(2.4)	663	(3.4)
	Switzerland	515	(3.2)	366	(5.9)	460	(3.6)	574	(3.1)	649	(4.6)
	United States	503	(3.1)	336	(5.3)	438	(3.4)	573	(2.9)	655	(3.4)
	OECD average	*514*	*(0.8)*	*350*	*(1.7)*	*454*	*(1.0)*	*580*	*(0.7)*	*657*	*(0.8)*
Partner countries	Hong Kong-China	513	(3.7)	363	(10.3)	463	(5.3)	572	(3.0)	634	(3.3)
	Macao-China	499	(5.1)	383	(8.8)	456	(6.9)	543	(5.3)	601	(6.8)
	Russian Federation	446	(4.0)	287	(5.4)	386	(5.1)	510	(3.9)	591	(3.9)
	Belgium (Flemish Community)	543	(3.0)	381	(7.7)	485	(4.2)	608	(2.2)	676	(2.1)
	Belgium (French Community)	494	(4.8)	300	(11.0)	430	(6.8)	570	(4.1)	644	(4.5)

Second-generation students

| | | Mean score | | Percentiles of the reading performance distribution | | | | | | | |
| | | | | 5th | | 25th | | 75th | | 95th | |
		Mean	S.E.	Score	S.E.	Score	S.E.	Score	S.E.	Score	S.E.
OECD countries	Australia	525	(4.6)	351	(10.1)	462	(5.9)	596	(5.2)	673	(7.5)
	Austria	428	(13.5)	c	c	355	(16.1)	512	(12.6)	591	(14.1)
	Belgium	439	(7.5)	253	(14.1)	365	(12.4)	519	(7.3)	606	(10.1)
	Canada	543	(4.2)	403	(8.0)	488	(5.0)	600	(4.3)	679	(7.8)
	Denmark	440	(13.8)	c	c	383	(20.8)	506	(15.5)	589	(21.2)
	France	458	(6.9)	287	(15.6)	400	(9.5)	523	(7.2)	599	(8.7)
	Germany	420	(9.9)	254	(20.8)	349	(16.2)	486	(12.2)	596	(12.3)
	Luxembourg	454	(4.0)	281	(8.1)	388	(6.0)	524	(4.9)	607	(6.1)
	Netherlands	475	(8.2)	353	(9.9)	418	(11.5)	527	(8.4)	598	(15.9)
	New Zealand	506	(8.3)	326	(14.9)	430	(11.0)	580	(9.8)	687	(13.6)
	Norway	446	(11.1)	260	(26.3)	375	(15.3)	517	(12.8)	c	c
	Sweden	502	(8.7)	333	(19.4)	439	(10.8)	566	(11.0)	649	(13.2)
	Switzerland	462	(5.2)	303	(11.6)	398	(6.5)	529	(5.7)	617	(7.1)
	United States	481	(8.7)	308	(14.7)	410	(10.6)	550	(9.5)	641	(11.7)
	OECD average	*475*	*(2.1)*	*295*	*(4.3)*	*407*	*(2.6)*	*546*	*(2.4)*	*637*	*(2.6)*
Partner countries	Hong Kong-China	522	(3.8)	364	(10.7)	479	(5.1)	577	(3.2)	632	(4.7)
	Macao-China	497	(2.9)	380	(5.7)	455	(4.4)	543	(4.2)	599	(4.2)
	Russian Federation	426	(6.9)	265	(15.6)	368	(8.7)	491	(8.2)	569	(7.3)
	Belgium (Flemish Community)	440	(10.2)	268	(17.3)	363	(11.8)	513	(13.1)	608	(19.0)
	Belgium (French Community)	439	(10.4)	246	(22.6)	365	(18.9)	521	(9.2)	604	(12.4)

First-generation students

| | | Mean score | | Percentiles of the reading performance distribution | | | | | | | |
| | | | | 5th | | 25th | | 75th | | 95th | |
		Mean	S.E.	Score	S.E.	Score	S.E.	Score	S.E.	Score	S.E.
OECD countries	Australia	517	(5.0)	331	(11.2)	452	(7.7)	590	(5.9)	675	(7.2)
	Austria	425	(8.0)	254	(15.9)	354	(9.8)	497	(8.0)	597	(12.7)
	Belgium	407	(11.9)	193	(24.0)	321	(21.2)	492	(10.1)	610	(13.9)
	Canada	515	(4.7)	353	(8.3)	457	(6.1)	579	(4.1)	654	(6.3)
	Denmark	454	(9.5)	291	(25.0)	389	(13.1)	526	(11.1)	c	c
	France	426	(15.3)	223	(18.5)	339	(25.5)	508	(14.4)	593	(18.1)
	Germany	431	(8.9)	248	(14.7)	351	(10.5)	514	(9.1)	599	(12.3)
	Luxembourg	431	(4.4)	253	(9.0)	355	(5.6)	511	(6.0)	600	(7.2)
	Netherlands	463	(8.1)	349	(16.6)	409	(8.2)	514	(11.0)	602	(17.5)
	New Zealand	503	(5.3)	310	(10.2)	430	(7.4)	580	(5.6)	675	(6.4)
	Norway	436	(11.5)	250	(31.3)	363	(15.0)	512	(12.8)	609	(21.2)
	Sweden	433	(11.3)	232	(29.3)	362	(17.1)	516	(10.6)	602	(11.9)
	Switzerland	422	(6.3)	255	(8.5)	349	(9.0)	492	(7.6)	594	(14.6)
	United States	453	(8.3)	267	(11.5)	369	(12.1)	538	(9.4)	629	(10.6)
	OECD average	*456*	*(2.1)*	*265*	*(4.0)*	*379*	*(2.9)*	*538*	*(2.1)*	*634*	*(2.5)*
Partner countries	Hong Kong-China	494	(4.8)	349	(11.8)	442	(5.5)	550	(3.9)	611	(5.2)
	Macao-China	499	(7.1)	382	(18.7)	451	(6.5)	548	(7.3)	609	(10.1)
	Russian Federation	413	(7.5)	251	(13.7)	346	(9.3)	479	(6.3)	561	(9.9)
	Belgium (Flemish Community)	450	(10.6)	253	(25.3)	379	(16.3)	527	(13.8)	633	(19.8)
	Belgium (French Community)	385	(15.8)	180	(19.8)	291	(28.7)	472	(12.0)	586	(20.8)

Table 2.4a
Percentage of native students at each level of proficiency on the mathematics scale

| | Native students - Proficiency levels | | | | | | | | | | | |
| | Below Level 1 (below 358 score points) | | Level 1 (from 358 to 420 score points) | | Level 2 (from 421 to 482 score points) | | Level 3 (from 483 to 544 score points) | | Level 4 (from 545 to 606 score points) | | Levels 5 and 6 (above 606 score points) | |
	%	S.E.	%	S.E.	%	S.E.	%	S.E.	%	S.E.	%	S.E.
Australia	3.7	(0.4)	9.5	(0.5)	18.5	(0.7)	24.4	(0.7)	23.9	(0.6)	20.0	(0.7)
Austria	4.0	(0.7)	11.6	(0.9)	20.6	(1.0)	25.9	(1.3)	21.9	(0.9)	16.0	(1.1)
Belgium	4.0	(0.4)	7.4	(0.5)	15.2	(0.7)	20.8	(0.8)	22.9	(0.7)	29.7	(1.0)
Canada	2.1	(0.3)	7.1	(0.4)	17.3	(0.6)	26.0	(0.8)	25.8	(0.6)	21.7	(0.7)
Denmark	3.8	(0.5)	9.8	(0.7)	20.0	(0.9)	26.6	(0.9)	22.8	(0.9)	17.0	(1.0)
France	3.8	(0.6)	9.7	(0.9)	19.5	(1.0)	26.5	(1.1)	23.7	(1.2)	16.8	(1.0)
Germany	3.6	(0.6)	9.4	(0.8)	18.9	(1.3)	24.8	(1.0)	23.9	(1.1)	19.4	(1.1)
Luxembourg	4.5	(0.5)	11.8	(1.0)	21.6	(1.4)	28.2	(1.0)	21.7	(1.1)	12.2	(0.8)
Netherlands	0.9	(0.3)	6.0	(0.7)	16.3	(1.2)	23.4	(1.2)	24.3	(1.4)	29.0	(1.5)
New Zealand	4.0	(0.5)	9.4	(0.7)	19.0	(0.7)	23.4	(0.9)	22.7	(0.9)	21.5	(0.9)
Norway	6.1	(0.5)	13.2	(0.8)	23.5	(1.1)	25.7	(1.1)	19.6	(1.1)	11.8	(0.7)
Sweden	3.8	(0.4)	10.5	(0.6)	21.2	(0.9)	26.2	(0.9)	21.1	(0.9)	17.2	(0.8)
Switzerland	2.6	(0.4)	6.7	(0.6)	15.8	(0.8)	25.3	(1.1)	25.3	(0.8)	24.2	(1.6)
United States	8.4	(0.7)	14.5	(0.9)	24.0	(0.8)	24.8	(0.9)	17.5	(0.8)	10.9	(0.8)
Hong Kong-China	3.5	(0.8)	5.8	(0.8)	12.8	(1.0)	19.6	(1.4)	25.0	(1.4)	33.2	(1.8)
Macao-China	1.5	(0.9)	7.8	(3.2)	21.1	(4.1)	27.3	(3.6)	23.8	(3.6)	18.5	(2.6)
Russian Federation	10.9	(1.1)	18.2	(1.2)	25.9	(1.1)	23.6	(1.0)	13.9	(1.0)	7.5	(0.8)
Belgium (Flemish Community)	2.1	(0.4)	5.2	(0.5)	12.3	(0.6)	19.1	(0.7)	24.1	(0.7)	37.3	(1.1)
Belgium (French Community)	6.9	(0.9)	10.6	(0.9)	19.4	(1.0)	23.3	(1.1)	21.2	(1.1)	18.6	(1.4)

OECD countries / Partner countries

Table 2.4b
Percentage of second-generation students at each level of proficiency on the mathematics scale

| | Second-generation students - Proficiency levels | | | | | | | | | | | |
| | Below Level 1 (below 358 score points) | | Level 1 (from 358 to 420 score points) | | Level 2 (from 421 to 482 score points) | | Level 3 (from 483 to 544 score points) | | Level 4 (from 545 to 606 score points) | | Levels 5 and 6 (above 606 score points) | |
	%	S.E.	%	S.E.	%	S.E.	%	S.E.	%	S.E.	%	S.E.
Australia	4.7	(1.0)	10.4	(1.0)	19.7	(1.6)	23.1	(2.0)	22.4	(2.3)	19.7	(2.0)
Austria	13.2	(3.4)	20.6	(3.6)	27.0	(3.9)	20.6	(3.5)	15.7	(3.6)	2.9	(1.5)
Belgium	17.4	(2.5)	20.7	(2.0)	23.1	(2.4)	19.0	(3.1)	11.9	(2.4)	7.8	(2.0)
Canada	1.4	(0.6)	5.9	(1.0)	16.3	(1.7)	28.0	(2.3)	25.5	(2.3)	22.9	(9.0)
Denmark	15.7	(3.9)	20.4	(4.6)	28.0	(6.9)	23.5	(6.7)	8.2	(3.6)	4.2	(2.6)
France	10.9	(2.3)	17.1	(2.3)	24.8	(3.5)	26.7	(2.8)	14.5	(2.6)	5.9	(2.3)
Germany	23.5	(4.2)	23.3	(3.3)	23.8	(3.4)	16.3	(2.7)	8.4	(2.3)	4.8	(1.4)
Luxembourg	9.3	(1.3)	17.4	(2.1)	27.3	(2.3)	24.5	(2.0)	13.1	(1.7)	8.5	(1.1)
Netherlands	4.2	(1.5)	16.4	(4.2)	27.9	(4.3)	23.9	(4.2)	18.6	(3.2)	9.0	(2.6)
New Zealand	8.7	(3.3)	15.6	(3.1)	21.8	(3.4)	22.2	(3.1)	17.4	(2.7)	14.4	(2.7)
Norway	15.2	(4.9)	19.5	(4.8)	25.0	(7.9)	17.7	(5.8)	13.6	(4.2)	9.0	(3.6)
Sweden	9.6	(2.4)	14.8	(3.4)	26.5	(3.2)	23.5	(4.9)	14.4	(3.7)	11.2	(3.3)
Switzerland	8.8	(1.6)	17.6	(2.3)	25.6	(2.7)	21.3	(2.4)	15.3	(1.7)	11.4	(2.3)
United States	12.5	(2.5)	21.0	(3.0)	23.3	(2.3)	21.0	(2.4)	14.2	(2.2)	8.0	(2.0)
Hong Kong-China	2.9	(0.8)	4.9	(0.9)	10.2	(1.4)	16.3	(1.5)	27.8	(1.9)	37.9	(2.2)
Macao-China	2.4	(0.7)	7.9	(1.2)	18.2	(1.8)	26.9	(2.4)	24.6	(2.2)	20.0	(2.1)
Russian Federation	10.0	(2.4)	21.9	(3.1)	31.0	(4.1)	22.8	(3.7)	10.3	(2.5)	4.0	(2.0)
Belgium (Flemish Community)	21.3	(3.4)	21.0	(3.1)	25.0	(2.9)	15.6	(2.9)	9.1	(2.3)	8.1	(2.3)
Belgium (French Community)	15.4	(2.9)	20.6	(2.4)	22.1	(2.5)	20.8	(2.7)	13.4	(2.5)	7.6	(1.7)

OECD countries / Partner countries

© OECD 2006 Where immigrant students succeed - A comparative review of performance and engagement in PISA 2003

Table 2.4c
Percentage of first-generation students at each level of proficiency on the mathematics scale

| | | First-generation students - Proficiency levels | | | | | | | | | |
| | Below Level 1 (below 358 score points) | | Level 1 (from 358 to 420 score points) | | Level 2 (from 421 to 482 score points) | | Level 3 (from 483 to 544 score points) | | Level 4 (from 545 to 606 score points) | | Levels 5 and 6 (above 606 score points) | |
	%	S.E.	%	S.E.	%	S.E.	%	S.E.	%	S.E.	%	S.E.
Australia	5.1	(1.0)	10.5	(1.5)	17.9	(1.5)	22.7	(1.9)	22.4	(2.0)	21.5	(2.0)
Austria	14.1	(2.4)	23.6	(3.9)	28.4	(3.2)	18.7	(2.2)	10.2	(1.8)	5.1	(1.4)
Belgium	25.0	(4.6)	18.6	(2.7)	21.2	(3.0)	17.9	(2.7)	10.0	(2.1)	7.3	(1.6)
Canada	3.3	(0.7)	8.3	(1.4)	18.0	(2.4)	25.7	(2.2)	22.8	(2.0)	22.0	(2.1)
Denmark	14.4	(4.3)	19.4	(4.7)	28.2	(4.5)	20.5	(4.4)	13.6	(3.8)	3.8	(2.3)
France	22.0	(5.3)	20.6	(4.1)	21.7	(4.2)	15.3	(3.7)	12.8	(3.9)	7.5	(2.7)
Germany	17.5	(2.8)	21.3	(3.4)	20.7	(2.9)	20.5	(2.4)	14.4	(2.7)	5.6	(2.0)
Luxembourg	15.0	(1.7)	20.4	(2.1)	24.4	(2.0)	18.9	(1.7)	12.9	(1.6)	8.5	(1.4)
Netherlands	6.3	(2.1)	21.4	(4.8)	32.2	(5.6)	21.3	(5.0)	12.9	(4.2)	5.8	(2.3)
New Zealand	5.5	(1.3)	10.0	(1.9)	18.2	(3.1)	24.1	(2.8)	20.7	(2.1)	21.6	(1.9)
Norway	18.9	(4.3)	26.8	(5.1)	23.5	(4.2)	17.3	(4.5)	8.9	(4.3)	4.6	(2.2)
Sweden	24.0	(4.2)	23.1	(3.9)	24.7	(4.2)	16.5	(2.7)	8.4	(2.4)	3.3	(1.5)
Switzerland	17.2	(2.1)	21.9	(2.4)	23.7	(2.7)	20.0	(2.0)	8.8	(1.3)	8.4	(1.7)
United States	19.5	(3.4)	18.3	(2.4)	22.4	(4.0)	20.6	(3.3)	12.7	(2.5)	6.5	(1.6)
Hong Kong-China	5.2	(1.3)	9.6	(1.3)	20.5	(2.3)	25.4	(2.5)	23.0	(2.2)	16.3	(1.6)
Macao-China	3.2	(1.8)	12.1	(4.0)	21.2	(4.0)	25.5	(4.2)	21.9	(3.8)	16.1	(3.7)
Russian Federation	14.1	(2.5)	21.9	(3.2)	30.1	(3.0)	19.3	(2.1)	9.5	(1.8)	5.2	(1.5)
Belgium (Flemish Community)	13.4	(4.0)	15.8	(3.1)	22.8	(3.3)	25.8	(5.0)	14.3	(2.6)	7.9	(2.4)
Belgium (French Community)	30.6	(6.1)	19.9	(2.8)	20.5	(3.4)	14.2	(2.5)	7.8	(1.8)	6.9	(1.8)

Table 2.4d
Percentage of native students at each level of proficiency on the reading scale

| | | Native students - Proficiency levels | | | | | | | | | |
| | Below Level 1 (below 335 score points) | | Level 1 (from 335 to 407 score points) | | Level 2 (from 408 to 480 score points) | | Level 3 (from 481 to 552 score points) | | Level 4 (from 553 to 626 score points) | | Level 5 (above 626 score points) | |
	%	S.E.	%	S.E.	%	S.E.	%	S.E.	%	S.E.	%	S.E.
Australia	3.1	(0.4)	7.7	(0.5)	17.9	(0.7)	28.6	(0.8)	27.8	(0.8)	14.9	(0.7)
Austria	5.4	(0.8)	11.7	(1.0)	22.1	(1.0)	28.6	(1.2)	22.9	(1.1)	9.3	(0.9)
Belgium	4.5	(0.6)	8.2	(0.6)	17.6	(0.7)	27.3	(0.8)	28.2	(0.9)	14.1	(0.6)
Canada	1.8	(0.2)	6.6	(0.4)	17.1	(0.6)	30.7	(0.8)	29.9	(0.6)	13.9	(0.6)
Denmark	3.9	(0.6)	11.2	(0.7)	24.4	(1.2)	34.3	(1.2)	20.8	(1.0)	5.5	(0.5)
France	4.6	(0.7)	10.1	(0.6)	22.0	(0.9)	30.4	(1.0)	24.6	(0.9)	8.3	(0.7)
Germany	3.3	(0.5)	10.3	(1.0)	19.5	(1.1)	29.3	(0.9)	25.9	(1.2)	11.6	(0.8)
Luxembourg	4.5	(0.4)	10.4	(0.7)	23.8	(0.9)	31.9	(1.3)	22.9	(1.4)	6.6	(0.5)
Netherlands	1.0	(0.3)	6.9	(0.8)	21.8	(1.2)	31.7	(1.4)	28.7	(1.3)	10.0	(0.8)
New Zealand	3.9	(0.5)	8.6	(0.7)	18.1	(1.0)	26.7	(1.1)	25.2	(1.1)	17.5	(0.8)
Norway	5.5	(0.5)	11.0	(0.8)	21.1	(1.3)	29.5	(1.1)	22.4	(0.9)	10.4	(0.8)
Sweden	2.6	(0.4)	8.3	(0.7)	20.2	(1.0)	30.5	(1.6)	26.1	(1.3)	12.3	(0.7)
Switzerland	2.5	(0.3)	8.5	(0.8)	21.5	(1.1)	33.4	(1.5)	25.1	(1.1)	9.1	(0.9)
United States	4.8	(0.6)	11.8	(0.9)	22.7	(1.1)	28.6	(1.1)	22.2	(0.9)	9.9	(0.7)
Hong Kong-China	3.1	(0.7)	8.2	(1.0)	20.1	(1.6)	34.5	(1.6)	27.7	(1.5)	6.5	(0.7)
Macao-China	0.8	(0.9)	9.5	(2.9)	25.9	(4.1)	43.6	(3.8)	18.3	(2.7)	2.0	(0.9)
Russian Federation	11.7	(1.0)	20.7	(1.0)	30.5	(1.0)	25.4	(1.1)	9.8	(0.9)	2.0	(0.3)
Belgium (Flemish Community)	2.1	(0.5)	6.2	(0.5)	15.3	(0.7)	26.7	(0.8)	31.8	(0.9)	17.9	(0.7)
Belgium (French Community)	8.2	(1.1)	11.2	(1.0)	21.1	(1.0)	28.2	(1.2)	23.0	(1.1)	8.4	(0.9)

Table 2.4e
Percentage of second-generation students at each level of proficiency on the reading scale

	Below Level 1 (below 335 score points)		Level 1 (from 335 to 407 score points)		Level 2 (from 408 to 480 score points)		Level 3 (from 481 to 552 score points)		Level 4 (from 553 to 626 score points)		Level 5 (above 626 score points)	
	%	S.E.	%	S.E.	%	S.E.	%	S.E.	%	S.E.	%	S.E.
Australia	3.7	(0.9)	8.7	(1.1)	17.7	(1.4)	28.9	(1.8)	26.0	(1.9)	15.0	(1.9)
Austria	18.7	(4.5)	20.6	(3.6)	25.0	(5.0)	23.7	(3.9)	10.3	(2.8)	1.7	(1.1)
Belgium	18.6	(2.5)	17.9	(2.2)	24.5	(3.0)	24.3	(2.6)	11.4	(2.1)	3.2	(1.2)
Canada	1.0	(0.3)	4.5	(0.9)	16.5	(1.7)	31.6	(2.2)	31.1	(2.2)	15.4	(2.1)
Denmark	15.3	(4.9)	17.2	(4.1)	34.1	(6.4)	22.3	(5.4)	9.4	(4.1)	1.7	(1.7)
France	10.6	(2.2)	16.8	(2.4)	29.6	(3.2)	27.6	(4.6)	12.8	(2.3)	2.6	(0.9)
Germany	21.6	(4.4)	22.5	(3.8)	28.9	(4.0)	15.9	(2.7)	8.7	(2.1)	2.5	(1.2)
Luxembourg	12.8	(1.4)	18.5	(1.9)	27.1	(2.2)	25.5	(1.9)	12.9	(1.7)	3.1	(0.7)
Netherlands	3.0	(1.4)	17.4	(4.0)	31.1	(3.8)	33.3	(4.2)	12.2	(2.6)	3.0	(1.3)
New Zealand	5.7	(1.7)	13.0	(3.0)	21.0	(3.2)	25.2	(3.2)	22.6	(4.5)	12.5	(2.6)
Norway	14.3	(4.8)	20.7	(5.5)	26.4	(6.2)	23.4	(5.6)	10.7	(3.4)	4.5	(2.4)
Sweden	4.9	(1.8)	10.6	(3.0)	22.7	(3.7)	31.7	(4.0)	20.7	(3.9)	9.4	(2.8)
Switzerland	9.6	(2.0)	19.5	(2.6)	28.6	(2.7)	24.7	(3.4)	13.6	(1.7)	4.0	(1.4)
United States	8.0	(2.1)	16.3	(2.6)	24.6	(3.3)	26.4	(2.8)	16.6	(3.0)	8.0	(2.1)
Hong Kong-China	3.0	(0.8)	6.0	(1.1)	16.3	(1.5)	35.7	(1.9)	32.6	(2.0)	6.4	(0.9)
Macao-China	1.1	(0.5)	8.8	(1.3)	27.0	(2.4)	42.0	(2.3)	19.6	(2.3)	1.4	(0.6)
Russian Federation	15.4	(2.7)	25.1	(3.3)	30.5	(4.1)	20.5	(3.2)	8.1	(2.1)	0.4	c
Belgium (Flemish Community)	16.4	(3.2)	22.2	(3.2)	25.3	(3.1)	22.1	(3.4)	10.3	(2.3)	3.7	(1.5)
Belgium (French Community)	19.7	(3.4)	15.7	(2.6)	24.1	(3.2)	25.4	(3.0)	12.0	(2.2)	3.0	(1.2)

OECD countries / Partner countries

Table 2.4f
Percentage of first-generation students at each level of proficiency on the reading scale

	Below Level 1 (below 335 score points)		Level 1 (from 335 to 407 score points)		Level 2 (from 408 to 480 score points)		Level 3 (from 481 to 552 score points)		Level 4 (from 553 to 626 score points)		Level 5 (above 626 score points)	
	%	S.E.	%	S.E.	%	S.E.	%	S.E.	%	S.E.	%	S.E.
Australia	5.3	(0.9)	9.5	(1.1)	19.3	(1.6)	26.8	(2.5)	24.5	(2.2)	14.7	(1.8)
Austria	18.9	(3.2)	24.7	(3.2)	25.9	(2.6)	19.6	(2.3)	8.6	(1.5)	2.3	(1.0)
Belgium	27.5	(4.6)	21.3	(2.5)	22.9	(3.6)	16.9	(2.2)	7.7	(1.8)	3.8	(1.1)
Canada	3.4	(0.8)	9.3	(1.7)	20.3	(2.0)	31.1	(2.3)	25.5	(2.1)	10.5	(1.4)
Denmark	11.5	(3.0)	19.9	(4.9)	27.5	(5.6)	24.9	(5.6)	13.8	(5.1)	2.5	(1.6)
France	23.3	(6.0)	17.8	(5.2)	22.9	(4.5)	23.3	(4.9)	10.0	(2.9)	2.7	(1.8)
Germany	20.1	(3.6)	21.8	(4.2)	21.4	(3.6)	22.8	(2.6)	11.4	(2.6)	2.5	(1.3)
Luxembourg	18.7	(1.6)	22.9	(1.8)	23.8	(2.3)	20.3	(2.2)	11.8	(1.7)	2.5	(0.7)
Netherlands	2.8	(2.0)	21.5	(4.5)	36.8	(5.5)	26.4	(5.3)	9.7	(3.0)	2.8	(1.6)
New Zealand	7.4	(1.4)	12.2	(1.5)	19.8	(2.3)	25.6	(2.0)	21.7	(2.5)	13.2	(1.9)
Norway	17.7	(4.4)	21.8	(4.5)	25.3	(4.2)	20.7	(4.4)	10.9	(3.9)	3.6	(2.2)
Sweden	19.6	(4.4)	19.1	(2.9)	24.6	(4.2)	21.3	(3.2)	12.9	(3.2)	2.5	(1.4)
Switzerland	21.7	(3.0)	22.8	(2.4)	26.2	(3.1)	18.7	(3.0)	7.7	(1.9)	2.8	(1.0)
United States	16.5	(3.0)	18.8	(2.7)	20.1	(2.7)	24.5	(3.1)	14.5	(2.7)	5.5	(1.5)
Hong Kong-China	3.5	(1.1)	11.7	(1.5)	24.1	(2.2)	37.1	(2.2)	20.5	(1.9)	3.2	(0.7)
Macao-China	1.0	(1.2)	7.7	(2.4)	32.1	(5.9)	36.1	(6.5)	20.8	(5.5)	2.2	(1.7)
Russian Federation	21.2	(3.6)	24.0	(2.4)	30.2	(3.0)	18.6	(2.2)	5.4	(1.2)	0.6	(0.5)
Belgium (Flemish Community)	14.7	(3.4)	19.4	(3.2)	26.4	(4.9)	22.9	(3.0)	10.2	(2.7)	6.4	(2.0)
Belgium (French Community)	33.7	(6.2)	22.3	(3.1)	21.3	(3.1)	13.8	(2.4)	6.3	(1.7)	2.5	(1.0)

OECD countries / Partner countries

© OECD 2006 *Where immigrant students succeed - A comparative review of performance and engagement in PISA 2003*

Table 2.5a

Performance on the mathematics scale by immigrant status and language spoken at home

Results based on students' self-reports

	Performance on the mathematics scale									
	Language spoken at home most of the time IS THE SAME as the language of assessment, other official languages or another national dialects						Language spoken at home most of the time IS DIFFERENT from the language of assessment, from other official languages or from other national dialects			
	Native students		Second-generation students		First-generation students		Second-generation students		First-generation students	
	Mean score	S.E.	Mean score	S.E.	Mean score	S.E.	Mean score	S.E.	Mean score	S.E.
Australia	528	(2.1)	528	(4.5)	527	(5.4)	514	(7.5)	523	(7.5)
Austria	515	(3.3)	471	(13.9)	468	(9.8)	460	(11.2)	453	(7.8)
Belgium	551	(2.4)	473	(11.4)	443	(16.4)	454	(11.7)	425	(11.4)
Canada	538	(1.6)	551	(5.0)	530	(6.0)	531	(6.2)	533	(5.4)
Denmark	520	(2.6)	455	(15.3)	446	(15.5)	438	(17.4)	458	(14.3)
France	521	(2.4)	488	(5.9)	461	(19.6)	455	(9.8)	441	(21.6)
Germany	528	(3.5)	458	(9.8)	480	(10.5)	427	(15.5)	435	(9.0)
Luxembourg	509	(1.5)	482	(6.6)	513	(11.1)	480	(5.2)	455	(3.8)
Netherlands	553	(3.1)	508	(11.4)	486	(14.1)	470	(13.1)	462	(10.4)
New Zealand	528	(2.6)	502	(9.4)	528	(6.2)	478	(13.4)	523	(6.8)
Norway	501	(2.3)	445	(19.8)	418	(24.3)	483	(15.2)	442	(10.8)
Sweden	519	(2.2)	499	(9.4)	445	(19.3)	484	(16.2)	427	(10.1)
Switzerland	545	(3.5)	495	(7.3)	480	(10.2)	487	(8.6)	447	(7.8)
United States	492	(2.8)	493	(8.4)	481	(11.3)	447	(9.7)	449	(8.0)
OECD average	525	(0.7)	500	(2.4)	495	(3.4)	474	(3.2)	470	(2.5)
Hong Kong-China	561	(4.4)	573	(4.7)	521	(5.3)	508	(23.3)	442	(14.5)
Macao-China	531	(6.1)	534	(4.2)	522	(9.6)	491	(21.8)	468	(20.2)
Russian Federation	474	(4.2)	460	(7.4)	460	(5.5)	419	(21.1)	400	(15.9)
Belgium (Flemish Community)	571	(2.8)	501	(18.1)	499	(9.6)	431	(15.0)	441	(18.4)
Belgium (French Community)	519	(4.1)	466	(13.2)	422	(20.0)	475	(14.4)	410	(15.5)

OECD countries / Partner countries

	Difference in the mathematics score							
	Second-generation minus native students				First-generation minus native students			
	Both sub-groups speak language of assessment at home		Second-generation students speak a different language at home		Both sub-groups speak language of assessment at home		First-generation students speak a different language at home	
	Difference.	S.E.	Difference.	S.E.	Difference.	S.E.	Difference.	S.E.
Australia	-1	(4.6)	-14	(7.4)	-1	(5.1)	-6	(7.6)
Austria	-44	(14.3)	-55	(11.5)	-48	(9.1)	-62	(7.9)
Belgium	-77	(11.7)	-96	(11.4)	-107	(16.5)	-126	(11.3)
Canada	13	(5.0)	-8	(6.6)	-8	(6.2)	-5	(5.5)
Denmark	-65	(15.1)	-81	(17.7)	-74	(15.3)	-61	(14.3)
France	-33	(6.3)	-66	(10.1)	-60	(19.4)	-80	(21.9)
Germany	-71	(10.2)	-102	(15.7)	-48	(11.0)	-93	(8.9)
Luxembourg	-27	(7.0)	-30	(5.4)	4	(11.2)	-54	(4.3)
Netherlands	-45	(12.2)	-83	(13.8)	-67	(14.5)	-92	(10.8)
New Zealand	-27	(9.9)	-50	(13.8)	-1	(6.4)	-5	(7.4)
Norway	-55	(19.7)	-17	(14.9)	-83	(24.2)	-58	(10.9)
Sweden	-20	(9.4)	-36	(15.7)	-75	(18.9)	-92	(10.5)
Switzerland	-50	(6.9)	-58	(8.6)	-65	(9.3)	-98	(7.6)
United States	2	(8.1)	-45	(9.8)	-11	(10.9)	-43	(8.4)
OECD average	-25	(2.3)	-51	(3.2)	-29	(3.4)	-54	(2.7)
Hong Kong-China	12	(4.5)	-53	(22.9)	-39	(4.5)	-119	(13.8)
Macao-China	3	(7.9)	-40	(22.8)	-9	(11.1)	-63	(21.4)
Russian Federation	-14	(7.4)	-55	(21.5)	-14	(5.4)	-74	(15.2)
Belgium (Flemish Community)	-70	(18.4)	-140	(15.7)	-72	(9.5)	-130	(18.2)
Belgium (French Community)	-53	(13.3)	-44	(13.1)	-98	(20.2)	-110	(15.4)

Note: Differences that are statistically significant are indicated in bold.

Table 2.5b

Performance on the reading scale by immigrant status and language spoken at home

Results based on students' self-reports

	Performance on the reading scale									
	Language spoken at home most of the time IS THE SAME as the language of assessment, other official languages or another national dialects						Language spoken at home most of the time IS DIFFERENT from the language of assessment, from other official languages or from other national dialects			
	Native students		Second-generation students		First-generation students		Second-generation students		First-generation students	
	Mean score	S.E.	Mean score	S.E.	Mean score	S.E.	Mean score	S.E.	Mean score	S.E.
Australia	530	(2.2)	531	(5.1)	524	(5.6)	516	(7.0)	508	(7.5)
Austria	502	(3.9)	461	(16.5)	460	(12.7)	413	(21.5)	421	(9.4)
Belgium	529	(2.6)	462	(12.0)	412	(18.6)	436	(12.8)	403	(15.1)
Canada	535	(1.6)	553	(4.3)	527	(6.1)	527	(7.0)	512	(5.7)
Denmark	497	(2.8)	443	(18.5)	452	(14.6)	443	(22.8)	458	(13.8)
France	507	(2.7)	477	(6.3)	450	(21.8)	435	(12.0)	412	(19.4)
Germany	520	(3.5)	457	(9.5)	463	(11.4)	404	(17.0)	404	(11.8)
Luxembourg	503	(1.8)	466	(6.9)	487	(10.7)	452	(5.8)	422	(4.7)
Netherlands	527	(3.0)	489	(9.1)	477	(13.4)	458	(11.7)	459	(10.0)
New Zealand	529	(2.9)	522	(10.0)	535	(6.9)	465	(12.8)	481	(6.8)
Norway	506	(2.6)	440	(22.0)	429	(27.3)	457	(17.1)	435	(12.6)
Sweden	524	(2.1)	512	(9.9)	466	(21.5)	507	(16.3)	431	(12.4)
Switzerland	517	(3.3)	473	(7.9)	455	(10.6)	464	(8.1)	412	(8.3)
United States	505	(3.0)	507	(8.6)	494	(11.7)	462	(11.8)	443	(8.8)
OECD average	*516*	*(0.8)*	*496*	*(2.4)*	*488*	*(3.7)*	*460*	*(3.4)*	*446*	*(2.6)*
Hong Kong-China	516	(3.4)	525	(3.9)	498	(4.9)	460	(21.5)	436	(13.2)
Macao-China	502	(5.3)	498	(3.0)	502	(7.7)	470	(13.5)	470	(20.9)
Russian Federation	449	(3.6)	430	(7.1)	420	(7.6)	377	(24.5)	367	(13.8)
Belgium (Flemish Community)	547	(2.9)	493	(17.5)	479	(15.5)	423	(14.7)	427	(22.2)
Belgium (French Community)	501	(4.5)	454	(14.8)	387	(22.6)	447	(19.1)	382	(20.9)

	Difference in the reading score							
	Second-generation minus native students				First-generation minus native students			
	Both sub-groups speak language of assessment at home		Second-generation students speak a different language at home		Both sub-groups speak language of assessment at home		First-generation students speak a different language at home	
	Difference	S.E.	Difference	S.E.	Difference	S.E.	Difference	S.E.
Australia	1	(5.2)	-14	(7.2)	-6	(5.4)	**-22**	(7.6)
Austria	**-41**	(17.0)	**-90**	(21.4)	**-42**	(12.5)	**-81**	(10.0)
Belgium	**-67**	(11.9)	**-93**	(12.3)	**-117**	(18.6)	**-125**	(15.1)
Canada	**18**	(4.2)	-8	(7.2)	-8	(6.3)	**-23**	(5.7)
Denmark	**-54**	(18.4)	**-53**	(23.2)	**-45**	(14.8)	**-39**	(14.1)
France	**-31**	(7.0)	**-72**	(12.1)	**-57**	(21.8)	**-95**	(19.6)
Germany	**-63**	(9.9)	**-115**	(17.3)	**-57**	(11.9)	**-116**	(11.5)
Luxembourg	**-36**	(7.2)	**-51**	(6.1)	-16	(11.1)	**-81**	(5.0)
Netherlands	**-38**	(9.6)	**-69**	(12.1)	**-49**	(13.8)	**-68**	(10.5)
New Zealand	-7	(10.7)	**-64**	(12.9)	6	(7.3)	**-48**	(7.5)
Norway	**-67**	(22.0)	**-49**	(17.0)	**-78**	(26.9)	**-71**	(12.4)
Sweden	-11	(9.8)	-17	(16.1)	**-58**	(21.3)	**-93**	(12.8)
Switzerland	**-45**	(7.2)	**-53**	(8.1)	**-63**	(9.3)	**-105**	(8.0)
United States	2	(8.3)	**-43**	(11.8)	-12	(11.7)	**-62**	(9.1)
OECD average	*-20*	*(2.4)*	*-56*	*(3.4)*	*-28*	*(3.7)*	*-70*	*(2.8)*
Hong Kong-China	8	(3.6)	-57	(21.2)	**-18**	(4.2)	**-80**	(13.4)
Macao-China	-4	(5.6)	-33	(14.9)	0	(10.1)	-32	(20.7)
Russian Federation	**-20**	(6.8)	-72	(24.5)	**-29**	(7.0)	**-82**	(13.2)
Belgium (Flemish Community)	**-54**	(18.0)	**-124**	(15.5)	**-69**	(15.7)	**-120**	(22.3)
Belgium (French Community)	**-47**	(14.4)	**-53**	(17.6)	**-114**	(22.5)	**-119**	(20.6)

Note: Differences that are statistically significant are indicated in bold.

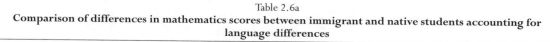

Table 2.6a
Comparison of differences in mathematics scores between immigrant and native students accounting for language differences

	Difference in the mathematics score							
	WITHOUT accounting for language differences				WITH accounting for language differences			
	Second-generation students minus native students		First-generation students minus native students		Second-generation students minus native students		First-generation students minus native students	
	Difference	S.E.	Difference	S.E.	Difference	S.E.	Difference	S.E.
Australia	-5	(4.4)	0	(5.0)	-3	(4.2)	4	(4.5)
Austria	-43	(10.1)	-56	(6.9)	-33	(11.1)	-44	(8.5)
Belgium	-76	(8.4)	-104	(11.0)	-62	(9.1)	-90	(12.5)
Canada	7	(4.5)	-1	(4.6)	13	(4.5)	11	(5.5)
Denmark	-70	(13.2)	-61	(10.9)	-71	(13.0)	-63	(11.6)
France	-42	(5.9)	-64	(17.6)	-34	(6.6)	-50	(18.1)
Germany	-86	(11.4)	-58	(8.9)	-68	(10.8)	-40	(9.3)
Luxembourg	-28	(4.2)	-44	(4.0)	-13	(6.3)	-25	(7.5)
Netherlands	-56	(11.7)	-77	(10.5)	-45	(11.4)	-57	(12.5)
New Zealand	-36	(10.4)	-7	(6.4)	-30	(10.6)	4	(7.7)
Norway	-32	(13.2)	-54	(10.6)	-33	(16.5)	-55	(18.2)
Sweden	-25	(9.6)	-79	(9.2)	-18	(8.0)	-67	(11.8)
Switzerland	-50	(5.9)	-80	(6.0)	-42	(6.3)	-65	(7.8)
United States	-16	(7.4)	-32	(7.6)	2	(7.5)	-4	(8.0)
OECD average	*-33*	*(2.2)*	*-42*	*(2.1)*	*-22*	*(2.2)*	*-25*	*(2.4)*
Hong Kong-China	14	(4.6)	-40	(4.7)	13	(4.6)	-39	(4.5)
Macao-China	5	(8.0)	-9	(10.8)	4	(8.0)	-10	(10.7)
Russian Federation	-14	(7.2)	-20	(5.6)	-14	(7.2)	-17	(5.4)
Belgium (Flemish Community)	-98	(14.8)	-90	(11.3)	-70	(16.1)	-66	(12.9)
Belgium (French Community)	-45	(9.5)	-93	(14.8)	-36	(9.7)	-84	(15.6)

Note: Differences that are statistically significant are indicated in bold.

Table 2.6b
Comparison of differences in reading scores between immigrant and native students accounting for language differences

	Difference in the reading score							
	WITHOUT accounting for language differences				WITH accounting for language differences			
	Second-generation students minus native students		First-generation students minus native students		Second-generation students minus native students		First-generation students minus native students	
	Difference	S.E.	Difference	S.E.	Difference	S.E.	Difference	S.E.
Australia	-3	(4.7)	-13	(4.9)	1	(4.8)	-7	(4.7)
Austria	-71	(14.8)	-71	(9.1)	-45	(12.0)	-40	(11.3)
Belgium	-76	(8.6)	-118	(14.1)	-61	(10.0)	-106	(16.4)
Canada	11	(4.2)	-17	(4.7)	19	(4.2)	1	(5.4)
Denmark	-54	(15.4)	-42	(10.9)	-57	(15.0)	-46	(12.1)
France	-45	(7.3)	-76	(17.6)	-28	(7.3)	-51	(17.0)
Germany	-86	(11.5)	-86	(9.3)	-60	(11.7)	-57	(9.8)
Luxembourg	-45	(4.8)	-69	(4.8)	-20	(6.3)	-37	(7.5)
Netherlands	-47	(8.7)	-59	(9.2)	-38	(8.7)	-42	(10.7)
New Zealand	-22	(9.0)	-22	(5.8)	-7	(9.3)	8	(7.2)
Norway	-57	(12.5)	-72	(11.9)	-51	(15.8)	-62	(21.3)
Sweden	-13	(8.7)	-85	(11.5)	-7	(7.8)	-73	(15.7)
Switzerland	-47	(5.7)	-90	(5.9)	-37	(6.8)	-70	(7.8)
United States	-19	(7.6)	-47	(8.3)	5	(7.6)	-11	(9.0)
OECD average	*-34*	*(2.2)*	*-54*	*(2.2)*	*-18*	*(2.3)*	*-29*	*(3.0)*
Hong Kong-China	9	(3.5)	-20	(4.2)	8	(3.5)	-19	(4.2)
Macao-China	-2	(5.6)	2	(9.4)	-3	(5.6)	1	(9.4)
Russian Federation	-20	(6.6)	-32	(6.8)	-20	(6.7)	-29	(6.6)
Belgium (Flemish Community)	-96	(13.0)	-92	(13.1)	-59	(14.8)	-64	(13.8)
Belgium (French Community)	-47	(11.0)	-113	(18.2)	-38	(11.7)	-106	(20.2)

Note: Differences that are statistically significant are indicated in bold.

Table 2.7

Mean score and gender differences in student performance on the mathematics and reading scales, by immigrant status

Native students

	Performance on the mathematics scale						Performance on the reading scale					
	Males		Females		Difference (F - M)		Males		Females		Difference (F - M)	
	Mean score	S.E.	Mean score	S.E.	Score dif.	S.E.	Mean score	S.E.	Mean score	S.E.	Score dif.	S.E.
OECD countries												
Australia	529	(2.9)	525	(2.5)	4	(3.3)	509	(2.8)	550	(2.2)	**-41**	(3.2)
Austria	520	(4.2)	510	(4.0)	**10**	(4.8)	479	(4.8)	523	(4.3)	**-44**	(5.9)
Belgium	550	(3.8)	540	(2.8)	**10**	(4.6)	507	(4.0)	541	(2.9)	**-34**	(4.7)
Canada	543	(2.0)	531	(1.9)	**12**	(2.3)	518	(2.1)	549	(1.9)	**-31**	(2.3)
Denmark	528	(3.2)	512	(2.8)	**17**	(3.2)	484	(3.2)	509	(3.0)	**-25**	(3.1)
France	525	(3.5)	515	(2.8)	**10**	(4.2)	486	(3.6)	524	(3.0)	**-38**	(4.2)
Germany	532	(4.1)	520	(4.0)	**12**	(4.0)	497	(4.3)	537	(3.8)	**-39**	(4.2)
Luxembourg	518	(2.4)	497	(2.0)	**22**	(3.7)	486	(2.9)	514	(2.3)	**-28**	(3.8)
Netherlands	553	(4.0)	549	(3.4)	4	(4.2)	513	(3.8)	536	(3.1)	**-22**	(3.9)
New Zealand	536	(3.2)	521	(3.4)	**15**	(4.0)	514	(3.8)	543	(3.5)	**-29**	(4.6)
Norway	503	(2.8)	495	(2.8)	7	(3.1)	480	(3.2)	529	(3.2)	**-50**	(3.4)
Sweden	520	(2.8)	515	(2.9)	5	(3.4)	503	(2.6)	541	(2.7)	**-39**	(3.3)
Switzerland	552	(4.7)	533	(3.8)	**18**	(5.2)	498	(4.5)	533	(3.0)	**-34**	(5.0)
United States	494	(3.2)	486	(3.2)	8	(3.0)	488	(3.6)	518	(3.5)	**-30**	(3.5)
OECD average	*529*	*(1.0)*	*517*	*(0.8)*	*11*	*(1.0)*	*497*	*(1.0)*	*531*	*(0.8)*	*-34*	*(1.0)*
Partner countries												
Hong Kong-China	558	(6.5)	556	(4.9)	2	(7.0)	496	(5.3)	529	(3.7)	**-33**	(5.8)
Macao-China	548	(8.1)	512	(7.6)	37	(10.9)	493	(6.9)	503	(6.5)	-10	(8.8)
Russian Federation	478	(5.5)	465	(4.4)	13	(4.4)	433	(4.7)	459	(4.0)	**-27**	(4.1)
Belgium (Flemish Community)	574	(4.6)	559	(3.2)	**-15**	(5.4)	529	(4.5)	557	(3.3)	28	(5.4)
Belgium (French Community)	516	(6.6)	512	(4.7)	-4	(7.8)	475	(7.0)	515	(5.3)	**40**	(8.8)

Second-generation students

	Males		Females		Difference (F - M)		Males		Females		Difference (F - M)	
	Mean score	S.E.	Mean score	S.E.	Score dif.	S.E.	Mean score	S.E.	Mean score	S.E.	Score dif.	S.E.
OECD countries												
Australia	526	(7.3)	518	(6.3)	8	(9.9)	505	(7.3)	544	(6.4)	**-38**	(9.9)
Austria	470	(10.9)	444	(13.2)	26	(16.5)	410	(11.7)	452	(22.6)	-42	(22.1)
Belgium	458	(9.5)	450	(8.4)	8	(10.1)	419	(10.0)	460	(9.4)	**-41**	(12.2)
Canada	553	(5.9)	534	(4.7)	**19**	(6.2)	532	(5.4)	554	(4.7)	**-22**	(5.7)
Denmark	470	(16.3)	432	(12.5)	**38**	(17.8)	425	(17.6)	452	(15.6)	-28	(18.7)
France	470	(10.0)	474	(7.1)	-5	(11.8)	433	(10.2)	476	(7.4)	**-43**	(12.4)
Germany	441	(11.2)	429	(10.4)	12	(11.9)	396	(11.9)	446	(10.2)	**-50**	(12.3)
Luxembourg	481	(5.2)	472	(4.2)	10	(6.7)	433	(5.9)	474	(4.9)	**-41**	(7.3)
Netherlands	510	(12.7)	476	(10.8)	**34**	(12.5)	478	(11.4)	472	(8.8)	5	(12.0)
New Zealand	490	(10.7)	502	(10.3)	-12	(12.6)	481	(11.0)	532	(10.3)	**-51**	(14.7)
Norway	476	(15.3)	443	(17.6)	33	(23.6)	446	(15.8)	446	(17.5)	1	(24.6)
Sweden	495	(12.1)	472	(11.8)	23	(14.4)	491	(11.9)	511	(10.0)	-20	(13.0)
Switzerland	491	(7.1)	475	(6.8)	16	(9.5)	447	(7.2)	479	(6.8)	**-32**	(9.8)
United States	474	(9.7)	461	(6.4)	13	(10.7)	471	(9.8)	493	(10.9)	-22	(11.6)
OECD average	*489*	*(2.6)*	*477*	*(2.5)*	*12*	*(2.8)*	*458*	*(2.8)*	*491*	*(2.6)*	*-33*	*(3.2)*
Partner countries												
Hong Kong-China	572	(7.1)	568	(5.6)	3	(9.0)	507	(6.0)	538	(4.7)	**-31**	(7.7)
Macao-China	540	(6.3)	524	(5.0)	16	(7.9)	491	(4.6)	503	(3.9)	-12	(6.2)
Russian Federation	455	(8.3)	461	(9.9)	-5	(11.1)	414	(8.7)	445	(7.1)	**-31**	(10.0)
Belgium (Flemish Community)	455	(15.9)	436	(11.2)	-18	(17.7)	423	(16.9)	454	(11.8)	31	(19.5)
Belgium (French Community)	459	(11.5)	458	(12.0)	-2	(13.4)	417	(12.6)	463	(13.7)	**47**	(16.5)

First-generation students

	Males		Females		Difference (F - M)		Males		Females		Difference (F - M)	
	Mean score	S.E.	Mean score	S.E.	Score dif.	S.E.	Mean score	S.E.	Mean score	S.E.	Score dif.	S.E.
OECD countries												
Australia	531	(7.6)	519	(8.1)	12	(12.3)	504	(7.9)	531	(7.5)	**-27**	(11.5)
Austria	451	(8.6)	452	(7.1)	-1	(10.6)	400	(10.0)	455	(9.5)	**-55**	(12.6)
Belgium	437	(14.0)	436	(12.6)	0	(16.5)	387	(14.7)	437	(14.2)	**-50**	(17.0)
Canada	533	(6.5)	528	(5.3)	5	(7.2)	498	(6.5)	532	(6.0)	**-34**	(8.5)
Denmark	450	(12.5)	459	(13.5)	-9	(16.6)	437	(13.7)	472	(12.9)	-35	(19.1)
France	449	(16.8)	446	(18.3)	3	(18.4)	403	(18.0)	449	(19.3)	**-46**	(20.9)
Germany	466	(9.3)	446	(9.0)	**21**	(10.5)	420	(11.3)	443	(10.6)	-23	(12.9)
Luxembourg	472	(5.7)	451	(4.8)	**22**	(7.6)	418	(6.7)	446	(5.4)	**-27**	(8.6)
Netherlands	482	(10.9)	463	(11.4)	19	(14.7)	458	(10.8)	469	(10.1)	-11	(13.2)
New Zealand	537	(5.9)	510	(7.3)	**26**	(9.2)	498	(7.6)	508	(7.9)	-10	(11.3)
Norway	431	(12.5)	446	(12.3)	-15	(16.5)	406	(14.6)	468	(14.1)	**-62**	(17.9)
Sweden	427	(14.0)	424	(9.4)	3	(14.1)	416	(15.4)	449	(10.9)	**-33**	(14.0)
Switzerland	459	(8.1)	447	(7.3)	12	(9.6)	405	(7.9)	441	(7.9)	**-37**	(9.9)
United States	460	(8.6)	445	(10.8)	15	(12.2)	440	(9.3)	469	(12.7)	**-29**	(14.6)
OECD average	*479*	*(2.8)*	*470*	*(2.3)*	*10*	*(3.4)*	*440*	*(3.0)*	*474*	*(2.8)*	*-34*	*(4.0)*
Partner countries												
Hong Kong-China	520	(9.4)	512	(4.9)	8	(10.2)	480	(8.2)	507	(4.3)	**-27**	(9.0)
Macao-China	523	(14.5)	510	(8.2)	13	(15.1)	487	(11.5)	512	(7.3)	-26	(13.1)
Russian Federation	454	(8.2)	449	(8.3)	6	(11.5)	401	(9.6)	429	(9.6)	-28	(12.4)
Belgium (Flemish Community)	483	(11.4)	459	(14.6)	-25	(18.0)	437	(13.2)	464	(15.3)	27	(18.7)
Belgium (French Community)	418	(17.2)	421	(17.5)	3	(20.2)	368	(18.1)	418	(20.5)	**50**	(21.6)

Note: Differences that are statistically significant are indicated in bold.

© OECD 2006 Where immigrant students succeed - A comparative review of performance and engagement in PISA 2003

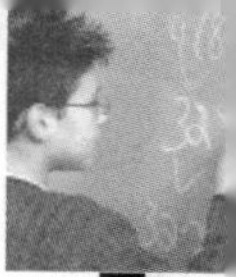

Table 2.8
Three most common countries of origin for immigrant students in each case country

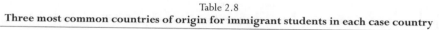

	Most common immigrant groups[1]	Participating students		Performance on the mathematics scale				Difference in mathematics score	
				Immigrant students		Native students		Immigrant students minus native students	
		Number	Weighted %	Mean score	S.E.	Mean score	S.E.	Difference	S.E.
OECD countries									
Australia	England	357	11.8	540	(7.3)			13	(7.5)
	New Zealand	189	7.0	516	(7.6)	527	(2.1)	-11	(7.5)
	China	130	5.0	576	(16.7)			**49**	(16.7)
Austria	Former Yugoslavia[2]	276	47.2	456	(6.7)			**-59**	(7.6)
	Turkey	141	25.9	423	(8.9)	515	(3.3)	**-92**	(9.1)
	Romania	19	c	c	c			c	c
Belgium	France	184	16.3	413	(25.3)			**-133**	(25.2)
	Turkey	140	14.8	421	(13.1)	546	(2.5)	**-125**	(12.8)
	Netherlands	54	5.8	521	(13.9)			**-24**	(14.1)
Canada	a	a	a	a	a	a	a	a	a
Denmark	Turkey	53	32.1	424	(12.4)			**-95**	(12.3)
	Pakistan	31	11.6	449	(14.3)	520	(2.5)	**-71**	(14.1)
	Former Yugoslavia	23	c	c	c			c	c
France	a	a	a	a	a	a	a	a	a
Germany	Turkey	197	32.1	405	(10.8)			**-120**	(11.6)
	Former Soviet Republic	180	28.3	466	(8.3)	525	(3.5)	**-59**	(9.3)
	Poland	100	16.1	486	(11.5)			**-39**	(11.2)
Luxembourg	Portugal	595	47.3	446	(3.2)			**-61**	(3.6)
	Italy	99	7.9	466	(9.0)	507	(1.3)	**-41**	(9.0)
	Former Yugoslavia	92	7.3	421	(10.2)			**-86**	(10.2)
Netherlands	a	a	a	a	a	a	a	a	a
New Zealand	Samoa	124	14.6	447	(10.3)			**-81**	(10.5)
	United Kingdom	103	11.2	546	(8.5)	528	(2.6)	18	(9.0)
	China	76	8.4	541	(17.7)			13	(18.1)
Norway	a	a	a	a	a	a	a	a	a
Portugal	a	a	a	a	a	a	a	a	a
Sweden	a	a	a	a	a	a	a	a	a
Switzerland	Former Yugoslavia	408	23.0	460	(7.3)			**-82**	(8.0)
	Albania/Kosovo	257	16.2	404	(6.8)	543	(3.3)	**-139**	(7.5)
	Italy	245	11.7	467	(8.3)			**-75**	(8.1)
United Kingdom	a	a	a	a	a	a	a	a	a
United States	Spanish speaking immigrants	270	35.0	423	(7.3)	490	(2.8)	**-66**	(7.5)
Partner countries									
Hong Kong-China	a	a	a	a	a	a	a	a	a
Macao-China	a	a	a	a	a	a	a	a	a
Russian Federation	a	a	a	a	a	a	a	a	a

Note: Differences that are statistically significant are indicated in bold.
1. These categories are chosen by countries.
2. Authors' calculations.

Table 2.9
Comparison of performance levels for immigrant students whose families came from Turkey and the former Yugoslavia

	Immigrant students								Native students		Difference in mathematics performance between native students and Turkish immigrant students		Difference in mathematics performance between native students and immigrant students from the former Yugoslavia	
	Turkey				Former Yugoslavia									
	Participating Students		Performance on the mathematics scale		Participating Students		Performance on the mathematics scale							
	N	Weighted %	Mean score	S.E.	N	Weighted %	Mean score	S.E.	Mean score	S.E.	Difference	S.E.	Difference	S.E.
Austria	141	25.9	423	(8.9)	276	47.2	456	(6.7)	515	(3.3)	**-92**	(9.1)	**-59**	(7.6)
Belgium	140	14.8	421	(13.1)	c	c	c	c	546	(2.5)	**-125**	(12.8)	c	c
Denmark	53	32.1	424	(12.4)	c	c	c	c	520	(2.5)	**-95**	(12.3)	c	c
Germany	197	32.1	405	(10.8)	45	7.0	448	(17.0)	525	(3.5)	**-120**	(11.6)	**-78**	(17.0)
Luxembourg	c	c	c	c	92	7.3	421	(10.2)	507	(1.3)	c	c	**-86**	(10.2)
Switzerland	142	8.5	436	(10.4)	408	23.0	460	(7.3)	543	(3.3)	**-106**	(10.3)	**-82**	(8.0)

Note: Differences that are statistically significant are indicated in bold.

© OECD 2006 Where immigrant students succeed - A comparative review of performance and engagement in PISA 2003

Table 3.1
Highest level of parental education (in years of schooling) by immigrant status

		Highest level of parental education in years of schooling[1]					
		Native students		Second-generation students		First-generation students	
		Mean	S.E.	Mean	S.E.	Mean	S.E.
OECD countries	Australia	13.1	(0.04)	**12.6**	(0.13)	**13.5**	(0.15)
	Austria	13.2	(0.06)	**11.1**	(0.31)	**12.3**	(0.24)
	Belgium	13.8	(0.05)	**10.7**	(0.33)	**12.1**	(0.30)
	Canada	14.5	(0.04)	14.4	(0.13)	**15.2**	(0.14)
	Denmark	14.6	(0.07)	**11.8**	(0.64)	**13.3**	(0.50)
	France	12.4	(0.05)	**9.3**	(0.29)	**9.7**	(0.54)
	Germany	13.9	(0.06)	**9.0**	(0.47)	**8.7**	(0.43)
	Luxembourg	14.5	(0.06)	**11.4**	(0.26)	**11.2**	(0.25)
	Netherlands	13.1	(0.06)	**10.0**	(0.39)	**11.6**	(0.46)
	New Zealand	13.5	(0.07)	**12.1**	(0.33)	13.8	(0.18)
	Norway	14.6	(0.04)	**13.7**	(0.43)	**13.7**	(0.39)
	Sweden	13.6	(0.05)	**12.2**	(0.37)	**12.3**	(0.36)
	Switzerland	12.6	(0.06)	**10.7**	(0.17)	**10.9**	(0.19)
	United States	13.8	(0.05)	**11.9**	(0.32)	**12.1**	(0.27)
	OECD average	***13.7***	***(0.02)***	***11.4***	***(0.09)***	***12.3***	***(0.08)***
Partner countries	Hong Kong-China	10.3	(0.12)	**9.2**	(0.11)	**8.7**	(0.12)
	Macao-China	10.0	(0.31)	9.3	(0.16)	9.3	(0.31)
	Russian Federation	13.3	(0.04)	13.2	(0.10)	13.3	(0.09)
	Belgium (Flemish Community)	13.7	(0.06)	**10.2**	(0.41)	**12.0**	(0.58)
	Belgium (French Community)	14.0	(0.08)	**11.0**	(0.48)	**12.2**	(0.37)

Note: Statistically significant differences from native students' scores are indicated in bold.
1. Table A1.1 in Annex A1 shows conversions used for years of schooling.

Table 3.2
Distribution of the index of economic, social and cultural status (ESCS) by immigrant status
(scores standardised within each country sample)

		Distribution of the index of economic, social and cultural status (ESCS)									
				Percentiles							
		ESCS mean		5th		25th		75th		95th	
		Index	S.E.	Index	S.E.	Index	S.E.	Index	S.E.	Index	S.E.
Australia	Native	0.03	(0.02)	-1.55	(0.03)	-0.62	(0.03)	0.73	(0.02)	1.64	(0.00)
	Second-generation	-0.20	(0.05)	-1.85	(0.09)	-0.88	(0.06)	0.54	(0.05)	1.57	(0.09)
	First-generation	0.04	(0.07)	-1.72	(0.30)	-0.68	(0.07)	0.84	(0.05)	1.63	(0.02)
Austria	Native	0.10	(0.03)	-1.30	(0.03)	-0.60	(0.03)	0.74	(0.04)	1.73	(0.03)
	Second-generation	-0.66	(0.11)	-2.56	(0.24)	-1.47	(0.14)	-0.05	(0.16)	1.67	(0.29)
	First-generation	-0.60	(0.07)	-2.17	(0.14)	-1.34	(0.09)	0.01	(0.08)	1.33	(0.16)
Belgium	Native	0.10	(0.02)	-1.42	(0.04)	-0.57	(0.03)	0.80	(0.02)	1.61	(0.03)
	Second-generation	-0.80	(0.08)	-2.82	(0.10)	-1.63	(0.10)	-0.04	(0.11)	1.19	(0.13)
	First-generation	-0.59	(0.07)	-2.55	(0.13)	-1.32	(0.11)	0.19	(0.08)	1.17	(0.15)
Canada	Native	0.00	(0.02)	-1.60	(0.03)	-0.70	(0.02)	0.73	(0.03)	1.66	(0.01)
	Second-generation	-0.07	(0.05)	-1.67	(0.07)	-0.83	(0.06)	0.70	(0.07)	1.65	(0.04)
	First-generation	0.15	(0.05)	-1.57	(0.09)	-0.54	(0.08)	0.89	(0.06)	1.67	(0.03)
Denmark	Native	0.06	(0.03)	-1.47	(0.04)	-0.61	(0.03)	0.72	(0.04)	1.64	(0.04)
	Second-generation	-0.81	(0.15)	c	c	-1.52	(0.16)	-0.08	(0.20)	c	c
	First-generation	-0.58	(0.11)	-3.10	(0.40)	-1.20	(0.08)	0.10	(0.11)	1.14	(0.23)
France	Native	0.12	(0.03)	-1.29	(0.05)	-0.54	(0.04)	0.77	(0.04)	1.66	(0.06)
	Second-generation	-0.76	(0.07)	-2.82	(0.11)	-1.44	(0.10)	0.01	(0.09)	1.07	(0.14)
	First-generation	-0.66	(0.15)	-2.95	(0.18)	-1.46	(0.24)	0.29	(0.26)	c	c
Germany	Native	0.18	(0.03)	-1.08	(0.03)	-0.43	(0.02)	0.77	(0.04)	1.69	(0.01)
	Second-generation	-0.91	(0.09)	-2.57	(0.08)	-1.89	(0.16)	-0.30	(0.13)	1.10	(0.17)
	First-generation	-0.90	(0.08)	-2.58	(0.07)	-1.89	(0.12)	-0.05	(0.12)	1.27	(0.19)
Luxembourg	Native	0.23	(0.01)	-1.26	(0.04)	-0.27	(0.02)	0.79	(0.02)	1.52	(0.01)
	Second-generation	-0.36	(0.05)	-2.12	(0.06)	-1.33	(0.06)	0.49	(0.05)	1.42	(0.05)
	First-generation	-0.54	(0.05)	-2.28	(0.06)	-1.52	(0.05)	0.46	(0.08)	1.50	(0.02)
Netherlands	Native	0.10	(0.03)	-1.36	(0.04)	-0.58	(0.04)	0.81	(0.03)	1.69	(0.05)
	Second-generation	-0.81	(0.12)	-3.01	(0.16)	-1.55	(0.12)	0.02	(0.15)	1.15	(0.33)
	First-generation	-0.58	(0.12)	-3.25	(0.40)	-1.30	(0.16)	0.17	(0.20)	1.15	(0.21)
New Zealand	Native	0.02	(0.02)	-1.56	(0.06)	-0.60	(0.02)	0.70	(0.03)	1.57	(0.03)
	Second-generation	-0.39	(0.08)	-2.54	(0.17)	-1.19	(0.12)	0.40	(0.11)	1.45	(0.12)
	First-generation	0.10	(0.04)	-2.17	(0.24)	-0.43	(0.05)	0.85	(0.05)	1.55	(0.05)
Norway	Native	0.03	(0.03)	-1.50	(0.04)	-0.65	(0.03)	0.73	(0.03)	1.61	(0.01)
	Second-generation	-0.39	(0.16)	-2.79	(0.36)	-1.37	(0.21)	0.51	(0.26)	c	c
	First-generation	-0.57	(0.13)	-3.19	(0.69)	-1.37	(0.15)	0.35	(0.16)	1.50	(0.13)
Sweden	Native	0.08	(0.03)	-1.45	(0.04)	-0.57	(0.02)	0.79	(0.04)	1.60	(0.02)
	Second-generation	-0.49	(0.09)	-2.77	(0.30)	-1.17	(0.12)	0.35	(0.13)	1.07	(0.13)
	First-generation	-0.62	(0.10)	-3.03	(0.26)	-1.37	(0.19)	0.30	(0.10)	1.29	(0.11)
Switzerland	Native	0.15	(0.03)	-1.32	(0.05)	-0.45	(0.03)	0.75	(0.04)	1.64	(0.03)
	Second-generation	-0.52	(0.04)	-2.50	(0.18)	-1.33	(0.06)	0.14	(0.08)	1.46	(0.08)
	First-generation	-0.68	(0.06)	-2.66	(0.12)	-1.44	(0.05)	0.00	(0.09)	1.33	(0.14)
United States	Native	0.10	(0.03)	-1.36	(0.03)	-0.55	(0.02)	0.79	(0.04)	1.56	(0.01)
	Second-generation	-0.46	(0.11)	-2.77	(0.21)	-1.27	(0.15)	0.36	(0.09)	1.47	(0.10)
	First-generation	-0.55	(0.08)	-2.58	(0.33)	-1.48	(0.09)	0.54	(0.13)	1.37	(0.17)
Hong Kong-China	Native	0.23	(0.04)	-1.38	(0.06)	-0.46	(0.04)	0.90	(0.06)	1.97	(0.10)
	Second-generation	-0.16	(0.03)	-1.65	(0.06)	-0.68	(0.03)	0.36	(0.05)	1.34	(0.09)
	First-generation	-0.45	(0.03)	-1.87	(0.11)	-1.06	(0.04)	0.05	(0.04)	1.12	(0.15)
Macao-China	Native	0.28	(0.08)	-1.80	(0.17)	-0.41	(0.14)	1.02	(0.09)	2.00	(0.11)
	Second-generation	-0.05	(0.04)	-1.79	(0.12)	-0.64	(0.05)	0.58	(0.04)	1.33	(0.06)
	First-generation	-0.15	(0.07)	-1.75	(0.17)	-0.78	(0.06)	0.46	(0.09)	1.33	(0.13)
Russian Federation	Native	0.01	(0.03)	-1.42	(0.03)	-0.78	(0.03)	0.80	(0.06)	1.70	(0.04)
	Second-generation	-0.03	(0.07)	-1.58	(0.10)	-0.79	(0.09)	0.75	(0.10)	1.63	(0.11)
	First-generation	-0.03	(0.07)	-1.61	(0.12)	-0.81	(0.09)	0.79	(0.08)	1.64	(0.17)
Belgium (Flemish Community)	Native	0.06	(0.03)	-1.43	(0.07)	-0.62	(0.04)	0.79	(0.02)	1.62	(0.03)
	Second-generation	-1.03	(0.10)	-2.78	(0.13)	-1.90	(0.14)	-0.33	(0.15)	0.76	(0.26)
	First-generation	-0.55	(0.14)	-2.90	(0.32)	-1.38	(0.26)	0.35	(0.13)	c	c
Belgium (French Community)	Native	0.14	(0.04)	-1.40	(0.07)	-0.52	(0.05)	0.82	(0.04)	1.59	(0.04)
	Second-generation	-0.64	(0.10)	-2.77	(0.13)	-1.39	(0.17)	0.10	(0.12)	1.33	(0.11)
	First-generation	-0.57	(0.08)	-2.35	(0.20)	-1.26	(0.15)	0.16	(0.12)	1.18	(0.17)

Note: Statistically significant differences from native students' scores are indicated in bold.

© OECD 2006 *Where immigrant students succeed - A comparative review of performance and engagement in PISA 2003*

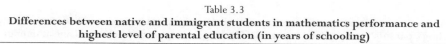

Table 3.3

Differences between native and immigrant students in mathematics performance and highest level of parental education (in years of schooling)

| | Difference in mathematics score | | | | Difference in highest parental education in years of schooling[1] | | | |
| | Second-generation students minus native students | | First-generation students minus native students | | Second-generation students minus native students | | First-generation students minus native students | |
	Difference	S.E.	Difference	S.E.	Difference	S.E.	Difference	S.E.
Australia	-5	(4.7)	-2	(4.9)	**-0.44**	(0.13)	**0.44**	(0.14)
Austria	**-56**	(9.3)	**-63**	(6.0)	**-2.18**	(0.31)	**-0.98**	(0.24)
Belgium	**-92**	(7.6)	**-109**	(10.9)	**-3.13**	(0.33)	**-1.70**	(0.30)
Canada	6	(4.4)	-7	(4.8)	-0.06	(0.13)	**0.71**	(0.14)
Denmark	**-70**	(11.1)	**-65**	(9.8)	**-2.83**	(0.62)	**-1.40**	(0.50)
France	**-48**	(6.6)	**-72**	(15.0)	**-3.04**	(0.29)	**-2.64**	(0.54)
Germany	**-93**	(9.6)	**-71**	(7.9)	**-4.85**	(0.48)	**-5.20**	(0.43)
Luxembourg	**-31**	(3.7)	**-45**	(4.1)	**-3.10**	(0.27)	**-3.33**	(0.25)
Netherlands	**-59**	(11.1)	**-79**	(8.8)	**-3.04**	(0.39)	**-1.43**	(0.47)
New Zealand	**-32**	(9.1)	-5	(5.6)	**-1.49**	(0.34)	0.26	(0.20)
Norway	**-39**	(11.3)	**-61**	(9.4)	**-0.97**	(0.42)	**-0.99**	(0.39)
Sweden	**-34**	(9.1)	**-92**	(9.7)	**-1.38**	(0.36)	**-1.36**	(0.36)
Switzerland	**-59**	(4.9)	**-89**	(6.0)	**-1.90**	(0.18)	**-1.78**	(0.20)
United States	**-22**	(7.2)	**-36**	(7.5)	**-1.86**	(0.32)	**-1.71**	(0.27)
OECD average	*-40*	*(2.0)*	*-48*	*(2.1)*	*-2.24*	*(0.09)*	*-1.41*	*(0.08)*
Hong Kong-China	13	(4.3)	**-41**	(4.5)	**-1.07**	(0.14)	**-1.58**	(0.17)
Macao-China	4	(7.9)	-11	(10.4)	-0.67	(0.37)	-0.67	(0.43)
Russian Federation	-14	(7.2)	**-20**	(5.4)	-0.10	(0.10)	0.00	(0.10)
Belgium (Flemish Community)	**-122**	(11.3)	**-95**	(9.9)	**-3.57**	(0.40)	**-1.76**	(0.58)
Belgium (French Community)	**-56**	(9.3)	**-94**	(14.4)	**-3.02**	(0.50)	**-1.83**	(0.37)

OECD countries / Partner countries

Note: Statistically significant differences are indicated in bold.
1. Table A1.1 in Annex A1 shows conversions used for years of schooling.

Table 3.4

Differences between native and immigrant students in mathematics performance and parents' economic, social and cultural status (ESCS)

| | Difference in mathematics score | | | | Difference in the index of economic, social and cultural status (ESCS) | | | |
| | Second-generation students minus native students | | First-generation students minus native students | | Second-generation students minus native students | | First-generation students minus native students | |
	Difference	S.E.	Difference	S.E.	Difference	S.E.	Difference	S.E.
Australia	-5	(4.7)	-2	(4.9)	**-0.20**	(0.04)	0.00	(0.05)
Austria	**-56**	(9.3)	**-63**	(6.0)	**-0.64**	(0.09)	**-0.59**	(0.05)
Belgium	**-92**	(7.6)	**-109**	(10.9)	**-0.85**	(0.07)	**-0.65**	(0.07)
Canada	6	(4.4)	-7	(4.8)	-0.06	(0.04)	**0.13**	(0.04)
Denmark	**-70**	(11.1)	**-65**	(9.8)	**-0.75**	(0.12)	**-0.55**	(0.10)
France	**-48**	(6.6)	**-72**	(15.0)	**-0.83**	(0.07)	**-0.74**	(0.13)
Germany	**-93**	(9.6)	**-71**	(7.9)	**-1.08**	(0.09)	**-1.07**	(0.08)
Luxembourg	**-31**	(3.7)	**-45**	(4.1)	**-0.64**	(0.06)	**-0.84**	(0.05)
Netherlands	**-59**	(11.1)	**-79**	(8.8)	**-0.78**	(0.10)	**-0.58**	(0.11)
New Zealand	**-32**	(9.1)	-5	(5.6)	**-0.37**	(0.08)	0.08	(0.05)
Norway	**-39**	(11.3)	**-61**	(9.4)	**-0.33**	(0.12)	**-0.47**	(0.10)
Sweden	**-34**	(9.1)	**-92**	(9.7)	**-0.50**	(0.07)	**-0.61**	(0.08)
Switzerland	**-59**	(4.9)	**-89**	(6.0)	**-0.57**	(0.05)	**-0.70**	(0.05)
United States	**-22**	(7.2)	**-36**	(7.5)	**-0.52**	(0.10)	**-0.59**	(0.08)
OECD average	*-40*	*(2.0)*	*-48*	*(2.1)*	*-0.58*	*(0.02)*	*-0.47*	*(0.02)*
Hong Kong-China	13	(4.3)	**-41**	(4.5)	**-0.31**	(0.03)	**-0.55**	(0.04)
Macao-China	4	(7.9)	-11	(10.4)	-0.28	(0.07)	-0.37	(0.09)
Russian Federation	-14	(7.2)	**-20**	(5.4)	-0.03	(0.05)	-0.03	(0.05)
Belgium (Flemish Community)	**-122**	(11.3)	**-95**	(9.9)	**-0.99**	(0.09)	**-0.55**	(0.13)
Belgium (French Community)	**-56**	(9.3)	**-94**	(14.4)	**-0.77**	(0.10)	**-0.70**	(0.08)

OECD countries / Partner countries

Note: Statistically significant differences are indicated in bold.

Table 3.5

Regression estimates of mathematics performance on immigrant status, parental education (in years of schooling), parents' occupational status (HISEI), language spoken at home and age at immigration

		Regression										Explained variance (unique) Percentage	Missing (un-weighted) Percentage
		Model 1		Model 2		Model 3		Model 4		Model 5			
		B	S.E.	B	S.E.	B	S.E.	B	S.E.	B	S.E.		
OECD countries													
Australia	Second-generation	-5.2	(4.43)	-1.9	(4.12)	1.8	(4.01)	1.9	(3.80)	1.6	(3.73)	0.0	
	First-generation	0.1	(5.01)	-5.4	(4.86)	-4.7	(4.84)	-4.4	(4.43)	2.6	(6.42)	0.0	
	Parental education in years of schooling			**8.5**	(0.62)	**4.1**	(0.57)	**4.1**	(0.57)	**4.1**	(0.58)	0.8	
	Parents' occupational status					**1.6**	(0.07)	**1.6**	(0.07)	**1.6**	(0.07)	6.1	
	Foreign language spoken at home							-0.6	(5.05)	0.8	(5.18)	0.0	
	Age at immigration									**-1.5**	(0.63)	0.1	
	R-squared		0.00		0.04		0.10		0.10		0.11		9.8
Austria	Second-generation	**-42.6**	(10.11)	**-27.6**	(9.80)	**-25.3**	(10.00)	**-23.5**	(10.74)	**-23.9**	(10.74)	0.2	
	First-generation	**-55.6**	(6.90)	**-48.1**	(6.82)	**-38.4**	(6.83)	**-36.3**	(7.72)	**-29.2**	(9.99)	0.2	
	Parental education in years of schooling			**7.1**	(0.85)	**3.3**	(0.80)	**3.3**	(0.80)	**3.4**	(0.80)	0.8	
	Parents' occupational status					**1.4**	(0.13)	**1.4**	(0.13)	**1.4**	(0.13)	5.2	
	Foreign language spoken at home							-2.9	(7.97)	-2.3	(8.01)	0.0	
	Age at immigration									-1.3	(1.56)	0.2	
	R-squared		0.03		0.07		0.12		0.12		0.13		8.5
Belgium	Second-generation	**-75.8**	(8.41)	**-55.0**	(7.95)	**-50.6**	(7.51)	**-40.9**	(7.92)	**-40.7**	(8.05)	0.6	
	First-generation	**-103.6**	(10.99)	**-89.0**	(10.38)	**-83.0**	(9.54)	**-73.7**	(10.55)	**-25.4**	(9.98)	0.1	
	Parental education in years of schooling			**7.9**	(0.51)	**3.0**	(0.49)	**2.9**	(0.49)	**2.9**	(0.48)	0.6	
	Parents' occupational status					**1.8**	(0.11)	**1.8**	(0.11)	**1.8**	(0.11)	7.2	
	Foreign language spoken at home							**-30.6**	(9.07)	**-32.1**	(9.14)	0.3	
	Age at immigration									**-5.2**	(1.05)	0.8	
	R-squared		0.06		0.11		0.18		0.19		0.19		19.1
Canada	Second-generation	7.4	(4.47)	8.0	(4.27)	10.6	(4.09)	**14.1**	(4.23)	**13.9**	(4.25)	0.2	
	First-generation	-1.1	(4.65)	-6.4	(4.68)	-6.0	(4.53)	1.9	(5.43)	7.0	(7.38)	0.0	
	Parental education in years of schooling			**6.8**	(0.45)	**3.3**	(0.43)	**3.3**	(0.43)	**3.3**	(0.43)	0.7	
	Parents' occupational status					**1.2**	(0.07)	**1.2**	(0.08)	**1.2**	(0.08)	4.1	
	Foreign language spoken at home							**-11.9**	(5.18)	**-11.4**	(5.18)	0.1	
	Age at immigration									-0.7	(0.77)	0.1	
	R-squared		0.00		0.04		0.08		0.08		0.08		10.8
Denmark	Second-generation	**-69.6**	(13.24)	**-49.4**	(13.98)	**-45.3**	(13.13)	**-47.4**	(12.89)	**-48.2**	(12.77)	0.7	
	First-generation	**-60.9**	(10.89)	**-55.3**	(12.21)	**-52.5**	(12.04)	**-55.3**	(12.77)	-18.0	(13.53)	0.0	
	Parental education in years of schooling			**8.2**	(0.74)	**5.1**	(0.70)	**5.1**	(0.70)	**5.2**	(0.69)	1.9	
	Parents' occupational status					**1.3**	(0.11)	**1.3**	(0.11)	**1.3**	(0.11)	4.5	
	Foreign language spoken at home							5.6	(10.06)	7.2	(9.72)	0.0	
	Age at immigration									**-6.5**	(1.53)	0.5	
	R-squared		0.03		0.08		0.13		0.13		0.13		9.0
France	Second-generation	**-42.3**	(5.94)	**-20.8**	(6.10)	**-18.4**	(5.90)	**-15.6**	(6.31)	**-15.9**	(6.33)	0.2	
	First-generation	**-64.4**	(17.56)	**-45.9**	(14.61)	**-47.4**	(14.35)	**-42.5**	(15.21)	-13.7	(14.65)	0.1	
	Parental education in years of schooling			**7.6**	(0.68)	**3.2**	(0.67)	**3.1**	(0.69)	**3.1**	(0.69)	0.7	
	Parents' occupational status					**1.5**	(0.13)	**1.5**	(0.13)	**1.5**	(0.13)	6.2	
	Foreign language spoken at home							-9.6	(9.52)	-8.8	(9.22)	0.1	
	Age at immigration									**-4.3**	(1.81)	0.3	
	R-squared		0.03		0.08		0.14		0.14		0.15		12.0
Germany	Second-generation	**-86.0**	(11.37)	**-57.2**	(10.31)	**-51.3**	(9.26)	**-35.9**	(9.89)	**-40.5**	(9.20)	0.7	
	First-generation	**-58.0**	(8.88)	**-24.9**	(9.36)	**-24.5**	(8.98)	-9.1	(9.05)	13.6	(11.51)	0.1	
	Parental education in years of schooling			**6.6**	(0.63)	**3.3**	(0.61)	**3.2**	(0.59)	**3.2**	(0.60)	1.1	
	Parents' occupational status					**1.8**	(0.11)	**1.8**	(0.11)	**1.8**	(0.11)	7.7	
	Foreign language spoken at home							**-35.6**	(9.20)	**-25.3**	(9.80)	0.2	
	Age at immigration									**-5.7**	(1.85)	0.4	
	R-squared		0.07		0.12		0.19		0.20		0.20		20.8
Luxembourg	Second-generation	**-28.3**	(4.23)	**-13.2**	(4.43)	**-10.1**	(4.36)	-9.9	(5.95)	-10.3	(6.05)	0.1	
	First-generation	**-44.3**	(4.03)	**-28.4**	(4.21)	**-20.9**	(4.19)	**-20.7**	(7.28)	-11.9	(8.30)	0.1	
	Parental education in years of schooling			**4.7**	(0.32)	**1.8**	(0.38)	**1.8**	(0.39)	**1.8**	(0.39)	0.6	
	Parents' occupational status					**1.7**	(0.13)	**1.7**	(0.13)	**1.7**	(0.13)	6.5	
	Foreign language spoken at home							-0.3	(7.42)	0.1	(7.58)	0.0	
	Age at immigration									-1.9	(1.08)	0.1	
	R-squared		0.04		0.09		0.16		0.16		0.16		21.1

Note: Statistically significant coefficients are indicated in bold. For the variable *Age at immigration* the number of missing values is particularly high, therefore mean substitution is used and a dummy variable indicating whether or not the age at immigration is missing was included in the regression model. Table A1.1 in Annex A1 shows the conversions used for the variable *Parental education in years of schooling*.

© OECD 2006 Where immigrant students succeed - A comparative review of performance and engagement in PISA 2003

Table 3.5 (*continued*)

Regression estimates of mathematics performance on immigrant status, parental education (in years of schooling), parents' occupational status (HISEI), language spoken at home and age at immigration

		Regression										Explained variance (unique)	Missing (un-weighted)
		Model 1		Model 2		Model 3		Model 4		Model 5			
		B	S.E.	B	S.E.	B	S.E.	B	S.E.	B	S.E.	Percentage	Percentage
Netherlands	Second-generation	**-55.6**	(11.69)	**-40.3**	(10.96)	**-38.1**	(9.85)	**-32.1**	(9.84)	**-33.0**	(9.88)	0.7	
	First-generation	**-77.3**	(10.48)	**-69.7**	(10.47)	**-66.3**	(9.95)	**-54.6**	(11.83)	**-36.4**	(13.99)	0.2	
	Parental education in years of schooling			**7.1**	(0.71)	**2.5**	(0.77)	**2.4**	(0.77)	**2.4**	(0.76)	0.4	
	Parents' occupational status					**1.6**	(0.13)	**1.6**	(0.13)	**1.6**	(0.13)	6.6	
	Foreign language spoken at home							-21.4	(10.92)	-19.0	(11.03)	0.1	
	Age at immigration									-3.2	(1.60)	0.2	
	R-squared		0.04		0.08		0.15		0.15		0.15		15.0
New Zealand	Second-generation	**-35.9**	(10.39)	**-25.8**	(10.47)	**-22.8**	(9.44)	**-20.0**	(9.51)	**-20.4**	(9.46)	0.3	
	First-generation	-7.5	(6.43)	-9.5	(6.22)	**-14.9**	(6.13)	-8.9	(7.07)	2.4	(10.66)	0.0	
	Parental education in years of schooling			**6.8**	(0.58)	**4.4**	(0.58)	**4.3**	(0.59)	**4.4**	(0.59)	2.0	
	Parents' occupational status					**1.5**	(0.11)	**1.5**	(0.11)	**1.5**	(0.11)	5.7	
	Foreign language spoken at home							-12.0	(8.63)	-10.7	(8.72)	0.1	
	Age at immigration									-1.3	(0.91)	0.1	
	R-squared		0.01		0.06		0.12		0.12		0.12		26.3
Norway	Second-generation	**-32.1**	(13.23)	-22.5	(11.88)	**-25.6**	(11.17)	-28.2	(15.07)	-29.7	(15.16)	0.1	
	First-generation	**-53.9**	(10.61)	**-47.1**	(10.27)	**-40.3**	(9.97)	**-44.5**	(16.61)	-30.2	(17.04)	0.1	
	Parental education in years of schooling			**8.2**	(0.74)	**3.2**	(0.77)	**3.2**	(0.77)	**3.3**	(0.77)	0.4	
	Parents' occupational status					**1.5**	(0.11)	**1.5**	(0.11)	**1.5**	(0.11)	5.4	
	Foreign language spoken at home							4.9	(15.75)	7.6	(15.99)	0.0	
	Age at immigration									-2.6	(1.45)	0.1	
	R-squared		0.01		0.04		0.10		0.10		0.10		8.6
Sweden	Second-generation	**-25.2**	(9.59)	**-20.1**	(9.27)	-12.5	(9.70)	-4.8	(8.36)	-5.3	(8.63)	0.0	
	First-generation	**-78.8**	(9.15)	**-74.7**	(9.06)	**-69.3**	(8.37)	**-56.2**	(11.54)	**-48.8**	(11.74)	0.5	
	Parental education in years of schooling			**5.3**	(0.61)	**2.2**	(0.58)	**2.2**	(0.59)	**2.2**	(0.60)	0.4	
	Parents' occupational status					**1.5**	(0.12)	**1.5**	(0.12)	**1.5**	(0.12)	5.9	
	Foreign language spoken at home							-17.7	(10.36)	-16.1	(10.59)	0.1	
	Age at immigration									-1.6	(1.75)	0.2	
	R-squared		0.04		0.06		0.12		0.12		0.12		12.4
Switzerland	Second-generation	**-49.9**	(5.92)	**-35.9**	(6.00)	**-31.0**	(5.84)	**-28.7**	(6.06)	**-29.7**	(6.04)	0.6	
	First-generation	**-79.9**	(6.00)	**-65.3**	(5.58)	**-56.7**	(5.50)	**-52.2**	(6.67)	**-34.9**	(10.64)	0.4	
	Parental education in years of schooling			**8.9**	(0.77)	**6.3**	(0.71)	**6.3**	(0.71)	**6.4**	(0.71)	2.6	
	Parents' occupational status					**1.1**	(0.10)	**1.1**	(0.10)	**1.1**	(0.10)	2.7	
	Foreign language spoken at home							-7.3	(7.48)	-4.5	(7.48)	0.0	
	Age at immigration									**-3.7**	(1.21)	0.4	
	R-squared		0.07		0.13		0.16		0.16		0.16		12.3
United States	Second-generation	**-16.1**	(7.43)	-3.0	(6.61)	-0.4	(6.06)	8.8	(6.21)	8.3	(6.17)	0.0	
	First-generation	**-32.1**	(7.58)	**-19.8**	(7.36)	**-14.7**	(6.58)	0.1	(7.32)	13.5	(10.16)	0.0	
	Parental education in years of schooling			**8.2**	(0.60)	**4.4**	(0.59)	**4.2**	(0.58)	**4.3**	(0.59)	1.1	
	Parents' occupational status					**1.5**	(0.10)	**1.5**	(0.10)	**1.5**	(0.10)	5.9	
	Foreign language spoken at home							-22.2	(7.13)	-21.0	(7.27)	0.2	
	Age at immigration									-2.2	(1.38)	0.1	
	R-squared		0.01		0.06		0.12		0.12		0.12		11.2
OECD average	*Second-generation*	*-32.9*	*(2.16)*	*-20.4*	*(2.19)*	*-17.3*	*(2.11)*	*-11.5*	*(2.10)*	*-11.8*	*(2.09)*	*0.1*	
	First-generation	*-42.1*	*(2.08)*	*-34.0*	*(2.10)*	*-30.4*	*(1.94)*	*-21.1*	*(2.13)*	*-14.1*	*(2.83)*	*0.1*	
	Parental education in years of schooling			*6.3*	*(0.14)*	*2.9*	*(0.15)*	*2.8*	*(0.15)*	*2.9*	*(0.15)*	*0.7*	
	Parents' occupational status					*1.5*	*(0.03)*	*1.5*	*(0.03)*	*1.5*	*(0.03)*	*5.6*	
	Foreign language spoken at home							*-15.3*	*(2.01)*	*-14.5*	*(2.02)*	*0.1*	
	Age at immigration									*-1.3*	*(0.36)*	*0.1*	
	R-squared		*0.02*		*0.06*		*0.12*		*0.12*		*0.12*		*14.1*

Note: Statistically significant coefficients are indicated in bold. For the variable *Age at immigration* the number of missing values is particularly high, therefore mean substitution is used and a dummy variable indicating whether or not the age at immigration is missing was included in the regression model. Table A1.1 in Annex A1 shows the conversions used for the variable *Parental education in years of schooling*.

Table 3.5 (*continued*)

Regression estimates of mathematics performance on immigrant status, parental education (in years of schooling), parents' occupational status (HISEI), language spoken at home and age at immigration

		Regression										Explained variance (unique)	Missing (un-weighted)
		Model 1		Model 2		Model 3		Model 4		Model 5			
		B	S.E.	B	S.E.	B	S.E.	B	S.E.	B	S.E.	Percentage	Percentage
Hong Kong-China	Second-generation	**13.6**	(4.62)	**17.1**	(4.61)	**21.0**	(4.65)	**20.1**	(4.63)	**17.4**	(4.55)	0.5	
	First-generation	**-39.6**	(4.71)	**-34.6**	(4.77)	**-27.3**	(4.91)	**-26.9**	(4.73)	10.4	(6.20)	0.0	
	Parental education in years of schooling			**3.3**	(0.76)	1.3	(0.69)	**1.4**	(0.68)	**1.4**	(0.67)	0.2	
	Parents' occupational status					**1.1**	(0.16)	**1.0**	(0.15)	**0.9**	(0.15)	1.2	
	Foreign language spoken at home							**-58.7**	(9.61)	**-54.5**	(9.31)	1.3	
	Age at immigration									**-4.9**	(0.55)	2.5	
	R-squared		0.04		0.05		0.06		0.08		0.10		9.3
Macao-China	Second-generation	5.3	(8.04)	6.6	(8.02)	9.1	(8.21)	7.7	(8.21)	7.1	(8.23)	0.1	
	First-generation	-9.5	(10.84)	-8.1	(10.83)	-5.0	(11.08)	-6.1	(10.98)	12.1	(15.62)	0.1	
	Parental education in years of schooling			**1.9**	(0.76)	1.3	(0.86)	1.2	(0.86)	1.0	(0.86)	0.2	
	Parents' occupational status					0.5	(0.29)	0.5	(0.29)	0.5	(0.29)	0.3	
	Foreign language spoken at home							**-41.9**	(15.38)	**-36.8**	(15.91)	0.8	
	Age at immigration									-2.6	(1.78)	2.0	
	R-squared		0.00		0.01		0.02		0.03		0.05		6.8
Russian Federation	Second-generation	-14.0	(7.21)	-13.1	(6.98)	-13.4	(7.02)	-13.0	(7.02)	-13.2	(7.05)	0.2	
	First-generation	**-19.6**	(5.62)	**-19.5**	(5.22)	**-20.5**	(5.38)	**-18.6**	(5.32)	-12.0	(7.97)	0.1	
	Parental education in years of schooling			**12.9**	(1.08)	**7.2**	(1.27)	**6.9**	(1.26)	**6.9**	(1.26)	1.0	
	Parents' occupational status					**1.0**	(0.13)	**0.9**	(0.13)	**0.9**	(0.13)	2.1	
	Foreign language spoken at home							**-32.9**	(12.98)	**-32.9**	(13.11)	0.6	
	Age at immigration									-1.3	(0.77)	0.1	
	R-squared		0.00		0.05		0.07		0.08		0.08		4.9
Belgium (Flemish Community)	Second-generation	**-98.3**	(14.85)	**-70.7**	(13.74)	**-64.7**	(13.10)	**-43.4**	(14.48)	**-44.0**	(14.79)	0.3	
	First-generation	**-90.1**	(11.31)	**-69.6**	(10.30)	**-70.6**	(10.02)	**-51.8**	(11.79)	2.1	(18.76)	0.0	
	Parental education in years of schooling			**9.4**	(0.69)	**4.1**	(0.66)	**1.8**	(0.13)	**4.0**	(0.67)	1.0	
	Parents' occupational status					**1.8**	(0.13)	**4.0**	(0.66)	**1.8**	(0.13)	7.2	
	Foreign language spoken at home							**-41.0**	(13.10)	**-40.2**	(13.32)	0.3	
	Age at immigration									**-6.3**	(1.57)	0.3	
	R-squared		0.04		0.11		0.19		0.19		0.19		16.4
Belgium (French Community)	Second-generation	**-45.1**	(9.46)	**-26.0**	(9.12)	**-22.0**	(8.69)	-16.7	(8.63)	**-17.1**	(8.70)	0.2	
	First-generation	**-92.5**	(14.76)	**-79.1**	(14.42)	**-69.1**	(13.39)	**-63.8**	(13.97)	**-31.3**	(14.55)	0.3	
	Parental education in years of schooling			**7.1**	(0.84)	**3.0**	(0.74)	**1.8**	(0.19)	**2.9**	(0.69)	0.6	
	Parents' occupational status					**1.8**	(0.19)	**3.0**	(0.74)	**1.8**	(0.19)	7.4	
	Foreign language spoken at home							**-23.5**	(10.63)	**-25.4**	(10.48)	0.3	
	Age at immigration									-3.5	(1.38)	0.7	
	R-squared		0.06		0.11		0.18		0.18		0.19		21.4

Note: Statistically significant coefficients are indicated in bold. For the variable *Age at immigration* the number of missing values is particularly high, therefore mean substitution is used and a dummy variable indicating whether or not the age at immigration is missing was included in the regression model. Table A1.1 in Annex A1 shows the conversions used for the variable *Parental education in years of schooling*.

© OECD 2006   Where immigrant students succeed - A comparative review of performance and engagement in PISA 2003

Table 3.6
Between- and within-school variance in student performance in mathematics

		Percentage of the total variance within the country that is:		Variance explained by students' immigrant status			
		Between schools	Within schools	Between-school variance explained	Within-school variance explained	Between-school variance explained expressed as a percentage of the total variance	Within-school variance explained expressed as a percentage of the total variance
OECD countries	Australia	20.9	79.1	0.09	0.05	0.02	0.04
	Austria	55.2	44.8	6.53	3.36	3.61	1.51
	Belgium	53.0	47.0	9.93	2.92	5.26	1.37
	Canada[1]	17.0	83.0	a	a	a	a
	Denmark	13.7	86.3	11.29	2.23	1.54	1.92
	France	46.1	53.9	4.44	2.20	2.04	1.18
	Germany	51.8	48.2	10.68	3.24	5.53	1.56
	Luxembourg	31.3	68.7	6.17	2.66	1.93	1.83
	Netherlands	57.9	42.1	6.70	3.34	3.88	1.41
	New Zealand	17.9	82.1	1.52	0.30	0.27	0.24
	Norway	6.7	93.3	5.31	1.55	0.36	1.45
	Sweden	10.9	89.1	28.33	3.25	3.09	2.90
	Switzerland	34.0	66.0	16.82	7.20	5.72	4.75
	United States	25.3	74.7	2.46	0.25	0.62	0.18
Partner countries	Hong Kong-China	46.5	53.5	2.83	2.22	1.32	1.19
	Macao-China	18.3	81.7	0.24	0.27	0.04	0.22
	Russian Federation	29.8	70.2	0.44	0.38	0.13	0.27

Note: The variance components were estimated for all students with data on immigrant status.
1. Accounting for immigrant student status slightly increases the school-level variance in Canada, thus resulting in a negative estimate for explained between-school variance.

Table 3.7a
Percentage of second-generation students attending schools with different sized immigrant student populations (first- and second-generation students combined)

		Proportion of immigrant students within the school															
		0% to <10%	S.E.	10% to <20%	S.E.	20% to <30%	S.E.	30% to <40%	S.E.	40% to <50%	S.E.	50% to <60%	S.E.	60% to <70%	S.E.	70% or higher	S.E.	Total
OECD countries	Australia	7.6	(1.07)	14.0	(2.23)	17.3	(3.04)	15.1	(3.06)	10.2	(3.49)	9.4	(3.06)	6.5	(2.84)	19.8	(5.01)	100.0
	Austria	12.6	(3.11)	14.3	(3.96)	16.9	(6.08)	11.6	(5.17)	3.6	(3.50)	15.9	(6.13)	9.8	(6.96)	15.3	(5.56)	100.0
	Belgium	17.6	(2.76)	21.3	(3.91)	19.9	(4.81)	10.7	(3.18)	5.5	(3.43)	7.1	(4.38)	2.1	(1.30)	15.8	(7.24)	100.0
	Canada	9.5	(1.20)	8.9	(1.47)	13.2	(2.05)	12.1	(3.02)	9.6	(2.25)	14.9	(3.52)	6.9	(2.72)	24.9	(4.38)	100.0
	Denmark	25.1	(5.35)	25.7	(6.81)	7.6	(4.48)	7.2	(4.11)	5.3	(3.60)	3.7	(3.67)	4.9	(4.87)	20.6	(11.64)	100.0
	France	10.4	(2.22)	21.9	(4.52)	13.6	(3.56)	14.8	(3.87)	20.9	(5.93)	4.5	(3.13)	6.5	(4.43)	7.5	(4.22)	100.0
	Germany	7.9	(1.85)	11.1	(3.06)	18.3	(4.31)	12.9	(3.77)	13.4	(4.97)	13.3	(5.46)	10.5	(5.22)	12.7	(6.96)	100.0
	Luxembourg	0.6	(0.32)	15.1	(1.29)	23.2	(1.39)	9.7	(1.02)	26.1	(1.72)	6.5	(0.89)	6.1	(0.82)	12.7	(1.05)	100.0
	Netherlands	15.6	(3.68)	25.9	(6.07)	11.8	(4.76)	0.0	c	3.9	(3.92)	16.4	(7.83)	5.0	(4.91)	21.3	(8.90)	100.0
	New Zealand	9.3	(2.11)	12.7	(2.50)	8.4	(2.50)	17.5	(4.87)	14.4	(4.13)	9.9	(2.95)	2.7	(2.64)	25.3	(7.98)	100.0
	Norway	26.3	(6.63)	23.9	(7.42)	12.4	(6.80)	6.4	(4.48)	24.4	(12.01)	6.7	(6.39)	0.0	c	0.0	c	100.0
	Sweden	14.4	(2.58)	22.4	(4.76)	23.4	(5.88)	12.1	(5.31)	11.3	(5.24)	0.6	(0.58)	9.2	(5.80)	6.6	(2.38)	100.0
	Switzerland	5.0	(1.14)	25.3	(3.59)	25.0	(3.67)	10.7	(2.80)	6.1	(1.57)	17.0	(3.73)	4.4	(1.40)	6.5	(2.87)	100.0
Partner countries	United States	7.6	(1.62)	12.1	(2.55)	11.5	(3.38)	13.5	(3.48)	19.5	(4.64)	6.7	(2.84)	9.6	(4.22)	19.5	(6.39)	100.0
	OECD average	**9.6**	**(0.48)**	**17.5**	**(0.99)**	**16.5**	**(1.13)**	**12.1**	**(0.94)**	**14.1**	**(1.21)**	**8.7**	**(0.97)**	**6.2**	**(1.03)**	**15.2**	**(1.54)**	**100.0**
	Hong Kong-China	0.0	c	2.5	(0.93)	7.4	(1.91)	23.7	(3.65)	29.4	(4.12)	20.6	(3.79)	11.2	(3.24)	5.1	(2.33)	100.0
	Macao-China	0.0	c	0.0	c	0.6	(0.17)	0.0	c	2.0	(0.48)	9.6	(0.90)	17.8	(0.95)	70.1	(1.11)	100.0
	Russian Federation	20.1	(3.43)	33.5	(4.97)	32.1	(5.47)	10.6	(4.31)	0.0	c	3.6	(2.73)	0.0	c	0.0	c	100.0
	Belgium (Flemish Community)	30.7	(5.64)	14.9	(4.25)	21.2	(5.64)	17.1	(6.42)	7.2	(6.88)	2.6	(2.35)	0.5	(0.54)	5.6	(5.41)	100.0
	Belgium (French Community)	10.9	(2.64)	24.7	(5.63)	19.0	(6.62)	7.3	(3.52)	4.6	(3.89)	9.4	(6.48)	2.9	(1.98)	21.1	(10.30)	100.0

Table 3.7b
Percentage of first-generation students attending schools with different sized immigrant student populations (first- and second-generation students combined)

| | Proportion of immigrant students within the school | | | | | | | | | | | | | | | | |
	0% to <10%	S.E.	10% to <20%	S.E.	20% to <30%	S.E.	30% to <40%	S.E.	40% to <50%	S.E.	50% to <60%	S.E.	60% to <70%	S.E.	70% or higher	S.E.	Total
Australia	5.4	(0.86)	14.2	(2.14)	19.3	(3.06)	15.6	(3.24)	9.4	(3.70)	11.0	(2.84)	5.0	(2.19)	20.1	(4.20)	100.0
Austria	19.2	(2.77)	26.5	(4.49)	15.0	(4.34)	10.6	(3.76)	2.2	(2.11)	10.3	(4.35)	4.6	(3.24)	11.7	(3.53)	100.0
Belgium	15.4	(2.57)	15.5	(2.84)	20.8	(4.72)	9.9	(3.04)	4.3	(3.43)	3.6	(2.31)	18.8	(7.11)	11.6	(5.16)	100.0
Canada	6.6	(1.02)	7.0	(1.26)	10.3	(2.03)	7.7	(1.94)	8.5	(2.25)	15.8	(3.46)	9.4	(3.25)	34.7	(5.35)	100.0
Denmark	38.1	(5.76)	29.5	(7.61)	6.4	(3.86)	7.5	(4.41)	6.8	(6.42)	0.8	(0.83)	2.9	(2.94)	8.1	(5.11)	100.0
France	11.6	(3.17)	17.8	(5.24)	14.9	(4.52)	17.2	(4.93)	17.3	(6.56)	0.0	c	3.5	(2.46)	17.7	(9.92)	100.0
Germany	16.3	(2.95)	13.2	(3.13)	20.0	(3.90)	17.8	(4.64)	6.8	(3.05)	10.2	(6.78)	6.1	(3.35)	9.5	(3.89)	100.0
Luxembourg	0.0	c	11.0	(1.02)	19.5	(1.31)	10.2	(0.99)	25.7	(1.62)	6.6	(0.87)	13.1	(0.88)	13.9	(1.02)	100.0
Netherlands	31.1	(6.25)	25.9	(5.81)	11.6	(4.81)	0.0	c	0.6	(0.64)	12.2	(6.01)	1.7	(1.67)	17.0	(7.41)	100.0
New Zealand	10.3	(1.55)	13.2	(2.20)	12.1	(2.43)	21.2	(3.20)	19.5	(2.84)	12.5	(2.29)	0.7	(0.66)	10.7	(2.91)	100.0
Norway	41.0	(6.52)	31.7	(7.13)	3.4	(2.17)	11.6	(4.98)	6.5	(3.76)	5.8	(5.55)	0.0	c	0.0	c	100.0
Sweden	13.7	(2.73)	23.1	(4.00)	13.3	(4.32)	15.6	(6.16)	3.1	(2.19)	1.1	(0.78)	6.1	(3.58)	24.0	(7.96)	100.0
Switzerland	6.9	(1.70)	21.4	(3.64)	28.1	(4.20)	11.1	(2.01)	5.2	(1.14)	14.8	(3.64)	4.6	(1.44)	7.9	(2.94)	100.0
United States	8.2	(1.93)	21.1	(3.13)	10.4	(3.05)	19.6	(5.14)	13.8	(3.59)	9.2	(4.11)	7.2	(3.61)	10.5	(3.63)	100.0
OECD average	*11.5*	*(0.64)*	*17.1*	*(0.99)*	*16.1*	*(0.99)*	*13.4*	*(0.86)*	*11.8*	*(0.93)*	*9.0*	*(0.87)*	*6.4*	*(0.79)*	*14.8*	*(1.25)*	*100.0*
Hong Kong-China	0.0	c	1.0	(0.55)	7.1	(2.03)	15.5	(2.89)	29.1	(5.05)	24.1	(4.31)	13.9	(5.02)	9.2	(4.21)	100.0
Macao-China	0.0	c	0.0	c	0.5	(0.33)	0.0	c	0.9	(0.64)	6.9	(1.67)	10.0	(2.12)	81.8	(2.58)	100.0
Russian Federation	15.7	(2.88)	41.2	(4.96)	26.9	(4.16)	11.0	(3.95)	0.0	c	5.3	(3.91)	0.0	c	0.0	c	100.0
Belgium (Flemish Community)	32.7	(7.19)	17.6	(5.04)	19.7	(4.69)	12.7	(4.88)	0.0	c	1.5	(1.39)	13.6	(12.02)	2.2	(2.21)	100.0
Belgium (French Community)	8.0	(2.49)	14.1	(3.53)	20.6	(6.67)	8.3	(3.82)	6.4	(5.01)	4.7	(3.35)	21.8	(9.06)	16.2	(7.54)	100.0

Table 3.7c
Percentage of native students attending schools with different sized immigrant student populations (first- and second-generation students combined)

| | Proportion of immigrant students within the school | | | | | | | | | | | | | | | | |
	0% to <10%	S.E.	10% to <20%	S.E.	20% to <30%	S.E.	30% to <40%	S.E.	40% to <50%	S.E.	50% to <60%	S.E.	60% to <70%	S.E.	70% or higher	S.E.	Total
Australia	42.8	(2.49)	24.0	(2.86)	16.1	(2.28)	8.5	(1.53)	3.6	(1.32)	2.6	(0.68)	1.0	(0.44)	1.3	(0.37)	100.0
Austria	66.3	(3.57)	20.1	(3.30)	7.5	(1.92)	3.4	(1.20)	0.5	(0.48)	1.4	(0.60)	0.4	(0.31)	0.5	(0.21)	100.0
Belgium	70.7	(2.77)	15.5	(2.12)	8.5	(1.67)	2.8	(0.83)	0.9	(0.49)	0.6	(0.38)	0.7	(0.30)	0.3	(0.15)	100.0
Canada	65.5	(1.99)	12.5	(1.59)	9.2	(1.30)	4.5	(1.01)	2.8	(0.60)	3.5	(0.75)	1.1	(0.31)	1.1	(0.25)	100.0
Denmark	84.9	(2.47)	11.3	(2.35)	1.7	(0.90)	1.1	(0.59)	0.5	(0.37)	0.1	(0.14)	0.2	(0.16)	0.1	(0.14)	100.0
France	61.0	(3.79)	21.2	(3.56)	7.1	(1.81)	5.0	(1.25)	4.3	(1.37)	0.5	(0.38)	0.5	(0.34)	0.5	(0.29)	100.0
Germany	63.5	(3.31)	14.1	(2.70)	11.5	(2.04)	5.4	(1.39)	2.3	(0.84)	2.0	(1.10)	0.8	(0.44)	0.5	(0.30)	100.0
Luxembourg	1.7	(0.11)	35.0	(0.38)	32.5	(0.47)	8.5	(0.30)	16.6	(0.50)	2.3	(0.26)	2.4	(0.21)	0.9	(0.18)	100.0
Netherlands	74.0	(3.94)	19.0	(3.52)	4.3	(1.66)	0.0	c	0.4	(0.40)	1.7	(0.90)	0.3	(0.29)	0.4	(0.19)	100.0
New Zealand	54.8	(3.07)	18.9	(2.47)	7.6	(1.69)	9.5	(1.50)	5.8	(1.05)	2.3	(0.58)	0.2	(0.16)	1.0	(0.35)	100.0
Norway	85.8	(2.56)	10.4	(2.31)	1.4	(0.82)	1.1	(0.58)	1.0	(0.59)	0.3	(0.30)	0.0	c	0.0	c	100.0
Sweden	68.0	(3.12)	19.0	(2.89)	7.2	(1.78)	3.5	(1.44)	1.4	(0.66)	0.1	(0.08)	0.6	(0.35)	0.2	(0.13)	100.0
Switzerland	34.7	(4.03)	33.1	(4.08)	20.7	(2.82)	5.3	(1.03)	1.8	(0.40)	3.4	(0.82)	0.6	(0.22)	0.5	(0.20)	100.0
United States	67.2	(2.35)	15.2	(2.18)	6.2	(1.55)	5.1	(1.25)	3.8	(0.91)	1.1	(0.45)	0.9	(0.41)	0.6	(0.21)	100.0
OECD average	*61.7*	*(0.87)*	*18.9*	*(0.83)*	*9.4*	*(0.50)*	*4.5*	*(0.29)*	*3.0*	*(0.23)*	*1.4*	*(0.14)*	*0.6*	*(0.09)*	*0.5*	*(0.07)*	
Hong Kong-China	0.0	c	6.5	(2.39)	17.5	(3.65)	27.7	(3.85)	26.9	(3.93)	14.3	(2.54)	5.3	(1.78)	1.7	(0.84)	100.0
Macao-China	0.0	c	0.0	c	4.5	(0.48)	0.0	c	6.1	(1.12)	23.9	(2.23)	26.6	(2.41)	38.9	(3.14)	100.0
Russian Federation	46.6	(4.37)	34.9	(3.96)	14.8	(2.57)	3.1	(1.14)	0.0	c	0.6	(0.43)	0.0	c	0.0	c	100.0
Belgium (Flemish Community)	84.9	(2.38)	7.6	(1.77)	4.5	(0.98)	2.1	(0.83)	0.3	(0.33)	0.2	(0.14)	0.3	(0.30)	0.1	(0.09)	100.0
Belgium (French Community)	50.4	(5.87)	26.9	(4.61)	14.1	(3.92)	3.7	(1.70)	1.8	(1.14)	1.3	(0.93)	1.3	(0.61)	0.6	(0.36)	100.0

OECD countries / Partner countries

© OECD 2006 Where immigrant students succeed - A comparative review of performance and engagement in PISA 2003

Table 3.8

Differences between native and immigrant students in mathematics performance and percentage of immigrant students within countries

		Difference in mathematics score (immigrant students minus native students)		Percentage of immigrant students in the country	
		Difference	S.E.	Percentage	S.E.
OECD countries	Australia	-3	(4.1)	22.7	(1.13)
	Austria	**-61**	(5.7)	13.3	(0.99)
	Belgium	**-100**	(7.0)	11.8	(0.91)
	Canada	-1	(3.9)	20.1	(1.14)
	Denmark	**-68**	(8.0)	6.5	(0.78)
	France	**-54**	(7.0)	14.3	(1.33)
	Germany	**-81**	(6.9)	15.4	(1.10)
	Luxembourg	**-38**	(2.8)	33.3	(0.61)
	Netherlands	**-66**	(9.0)	11.0	(1.39)
	New Zealand	**-14**	(6.0)	19.8	(1.14)
	Norway	**-52**	(7.6)	5.6	(0.73)
	Sweden	**-64**	(8.3)	11.5	(0.87)
	Switzerland	**-76**	(4.5)	20.0	(0.91)
	United States	**-28**	(6.3)	14.4	(0.95)
	OECD average	*-44*	*(1.7)*	*15.7*	*(0.30)*
Partner countries	Hong Kong-China	-12	(3.6)	43.3	(1.41)
	Macao-China	1	(7.3)	76.1	(1.41)
	Russian Federation	-17	(4.8)	13.5	(0.71)
	Belgium (Flemish Community)	**-110**	(8.8)	6.8	(0.72)
	Belgium (French Community)	**-74**	(9.4)	18.3	(1.87)

Note: Statistically significant differences are indicated in bold.

Table 3.9
**Characteristics of schools attended by native and immigrant students
(scores standardised within each country sample)**

Characteristics of schools attended by native students and immigrant students

	Economic, social and cultural status of students within the school (ESCS)		Human resources				Physical and educational resources			
			Student/teacher ratio		Teacher shortage		Quality of the school's physical infrastructure		Quality of the school's educational resources	
	Native students	Immigrant students	Native students	Immigrant students	Native students	Immigrant students	Native students	Immigrant students	Native students	Immigrant students
	Mean index S.E.	Mean index S.E.	Mean index S.E.	Mean index S.E.	Mean index S.E.	Mean index S.E.	Mean index S.E.	Mean index S.E.	Mean index S.E.	Mean index S.E.
Australia	0.02 (0.04)	-0.06 (0.08)	0.02 (0.08)	-0.07 (0.09)	0.01 (0.05)	-0.02 (0.08)	-0.02 (0.06)	0.07 (0.11)	-0.02 (0.06)	0.08 (0.11)
Austria	0.05 (0.06)	**-0.35** (0.09)	0.01 (0.06)	-0.08 (0.06)	-0.02 (0.08)	0.11 (0.11)	0.02 (0.09)	-0.15 (0.10)	0.03 (0.09)	-0.17 (0.11)
Belgium	0.09 (0.04)	**-0.66** (0.12)	0.04 (0.05)	**-0.29** (0.08)	-0.04 (0.06)	**0.30** (0.11)	0.01 (0.07)	-0.05 (0.09)	0.01 (0.06)	-0.08 (0.10)
Canada	-0.05 (0.04)	**0.22** (0.09)	-0.02 (0.06)	0.09 (0.09)	0.04 (0.05)	-0.17 (0.08)	0.03 (0.04)	-0.12 (0.08)	0.01 (0.05)	-0.02 (0.10)
Denmark	0.05 (0.06)	**-0.70** (0.29)	0.00 (0.06)	0.04 (0.11)	0.01 (0.08)	-0.17 (0.14)	0.01 (0.08)	-0.21 (0.23)	0.01 (0.08)	-0.16 (0.24)
France	0.08 (0.06)	**-0.49** (0.12)	w w	w w	w w	w w	w w	w w	w w	w w
Germany	0.12 (0.04)	**-0.67** (0.08)	0.00 (0.07)	-0.02 (0.12)	-0.01 (0.08)	0.07 (0.13)	0.00 (0.08)	-0.02 (0.14)	0.00 (0.07)	0.02 (0.14)
Luxembourg	0.06 (0.01)	**-0.12** (0.02)	-0.19 (0.01)	**0.35** (0.02)	0.08 (0.01)	**-0.17** (0.02)	0.04 (0.01)	**-0.09** (0.02)	-0.05 (0.01)	**0.10** (0.02)
Netherlands	0.08 (0.06)	**-0.61** (0.17)	0.03 (0.08)	-0.27 (0.18)	-0.05 (0.08)	0.38 (0.17)	0.01 (0.08)	-0.09 (0.18)	-0.01 (0.07)	0.09 (0.18)
New Zealand	-0.02 (0.05)	0.08 (0.07)	-0.09 (0.07)	**0.37** (0.10)	-0.02 (0.05)	0.08 (0.09)	-0.01 (0.06)	0.05 (0.09)	-0.05 (0.06)	0.22 (0.09)
Norway	0.01 (0.06)	-0.11 (0.18)	0.01 (0.08)	-0.13 (0.15)	0.00 (0.08)	0.03 (0.11)	-0.01 (0.07)	0.12 (0.15)	0.01 (0.08)	-0.16 (0.16)
Sweden	0.05 (0.07)	-0.38 (0.19)	0.03 (0.08)	-0.23 (0.09)	-0.01 (0.07)	0.06 (0.13)	0.02 (0.07)	-0.16 (0.14)	0.02 (0.08)	-0.18 (0.10)
Switzerland	0.08 (0.06)	**-0.31** (0.06)	0.03 (0.09)	-0.11 (0.11)	-0.04 (0.08)	0.17 (0.10)	0.01 (0.07)	-0.02 (0.08)	0.01 (0.08)	-0.04 (0.09)
United States	0.08 (0.05)	**-0.46** (0.15)	-0.05 (0.04)	**0.35** (0.14)	-0.02 (0.07)	0.14 (0.11)	0.03 (0.07)	-0.18 (0.11)	0.01 (0.08)	-0.06 (0.12)
OECD average	*0.06 (0.01)*	***-0.30 (0.03)***	*-0.01 (0.02)*	*0.06 (0.02)*	*-0.02 (0.02)*	***0.10 (0.02)***	*0.00 (0.02)*	*-0.03 (0.03)*	*-0.01 (0.02)*	*0.04 (0.03)*
Hong Kong-China	0.14 (0.09)	**-0.18** (0.06)	-0.02 (0.07)	0.02 (0.08)	0.01 (0.09)	-0.02 (0.08)	-0.03 (0.09)	0.03 (0.09)	-0.01 (0.10)	0.01 (0.07)
Macao-China	0.44 (0.06)	**-0.14** (0.02)	0.17 (0.05)	**-0.06** (0.02)	-0.02 (0.05)	0.01 (0.02)	-0.11 (0.05)	**0.04** (0.02)	-0.18 (0.05)	**0.06** (0.02)
Russian Federation	0.01 (0.07)	-0.06 (0.09)	-0.01 (0.11)	0.07 (0.12)	-0.02 (0.09)	0.10 (0.11)	-0.01 (0.10)	0.03 (0.10)	-0.02 (0.08)	0.10 (0.09)
Belgium (Flemish Community)	0.05 (0.06)	**-0.54** (0.11)	0.03 (0.07)	**-0.43** (0.07)	-0.02 (0.08)	0.25 (0.14)	0.01 (0.09)	-0.08 (0.14)	0.01 (0.09)	-0.20 (0.15)
Belgium (French Community)	0.08 (0.11)	-0.40 (0.16)	0.06 (0.08)	-0.27 (0.13)	0.00 (0.10)	0.00 (0.16)	-0.03 (0.11)	0.12 (0.12)	-0.06 (0.11)	0.28 (0.15)

Characteristics of schools attended by native students and immigrant students

	Students' perceptions of classroom climate				Principals' perceptions of school climate					
	Teacher support		Disciplinary climate		Student-related factors		Teacher-related factors		Teacher morale and commitment	
	Native students	Immigrant students	Native students	Immigrant students	Native students	Immigrant students	Native students	Immigrant students	Native students	Immigrant students
	Mean index S.E.	Mean index S.E.	Mean index S.E.	Mean index S.E.	Mean index S.E.	Mean index S.E.	Mean index S.E.	Mean index S.E.	Mean index S.E.	Mean index S.E.
Australia	-0.01 (0.08)	0.03 (0.07)	0.00 (0.06)	0.01 (0.09)	-0.02 (0.05)	0.05 (0.07)	0.01 (0.05)	-0.04 (0.10)	0.03 (0.07)	-0.09 (0.09)
Austria	-0.02 (0.07)	0.13 (0.10)	0.07 (0.06)	**-0.44** (0.08)	0.05 (0.08)	**-0.31** (0.11)	0.03 (0.09)	-0.19 (0.09)	0.04 (0.08)	-0.23 (0.13)
Belgium	-0.02 (0.07)	0.15 (0.09)	0.05 (0.06)	**-0.38** (0.10)	0.06 (0.06)	**-0.46** (0.09)	0.04 (0.06)	**-0.28** (0.10)	0.05 (0.06)	**-0.39** (0.08)
Canada	0.00 (0.04)	0.01 (0.08)	-0.01 (0.04)	0.05 (0.07)	0.00 (0.05)	0.01 (0.09)	0.04 (0.05)	-0.14 (0.10)	0.02 (0.04)	-0.07 (0.08)
Denmark	0.02 (0.06)	-0.33 (0.17)	0.01 (0.07)	-0.09 (0.14)	0.02 (0.07)	-0.36 (0.18)	0.03 (0.07)	-0.39 (0.15)	0.02 (0.08)	-0.28 (0.13)
France	0.00 (0.06)	0.00 (0.10)	0.03 (0.07)	-0.15 (0.10)	w w	w w	w w	w w	w w	w w
Germany	-0.04 (0.07)	0.22 (0.11)	0.07 (0.07)	**-0.37** (0.11)	0.05 (0.07)	-0.27 (0.12)	-0.02 (0.08)	0.11 (0.15)	0.00 (0.07)	0.01 (0.12)
Luxembourg	-0.14 (0.01)	**0.29** (0.02)	0.06 (0.01)	**-0.11** (0.02)	0.03 (0.01)	**-0.05** (0.02)	0.02 (0.01)	**-0.04** (0.02)	-0.06 (0.01)	**0.12** (0.02)
Netherlands	-0.01 (0.09)	0.04 (0.17)	0.03 (0.09)	-0.26 (0.14)	0.06 (0.09)	**-0.44** (0.12)	0.03 (0.09)	-0.22 (0.15)	0.01 (0.08)	-0.09 (0.15)
New Zealand	-0.01 (0.08)	0.05 (0.08)	-0.02 (0.06)	0.09 (0.07)	-0.03 (0.06)	0.11 (0.06)	-0.02 (0.07)	0.08 (0.10)	-0.03 (0.08)	0.13 (0.08)
Norway	0.02 (0.07)	-0.28 (0.14)	-0.01 (0.07)	0.14 (0.15)	0.00 (0.08)	-0.05 (0.12)	-0.01 (0.09)	0.21 (0.13)	0.00 (0.08)	0.05 (0.13)
Sweden	0.02 (0.07)	-0.18 (0.14)	0.03 (0.08)	-0.22 (0.13)	0.05 (0.07)	**-0.38** (0.11)	0.03 (0.08)	-0.26 (0.13)	0.00 (0.08)	-0.02 (0.14)
Switzerland	-0.04 (0.06)	0.15 (0.07)	0.05 (0.08)	-0.21 (0.07)	0.05 (0.11)	-0.22 (0.08)	0.02 (0.07)	-0.09 (0.08)	0.04 (0.08)	-0.14 (0.08)
United States	0.01 (0.07)	-0.04 (0.09)	0.02 (0.06)	-0.12 (0.09)	0.03 (0.08)	-0.19 (0.10)	0.01 (0.07)	-0.09 (0.10)	-0.01 (0.07)	0.08 (0.11)
OECD average	*-0.01 (0.01)*	***0.06 (0.02)***	*0.03 (0.02)*	***-0.15 (0.02)***	*0.03 (0.02)*	***-0.19 (0.03)***	*0.02 (0.02)*	***-0.12 (0.03)***	*0.02 (0.02)*	***-0.09 (0.03)***
Hong Kong-China	0.03 (0.08)	-0.03 (0.08)	0.02 (0.09)	-0.02 (0.09)	-0.01 (0.09)	0.01 (0.07)	-0.02 (0.08)	0.02 (0.07)	0.03 (0.08)	-0.04 (0.08)
Macao-China	-0.20 (0.05)	**0.06** (0.02)	-0.16 (0.05)	**0.05** (0.02)	0.11 (0.05)	**-0.03** (0.02)	0.25 (0.06)	**-0.08** (0.02)	0.06 (0.05)	-0.02 (0.02)
Russian Federation	0.01 (0.08)	-0.09 (0.08)	0.02 (0.08)	-0.14 (0.11)	-0.01 (0.08)	0.06 (0.11)	-0.01 (0.08)	0.05 (0.08)	0.01 (0.07)	-0.09 (0.11)
Belgium (Flemish Community)	-0.01 (0.08)	0.04 (0.16)	0.03 (0.07)	-0.27 (0.12)	0.04 (0.07)	**-0.50** (0.16)	0.01 (0.08)	-0.10 (0.13)	0.02 (0.07)	-0.21 (0.15)
Belgium (French Community)	-0.06 (0.12)	0.30 (0.13)	0.07 (0.12)	-0.21 (0.13)	0.04 (0.11)	-0.19 (0.13)	0.02 (0.12)	-0.10 (0.16)	0.06 (0.11)	-0.29 (0.10)

Note: Statistically significant differences from native students' scores are indicated in bold.

© OECD 2006 *Where immigrant students succeed - A comparative review of performance and engagement in PISA 2003*

Table 4.1

Index of interest in and enjoyment of mathematics and student performance on the mathematics scale

Results based on students' self-reports

Index of interest in and enjoyment of mathematics

	Native students		Second-generation students		First-generation students	
	Mean index	S.E.	Mean index	S.E.	Mean index	S.E.
Australia	-0.06	(0.02)	**0.22**	(0.04)	**0.30**	(0.04)
Austria	-0.32	(0.02)	-0.15	(0.08)	**-0.09**	(0.06)
Belgium	-0.20	(0.02)	**-0.01**	(0.05)	**0.16**	(0.07)
Canada	-0.09	(0.01)	**0.13**	(0.04)	**0.49**	(0.05)
Denmark	0.40	(0.02)	0.58	(0.09)	**0.66**	(0.10)
France	0.04	(0.02)	0.07	(0.05)	**0.32**	(0.10)
Germany	0.00	(0.02)	**0.24**	(0.07)	**0.27**	(0.07)
Luxembourg	-0.34	(0.02)	**-0.21**	(0.04)	**0.04**	(0.04)
Netherlands	-0.25	(0.02)	**0.19**	(0.06)	**0.23**	(0.11)
New Zealand	0.03	(0.02)	**0.35**	(0.07)	**0.54**	(0.04)
Norway	-0.19	(0.02)	**0.17**	(0.11)	**0.14**	(0.08)
Sweden	0.05	(0.02)	0.20	(0.08)	**0.45**	(0.06)
Switzerland	0.08	(0.02)	0.16	(0.05)	**0.38**	(0.04)
United States	0.00	(0.02)	0.23	(0.06)	**0.40**	(0.07)
OECD average	*-0.05*	*(0.01)*	*0.12*	*(0.02)*	*0.29*	*(0.02)*
Hong Kong-China	0.19	(0.03)	**0.27**	(0.03)	0.26	(0.02)
Macao-China	0.05	(0.05)	0.11	(0.05)	**0.27**	(0.06)
Russian Federation	0.25	(0.02)	0.21	(0.05)	0.23	(0.06)
Belgium (Flemish Community)	-0.24	(0.02)	**-0.04**	(0.07)	**0.04**	(0.11)
Belgium (French Community)	-0.12	(0.03)	0.00	(0.07)	**0.24**	(0.08)

Change in the mathematics score per unit of the index of interest in and enjoyment of mathematics

	Native students		Explained variance in student performance (r-squared x 100)	Second-generation students		Explained variance in student performance (r-squared x 100)	First-generation students		Explained variance in student performance (r-squared x 100)
	Effect	S.E.	%	Effect	S.E.	%	Effect	S.E.	%
Australia	**20.5**	(1.5)	4.2	**15.5**	(3.8)	2.3	**12.9**	(2.9)	1.7
Austria	**13.0**	(2.0)	2.2	5.0	(5.9)	0.4	-3.4	(5.0)	0.2
Belgium	**20.8**	(1.5)	4.0	2.4	(6.4)	0.1	-11.0	(6.5)	1.1
Canada	**21.9**	(1.0)	6.7	**24.2**	(2.9)	8.2	**16.0**	(3.2)	3.6
Denmark	**30.8**	(1.7)	11.1	2.0	(8.5)	0.1	8.6	(7.9)	1.0
France	**21.7**	(2.0)	5.6	**17.4**	(4.5)	3.9	**26.4**	(12.4)	6.1
Germany	**13.7**	(1.8)	2.8	**21.4**	(5.4)	6.7	5.8	(4.6)	0.5
Luxembourg	**12.4**	(1.7)	2.5	6.8	(4.0)	0.7	-2.3	(4.2)	0.1
Netherlands	**21.3**	(1.7)	4.6	2.7	(7.0)	0.1	6.5	(6.7)	0.8
New Zealand	**15.1**	(2.1)	2.1	2.6	(5.8)	0.1	8.3	(4.8)	0.7
Norway	**36.5**	(1.4)	18.5	**36.7**	(9.5)	17.6	**16.3**	(7.2)	4.0
Sweden	**30.7**	(1.8)	11.7	**29.8**	(7.9)	8.6	10.9	(5.9)	1.3
Switzerland	**17.2**	(1.7)	3.8	-1.9	(5.0)	0.1	-6.6	(5.3)	0.5
United States	**9.9**	(1.7)	1.2	**12.7**	(4.8)	2.1	0.9	(6.3)	0.1
OECD average	*19.8*	*(0.5)*	*4.8*	*12.1*	*(1.3)*	*1.7*	*7.4*	*(1.3)*	*0.6*
Hong Kong-China	**32.4**	(2.3)	9.9	**33.2**	(3.5)	10.8	**30.2**	(4.3)	7.8
Macao-China	12.1	(6.7)	1.7	**24.7**	(5.0)	6.8	17.0	(9.2)	2.0
Russian Federation	**15.1**	(2.2)	1.7	-2.5	(5.5)	0.1	9.2	(6.6)	0.7
Belgium (Flemish Community)	**30.0**	(1.8)	8.9	0.8	(9.0)	0.1	-10.4	(8.5)	1.4
Belgium (French Community)	**11.7**	(2.7)	1.3	2.9	(7.7)	0.2	-9.9	(9.2)	0.8

Regression estimates of the index of interest in and enjoyment of mathematics

	Accounting for ESCS				Accounting for mathematics performance			
	Second-generation students		First-generation students		Second-generation students		First-generation students	
	Coef.	S.E.	Coef.	S.E.	Coef.	S.E.	Coef.	S.E.
Australia	**0.29**	(0.04)	**0.36**	(0.04)	**0.29**	(0.04)	**0.36**	(0.04)
Austria	**0.17**	(0.08)	**0.21**	(0.07)	**0.26**	(0.08)	**0.32**	(0.07)
Belgium	**0.26**	(0.06)	**0.39**	(0.07)	**0.35**	(0.06)	**0.52**	(0.08)
Canada	**0.23**	(0.04)	**0.57**	(0.05)	**0.20**	(0.04)	**0.60**	(0.05)
Denmark	**0.30**	(0.09)	**0.33**	(0.10)	**0.43**	(0.10)	**0.49**	(0.10)
France	0.09	(0.06)	**0.34**	(0.11)	0.15	(0.06)	**0.46**	(0.10)
Germany	**0.27**	(0.08)	**0.32**	(0.08)	**0.45**	(0.08)	**0.41**	(0.09)
Luxembourg	**0.16**	(0.05)	**0.40**	(0.05)	**0.19**	(0.05)	**0.45**	(0.05)
Netherlands	**0.47**	(0.06)	**0.52**	(0.12)	**0.55**	(0.06)	**0.65**	(0.11)
New Zealand	**0.33**	(0.07)	**0.51**	(0.05)	**0.37**	(0.07)	**0.52**	(0.05)
Norway	**0.46**	(0.11)	**0.46**	(0.08)	**0.55**	(0.12)	**0.63**	(0.09)
Sweden	**0.22**	(0.09)	**0.50**	(0.07)	**0.27**	(0.08)	**0.72**	(0.07)
Switzerland	0.09	(0.06)	**0.31**	(0.06)	**0.20**	(0.06)	**0.47**	(0.06)
United States	**0.24**	(0.07)	**0.41**	(0.08)	**0.26**	(0.06)	**0.44**	(0.08)
OECD average	*0.21*	*(0.02)*	*0.37*	*(0.02)*	*0.27*	*(0.02)*	*0.45*	*(0.02)*
Hong Kong-China	**0.10**	(0.03)	**0.10**	(0.04)	0.03	(0.03)	**0.19**	(0.04)
Macao-China	0.07	(0.08)	**0.23**	(0.07)	0.06	(0.07)	**0.24**	(0.07)
Russian Federation	-0.04	(0.05)	-0.02	(0.06)	-0.03	(0.05)	0.01	(0.06)
Belgium (Flemish Community)	**0.35**	(0.08)	**0.36**	(0.11)	**0.55**	(0.08)	**0.55**	(0.12)
Belgium (French Community)	0.14	(0.08)	**0.34**	(0.09)	0.18	(0.09)	**0.42**	(0.09)

Note: Values that are statistically significant are indicated in bold.

Table 4.2
Index of instrumental motivation in mathematics and student performance on the mathematics scale

Results based on students' self-reports

Index of instrumental motivation in mathematics

	Native students		Second-generation students		First-generation students	
	Mean index	S.E.	Mean index	S.E.	Mean index	S.E.
OECD countries						
Australia	0.19	(0.02)	**0.35**	(0.04)	**0.37**	(0.03)
Austria	-0.53	(0.03)	-0.32	(0.10)	**-0.29**	(0.07)
Belgium	-0.35	(0.02)	**-0.19**	(0.07)	0.03	(0.06)
Canada	0.17	(0.01)	**0.36**	(0.05)	**0.52**	(0.04)
Denmark	0.37	(0.02)	0.39	(0.09)	0.37	(0.10)
France	-0.11	(0.02)	**0.02**	(0.05)	**0.30**	(0.10)
Germany	-0.08	(0.02)	**0.09**	(0.06)	**0.17**	(0.06)
Luxembourg	-0.52	(0.02)	**-0.30**	(0.05)	-0.04	(0.05)
Netherlands	-0.30	(0.02)	**0.08**	(0.07)	-0.03	(0.09)
New Zealand	0.25	(0.02)	**0.45**	(0.06)	**0.47**	(0.04)
Norway	0.15	(0.02)	0.33	(0.12)	0.24	(0.09)
Sweden	-0.01	(0.02)	**0.21**	(0.07)	**0.28**	(0.04)
Switzerland	-0.09	(0.02)	**0.05**	(0.04)	**0.21**	(0.05)
United States	0.16	(0.02)	**0.26**	(0.05)	**0.33**	(0.06)
OECD average	*-0.04*	*(0.01)*	*0.10*	*(0.02)*	*0.20*	*(0.02)*
Hong Kong-China	-0.16	(0.02)	-0.12	(0.03)	0.02	(0.03)
Macao-China	-0.11	(0.05)	-0.02	(0.04)	0.02	(0.06)
Russian Federation	0.00	(0.02)	-0.01	(0.05)	0.01	(0.06)
Belgium (Flemish Community)	-0.45	(0.02)	-0.31	(0.08)	**-0.23**	(0.07)
Belgium (French Community)	-0.20	(0.02)	-0.13	(0.09)	**0.18**	(0.08)

Change in the mathematics score per unit of the index of instrumental motivation in mathematics

	Native students		Explained variance in student performance (r-squared x 100)	Second-generation students		Explained variance in student performance (r-squared x 100)	First-generation students		Explained variance in student performance (r-squared x 100)
	Effect	S.E.	%	Effect	S.E.	%	Effect	S.E.	%
OECD countries									
Australia	**17.4**	(1.2)	3.3	**17.4**	(3.3)	3.1	**16.3**	(2.8)	2.5
Austria	-0.6	(1.7)	0.0	-4.9	(7.1)	0.5	-7.1	(4.5)	0.8
Belgium	**15.8**	(1.6)	2.4	3.2	(6.3)	0.2	-4.0	(5.6)	0.2
Canada	**20.8**	(1.1)	6.1	**17.6**	(3.2)	4.7	**16.6**	(3.4)	3.4
Denmark	**22.2**	(1.7)	5.0	15.1	(10.5)	2.7	5.9	(9.2)	0.5
France	**15.5**	(1.6)	3.2	**11.4**	(3.8)	1.9	14.4	(10.9)	2.1
Germany	**4.4**	(2.2)	0.2	4.6	(5.8)	0.3	0.7	(6.3)	0.0
Luxembourg	**6.6**	(1.9)	0.8	-5.9	(3.5)	0.5	-7.2	(3.8)	0.6
Netherlands	**10.3**	(1.9)	1.0	2.2	(8.5)	0.1	10.7	(7.6)	1.8
New Zealand	**18.3**	(2.1)	3.1	-2.8	(6.9)	0.1	**12.5**	(5.1)	1.3
Norway	**28.8**	(1.5)	10.5	**30.5**	(10.2)	12.1	**30.9**	(7.9)	12.1
Sweden	**26.1**	(1.8)	7.3	**31.5**	(8.8)	8.8	7.2	(7.6)	0.5
Switzerland	2.8	(1.8)	0.1	-7.6	(4.0)	0.6	**-12.5**	(4.2)	1.7
United States	**13.8**	(1.7)	2.2	**18.2**	(5.0)	3.4	**15.7**	(6.4)	2.2
OECD average	*12.4*	*(0.5)*	*1.9*	*9.6*	*(1.2)*	*1.1*	*8.2*	*(1.6)*	*0.7*
Hong Kong-China	28.7	(2.3)	6.2	27.6	(4.0)	6.6	22.5	(5.2)	3.4
Macao-China	-9.1	(7.5)	0.8	10.7	(4.6)	1.2	-8.0	(10.8)	0.5
Russian Federation	14.4	(1.6)	2.1	13.4	(5.2)	2.2	6.8	(4.7)	0.6
Belgium (Flemish Community)	**25.9**	(2.1)	6.3	5.1	(10.2)	0.3	-10.3	(8.8)	1.2
Belgium (French Community)	**11.3**	(2.5)	1.4	1.9	(7.4)	0.1	2.0	(8.0)	0.0

Regression estimate of the index of instrumental motivation in mathematics

	Accounting for ESCS				Accounting for mathematics performance			
	Second-generation students		First-generation students		Second-generation students		First-generation students	
	Coef.	S.E.	Coef.	S.E.	Coef.	S.E.	Coef.	S.E.
OECD countries								
Australia	**0.18**	(0.04)	**0.19**	(0.03)	**0.17**	(0.04)	**0.19**	(0.03)
Austria	0.14	(0.10)	**0.16**	(0.07)	0.20	(0.10)	**0.22**	(0.08)
Belgium	**0.24**	(0.07)	**0.43**	(0.07)	**0.29**	(0.08)	**0.51**	(0.07)
Canada	**0.19**	(0.05)	**0.33**	(0.04)	**0.17**	(0.05)	**0.36**	(0.04)
Denmark	0.12	(0.09)	0.06	(0.10)	0.18	(0.10)	0.14	(0.10)
France	**0.19**	(0.06)	**0.48**	(0.11)	**0.23**	(0.06)	**0.55**	(0.12)
Germany	**0.16**	(0.06)	**0.24**	(0.07)	**0.22**	(0.07)	**0.29**	(0.07)
Luxembourg	**0.21**	(0.06)	**0.48**	(0.06)	**0.24**	(0.05)	**0.51**	(0.05)
Netherlands	**0.42**	(0.07)	**0.30**	(0.09)	**0.44**	(0.07)	**0.36**	(0.09)
New Zealand	**0.24**	(0.07)	**0.20**	(0.04)	**0.25**	(0.07)	**0.22**	(0.04)
Norway	**0.27**	(0.12)	**0.25**	(0.07)	**0.32**	(0.11)	**0.32**	(0.08)
Sweden	**0.30**	(0.08)	**0.39**	(0.05)	**0.31**	(0.07)	**0.53**	(0.05)
Switzerland	**0.10**	(0.05)	**0.25**	(0.05)	**0.15**	(0.05)	**0.31**	(0.05)
United States	**0.14**	(0.05)	**0.21**	(0.06)	**0.14**	(0.05)	**0.23**	(0.06)
OECD average	*0.29*	*(0.02)*	*0.28*	*(0.04)*	*0.20*	*(0.02)*	*0.31*	*(0.02)*
Hong Kong-China	0.07	(0.03)	**0.22**	(0.03)	0.00	(0.03)	**0.26**	(0.03)
Macao-China	0.09	(0.07)	0.10	(0.08)	0.09	(0.06)	0.13	(0.08)
Russian Federation	-0.01	(0.06)	0.02	(0.06)	0.01	(0.06)	0.05	(0.06)
Belgium (Flemish Community)	**0.26**	(0.09)	**0.30**	(0.08)	**0.42**	(0.09)	**0.44**	(0.08)
Belgium (French Community)	0.11	(0.10)	**0.38**	(0.08)	0.14	(0.10)	**0.47**	(0.09)

Note: Values that are statistically significant are indicated in bold.

© OECD 2006   Where immigrant students succeed - A comparative review of performance and engagement in PISA 2003

Table 4.3a

Performance in mathematics and reading by students' expected level of education

Results based on students' self-reports

| | | Students expecting to complete lower secondary education (ISCED Level 2) | | | | | | Students expecting to complete upper secondary education, not providing access to university-level programmes (ISCED Levels 3B and 3C) | | | | | | Students expecting to complete upper secondary education, providing access to university-level programmes (ISCED Levels 3A and 4) | | | | | |
		Percentage of students	S.E.	Performance on the mathematics scale Mean score	S.E.	Performance on the reading scale Mean score	S.E.	Percentage of students	S.E.	Performance on the mathematics scale Mean score	S.E.	Performance on the reading scale Mean score	S.E.	Percentage of students	S.E.	Performance on the mathematics scale Mean score	S.E.	Performance on the reading scale Mean score	S.E.
OECD countries																			
Australia	Native	3.0	(0.2)	427	(5.8)	406	(5.6)	4.1	(0.3)	456	(5.3)	446	(5.4)	25.1	(0.6)	485	(3.1)	482	(3.1)
	Second-generation	1.2	(0.3)	427	(20.1)	402	(31.9)	2.9	(0.7)	462	(22.0)	450	(22.6)	14.2	(1.3)	463	(9.2)	457	(10.0)
	First-generation	1.5	(0.4)	402	(23.3)	378	(31.8)	1.5	(0.4)	429	(19.6)	416	(15.0)	13.9	(1.1)	466	(8.3)	458	(9.2)
Austria	Native	3.2	(0.3)	471	(10.3)	463	(10.0)	26.3	(1.5)	459	(3.9)	439	(4.3)	28.0	(1.1)	535	(3.6)	537	(3.1)
	Second-generation	7.1	(1.9)	402	(23.7)	349	(27.6)	30.8	(4.4)	427	(11.9)	390	(15.5)	31.4	(4.0)	461	(10.5)	456	(12.2)
	First-generation	5.7	(1.3)	423	(19.8)	383	(27.4)	36.2	(2.7)	407	(7.2)	377	(8.8)	27.5	(2.5)	479	(9.1)	459	(11.5)
Belgium	Native	5.9	(0.4)	458	(7.2)	441	(7.7)	6.6	(0.4)	431	(5.3)	411	(7.3)	27.5	(0.9)	505	(2.9)	483	(3.4)
	Second-generation	12.0	(1.8)	433	(16.7)	415	(18.1)	12.9	(1.9)	383	(12.2)	363	(12.8)	29.3	(2.7)	426	(9.5)	416	(10.5)
	First-generation	12.0	(2.0)	396	(11.9)	374	(18.6)	13.8	(2.4)	409	(14.5)	382	(14.0)	28.8	(2.9)	445	(10.3)	407	(11.1)
Canada	Native	0.7	(0.1)	460	(11.5)	439	(12.3)	7.2	(0.3)	470	(4.4)	462	(4.1)	8.9	(0.4)	504	(3.7)	487	(3.6)
	Second-generation	0.5	(0.2)	424	(29.6)	440	(38.9)	5.8	(0.9)	476	(10.9)	474	(11.0)	1.9	(0.5)	481	(13.5)	477	(15.3)
	First-generation	0.6	(0.3)	471	(25.6)	419	(23.9)	2.1	(0.5)	443	(11.6)	426	(15.0)	2.0	(0.5)	470	(26.7)	441	(26.5)
Denmark	Native	9.6	(0.5)	443	(4.9)	418	(5.3)	12.5	(0.6)	480	(4.5)	445	(5.2)	35.0	(0.8)	508	(2.8)	491	(2.7)
	Second-generation	6.7	(2.0)	423	(36.0)	368	(39.7)	11.6	(2.1)	385	(18.4)	371	(34.5)	36.1	(4.1)	444	(15.3)	434	(17.2)
	First-generation	11.3	(2.9)	357	(23.6)	329	(24.1)	6.1	(2.2)	441	(29.7)	440	(39.4)	27.8	(4.7)	471	(15.9)	465	(14.8)
France	Native	1.5	(0.2)	442	(12.4)	409	(13.8)	24.6	(1.0)	445	(3.4)	423	(4.5)	22.4	(0.9)	531	(3.5)	519	(4.4)
	Second-generation	2.9	(0.9)	403	(23.5)	368	(28.1)	18.7	(2.6)	388	(9.8)	368	(11.5)	20.6	(1.9)	483	(10.1)	475	(9.2)
	First-generation	0.9	(0.9)	350	(44.3)	262	(48.7)	32.7	(4.7)	392	(16.5)	361	(17.5)	17.8	(3.1)	447	(21.6)	442	(23.4)
Germany	Native	40.6	(1.7)	469	(3.2)	459	(3.3)	3.3	(0.3)	504	(8.1)	493	(7.9)	33.7	(1.0)	552	(2.8)	546	(3.1)
	Second-generation	61.9	(3.6)	397	(9.0)	384	(10.3)	1.7	(0.7)	451	(38.8)	440	(26.1)	22.2	(2.6)	472	(13.4)	469	(13.8)
	First-generation	53.4	(3.4)	416	(8.1)	386	(9.3)	5.8	(1.3)	453	(21.7)	428	(19.8)	24.6	(2.7)	496	(10.2)	482	(11.3)
Luxembourg	Native	6.6	(0.5)	479	(5.4)	479	(6.0)	16.3	(0.7)	436	(3.6)	422	(4.2)	17.0	(0.7)	484	(3.6)	477	(4.0)
	Second-generation	4.0	(0.7)	440	(16.5)	415	(16.3)	19.4	(1.4)	403	(6.5)	372	(8.6)	21.4	(1.7)	454	(7.3)	427	(8.4)
	First-generation	2.3	(0.5)	436	(25.1)	400	(22.8)	25.5	(1.5)	391	(6.2)	351	(7.9)	20.1	(1.6)	442	(6.0)	415	(7.2)
Netherlands	Native	29.9	(1.6)	479	(4.1)	460	(4.1)	a	a	a	a	a	a	29.1	(1.1)	546	(3.2)	521	(3.1)
	Second-generation	27.9	(4.2)	449	(13.9)	434	(12.3)	a	a	a	a	a	a	26.8	(3.4)	479	(11.0)	466	(11.3)
	First-generation	30.5	(5.0)	428	(10.9)	420	(12.3)	a	a	a	a	a	a	29.0	(4.3)	466	(11.9)	453	(11.5)
New Zealand	Native	1.7	(0.3)	437	(12.1)	421	(14.2)	13.4	(0.7)	453	(4.7)	442	(6.0)	36.1	(0.9)	510	(2.8)	508	(3.1)
	Second-generation	0.3	(0.3)	334	(32.4)	334	(56.0)	7.2	(1.6)	447	(21.1)	445	(23.8)	30.6	(2.5)	464	(12.9)	478	(13.8)
	First-generation	2.0	(0.7)	402	(23.3)	368	(29.4)	5.9	(1.0)	443	(16.6)	382	(26.6)	22.9	(1.8)	490	(8.4)	468	(8.7)
Norway	Native	0.9	(0.2)	414	(15.8)	404	(20.1)	25.4	(0.8)	456	(2.8)	452	(3.5)	18.0	(0.7)	472	(4.1)	474	(4.9)
	Second-generation	1.0	(0.9)	520	(28.4)	688	(73.1)	14.9	(3.4)	420	(22.0)	416	(24.1)	18.8	(4.2)	461	(26.1)	429	(27.7)
	First-generation	2.8	(1.3)	397	(33.6)	329	(43.5)	24.7	(4.3)	413	(16.8)	403	(21.9)	20.1	(3.7)	402	(17.5)	395	(26.5)
Sweden	Native	4.1	(0.3)	445	(6.4)	446	(7.3)	15.5	(0.7)	488	(3.9)	490	(5.1)	23.8	(0.8)	478	(3.4)	482	(3.3)
	Second-generation	3.9	(1.4)	359	(32.6)	361	(37.2)	14.8	(2.4)	464	(15.7)	490	(17.4)	12.2	(2.4)	440	(15.1)	448	(15.8)
	First-generation	6.2	(1.7)	368	(33.5)	351	(39.6)	11.4	(2.3)	373	(12.9)	395	(17.0)	16.2	(3.0)	393	(16.9)	387	(16.0)
Switzerland	Native	7.9	(0.6)	459	(5.7)	451	(5.3)	47.3	(1.9)	511	(2.3)	488	(2.6)	19.1	(0.8)	582	(3.6)	552	(3.5)
	Second-generation	12.5	(1.7)	420	(11.1)	414	(12.9)	51.4	(2.8)	455	(5.5)	432	(6.9)	15.2	(1.8)	534	(11.7)	509	(10.2)
	First-generation	10.7	(1.3)	397	(13.4)	385	(14.6)	53.9	(2.5)	428	(5.8)	396	(6.6)	11.9	(1.3)	489	(10.2)	464	(13.7)
United States	Native	0.6	(0.1)	386	(20.2)	378	(22.9)	a	a	a	a	a	a	21.9	(0.8)	436	(3.8)	444	(4.0)
	Second-generation	0.6	(0.4)	368	(61.8)	322	(44.5)	a	a	a	a	a	a	23.3	(2.5)	402	(9.2)	409	(11.9)
	First-generation	2.0	(0.9)	341	(24.1)	318	(22.2)	a	a	a	a	a	a	29.2	(2.4)	387	(11.3)	374	(11.4)
Partner countries																			
Hong Kong-China	Native	0.7	(0.2)	424	(32.9)	377	(27.7)	11.7	(0.9)	459	(7.5)	432	(7.8)	21.5	(1.1)	518	(6.1)	483	(5.5)
	Second-generation	0.8	(0.2)	423	(31.4)	367	(34.3)	11.5	(1.2)	481	(13.0)	439	(12.1)	23.3	(1.3)	532	(7.2)	495	(6.4)
	First-generation	3.3	(0.5)	443	(19.9)	412	(17.1)	11.3	(1.2)	426	(14.3)	421	(15.0)	28.6	(1.2)	489	(6.3)	471	(6.6)
Macao-China	Native	2.9	(1.4)	432	(17.5)	423	(22.5)	1.9	(0.9)	516	(21.5)	421	(37.7)	29.8	(3.1)	496	(9.7)	472	(7.6)
	Second-generation	3.2	(0.6)	418	(14.8)	409	(12.7)	1.8	(0.7)	499	(29.8)	423	(28.4)	27.2	(2.0)	500	(7.9)	467	(6.6)
	First-generation	5.3	(1.9)	431	(25.2)	410	(28.8)	2.4	(1.2)	461	(13.0)	454	(21.9)	32.1	(3.5)	482	(15.9)	470	(11.5)
Russian Federation	Native	2.2	(0.3)	371	(10.5)	321	(11.9)	6.9	(1.2)	398	(8.7)	372	(8.5)	26.5	(1.1)	433	(4.7)	408	(4.6)
	Second-generation	1.4	(0.6)	393	(49.5)	323	(55.8)	8.1	(2.1)	413	(21.1)	365	(26.7)	30.7	(3.2)	430	(11.0)	391	(9.7)
	First-generation	0.8	(0.3)	385	(35.3)	297	(58.8)	9.2	(1.9)	410	(14.4)	338	(20.4)	32.5	(2.6)	419	(9.2)	391	(12.3)
Belgium (Flemish Community)	Native	0.9	(0.2)	517	(20.1)	504	(19.7)	7.4	(0.6)	440	(6.3)	423	(8.7)	26.4	(1.1)	515	(3.2)	493	(3.5)
	Second-generation	0.6	(0.4)	591	(10.8)	493	(22.1)	23.2	(4.0)	390	(11.1)	366	(15.4)	27.0	(4.0)	412	(13.3)	421	(12.1)
	First-generation	4.6	(2.3)	427	(36.9)	425	(62.1)	17.1	(3.2)	430	(23.7)	403	(25.0)	24.6	(5.3)	471	(13.6)	434	(14.5)
Belgium (French Community)	Native	13.8	(1.0)	453	(7.6)	435	(8.1)	5.3	(0.6)	410	(10.9)	386	(12.4)	29.0	(1.3)	491	(5.4)	469	(6.1)
	Second-generation	18.0	(2.4)	431	(17.2)	414	(18.4)	7.5	(1.8)	371	(25.8)	356	(24.3)	30.5	(3.6)	432	(12.1)	413	(14.0)
	First-generation	15.8	(2.8)	391	(12.5)	366	(19.2)	12.4	(3.4)	393	(16.3)	366	(14.1)	30.7	(3.6)	432	(12.1)	392	(14.4)

Table 4.3a (*continued*)
Performance in mathematics and reading by students' expected level of education
Results based on students' self-reports

| | | Students expecting to complete a non-university tertiary-level programme (ISCED Level 5B) | | | | | | Students expecting to complete a university-level programme (ISCED Levels 5A and 6) | | | | | |
| | | Percentage of students | S.E. | Performance on the mathematics scale | | Performance on the reading scale | | Percentage of students | S.E. | Performance on the mathematics scale | | Performance on the reading scale | |
				Mean score	S.E.	Mean score	S.E.			Mean score	S.E.	Mean score	S.E.
OECD countries													
Australia	Native	8.5	(0.3)	504	(4.1)	508	(4.7)	58.9	(0.8)	559	(2.1)	565	(2.1)
	Second-generation	7.2	(0.8)	483	(11.8)	481	(13.7)	74.5	(1.6)	541	(4.9)	547	(4.5)
	First-generation	5.2	(0.6)	489	(12.8)	489	(15.9)	77.4	(1.5)	543	(5.4)	535	(5.2)
Austria	Native	17.7	(0.9)	487	(4.7)	460	(5.3)	24.7	(1.4)	583	(3.8)	572	(3.7)
	Second-generation	5.2	(1.5)	450	(26.3)	426	(35.0)	25.4	(3.4)	536	(12.1)	516	(14.9)
	First-generation	10.4	(1.5)	442	(13.5)	406	(17.7)	18.7	(2.4)	520	(12.0)	507	(11.6)
Belgium	Native	23.2	(0.7)	562	(2.7)	545	(2.5)	36.4	(1.0)	609	(2.4)	582	(2.2)
	Second-generation	19.4	(2.4)	486	(12.6)	481	(12.4)	25.5	(2.5)	522	(11.9)	508	(12.8)
	First-generation	14.3	(1.8)	487	(14.9)	460	(16.3)	28.7	(2.7)	505	(13.1)	487	(13.7)
Canada	Native	24.8	(0.6)	514	(2.1)	517	(2.3)	58.3	(0.8)	562	(1.8)	559	(1.6)
	Second-generation	15.6	(1.3)	496	(6.6)	502	(7.5)	76.2	(1.8)	561	(4.5)	560	(4.2)
	First-generation	13.1	(1.3)	474	(10.3)	472	(10.4)	81.9	(1.5)	544	(5.0)	527	(4.6)
Denmark	Native	18.3	(0.7)	538	(3.6)	518	(3.7)	24.5	(0.9)	574	(3.2)	547	(3.3)
	Second-generation	9.1	(2.8)	472	(27.9)	467	(20.4)	36.4	(5.4)	474	(16.7)	473	(18.8)
	First-generation	12.2	(3.2)	462	(24.4)	468	(26.7)	41.9	(5.0)	473	(13.8)	482	(12.9)
France	Native	16.7	(0.8)	517	(3.5)	501	(3.6)	34.3	(1.0)	575	(3.0)	562	(2.8)
	Second-generation	19.4	(2.0)	463	(10.3)	444	(8.0)	38.1	(3.0)	520	(6.4)	506	(7.5)
	First-generation	15.1	(3.6)	447	(22.3)	419	(25.2)	30.9	(4.6)	536	(15.7)	515	(17.1)
Germany	Native	2.1	(0.2)	547	(12.1)	537	(10.5)	19.8	(1.0)	598	(3.1)	588	(3.0)
	Second-generation	1.0	(0.7)	537	(27.8)	519	(43.7)	12.4	(2.2)	518	(22.8)	500	(23.7)
	First-generation	0.7	(0.4)	523	(18.8)	555	(31.1)	14.8	(2.1)	533	(14.6)	517	(14.2)
Luxembourg	Native	15.2	(0.7)	517	(4.4)	521	(4.6)	40.9	(0.8)	554	(2.2)	545	(2.8)
	Second-generation	10.0	(1.3)	494	(8.7)	481	(9.2)	41.3	(1.8)	527	(6.0)	510	(6.6)
	First-generation	6.7	(0.9)	484	(14.0)	467	(15.1)	41.2	(2.0)	524	(5.3)	496	(6.1)
Netherlands	Native	a	a	a	a	a	a	40.6	(1.5)	610	(2.8)	576	(2.6)
	Second-generation	a	a	a	a	a	a	44.2	(4.9)	529	(13.3)	507	(9.8)
	First-generation	a	a	a	a	a	a	39.9	(4.5)	512	(13.1)	504	(12.0)
New Zealand	Native	13.5	(0.6)	545	(4.1)	559	(4.0)	35.3	(1.1)	576	(3.0)	579	(3.3)
	Second-generation	13.0	(1.9)	491	(17.4)	510	(17.9)	48.8	(2.7)	526	(10.5)	534	(12.3)
	First-generation	12.3	(1.5)	502	(10.5)	492	(13.0)	56.3	(2.2)	556	(6.4)	540	(6.7)
Norway	Native	29.9	(0.8)	517	(3.2)	528	(3.8)	25.3	(0.9)	546	(3.5)	559	(4.0)
	Second-generation	24.6	(3.8)	449	(20.6)	430	(26.7)	39.8	(4.2)	485	(19.3)	476	(15.9)
	First-generation	24.2	(3.3)	431	(17.8)	438	(18.3)	27.6	(3.9)	497	(15.0)	503	(19.7)
Sweden	Native	24.7	(0.7)	538	(2.6)	546	(2.8)	31.4	(1.1)	558	(3.2)	562	(2.8)
	Second-generation	24.4	(3.0)	504	(12.0)	528	(12.7)	43.8	(4.3)	506	(16.3)	525	(13.3)
	First-generation	16.2	(2.5)	448	(14.6)	458	(17.2)	47.0	(4.0)	457	(9.2)	473	(10.4)
Switzerland	Native	7.5	(0.5)	564	(5.9)	518	(6.0)	17.9	(1.5)	616	(5.1)	576	(4.5)
	Second-generation	4.6	(0.8)	542	(14.6)	511	(23.3)	15.9	(1.7)	564	(10.3)	538	(10.3)
	First-generation	6.3	(1.8)	460	(12.6)	425	(17.5)	16.3	(2.1)	558	(14.1)	525	(12.9)
United States	Native	12.6	(0.6)	486	(4.5)	497	(4.4)	64.7	(0.9)	510	(2.8)	526	(3.0)
	Second-generation	8.2	(1.3)	469	(17.1)	485	(16.1)	67.8	(2.7)	492	(7.9)	508	(8.4)
	First-generation	9.5	(1.9)	465	(18.7)	466	(23.7)	58.4	(2.9)	490	(7.5)	497	(8.6)
Partner countries													
Hong Kong-China	Native	12.1	(0.6)	553	(7.1)	510	(6.3)	53.8	(1.8)	597	(3.8)	546	(2.8)
	Second-generation	9.3	(0.9)	560	(7.8)	519	(7.0)	55.2	(1.9)	608	(4.6)	553	(3.3)
	First-generation	10.4	(1.0)	526	(9.5)	499	(9.0)	46.3	(1.5)	558	(5.3)	531	(4.2)
Macao-China	Native	16.7	(2.4)	517	(12.9)	500	(11.9)	48.9	(2.9)	556	(7.4)	522	(5.9)
	Second-generation	18.2	(1.7)	535	(7.4)	500	(6.9)	49.2	(1.9)	557	(6.6)	522	(3.8)
	First-generation	11.7	(2.6)	544	(23.8)	529	(18.0)	48.1	(4.2)	547	(10.1)	523	(6.4)
Russian Federation	Native	a	a	a	a	a	a	64.4	(2.0)	499	(3.9)	475	(3.6)
	Second-generation	a	a	a	a	a	a	59.8	(3.3)	479	(7.9)	455	(9.0)
	First-generation	a	a	a	a	a	a	57.0	(3.5)	480	(7.2)	441	(7.2)
Belgium (Flemish Community)	Native	26.6	(0.9)	575	(3.1)	556	(2.5)	38.3	(1.3)	629	(2.2)	598	(2.3)
	Second-generation	23.5	(3.5)	460	(18.3)	466	(16.1)	24.5	(3.7)	530	(19.2)	521	(17.2)
	First-generation	18.2	(3.6)	507	(16.2)	494	(18.6)	33.3	(4.2)	508	(14.1)	496	(17.3)
Belgium (French Community)	Native	18.0	(1.0)	532	(6.1)	520	(6.2)	33.6	(1.5)	575	(5.0)	554	(4.5)
	Second-generation	17.2	(3.3)	505	(16.3)	491	(18.3)	26.0	(3.0)	518	(14.5)	502	(16.4)
	First-generation	12.4	(2.2)	472	(23.3)	434	(25.3)	26.3	(3.8)	503	(20.1)	479	(22.5)

© OECD 2006 *Where immigrant students succeed - A comparative review of performance and engagement in PISA 2003*

Table 4.3b

Index of instrumental motivation in mathematics by students' expected level of education

Results based on students' self-reports

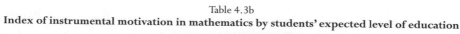

		Index of instrumental motivation in mathematics for students expecting to complete :								
		Lower secondary education (ISCED Level 2)		Upper secondary education, not providing access to university-level programmes (ISCED Levels 3B and 3C)		Upper secondary education, providing access to university-level programmes (ISCED Levels 3A and 4)		A non-university tertiary-level programme (ISCED Level 5B)		A university-level programme (ISCED Levels 5A and 6)	
		Mean index	S.E.	Mean index	S.E.	Mean index	S.E.	Mean index	S.E.	Mean index	S.E.
Australia	Native	-0.07	(0.08)	-0.03	(0.05)	-0.10	(0.03)	-0.07	(0.04)	0.38	(0.02)
	Second-generation	-0.47	(0.25)	0.29	(0.38)	0.02	(0.09)	-0.12	(0.09)	0.47	(0.04)
	First-generation	-0.56	(0.30)	-0.12	(0.17)	-0.10	(0.08)	0.07	(0.09)	0.50	(0.04)
Austria	Native	-0.41	(0.10)	-0.46	(0.04)	-0.71	(0.04)	-0.26	(0.05)	-0.60	(0.04)
	Second-generation	-0.51	(0.47)	-0.24	(0.18)	-0.29	(0.14)	-0.33	(0.37)	-0.44	(0.19)
	First-generation	-0.18	(0.26)	-0.13	(0.09)	-0.28	(0.10)	-0.20	(0.15)	-0.75	(0.16)
Belgium	Native	-0.39	(0.05)	-0.55	(0.06)	-0.48	(0.03)	-0.47	(0.03)	-0.14	(0.02)
	Second-generation	-0.02	(0.14)	-0.48	(0.18)	-0.19	(0.10)	-0.47	(0.11)	0.09	(0.12)
	First-generation	-0.10	(0.17)	0.10	(0.17)	0.20	(0.10)	-0.22	(0.10)	0.00	(0.13)
Canada	Native	-0.58	(0.15)	-0.35	(0.04)	-0.11	(0.04)	-0.04	(0.03)	0.38	(0.02)
	Second-generation	-0.06	(0.28)	-0.14	(0.18)	0.03	(0.20)	-0.10	(0.08)	0.51	(0.05)
	First-generation	0.49	(0.40)	-0.18	(0.33)	0.10	(0.17)	0.17	(0.10)	0.60	(0.04)
Denmark	Native	0.05	(0.04)	0.28	(0.05)	0.29	(0.03)	0.31	(0.04)	0.70	(0.03)
	Second-generation	0.51	(0.38)	0.17	(0.32)	0.32	(0.12)	0.33	(0.18)	0.51	(0.22)
	First-generation	0.31	(0.27)	0.03	(0.23)	0.38	(0.14)	0.05	(0.26)	0.50	(0.15)
France	Native	0.00	(0.13)	-0.24	(0.04)	-0.20	(0.04)	-0.14	(0.05)	0.11	(0.04)
	Second-generation	-0.15	(0.43)	-0.01	(0.12)	0.10	(0.14)	-0.19	(0.13)	0.14	(0.09)
	First-generation	0.89	(0.00)	-0.08	(0.19)	0.03	(0.23)	0.30	(0.27)	0.73	(0.13)
Germany	Native	-0.09	(0.03)	-0.20	(0.08)	-0.12	(0.03)	-0.08	(0.12)	0.01	(0.05)
	Second-generation	0.09	(0.07)	-0.79	(0.43)	0.03	(0.16)	-0.39	(0.68)	0.30	(0.24)
	First-generation	0.17	(0.08)	0.07	(0.16)	0.10	(0.14)	0.75	(0.74)	0.37	(0.17)
Luxembourg	Native	-0.75	(0.08)	-0.57	(0.06)	-0.48	(0.05)	-0.63	(0.05)	-0.43	(0.04)
	Second-generation	-0.59	(0.29)	-0.02	(0.10)	-0.31	(0.10)	-0.44	(0.14)	-0.36	(0.07)
	First-generation	-0.44	(0.37)	0.22	(0.08)	-0.16	(0.08)	-0.13	(0.20)	-0.07	(0.07)
Netherlands	Native	-0.31	(0.04)	a	a	-0.35	(0.03)	a	a	-0.26	(0.02)
	Second-generation	0.06	(0.13)	a	a	-0.03	(0.13)	a	a	0.16	(0.12)
	First-generation	0.06	(0.14)	a	a	0.05	(0.18)	a	a	-0.15	(0.15)
New Zealand	Native	-0.22	(0.14)	-0.05	(0.04)	0.16	(0.02)	0.34	(0.04)	0.46	(0.03)
	Second-generation	0.10	(0.00)	0.19	(0.25)	0.23	(0.09)	0.41	(0.13)	0.63	(0.08)
	First-generation	0.13	(0.30)	0.25	(0.14)	0.16	(0.07)	0.37	(0.10)	0.65	(0.05)
Norway	Native	-0.45	(0.24)	-0.15	(0.04)	-0.05	(0.04)	0.20	(0.03)	0.54	(0.04)
	Second-generation	0.10	(0.00)	-0.33	(0.25)	0.26	(0.26)	0.43	(0.19)	0.57	(0.30)
	First-generation	-0.36	(0.44)	0.03	(0.20)	-0.01	(0.20)	0.24	(0.21)	0.70	(0.15)
Sweden	Native	-0.28	(0.08)	-0.23	(0.04)	-0.23	(0.03)	-0.03	(0.03)	0.32	(0.04)
	Second-generation	-0.53	(0.39)	-0.11	(0.20)	-0.16	(0.12)	0.18	(0.11)	0.49	(0.08)
	First-generation	0.11	(0.16)	0.24	(0.16)	-0.05	(0.09)	0.07	(0.14)	0.49	(0.08)
Switzerland	Native	-0.17	(0.05)	-0.03	(0.03)	-0.25	(0.03)	0.26	(0.09)	-0.18	(0.06)
	Second-generation	-0.10	(0.09)	0.22	(0.07)	-0.10	(0.12)	-0.18	(0.17)	-0.17	(0.08)
	First-generation	-0.04	(0.17)	0.37	(0.07)	0.08	(0.12)	0.46	(0.14)	-0.10	(0.10)
United States	Native	0.04	(0.24)	a	a	-0.10	(0.04)	0.04	(0.05)	0.27	(0.02)
	Second-generation	-0.99	(0.35)	a	a	-0.12	(0.06)	0.21	(0.20)	0.41	(0.06)
	First-generation	-0.01	(0.57)	a	a	0.12	(0.14)	0.11	(0.13)	0.50	(0.08)
Hong Kong-China	Native	-0.81	(0.28)	-0.49	(0.06)	-0.28	(0.03)	-0.23	(0.06)	-0.01	(0.03)
	Second-generation	-0.75	(0.14)	-0.47	(0.09)	-0.23	(0.07)	-0.29	(0.10)	0.03	(0.05)
	First-generation	-0.44	(0.20)	-0.20	(0.06)	-0.08	(0.05)	0.01	(0.08)	0.17	(0.04)
Macao-China	Native	-0.21	(0.25)	-0.23	(0.39)	-0.14	(0.09)	-0.13	(0.12)	-0.08	(0.07)
	Second-generation	-0.32	(0.19)	-0.83	(0.40)	-0.18	(0.07)	0.02	(0.09)	0.11	(0.06)
	First-generation	0.01	(0.19)	0.13	(0.18)	0.00	(0.09)	-0.30	(0.20)	0.11	(0.09)
Russian Federation	Native	-0.18	(0.10)	-0.36	(0.06)	-0.12	(0.02)	a	a	0.09	(0.03)
	Second-generation	-0.34	(0.21)	-0.21	(0.22)	-0.04	(0.11)	a	a	0.03	(0.08)
	First-generation	-0.62	(0.24)	0.18	(0.20)	-0.14	(0.10)	a	a	0.09	(0.07)
Belgium (Flemish Community)	Native	-0.58	(0.2)	-0.72	(0.1)	-0.64	(0.0)	-0.54	(0.0)	-0.21	(0.0)
	Second-generation	-0.38	(0.1)	-0.19	(0.1)	-0.26	(0.0)	-0.32	(0.1)	-0.01	(0.0)
	First-generation	-0.36	(0.0)	-0.38	(0.2)	-0.33	(0.1)	-0.59	(0.2)	0.07	(0.1)
Belgium (French Community)	Native	-0.01	(0.1)	-0.61	(0.4)	-0.13	(0.1)	-0.37	(0.2)	0.10	(0.2)
	Second-generation	-1.16	(0.7)	-0.22	(0.1)	-0.18	(0.2)	-0.29	(0.1)	-0.14	(0.1)
	First-generation	0.06	(0.2)	0.33	(0.3)	0.39	(0.1)	-0.16	(0.1)	0.11	(0.2)

OECD countries / *Partner countries*

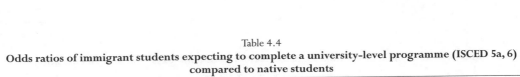

Table 4.4
Odds ratios of immigrant students expecting to complete a university-level programme (ISCED 5a, 6) compared to native students

	Meaning of one unit increase	Model 1 Odds	Model 2 Odds	Model 3 Odds
Australia				
Second-generation		**2.03**	**2.46**	**2.92**
First-generation		**2.39**	**2.97**	**3.16**
Math. performance	1 SD		**2.69**	**2.27**
ESCS	1 SD			**2.10**
Austria				
Second-generation		1.04	**2.18**	**3.49**
First-generation		**0.70**	**1.58**	**2.39**
Math. performance	1 SD		**3.71**	**2.94**
ESCS	1 SD			**2.92**
Belgium				
Second-generation		**0.60**	**1.60**	**2.41**
First-generation		**0.70**	**2.05**	**2.56**
Math. performance	1 SD		**3.32**	**2.64**
ESCS	1 SD			**2.36**
Canada				
Second-generation		**2.29**	**2.39**	**2.77**
First-generation		**3.22**	**4.06**	**3.90**
Math. performance	1 SD		**2.44**	**2.05**
ESCS	1 SD			**2.25**
Denmark				
Second-generation		**1.77**	**3.78**	**6.23**
First-generation		**2.23**	**4.81**	**6.96**
Math. performance	1 SD		**2.53**	**2.05**
ESCS	1 SD			**2.18**
France				
Second-generation		1.19	**2.34**	**3.63**
First-generation		0.85	**1.99**	**2.64**
Math. performance	1 SD		**3.63**	**2.97**
ESCS	1 SD			**1.97**
Germany				
Second-generation		**0.58**	**1.68**	**3.16**
First-generation		0.70	**1.58**	**3.03**
Math. performance	1 SD		**3.78**	**2.86**
ESCS	1 SD			**2.56**
Luxembourg				
Second-generation		1.02	**1.58**	**2.34**
First-generation		1.01	**1.90**	**3.35**
Math. performance	1 SD		**3.78**	**3.06**
ESCS	1 SD			**2.05**
Netherlands				
Second-generation		1.16	**3.71**	**5.47**
First-generation		0.97	**4.35**	**5.21**
Math. performance	1 SD		**5.70**	**4.85**
ESCS	1 SD			**1.86**
New Zealand				
Second-generation		**1.75**	**2.56**	**3.19**
First-generation		**2.36**	**2.83**	**2.77**
Math. performance	1 SD		**2.36**	**2.01**
ESCS	1 SD			**1.72**
Norway				
Second-generation		**1.95**	**2.86**	**3.86**
First-generation		1.13	**1.90**	**2.44**
Math. performance	1 SD		**2.23**	**1.77**
ESCS	1 SD			**2.56**
Sweden				
Second-generation		**1.70**	**2.32**	**3.29**
First-generation		**1.93**	**4.06**	**5.70**
Math. performance	1 SD		**2.03**	**1.67**
ESCS	1 SD			**2.18**
Switzerland				
Second-generation		0.87	**1.84**	**2.66**
First-generation		0.90	**2.51**	**3.67**
Math. performance	1 SD		**3.53**	**2.89**
ESCS	1 SD			**3.13**
United States				
Second-generation		1.15	**1.39**	**2.05**
First-generation		**0.76**	1.00	**1.43**
Math. performance	1 SD		**2.05**	**1.60**
ESCS	1 SD			**2.18**

	Meaning of one unit increase	Model 1 Odds	Model 2 Odds	Model 3 Odds
Hong Kong-China				
Second-generation		1.06	0.90	1.12
First-generation		**0.74**	1.09	1.49
Math. performance	1 SD		**2.94**	**2.75**
ESCS	1 SD			**1.88**
Macao-China				
Second-generation		1.01	1.01	1.11
First-generation		0.97	1.07	1.20
Math. performance	1 SD		**2.12**	**2.03**
ESCS	1 SD			**1.38**
Russian Federation				
Second-generation		0.83	0.90	0.90
First-generation		**0.73**	0.86	0.83
Math. performance	1 SD		**2.77**	**2.39**
ESCS	1 SD			**3.03**
Belgium (Flemish Community)				
Second-generation		**0.52**	**2.44**	**4.66**
First-generation		0.80	**2.92**	**3.39**
Math. performance	1 SD		**4.22**	**3.35**
ESCS	1 SD			**2.56**
Belgium (French Community)				
Second-generation		**0.70**	1.15	**1.62**
First-generation		0.70	1.46	**1.93**
Math. performance	1 SD		**2.83**	**2.20**
ESCS	1 SD			**2.12**

Note: Values that are statistically significant are indicated in bold.

© OECD 2006 *Where immigrant students succeed - A comparative review of performance and engagement in PISA 2003*

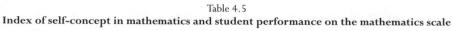

Table 4.5
Index of self-concept in mathematics and student performance on the mathematics scale

Results based on students' self-reports

Index of self-concept in mathematics

	Native students		Second-generation students		First-generation students	
	Mean index	S.E.	Mean index	S.E.	Mean index	S.E.
OECD countries						
Australia	0.10	(0.02)	**0.23**	(0.03)	**0.28**	(0.03)
Austria	0.07	(0.02)	0.10	(0.07)	0.09	(0.06)
Belgium	-0.04	(0.02)	0.02	(0.04)	0.07	(0.05)
Canada	0.16	(0.01)	0.20	(0.05)	**0.42**	(0.05)
Denmark	0.25	(0.02)	**0.03**	(0.09)	0.21	(0.10)
France	-0.17	(0.02)	-0.20	(0.06)	0.02	(0.10)
Germany	0.12	(0.02)	0.18	(0.07)	**0.30**	(0.05)
Luxembourg	0.05	(0.02)	0.05	(0.04)	**0.17**	(0.04)
Netherlands	-0.01	(0.03)	0.01	(0.07)	0.04	(0.10)
New Zealand	0.12	(0.02)	0.11	(0.05)	**0.38**	(0.04)
Norway	-0.18	(0.02)	0.06	(0.14)	-0.21	(0.08)
Sweden	0.12	(0.02)	0.12	(0.08)	0.22	(0.06)
Switzerland	0.13	(0.02)	0.09	(0.04)	**0.26**	(0.05)
United States	0.26	(0.02)	0.27	(0.06)	0.33	(0.06)
OECD average	*0.07*	*(0.01)*	*0.09*	*(0.02)*	*0.23*	*(0.02)*
Partner countries						
Hong Kong-China	-0.27	(0.03)	-0.24	(0.04)	-0.25	(0.03)
Macao-China	-0.40	(0.06)	**-0.16**	(0.04)	**-0.07**	(0.07)
Russian Federation	0.14	(0.02)	0.07	(0.04)	0.08	(0.05)
Belgium (Flemish Community)	-0.07	(0.02)	-0.02	(0.06)	0.05	(0.08)
Belgium (French Community)	0.01	(0.03)	0.04	(0.06)	0.08	(0.07)

Change in the mathematics score per unit of the index of self-concept in mathematics

	Native students		Explained variance in student performance (r-squared x 100)	Second-generation students		Explained variance in student performance (r-squared x 100)	First-generation students		Explained variance in student performance (r-squared x 100)
	Effect	S.E.	%	Effect	S.E.	%	Effect	S.E.	%
OECD countries									
Australia	**43.0**	(1.3)	18.1	**41.5**	(4.1)	14.5	**37.7**	(3.0)	11.5
Austria	**28.1**	(1.8)	11.2	**20.5**	(4.6)	6.5	11.4	(5.9)	1.9
Belgium	**25.4**	(1.5)	6.2	7.4	(6.2)	0.5	**16.0**	(6.4)	2.3
Canada	**35.9**	(0.8)	20.5	**39.7**	(3.0)	24.2	**33.9**	(2.7)	16.0
Denmark	**46.7**	(1.3)	29.1	**29.9**	(7.7)	10.2	**36.8**	(10.3)	15.1
France	**29.0**	(1.8)	11.3	**23.4**	(4.1)	8.2	**37.4**	(10.5)	12.5
Germany	**23.2**	(1.6)	8.6	**35.1**	(5.6)	15.9	**26.2**	(4.9)	9.3
Luxembourg	**19.9**	(1.5)	6.8	**20.3**	(3.7)	5.4	**21.6**	(4.1)	5.2
Netherlands	**23.5**	(1.7)	7.2	12.8	(7.3)	2.0	**20.4**	(6.4)	7.3
New Zealand	**45.1**	(1.8)	17.8	**45.6**	(6.4)	15.5	**44.8**	(5.4)	15.9
Norway	**47.4**	(1.2)	33.6	**47.0**	(5.6)	33.9	**35.2**	(7.5)	16.5
Sweden	**47.9**	(1.6)	27.9	**54.7**	(7.0)	27.9	**35.2**	(7.2)	11.2
Switzerland	**26.3**	(1.7)	9.7	**12.6**	(3.8)	1.8	**21.6**	(4.9)	4.7
United States	**34.5**	(1.6)	15.0	**42.4**	(4.9)	20.1	**33.9**	(6.9)	10.7
OECD average	*33.3*	*(0.5)*	*14.1*	*30.2*	*(1.3)*	*9.8*	*30.6*	*(1.6)*	*9.1*
Partner countries									
Hong Kong-China	**39.6**	(2.3)	14.0	**39.6**	(3.8)	14.5	**29.8**	(4.1)	6.3
Macao-China	**29.2**	(5.5)	9.9	**34.4**	(4.6)	13.8	**32.7**	(9.5)	10.2
Russian Federation	**40.9**	(1.9)	11.6	17.9	(6.3)	2.9	**29.7**	(7.3)	5.6
Belgium (Flemish Community)	**32.3**	(2.0)	10.0	1.5	(10.3)	0.1	7.0	(10.4)	0.5
Belgium (French Community)	**19.4**	(2.4)	4.3	9.7	(7.6)	0.9	**19.6**	(8.8)	3.7

Regression estimate of the index of self-concept in mathematics

	Accounting for ESCS				Accounting for mathematics performance			
	Second-generation students		First-generation students		Second-generation students		First-generation students	
	Coef.	S.E.	Coef.	S.E.	Coef.	S.E.	Coef.	S.E.
OECD countries								
Australia	**0.16**	(0.04)	**0.18**	(0.03)	**0.15**	(0.03)	**0.19**	(0.03)
Austria	0.09	(0.07)	0.08	(0.07)	**0.24**	(0.07)	**0.26**	(0.07)
Belgium	**0.09**	(0.04)	**0.13**	(0.06)	**0.27**	(0.05)	**0.32**	(0.06)
Canada	0.05	(0.05)	**0.24**	(0.05)	0.00	(0.04)	**0.30**	(0.05)
Denmark	-0.01	(0.10)	0.11	(0.10)	0.21	(0.11)	**0.35**	(0.10)
France	0.06	(0.07)	**0.29**	(0.10)	**0.14**	(0.07)	**0.46**	(0.09)
Germany	0.14	(0.08)	**0.28**	(0.06)	**0.41**	(0.07)	**0.43**	(0.06)
Luxembourg	0.04	(0.05)	**0.18**	(0.05)	**0.10**	(0.05)	**0.26**	(0.04)
Netherlands	0.05	(0.08)	0.07	(0.10)	**0.18**	(0.07)	**0.29**	(0.10)
New Zealand	0.06	(0.06)	**0.24**	(0.04)	**0.12**	(0.06)	**0.27**	(0.04)
Norway	**0.38**	(0.12)	0.17	(0.09)	**0.52**	(0.12)	**0.40**	(0.09)
Sweden	0.12	(0.07)	**0.25**	(0.06)	**0.19**	(0.06)	**0.60**	(0.06)
Switzerland	-0.02	(0.04)	**0.16**	(0.06)	**0.16**	(0.04)	**0.44**	(0.06)
United States	0.10	(0.06)	**0.18**	(0.06)	0.10	(0.06)	**0.22**	(0.06)
OECD average	*0.10*	*(0.02)*	*0.23*	*(0.02)*	*0.18*	*(0.02)*	*0.35*	*(0.02)*
Partner countries								
Hong Kong-China	0.05	(0.03)	0.07	(0.04)	-0.02	(0.03)	**0.15**	(0.04)
Macao-China	**0.23**	(0.08)	**0.33**	(0.09)	**0.22**	(0.07)	**0.36**	(0.08)
Russian Federation	-0.06	(0.05)	-0.05	(0.05)	-0.03	(0.04)	0.00	(0.05)
Belgium (Flemish Community)	**0.13**	(0.06)	**0.18**	(0.08)	**0.41**	(0.07)	**0.40**	(0.09)
Belgium (French Community)	0.02	(0.07)	0.05	(0.08)	0.14	(0.07)	**0.22**	(0.08)

Note: Values that are statistically significant are indicated in bold.

Table 4.6

Index of self-efficacy in mathematics and student performance on the mathematics scale

Results based on students' self-reports

Index of self-efficacy in mathematics

	Native students		Second-generation students		First-generation students	
	Mean index	S.E.	Mean index	S.E.	Mean index	S.E.
OECD countries						
Australia	0.08	(0.02)	**0.21**	(0.04)	**0.24**	(0.04)
Austria	0.20	(0.02)	**-0.17**	(0.09)	**-0.10**	(0.05)
Belgium	-0.04	(0.02)	-0.03	(0.06)	**-0.19**	(0.06)
Canada	0.24	(0.02)	0.23	(0.04)	**0.40**	(0.04)
Denmark	-0.06	(0.02)	**-0.23**	(0.07)	-0.10	(0.07)
France	0.01	(0.03)	**-0.13**	(0.05)	-0.09	(0.11)
Germany	0.19	(0.02)	**-0.09**	(0.07)	0.01	(0.06)
Luxembourg	0.19	(0.02)	**-0.05**	(0.04)	**-0.07**	(0.04)
Netherlands	-0.08	(0.02)	-0.15	(0.06)	-0.17	(0.08)
New Zealand	-0.02	(0.02)	-0.07	(0.05)	**0.23**	(0.04)
Norway	-0.04	(0.03)	0.13	(0.13)	-0.18	(0.08)
Sweden	0.03	(0.03)	0.16	(0.08)	-0.04	(0.07)
Switzerland	0.38	(0.03)	**0.13**	(0.04)	**0.13**	(0.04)
United States	0.29	(0.02)	0.22	(0.07)	0.24	(0.07)
OECD average	*0.09*	*(0.01)*	*0.02*	*(0.02)*	*0.07*	*(0.02)*
Partner countries						
Hong Kong-China	0.15	(0.03)	0.18	(0.03)	-0.05	(0.03)
Macao-China	0.00	(0.06)	0.09	(0.05)	0.17	(0.07)
Russian Federation	-0.07	(0.02)	-0.14	(0.05)	-0.13	(0.05)
Belgium (Flemish Community)	-0.15	(0.02)	-0.25	(0.06)	**-0.36**	(0.07)
Belgium (French Community)	0.13	(0.03)	0.08	(0.08)	**-0.11**	(0.09)

Change in the mathematics score per unit of the index of self-efficacy in mathematics

	Native students		Explained variance in student performance (r-squared x 100)	Second-generation students		Explained variance in student performance (r-squared x 100)	First-generation students		Explained variance in student performance (r-squared x 100)
	Effect	S.E.	%	Effect	S.E.	%	Effect	S.E.	%
OECD countries									
Australia	**49.5**	(1.2)	27.4	**47.6**	(3.3)	24.2	**52.2**	(3.7)	29.2
Austria	**45.7**	(1.8)	26.6	**38.9**	(6.8)	18.8	**29.4**	(5.9)	9.3
Belgium	**45.9**	(1.3)	19.5	**39.2**	(4.6)	15.9	**34.8**	(5.9)	12.9
Canada	**42.8**	(0.9)	28.4	**47.5**	(2.6)	33.9	**48.1**	(2.8)	30.3
Denmark	**50.7**	(1.9)	28.6	**43.5**	(9.8)	15.3	**41.8**	(10.9)	14.8
France	**46.1**	(1.6)	25.8	**44.2**	(5.1)	22.7	**62.8**	(9.0)	31.0
Germany	**48.2**	(1.8)	26.5	**42.8**	(6.2)	23.8	**51.5**	(6.1)	26.1
Luxembourg	**37.0**	(1.6)	20.6	**40.8**	(3.8)	20.4	**49.0**	(3.4)	25.3
Netherlands	**44.4**	(2.2)	22.4	**36.2**	(6.2)	11.7	**45.4**	(9.9)	21.1
New Zealand	**52.8**	(1.6)	28.4	**57.4**	(6.6)	28.7	**46.4**	(4.6)	22.9
Norway	**46.8**	(1.6)	30.9	**49.0**	(5.3)	36.7	**41.1**	(6.7)	20.8
Sweden	**53.7**	(1.7)	35.0	**52.1**	(6.0)	29.6	**41.3**	(6.1)	22.0
Switzerland	**50.7**	(2.2)	31.5	**46.0**	(5.9)	21.8	**53.9**	(5.2)	24.3
United States	**45.9**	(1.4)	27.2	**53.1**	(4.5)	37.7	**43.4**	(5.2)	22.6
OECD average	*45.9*	*(0.5)*	*25.1*	*47.2*	*(1.4)*	*24.0*	*49.8*	*(1.5)*	*24.1*
Partner countries									
Hong Kong-China	**53.7**	(2.5)	31.5	**51.5**	(2.8)	31.3	**52.6**	(4.2)	25.3
Macao-China	**40.1**	(6.3)	16.9	**43.4**	(3.8)	19.3	**45.8**	(7.2)	22.8
Russian Federation	**49.1**	(2.0)	20.5	**28.5**	(5.6)	8.1	**39.3**	(5.9)	13.3
Belgium (Flemish Community)	**54.1**	(1.8)	23.8	**44.2**	(11.7)	11.8	**35.2**	(11.2)	11.0
Belgium (French Community)	**47.3**	(2.3)	26.4	**37.8**	(5.0)	17.8	**36.6**	(7.4)	15.6

Regression estimate of the index of self-efficacy in mathematics

	Accounting for ESCS				Accounting for mathematics performance			
	Second-generation students		First-generation students		Second-generation students		First-generation students	
	Coef.	S.E.	Coef.	S.E.	Coef.	S.E.	Coef.	S.E.
OECD countries								
Australia	**0.20**	(0.04)	**0.17**	(0.04)	**0.16**	(0.03)	**0.17**	(0.03)
Austria	**-0.17**	(0.09)	**-0.12**	(0.05)	-0.07	(0.08)	0.05	(0.06)
Belgium	**0.28**	(0.05)	0.04	(0.06)	**0.39**	(0.05)	**0.23**	(0.06)
Canada	0.01	(0.04)	**0.13**	(0.04)	-0.05	(0.03)	**0.20**	(0.03)
Denmark	0.08	(0.07)	**0.15**	(0.07)	**0.22**	(0.07)	**0.31**	(0.07)
France	**0.13**	(0.06)	0.16	(0.09)	**0.12**	(0.05)	**0.29**	(0.07)
Germany	0.06	(0.08)	**0.18**	(0.06)	**0.24**	(0.06)	**0.20**	(0.05)
Luxembourg	**-0.11**	(0.05)	-0.06	(0.05)	**-0.08**	(0.04)	-0.02	(0.04)
Netherlands	**0.12**	(0.06)	0.05	(0.08)	**0.22**	(0.06)	**0.30**	(0.08)
New Zealand	0.08	(0.05)	**0.23**	(0.04)	**0.12**	(0.05)	**0.27**	(0.04)
Norway	**0.32**	(0.11)	0.08	(0.08)	**0.43**	(0.09)	**0.27**	(0.08)
Sweden	**0.33**	(0.07)	**0.17**	(0.07)	**0.34**	(0.05)	**0.51**	(0.07)
Switzerland	-0.06	(0.05)	-0.01	(0.04)	**0.11**	(0.05)	**0.28**	(0.04)
United States	**0.13**	(0.06)	**0.18**	(0.06)	0.06	(0.05)	**0.15**	(0.07)
OECD average	*0.12*	*(0.02)*	*0.13*	*(0.02)*	*0.15*	*(0.01)*	*0.23*	*(0.01)*
Partner countries								
Hong Kong-China	0.12	(0.03)	-0.04	(0.04)	-0.04	(0.04)	0.04	(0.03)
Macao-China	0.12	(0.08)	0.20	(0.08)	0.07	(0.07)	0.21	(0.08)
Russian Federation	-0.06	(0.05)	-0.05	(0.05)	-0.01	(0.05)	0.03	(0.04)
Belgium (Flemish Community)	**0.17**	(0.06)	-0.05	(0.08)	**0.41**	(0.05)	**0.20**	(0.08)
Belgium (French Community)	**0.24**	(0.06)	0.00	(0.09)	**0.26**	(0.07)	**0.16**	(0.08)

Note: Values that are statistically significant are indicated in bold.

© OECD 2006 Where immigrant students succeed - A comparative review of performance and engagement in PISA 2003

Annex B

Table 4.7
Index of anxiety in mathematics and student performance on the mathematics scale
Results based on students' self-reports

Index of anxiety in mathematics

	Native students		Second-generation students		First-generation students	
	Mean index	S.E.	Mean index	S.E.	Mean index	S.E.
Australia	-0.05	(0.01)	-0.09	(0.03)	-0.07	(0.03)
Austria	-0.29	(0.03)	-0.21	(0.09)	**-0.08**	(0.06)
Belgium	0.06	(0.02)	**0.31**	(0.05)	**0.20**	(0.05)
Canada	-0.05	(0.01)	0.01	(0.05)	-0.12	(0.04)
Denmark	-0.48	(0.02)	**-0.02**	(0.08)	**-0.21**	(0.09)
France	0.31	(0.02)	**0.50**	(0.05)	0.42	(0.11)
Germany	-0.28	(0.02)	**-0.06**	(0.08)	-0.19	(0.06)
Luxembourg	-0.08	(0.02)	**0.20**	(0.05)	**0.09**	(0.04)
Netherlands	-0.42	(0.02)	**-0.13**	(0.06)	**-0.13**	(0.10)
New Zealand	-0.11	(0.02)	**0.11**	(0.07)	-0.17	(0.04)
Norway	-0.06	(0.02)	-0.13	(0.13)	**0.26**	(0.09)
Sweden	-0.53	(0.02)	**-0.25**	(0.08)	**-0.25**	(0.07)
Switzerland	-0.35	(0.03)	**-0.04**	(0.05)	**-0.12**	(0.06)
United States	-0.12	(0.02)	-0.09	(0.06)	0.00	(0.07)
OECD average	*-0.18*	*(0.01)*	*0.05*	*(0.02)*	*-0.05*	*(0.02)*
Hong Kong-China	0.24	(0.02)	0.21	(0.04)	0.22	(0.03)
Macao-China	0.48	(0.05)	**0.20**	(0.05)	0.02	(0.08)
Russian Federation	0.14	(0.02)	0.10	(0.05)	0.22	(0.04)
Belgium (Flemish Community)	0.01	(0.02)	**0.31**	(0.08)	0.00	(0.06)
Belgium (French Community)	0.15	(0.03)	**0.31**	(0.06)	**0.31**	(0.06)

Change in the mathematics score per unit of the index of anxiety in mathematics

	Native students		Explained variance in student performance (r-squared x 100)	Second-generation students		Explained variance in student performance (r-squared x 100)	First-generation students		Explained variance in student performance (r-squared x 100)
	Effect	S.E.	%	Effect	S.E.	%	Effect	S.E.	%
Australia	**-38.0**	(1.5)	12.9	**-33.0**	(3.7)	9.6	**-36.9**	(3.7)	10.6
Austria	**-24.5**	(1.8)	10.0	**-23.8**	(4.6)	10.5	**-17.8**	(5.1)	4.8
Belgium	**-24.0**	(1.5)	5.2	**-16.6**	(5.6)	2.6	**-30.7**	(4.1)	7.5
Canada	**-32.1**	(0.8)	15.8	**-32.8**	(3.1)	17.2	**-34.7**	(2.8)	16.8
Denmark	**-43.8**	(1.5)	26.6	**-33.8**	(8.9)	11.7	**-43.5**	(8.4)	22.4
France	**-23.1**	(1.7)	5.8	**-22.1**	(6.1)	5.0	**-41.2**	(8.3)	14.9
Germany	**-25.0**	(1.3)	10.7	**-33.7**	(5.4)	15.1	**-38.9**	(4.8)	19.9
Luxembourg	**-23.1**	(1.5)	10.0	**-26.7**	(3.9)	9.0	**-28.4**	(4.3)	9.1
Netherlands	**-20.9**	(2.3)	4.3	-16.5	(7.4)	2.6	**-21.4**	(6.2)	7.8
New Zealand	**-46.6**	(1.7)	18.1	**-53.7**	(5.7)	22.1	**-48.7**	(4.9)	21.9
Norway	**-42.6**	(1.3)	25.3	**-31.1**	(7.4)	16.5	**-43.1**	(7.2)	26.8
Sweden	**-41.2**	(1.6)	19.6	**-42.4**	(7.4)	18.8	**-46.4**	(6.0)	24.1
Switzerland	**-25.6**	(2.0)	9.3	**-20.7**	(4.7)	4.6	**-34.8**	(4.3)	13.8
United States	**-32.4**	(1.6)	14.7	**-42.9**	(4.6)	20.5	**-40.3**	(6.2)	17.7
OECD average	*-30.5*	*(0.5)*	*12.0*	*-30.1*	*(1.4)*	*9.7*	*-35.6*	*(1.4)*	*12.9*
Hong Kong-China	**-30.4**	(2.9)	7.8	**-36.4**	(3.8)	11.1	**-27.2**	(4.3)	5.9
Macao-China	**-28.4**	(5.2)	9.0	**-30.1**	(4.5)	12.7	-21.3	(10.2)	4.8
Russian Federation	**-46.2**	(1.8)	15.7	**-20.7**	(6.6)	4.3	**-33.5**	(7.3)	7.8
Belgium (Flemish Community)	**-22.2**	(1.9)	4.5	**-22.5**	(10.3)	4.2	-17.5	(8.7)	2.4
Belgium (French Community)	**-22.5**	(2.8)	5.1	-13.9	(7.0)	2.0	**-34.8**	(6.3)	9.3

Regression estimate of the index of anxiety in mathematics

	Accounting for ESCS				Accounting for mathematics performance			
	Second-generation students		First-generation students		Second-generation students		First-generation students	
	Coef.	S.E.	Coef.	S.E.	Coef.	S.E.	Coef.	S.E.
Australia	**-0.07**	(0.03)	-0.02	(0.03)	-0.06	(0.03)	-0.02	(0.03)
Austria	0.02	(0.09)	**0.16**	(0.06)	-0.12	(0.09)	-0.03	(0.07)
Belgium	**0.23**	(0.04)	**0.12**	(0.05)	0.06	(0.05)	-0.05	(0.04)
Canada	0.05	(0.05)	-0.07	(0.04)	0.09	(0.05)	**-0.11**	(0.04)
Denmark	**0.23**	(0.09)	0.10	(0.09)	0.04	(0.09)	-0.13	(0.09)
France	**0.14**	(0.05)	0.05	(0.12)	0.07	(0.05)	-0.06	(0.10)
Germany	0.08	(0.08)	-0.06	(0.07)	**-0.18**	(0.07)	**-0.21**	(0.06)
Luxembourg	**0.23**	(0.05)	0.07	(0.05)	**0.16**	(0.04)	-0.01	(0.04)
Netherlands	**0.28**	(0.06)	**0.28**	(0.10)	**0.17**	(0.05)	0.11	(0.09)
New Zealand	**0.16**	(0.07)	-0.06	(0.04)	0.09	(0.07)	**-0.08**	(0.04)
Norway	-0.16	(0.13)	0.15	(0.08)	**-0.30**	(0.12)	-0.05	(0.07)
Sweden	**0.19**	(0.07)	**0.15**	(0.07)	0.12	(0.06)	**-0.16**	(0.05)
Switzerland	**0.29**	(0.06)	**0.21**	(0.07)	0.11	(0.06)	-0.10	(0.08)
United States	-0.06	(0.07)	0.00	(0.07)	-0.06	(0.06)	-0.03	(0.07)
OECD average	*0.16*	*(0.02)*	*0.06*	*(0.02)*	*0.08*	*(0.02)*	*-0.05*	*(0.02)*
Hong Kong-China	-0.04	(0.04)	-0.05	(0.04)	0.01	(0.04)	**-0.12**	(0.04)
Macao-China	**-0.28**	(0.07)	**-0.44**	(0.09)	**-0.26**	(0.07)	**-0.49**	(0.10)
Russian Federation	-0.04	(0.05)	0.08	(0.05)	-0.08	(0.04)	0.02	(0.05)
Belgium (Flemish Community)	**0.26**	(0.08)	-0.05	(0.06)	0.06	(0.08)	**-0.20**	(0.06)
Belgium (French Community)	**0.16**	(0.05)	**0.15**	(0.06)	0.04	(0.06)	0.01	(0.06)

Note: Values that are statistically significant are indicated in bold.

© OECD 2006 Where immigrant students succeed - A comparative review of performance and engagement in PISA 2003

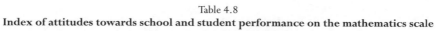

Table 4.8

Index of attitudes towards school and student performance on the mathematics scale

Results based on students' self-reports

	Index of attitudes towards school					
	Native students		Second-generation students		First-generation students	
	Mean index	S.E.	Mean index	S.E.	Mean index	S.E.
OECD countries						
Australia	0.24	(0.02)	**0.33**	(0.03)	0.29	(0.04)
Austria	0.09	(0.02)	0.20	(0.09)	**0.31**	(0.06)
Belgium	-0.21	(0.02)	**-0.01**	(0.05)	0.03	(0.08)
Canada	0.02	(0.01)	**0.14**	(0.04)	**0.25**	(0.04)
Denmark	-0.04	(0.02)	0.09	(0.09)	0.05	(0.10)
France	0.12	(0.02)	**0.26**	(0.06)	**0.35**	(0.08)
Germany	-0.12	(0.02)	**0.08**	(0.08)	**0.13**	(0.07)
Luxembourg	-0.33	(0.02)	**-0.09**	(0.04)	**0.05**	(0.04)
Netherlands	-0.22	(0.02)	**-0.02**	(0.06)	**0.19**	(0.08)
New Zealand	0.05	(0.02)	**0.39**	(0.06)	**0.20**	(0.04)
Norway	-0.22	(0.02)	-0.15	(0.16)	**0.04**	(0.09)
Sweden	0.00	(0.02)	0.17	(0.08)	**0.27**	(0.06)
Switzerland	0.00	(0.02)	0.13	(0.06)	**0.21**	(0.04)
United States	0.09	(0.02)	0.16	(0.05)	0.17	(0.08)
OECD average	*-0.04*	*(0.00)*	*0.13*	*(0.02)*	*0.18*	*(0.02)*
Partner countries						
Hong Kong-China	-0.52	(0.02)	-0.54	(0.02)	-0.50	(0.02)
Macao-China	-0.35	(0.04)	-0.37	(0.05)	-0.41	(0.07)
Russian Federation	0.20	(0.03)	0.09	(0.05)	0.18	(0.05)
Belgium (Flemish Community)	-0.27	(0.02)	**-0.03**	(0.07)	-0.13	(0.10)
Belgium (French Community)	-0.11	(0.03)	0.00	(0.07)	0.11	(0.11)

	Change in the mathematics score per unit of the index of attitudes towards school								
	Native students		Explained variance in student performance (r-squared x 100)	Second-generation students		Explained variance in student performance (r-squared x 100)	First-generation students		Explained variance in student performance (r-squared x 100)
	Effect	S.E.	%	Effect	S.E.	%	Effect	S.E.	%
OECD countries									
Australia	**15.4**	(1.2)	3.1	**5.0**	(2.2)	0.3	**11.0**	(3.5)	1.4
Austria	0.6	(1.6)	0.0	**-15.6**	(6.9)	4.8	**-10.4**	(5.1)	1.7
Belgium	-1.3	(2.0)	0.0	-6.4	(5.5)	0.4	-0.6	(6.8)	0.0
Canada	**8.2**	(0.9)	1.0	**11.1**	(3.7)	1.8	-2.7	(3.3)	0.1
Denmark	**8.6**	(1.9)	0.8	10.1	(12.4)	1.4	-12.1	(8.0)	2.4
France	**9.7**	(1.9)	1.2	1.2	(4.8)	0.0	**-13.9**	(6.6)	2.4
Germany	**-4.6**	(1.8)	0.3	-7.8	(7.0)	0.7	**-18.1**	(5.8)	4.1
Luxembourg	**-4.9**	(1.9)	0.3	**-9.2**	(4.1)	1.1	**-11.7**	(3.6)	1.6
Netherlands	**9.0**	(2.6)	0.6	-4.2	(8.9)	0.2	-8.8	(7.4)	1.1
New Zealand	**16.8**	(1.8)	3.1	3.7	(5.8)	0.2	**13.3**	(5.2)	1.9
Norway	**17.0**	(1.9)	3.2	12.1	(10.5)	2.3	**17.0**	(7.8)	4.1
Sweden	**17.1**	(1.5)	3.3	4.1	(9.4)	0.2	**16.4**	(7.1)	3.4
Switzerland	**5.7**	(1.9)	0.4	**-10.3**	(4.5)	1.3	-4.1	(6.1)	0.2
United States	**5.7**	(1.4)	0.4	-1.0	(5.4)	0.0	**15.8**	(7.2)	2.8
OECD average	*7.2*	*(0.4)*	*0.6*	*0.1*	*(1.4)*	*0.0*	*0.1*	*(1.6)*	*0.0*
Partner countries									
Hong Kong-China	**11.4**	(3.3)	0.8	**20.7**	(5.1)	2.6	**13.3**	(4.4)	1.0
Macao-China	4.6	(7.2)	0.2	2.1	(7.0)	0.0	-2.5	(14.2)	0.3
Russian Federation	**5.4**	(1.8)	0.3	-0.5	(5.6)	0.1	3.1	(5.4)	0.1
Belgium (Flemish Community)	0.7	(3.0)	0.0	-8.3	(8.6)	0.6	**-23.7**	(10.0)	5.4
Belgium (French Community)	1.4	(2.5)	0.0	-5.7	(6.8)	0.3	11.4	(9.0)	1.2

	Regression estimate of the index of attitudes towards school							
	Accounting for ESCS				Accounting for mathematics performance			
	Second-generation students		First-generation students		Second-generation students		First-generation students	
	Coef.	S.E.	Coef.	S.E.	Coef.	S.E.	Coef.	S.E.
OECD countries								
Australia	**0.13**	(0.03)	0.05	(0.04)	**0.09**	(0.03)	0.05	(0.04)
Austria	0.11	(0.09)	**0.21**	(0.07)	0.11	(0.09)	**0.21**	(0.07)
Belgium	**0.27**	(0.06)	**0.30**	(0.07)	**0.19**	(0.06)	**0.23**	(0.07)
Canada	**0.13**	(0.04)	**0.22**	(0.04)	**0.11**	(0.04)	**0.24**	(0.04)
Denmark	**0.24**	(0.10)	0.16	(0.10)	**0.20**	(0.09)	0.15	(0.10)
France	**0.20**	(0.07)	**0.30**	(0.09)	**0.20**	(0.07)	**0.31**	(0.10)
Germany	**0.22**	(0.08)	**0.26**	(0.07)	**0.15**	(0.08)	**0.21**	(0.07)
Luxembourg	**0.21**	(0.05)	**0.34**	(0.05)	**0.22**	(0.05)	**0.34**	(0.05)
Netherlands	**0.24**	(0.06)	**0.44**	(0.09)	**0.23**	(0.06)	**0.46**	(0.08)
New Zealand	**0.40**	(0.07)	**0.13**	(0.05)	**0.39**	(0.07)	**0.15**	(0.05)
Norway	0.13	(0.17)	**0.37**	(0.08)	0.14	(0.17)	**0.37**	(0.09)
Sweden	**0.28**	(0.09)	**0.40**	(0.06)	**0.23**	(0.09)	**0.44**	(0.05)
Switzerland	**0.19**	(0.07)	**0.27**	(0.05)	**0.16**	(0.07)	**0.26**	(0.06)
United States	**0.15**	(0.06)	0.16	(0.09)	0.09	(0.05)	0.11	(0.08)
OECD average	*0.22*	*(0.02)*	*0.26*	*(0.02)*	*0.20*	*(0.02)*	*0.26*	*(0.02)*
Partner countries								
Hong Kong-China	0.01	(0.03)	**0.07**	(0.03)	-0.03	(0.03)	0.05	(0.03)
Macao-China	-0.01	(0.06)	-0.04	(0.09)	-0.01	(0.06)	-0.05	(0.08)
Russian Federation	-0.11	(0.06)	-0.02	(0.05)	-0.10	(0.06)	-0.01	(0.05)
Belgium (Flemish Community)	**0.29**	(0.08)	0.16	(0.10)	**0.25**	(0.08)	0.14	(0.10)
Belgium (French Community)	**0.20**	(0.07)	**0.32**	(0.10)	0.12	(0.07)	**0.25**	(0.10)

Note: Values that are statistically significant are indicated in bold.

© OECD 2006 **Where immigrant students succeed - A comparative review of performance and engagement in PISA 2003**

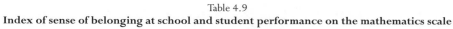

Table 4.9

Index of sense of belonging at school and student performance on the mathematics scale

Results based on students' self-reports

	Index of sense of belonging at school					
	Native students		Second-generation students		First-generation students	
	Mean index	S.E.	Mean index	S.E.	Mean index	S.E.
OECD countries						
Australia	0.04	(0.02)	**0.20**	(0.04)	-0.04	(0.03)
Austria	0.46	(0.02)	0.29	(0.11)	0.36	(0.06)
Belgium	-0.28	(0.01)	-0.22	(0.04)	-0.42	(0.08)
Canada	0.02	(0.01)	0.05	(0.04)	-0.06	(0.04)
Denmark	0.02	(0.02)	0.03	(0.08)	-0.11	(0.09)
France	-0.19	(0.02)	-0.10	(0.05)	-0.13	(0.08)
Germany	0.24	(0.02)	0.38	(0.09)	0.12	(0.05)
Luxembourg	0.36	(0.02)	**-0.01**	(0.04)	**-0.04**	(0.04)
Netherlands	-0.05	(0.02)	-0.07	(0.07)	-0.11	(0.08)
New Zealand	0.01	(0.02)	**0.21**	(0.06)	**-0.21**	(0.04)
Norway	0.25	(0.02)	0.02	(0.12)	0.04	(0.11)
Sweden	0.24	(0.02)	0.22	(0.08)	0.30	(0.07)
Switzerland	0.22	(0.03)	0.14	(0.05)	**0.09**	(0.04)
United States	m	m	m	m	m	m
OECD average	*0.10*	*(0.01)*	*0.07*	*(0.02)*	*-0.01*	*(0.02)*
Partner countries						
Hong Kong-China	-0.57	(0.02)	-0.59	(0.02)	-0.70	(0.02)
Macao-China	-0.64	(0.06)	-0.57	(0.03)	-0.71	(0.06)
Russian Federation	-0.29	(0.02)	-0.31	(0.04)	-0.22	(0.05)
Belgium (Flemish Community)	-0.27	(0.01)	-0.30	(0.08)	-0.35	(0.09)
Belgium (French Community)	-0.31	(0.03)	**-0.18**	(0.04)	-0.46	(0.11)

	Change in the mathematics score per unit of the index of sense of belonging at school								
	Native students		Explained variance in student performance (r-squared x 100)	Second-generation students		Explained variance in student performance (r-squared x 100)	First-generation students		Explained variance in student performance (r-squared x 100)
	Effect	S.E.	%	Effect	S.E.	%	Effect	S.E.	%
OECD countries									
Australia	**3.7**	(1.6)	0.2	-5.9	(3.1)	0.4	3.8	(3.6)	0.2
Austria	1.7	(1.5)	0.0	2.1	(6.7)	0.2	2.5	(5.3)	0.1
Belgium	**5.3**	(1.7)	0.2	6.0	(4.8)	0.3	10.0	(8.8)	0.8
Canada	-0.6	(1.0)	0.0	-2.2	(2.6)	0.1	**-7.8**	(2.9)	0.8
Denmark	3.1	(1.9)	0.1	2.9	(11.1)	0.1	5.0	(8.6)	0.6
France	**3.3**	(1.4)	0.1	-5.1	(5.3)	0.4	-5.9	(9.3)	0.4
Germany	-0.7	(1.9)	0.0	-2.7	(6.1)	0.1	-3.6	(7.0)	0.2
Luxembourg	3.3	(1.7)	0.2	3.8	(3.7)	0.2	3.3	(4.3)	0.1
Netherlands	**7.9**	(2.6)	0.6	-5.2	(5.7)	0.3	3.8	(7.4)	0.2
New Zealand	2.6	(1.6)	0.1	-6.4	(5.7)	0.5	**12.9**	(4.9)	1.5
Norway	-0.6	(1.6)	0.0	-8.4	(9.0)	1.1	2.3	(6.2)	0.1
Sweden	-0.3	(1.5)	0.0	-2.3	(9.2)	0.1	**15.1**	(6.3)	3.2
Switzerland	**6.7**	(1.9)	0.6	-0.3	(5.2)	0.0	**14.5**	(5.0)	2.3
United States	m	m	m	m	m	m	m	m	m
OECD average	*0.7*	*(0.5)*	*0.0*	*-1.4*	*(1.5)*	*0.0*	*2.1*	*(1.7)*	*0.0*
Partner countries									
Hong Kong-China	**12.4**	(2.8)	0.8	**14.6**	(4.4)	1.2	**19.3**	(5.3)	1.7
Macao-China	12.4	(9.1)	1.2	8.4	(6.9)	0.6	-8.2	(10.9)	0.6
Russian Federation	**11.5**	(1.5)	1.2	5.0	(6.4)	0.3	8.8	(5.4)	0.9
Belgium (Flemish Community)	2.8	(1.9)	0.1	8.4	(7.7)	0.6	6.7	(8.6)	0.4
Belgium (French Community)	**7.1**	(2.8)	0.4	4.1	(5.4)	0.2	9.4	(11.0)	0.7

	Regression estimate of the index of sense of belonging at school							
	Accounting for ESCS				Accounting for mathematics performance			
	Second-generation students		First-generation students		Second-generation students		First-generation students	
	Coef.	S.E.	Coef.	S.E.	Coef.	S.E.	Coef.	S.E.
OECD countries								
Australia	**0.18**	(0.04)	**-0.07**	(0.04)	**0.16**	(0.01)	**-0.07**	(0.01)
Austria	-0.11	(0.11)	-0.06	(0.07)	**-0.16**	(0.02)	**-0.09**	(0.01)
Belgium	**0.13**	(0.04)	-0.09	(0.09)	**0.10**	(0.01)	**-0.09**	(0.02)
Canada	0.03	(0.04)	**-0.09**	(0.04)	0.03	(0.01)	**-0.08**	(0.01)
Denmark	0.11	(0.08)	-0.06	(0.10)	**0.04**	(0.02)	**-0.10**	(0.02)
France	**0.16**	(0.05)	0.14	(0.09)	**0.10**	(0.01)	**0.09**	(0.02)
Germany	**0.22**	(0.09)	-0.05	(0.06)	**0.13**	(0.02)	**-0.13**	(0.01)
Luxembourg	**-0.32**	(0.04)	**-0.33**	(0.05)	**-0.35**	(0.01)	**-0.37**	(0.01)
Netherlands	0.05	(0.08)	0.00	(0.09)	0.02	(0.02)	0.00	(0.02)
New Zealand	**0.26**	(0.06)	**-0.21**	(0.04)	**0.21**	(0.01)	**-0.21**	(0.01)
Norway	-0.20	(0.14)	-0.15	(0.11)	**-0.24**	(0.03)	**-0.22**	(0.03)
Sweden	0.03	(0.08)	0.13	(0.07)	-0.02	(0.02)	**0.07**	(0.02)
Switzerland	0.03	(0.08)	-0.06	(0.05)	**-0.03**	(0.01)	**-0.04**	(0.01)
United States	m	m	m	m	m	m	m	m
OECD average	*0.04*	*(0.02)*	*-0.05*	*(0.02)*	*-0.02*	*(0.02)*	*-0.10*	*(0.02)*
Partner countries								
Hong Kong-China	0.02	(0.03)	**-0.07**	(0.03)	-0.02	(0.01)	**-0.10**	(0.01)
Macao-China	0.09	(0.07)	-0.06	(0.08)	**0.07**	(0.02)	**-0.07**	(0.02)
Russian Federation	-0.02	(0.05)	0.06	(0.05)	-0.01	(0.01)	**0.08**	(0.01)
Belgium (Flemish Community)	0.05	(0.09)	-0.03	(0.09)	0.00	(0.08)	-0.06	(0.09)
Belgium (French Community)	**0.19**	(0.06)	-0.11	(0.12)	**0.16**	(0.05)	-0.10	(0.11)

Note: Values that are statistically significant are indicated in bold.

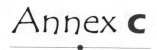

Annex C

LIST OF CONTRIBUTORS TO PISA

Annex C: The development and implementation of PISA —
a collaborative effort

Members of the PISA Governing Board

Chair: Ryo Watanabe

Australia: Wendy Whitham

Austria: Helmut Bachmann and Jürgen Horschinegg

Belgium: Dominique Barthélémy, Christiane Blondin and Liselotte van de Perre

Brazil: Eliezer Pacheco

Canada: Satya Brink and Dianne Pennock

Czech Republic: Jan Koucky

Denmark: Jørgen Balling Rasmussen

Finland: Jari Rajanen

France: Gérard Bonnet

Germany: Hans Konrad Koch, Elfriede Ohrnberger and Botho Priebe

Greece: Vassilis Koulaidis

Hong Kong-China: Esther Ho Sui Chu

Hungary: Péter Vári

Iceland: Júlíus K. Björnsson

Indonesia: Bahrul Hayat

Ireland: Gerry Shiel

Italy: Giacomo Elias and Angela Vegliante

Japan: Ryo Watanabe

Korea: Kye Young Lee

Latvia: Andris Kangro

Luxembourg: Michel Lanners

Macao-China: Lam Fat Lo

Mexico: Felipe Martínez Rizo

Netherlands: Jules L. Peschar

New Zealand: Lynne Whitney

Norway: Alette Schreiner

Poland: Stanislaw Drzazdzewski

Portugal: Glória Ramalho

Russian Federation: Galina Kovalyova

Serbia: Dragica Pavlovic Babic

Slovak Republic: Vladimir Repas

Spain: Carme Amorós Basté, Guillermo Gil and Josu Sierra Orrantia

Sweden: Anita Wester

Switzerland: Katrin Holenstein and Heinz Rhyn

Thailand: Sunee Klainin

Tunisia: Néjib Ayed

Turkey: Sevki Karaca and Ruhi Kilç

United Kingdom: Lorna Bertrand and Liz Levy

United States: Mariann Lemke and Elois Scott

Uruguay: Pedro Ravela

Special Advisor: Eugene Owen

PISA 2003 National Project Managers

Australia: John Cresswell and Sue Thomson

Austria: Günter Haider and Claudia Reiter

Belgium: Luc van de Poele

Brazil: Mariana Migliari

Canada: Tamara Knighton and Dianne Pennock

Czech Republic: Jana Paleckova

Denmark: Jan Mejding

Finland: Jouni Välijärvi

France: Anne-Laure Monnier

Germany: Manfred Prenzel

Greece: Vassilia Hatzinikita

Hong Kong-China: Esther Ho Sui Chu

Hungary: Péter Vári

Iceland: Almar Midvik Halldorsson

Indonesia: Bahrul Hayat

Ireland: Judith Cosgrove

Italy: Maria Teresa Siniscalco

Japan: Ryo Watanabe

Korea: Mee-Kyeong Lee

Latvia: Andris Kangro

Luxembourg: Iris Blanke

Macao-China: Esther Ho Sui Chu (2003) and Lam Fat Lo (2006)

Mexico: Rafael Vidal

Netherlands: Erna Gille

New Zealand: Fiona Sturrock

Norway: Marit Kjaernsli

Poland: Michal Federowicz

Portugal: Lídia Padinha

Russian Federation: Galina Kovalyova

Serbia: Dragica Pavlovic Babic

Slovak Republic: Paulina Korsnakova

Spain: Guillermo Gil

Sweden: Karin Taube

Switzerland: Huguette McCluskey

Thailand: Sunee Klainin

Tunisia: Néjib Ayed

Turkey: Sevki Karaca

United Kingdom: Rachael Harker and Graham Thorpe

United States: Mariann Lemke

Uruguay: Pedro Ravela

© OECD 2006   Where immigrant students succeed - A comparative review of performance and engagement in PISA 2003

OECD Secretariat

Andreas Schleicher (overall co-ordination of PISA and member country relations)

Cécile Bily (administrative support)

John Cresswell (project management)

Miyako Ikeda (project management)

Juliet Evans (editorial support)

Claire Shewbridge (project management)

Sophie Vayssettes (statistical support)

PISA Editorial Group
(Subgroup of the PISA Governing Board)

Wendy Whitham (Chair) (Australia)

Stanislaw Drzazdzewski (Poland)

Jürgen Horschinegg (Austria)

Dianne Pennock (Canada)

Heinz Rhyn (Switzerland)

Gerry Shiel (Ireland)

PISA Expert Groups

Mathematics Expert Group

Jan de Lange (Chair) (Utrecht University, Netherlands)

Werner Blum (Chair) (University of Kassel, Germany)

Vladimir Burjan (National Institute for Education, Slovak Republic)

Sean Close (St Patrick's College, Ireland)

John Dossey (Consultant, United States)

Mary Lindquist (Columbus State University, United States)

Zbigniew Marciniak (Warsaw University, Poland)

Mogens Niss (Roskilde University, Denmark)

Kyung-Mee Park (Hongik University, Korea)

Luis Rico (University of Granada, Spain)

Yoshinori Shimizu (Tokyo Gakugei University, Japan)

Reading Expert Group

Irwin Kirsch (Chair) (Educational Testing Service, United States)

Marilyn Binkley (National Center for Educational Statistics, United States)

Alan Davies (University of Edinburgh, United Kingdom)

Stan Jones (Statistics Canada, Canada)

John de Jong (Language Testing Services, Netherlands)

Dominique Lafontaine (Université de Liège Sart Tilman, Belgium)

Pirjo Linnakylä (University of Jyväskylä, Finland)

Martine Rémond (Institut National de Recherche Pédagogique, France)

Science Expert Group

Wynne Harlen (Chair) (University of Bristol, United Kingdom)

Peter Fensham (Monash University, Australia)

Raul Gagliardi (University of Geneva, Switzerland)

Svein Lie (University of Oslo, Norway)

Manfred Prenzel (Universität Kiel, Germany)

Senta A. Raizen (National Center for Improving Science Education (NCISE), United States)

Donghee Shin (KICE, Korea)

Elizabeth Stage (University of California, United States)

Problem Solving Expert Group

John Dossey (Chair) (Consultant, United States)

Beno Csapo (University of Szeged, Hungary)

Jan De Lange (Utrecht University, Netherlands)

Eckhard Klieme (German Institute for International Educational Research, Germany)

Wynne Harlen (University of Bristol, United Kingdom)

Ton de Jong (University of Twente, Netherlands)

Irwin Kirsch (Educational Training Service, United States)

Stella Vosniadou (University of Athens, Greece)

PISA Technical Advisory Group

Keith Rust (Chair) (Westat)

Ray Adams (ACER, Australia)

Pierre Foy (Statistics Canada, Canada)

Aletta Grisay (Belgium)

Larry Hedges (The University of Chicago, United States)

Eugene Johnson (American Institutes for Research, United States)

John de Jong (Language Testing Services, Netherlands)

Irwin Kirsch (Educational Testing Service, United States)

Steve May (Ministry of Education, New Zealand)

Christian Monseur (HallStat SPRL, Belgium)

Norman Verhelst (Citogroep, Netherlands)

J. Douglas Willms (University of New Brunswick, Canada)

PISA Consortium

Australian Council for Educational Research

Ray Adams (Project Director of the PISA Consortium)

Alla Berezner (data management, data analysis)

Eveline Gebhardt (data processing, data analysis)

Marten Koomen (management)

Dulce Lay (data processing)

Le Tu Luc (data processing)

Greg Macaskill (data processing)

Barry McCrae (science instruments, test development mathematics and problem solving)

Martin Murphy (field operations and sampling)

Van Nguyen (data processing)

Alla Routitsky (data processing)

Wolfram Schulz (Coordinator questionnaire development, data processing, data analysis)

Ross Turner (Coordinator test development)

Maurice Walker (sampling, data processing, questionnaire development)

Margaret Wu (test development mathematics and problem solving, data analysis)

John Cresswell (test development science)

Juliette Mendelovits (test development reading)

Joy McQueen (test development reading)

Beatrice Halleux (translation quality control)

Westat

Nancy Caldwell (Director of the PISA Consortium for field operations and quality monitoring)

Ming Chen (weighting)

Fran Cohen (weighting)

Susan Fuss (weighting)

Brice Hart (weighting)

Sharon Hirabayashi (weighting)

Sheila Krawchuk (sampling and weighting)

Christian Monseur (consultant) (weighting)

Phu Nguyen (weighting)

Mats Nyfjall (weighting)

Merl Robinson (field operations and quality monitoring)

Keith Rust (Director of the PISA Consortium for sampling and weighting)

Leslie Wallace (weighting)

Erin Wilson (weighting)

Citogroep

Steven Bakker (science test development)

Bart Bossers (reading test development)

Truus Decker (mathematics test development)

Janny Harmsen (office/meeting support)

Erna van Hest (reading test development and quality monitoring)

Kees Lagerwaard (mathematics test development)

Gerben van Lent (mathematics test development)

Ger Limpens (mathematical test development)

Ico de Roo (science test development)

Maria van Toor (office support and quality monitoring)

Norman Verhelst (technical advice, data analysis)

Educational Testing Service

Irwin Kirsch (reading test development)

National Institute for Educational Policy Research of Japan

Hanako Senuma (mathematics test development)

Other experts

Kai von Ahlefeld (layout)

Cordula Adelt (questionnaire development)

Aletta Grisay (technical advice, data analysis, translation, questionnaire development)

Anne-Lise Prigent (editorial review)

© OECD 2006   **Where immigrant students succeed - A comparative review of performance and engagement in PISA 2003**

WITHDRAWN

REFERENCE BOOK
DO NOT REMOVE

MAY   2007

REF LC 3715 .S73 2006

Stanat, Petra.
Where immigrant students succeed :

WITHDRAWN

OECD PUBLICATIONS, 2, rue André-Pascal, 75775 PARIS CEDEX 16
PRINTED IN FRANCE
(98 2006 02 1 P) ISBN 92-64-02360-7 No. 55063 2006

REFERENCE BOOK
DO NOT REMOVE

MIDDLESEX COUNTY COLLEGE
NEW BRUNSWICK CENTER
NEW BRUNSWICK, NJ 08901